The Conflict in Iraq 2003

The Conflict in Iraq 2003

Edited by

Paul Cornish
Director, Centre for Defence Studies, King's College London, UK

First published 2004 by
PALGRAVE MACMILLAN
Houndmills, Basingstoke, Hampshire RG21 6XS and
175 Fifth Avenue, New York, N.Y. 10010
Companies and representatives throughout the world

PALGRAVE MACMILLAN is the global academic imprint of the Palgrave
Macmillan division of St. Martin's Press, LLC and of Palgrave Macmillan Ltd.
Macmillan® is a registered trademark in the United States, United Kingdom
and other countries. Palgrave is a registered trademark in the European Union
and other countries.

ISBN 1–4039–3525–4 hardback
ISBN 1–4039–3526–2 paperback

This book is printed on paper suitable for recycling and
made from fully managed and sustained forest sources.

A catalogue record for this book is available
from the British Library.

Library of Congress Cataloging-in-Publication Data
The conflict in Iraq 2003 / edited by Paul Cornish.
    p. cm.
    ISBN 1–4039–3525–4 (cloth) — ISBN 1–4039–3526–2 (paper)
    1. Iraq War, 2003. I. Cornish, Paul.

DS79.76.C66 2005
956.7044'3—dc22

                                                        2004058656

10 9 8 7 6 5 4 3 2 1
14 13 12 11 10 09 08 07 06 05

Printed and bound in Great Britain by
Antony Rowe Ltd, Chippenham and Eastbourne

Contents

Part Three   Consequences

Foreword

It is an iron law of warfare that the unintended consequences, for good and bad, are as important if not more so than the intended. Because these consequences take time to work themselves through, the long-term reputations of wars rarely reflect the first reviews. Take the case of the 1991 war against Iraq. The early reviews were positive for a war fought with controlled moderation by a broad-based coalition sponsored by the UN. Eventually, the assessment darkened and moderation was recast as timidity that created more problems than it solved. Its neat conclusion, with a negotiated cease-fire, the return of prisoners and gradual disengagement, unfortunately left the problem of Saddam Hussein's regime unaddressed and helped create the conditions for the 2003 war. By contrast, the early reviews of the 2003 war have been terrible. Its radicalism appears as recklessness, based on exaggerated intelligence and unwarranted optimism about post-war Iraq.

A central issue here is that of limitations in war. The first Bush Administration assumed that Saddam Hussein's failed Kuwaiti adventure would be followed by the normal processes of political succession in Iraq. If the coalition tried to force the pace then they were anxious that they might trigger a disruptive civil war. Nor were they inclined to accept the potential cost and bother of trying to occupy and then run the country. In addition, the international licence for the war did not extend beyond the liberation of Kuwait.

The judgement of 1991 was neither unreasonable nor controversial. Indeed, given the experience of the US over 2003–4 it seems prudent. The respect for limitations was at the time seen to offer a model for the new world order by setting standards for the use of force by the great powers. Such force must be sanctioned by the UN, mounted by an international coalition in pursuit of limited objectives from which it must not stray, and show great care for civilian life and property. These are the standards against which the 2003 war has been evaluated, and so often found wanting.

It is important, however, to note that the 1991 war was the historical oddity and its aftermath must at least lead to some questioning of whether the model was either realistic or appropriate. Prior to this date the only war approved by the UN was in 1950, and then by a fluke, because the Soviet Union was boycotting the Security Council when the US gained agreement to push back North Korea's invasion of the South. The UN conspicuously failed to condemn Iraq's invasion of Iran in 1980, in a move of unanimous hypocrisy. This was compounded more than a decade later, in changed political circumstances, when the UN decided, retrospectively, that this was, after all, aggression. The UN did manage to deplore Israel's 1981 destruction of the Iraqi nuclear reactor at Osiraq, sold by France with scant regard for a non-proliferation treaty, which it was itself then refusing to sign. All this confirmed the pattern that has dominated the Security Council deliberations since 1945. The veto-wielding countries on the Security Council protect themselves and their friends – and so with most armed conflicts little has been condemned and even less approved. Force has normally been justified, albeit often only at a pinch, by reference to the 'inherent right of self-defence' as enshrined in Article 51 of the UN Charter. Even in 2003 a defensive motive could be claimed, even though it was in anticipation of a malign combination of terrorism and weapons of mass destruction (WMD) that had yet to be formed.

In 1991 Iraqi aggression against Kuwait was unambiguous. The Emir, having just escaped the invaders, initially relied on Article 51 but the unprecedented degree of harmony on the Security Council, following the end of the Cold War, made possible a series of UN resolutions which culminated in resolution 678 of November 1990, allowing member states to use 'all necessary means' to reverse the aggression. The mandate went no further. This was to be a truly limited war in both ends and means, which meant that in important respects it was to be inconclusive. The same had been true of the Korean War. At one point, until the Chinese intervened, it looked as if the US might use the opportunity to engineer a regime change in North Korea. The Chinese sent the 'UN Forces' scurrying back towards the south until they regrouped and the position stabilised at a line close to the boundaries with which the whole affair began. This was better than the third world war which many had feared as a result of the developing clash, and better than domination of the South by the North, but the underlying conflict was left unresolved, and it grumbles on, still posing serious risks to international peace and security, half a century later. This became the prototype limited war and demonstrated the prudence of not pushing for victory at all costs but also the problems of settling without a decisive conclusion.

After the war, the strategic response to Korea was to contain but not eliminate the danger. This strategy remains in place and still requires constant attention. This was also the case with Iraq, and again the continuation in power of the adversary meant that it was impossible to consider the problem solved and move on to other issues. Saddam used his survival to demonstrate that, despite appearances and Kuwait's return to its previous owners, the 1991 war had not been anything other than a victory. The coalition that fought the war had assumed that Saddam would not survive such a humiliating defeat. If he hung on to power he could be contained through a combination of UN monitoring, coercive sanctions and a local US military presence. So the whole experience, in its restraint and multilateralism, offered a model for future crisis management.

The reluctance to contemplate radical change, essential if the anti-Saddam coalition was to hold, created the conditions for growing acrimony among the major powers and helped legitimise anti-Americanism. The conservative Gulf states reverted to their pre-war, authoritarian complacency. When the Kurds and Shia rose up against Saddam's regime, the Americans and British decided, in what now appears as a mistake of historic proportions, not to help. Only when the Kurds were about to be pushed into Turkey was there a response, which led in practice to the creation of a quasi-autonomous Kurdistan within Iraq under coalition protection. Despite themselves, coalition members became involved in the internal affairs of Iraq. Saddam fought against the UN-imposed constraints. Sanctions became deeply unpopular while the US garrison in Saudi Arabia appeared, at least to Osama bin Laden and his followers, as the ultimate anti-Islamic provocation. The maintenance of sanctions added to the misery of the Iraqi people and strengthened the regime's control of the economy. Saddam's refusal to cooperate with efforts to disarm him of his most dangerous weapons added to the continuing sense of instability. There was no real peace after 1991, but continuing threats and occasional military action, with a substantial if short air campaign in December 1998 (Operation Desert Fox) followed by continuing skirmishing between coalition air forces and Iraqi air defences thereafter.

The 1991 war concluded with a promise for a new world order that turned out to be illusory and created expectations for the United Nations that it proved unable to meet. For example when it came to deciding on whether armed force was an appropriate military response to the turmoil in Kosovo, a war which by and large has had a better press than the Iraq War, the Security Council could not agree. This campaign also failed to meet the strict test of legality, although, like Iraq, there had been a series of tamer UN resolutions which could provide the basis for a case in international law. The real difference was that the coalition supporting the Kosovo War was larger and more cohesive than that supporting the Iraq War, and the 'facts of the case' were less disputed. The test of legitimacy, as opposed to legality, is therefore more clearly political. It does not depend on the rather non-judicial process of Security Council manoeuvring but on the ability of the major powers to convince key domestic and international constituencies that they are doing the right thing and that their motives are honourable. This will always involve compromises. There remains an inherent tension between a limited war most likely to have wide backing without providing the conditions for a lasting solution, and a more decisive war which may transform the situation but only at a cost of considerable international tension and division.

If President George W. Bush had decided to steer clear of Iraq over 2002–3 the picture now would not have been of continuing containment. Prior to 2002, France and Russia had been content to see the end of sanctions and UN inspections. Containment was in decline and was only reinforced as members of the Security Council scrambled to develop an alternative to war in late 2002. If matters had not been brought to a head, Saddam's Iraq would gradually have reasserted itself. In contrast to claims made prior to the war, Iraq had been effectively disarmed through a combination of sanctions and UN inspections. This did not mean that Saddam had no interest in reconstituting his programmes to construct deadly weapons, once the pressure was off. He did not go out of his way to encourage the view that he was compliant with UN resolutions, although his behaviour may have had as much to do with his generally antagonistic attitude to the coalition that had acted to thwart his ambitions as well as sustain some deterrent effect from the thought that WMD might be hidden.

In the end the inspections issue provided the pretext for the second war, and for some such as Tony Blair the actual reason. The Bush Administration was undoubtedly animated by its own highly antagonistic relationship with Saddam's regime, in part reflecting the past frustration with his survival and in part their future fear of some link with al-Qaeda. It is the failure to find the stocks of chemical and biological weapons that they assumed to have been successfully hidden from inspectors that has done so much to encourage the view (strong enough before this failure) that the war was based on a big lie. By the time that this had become evident, the rationale for the war had come to be based on the toppling of an outlaw regime, hated by its own population.

Unfortunately against this had then to be set the mess of a post-war Iraq. The poor security situation, aggravated by extraordinarily feeble American preparations for the role of occupying power, delayed reconstruction. This delay exacerbated Iraqi anger and exasperation with their 'liberators'. The sacking of Ba'athist officials and the disbanding of the Iraqi army created the recruits and the weapons for what has turned into a substantial insurgency. Though there was never much of a link between Saddam's Iraq and al-Qaeda, America's Iraq turned into something of a magnet for Islamic militants. Few of those trying to cope with the situation appreciated one of the more fatuous *post hoc* rationalisations that implied that somehow this was always intended, so that the bad guys could be corralled in one location from where they would be unable to bother the rest of the world. The promises that Iraq would emerge quickly as a beacon of Arab democracy subsidised by healthy oil exports soon appeared hopelessly far-fetched. Furthermore, because of their determination to solve the Saddam problem once and for all, with or without international support, the Americans and British had to manage the new Iraq largely alone. Only with significant concessions to local and international sentiment were they able by June 2004 to get a moderately representative Iraqi government in place with UN backing.

All this suggests that the 1991 model may not have been so bad after all, or at least it demonstrates the complexity of the trade between the legitimacy of an operation, in setting sufficiently limited war aims to ensure the widest possible backing, and decisiveness, in setting sufficiently ambitious war aims to deal with the causes of the conflict. Most observers would now add another factor, to the effect that the greater the ambition the higher the premium that has to be placed on basic competence and political acumen. The sheer ineptitude of the American performance, culminating in May 2004 with an aggressive approach to the insurgency in Fallujah, that ended in withdrawal because of the inability to gain a tactical victory without enormous civilian casualty, the mishandling of Shia militants, and, most of all, the damaging revelations about the treatment of prisoners of Abu Ghraib, left many supporters of the war in despair. These problems can be traced back to the lack of preparation for such a role in US military doctrine, and the stress placed on force protection to the exclusion of the political demands of the mission. Much blame must also be attached to the cheery optimism which afflicted senior civilian officials in the Pentagon when contemplating Iraqi responses to American (and British) soldiers blasting their way into their country and which led them to underestimate the requirements of occupation.

With so much to play for in Iraq itself it remains to be seen whether in the end the war will be seen as a starting point for the slow, painful but ultimately triumphant climb to a strong, moderately democratic (at least legitimate) Iraqi state or whether it is instead the start of the gradual break-up of the country into a Lebanon-style disarray (or even a combination of the two with the bloody disarray giving way to a local political settlement born of exhaustion). Much depends on decisions yet to be taken and on events which are currently beyond prediction. What is certainly the case is that, in contrast to 1991, and despite an even quicker military victory, this time round the sense of satisfaction at a job well done has been remarkably short-lived.

Meanwhile, some unintended consequences are starting to become evident. With its hands full in Iraq and Afghanistan Washington is bound to hesitate before taking on another adventure, especially if it has to be justified on the basis of intelligence. The US is tentatively returning to a more multilateral approach and treading carefully in its dealings over North Korea and Iran. Indeed the need to keep the Shia calm in Iraq requires Iranian connivance. Rather than an assertive America removing one rogue regime after the other, the complaint from allies may soon be about excessive caution and passivity in the face of the severe challenges that can not be met without a fully engaged United States. In ten years' time the view of the war will no doubt have been through a number of transformations. All the more reason to have as considered a view available now, in its painful aftermath, to record what has been one of the most extraordinary and divisive international crises for a generation.

Lawrence Freedman
Professor of War Studies
King's College London
July 2004

Notes on Contributors

Dr **Wyn Q. Bowen** is Director of Research, Defence Studies Department, King's College London at the Joint Services Command and Staff College, Defence Academy of the United Kingdom. He was Specialist Advisor to the House of Commons Foreign Affairs Committee in June–July 2003 for its inquiry into the decision to go to war in Iraq and during 1997 and 1998 he participated in three weapons inspection missions with the United Nations Special Commission in Iraq. From 1995 to 1997 he was a Senior Research Associate of the Center for Nonproliferation Studies, Monterey Institute of International Studies, California. He has written widely on issues related to proliferation and asymmetric conflict.

Michael Clarke is Professor of Defence Studies at King's College London and the Director of the International Policy Institute at KCL. He is Specialist Advisor to the House of Commons Defence Committee, having previously served on the House of Commons Foreign Affairs Committee. He is also the UK member of the UN Secretary General's Advisory Board on Disarmament Matters. He has previously been the Director of the Centre for Defence Studies, and also the Head of the School of Social Science and Public Policy at King's. He writes on defence issues with particular emphasis on UK defence policy and transatlantic relations.

Dr **Paul Cornish** was educated at St Andrews, the London School of Economics, the Royal Military Academy Sandhurst, and Cambridge. On leaving the British Army in 1989, he worked as an arms control and disarmament analyst at the Foreign and Commonwealth Office and then as Senior Research Fellow at Chatham House. He has lectured in defence studies at King's College London (Joint Services Command and Staff College), and strategic studies at the University of Cambridge, where he was a Fellow of Wolfson College. In March 2001 Dr Cornish joined the Conflict, Security and Development Group at King's College London, becoming Director of the Group in July 2001. In January 2002 he moved permanently to King's College London as Research Director, and subsequently Director of the Centre for Defence Studies. His research interests include British defence policy and practice, European security and defence industry, arms control and international arms exports, and the moral dimensions of the use of armed force. Publications include *The Arms Trade and Europe* (Pinter, 1995), *British Military Planning for the Defence of Germany, 1945–50* (Macmillan, 1996), *Controlling the Arms Trade:*

the West versus the Rest (Bowerdean, 1996), and *Partnership in Crisis? The United States, Europe and the Fall and Rise of NATO* (Cassell, 1997).

Dr **Andrew Dorman** is a Lecturer in the Defence Studies Department, King's College London based at the United Kingdom's Joint Services Command and Staff College. He is also a Senior Research Associate at the Centre for Defence Studies and Deputy Editor of *World Defence Systems*. He trained as a Chartered Accountant with KPMG Peat Marwick at their Cambridge office qualifying in 1990 before returning to academia. He has previously taught at the Royal Naval Staff College, Greenwich and at the University of Birmingham where he completed his masters and doctoral degrees and is currently on secondment to the Ministry of Defence. His most recent books include *Defence under Thatcher, 1979–89*, Southampton Studies in International Policy (Palgrave Macmillan, 2002); co-editor, *The Changing Face of Military Power*, JSCSC Series (Palgrave Macmillan, 2002); co-author, *Britain and Defence 1945–2000: A Policy Re-evaluation* (Pearson Longman, 2001).

Professor **John C. Garnett** was educated at the London School of Economics where he was awarded a First Class Honours degree in International Relations and an MSc (Econ). He held the Woodrow Wilson Chair in International Politics at the University of Wales and was head of department for 15 years. Currently he is Chairman and Acting Head of the International Policy Institute at King's College London, and Director of Academic Support at the Royal College of Defence Studies. Professor Garnett has specialised in strategic studies and his main interests lie in the field of security policy and international theory. His most recent book (with L.W. Martin) was *British Foreign Policy, Challenges and Choices for the 21st Century* (Royal Institute of International Affairs, 1997).

Tim Garden is currently working on European defence, transatlantic security, Middle East and North Africa conflict prevention and international terrorism. He was a pilot in the Royal Air Force for 32 years, eventually becoming the assistant chief of the UK defence staff, and was awarded his knighthood in 1994. His final military post was as the air marshal commandant of the Royal College of Defence Studies in London. He went on to be Director of the Royal Institute of International Affairs at Chatham House until 1998. He was appointed Chevalier de l'Ordre National de la Légion d'Honneur in 2003 for his work on European defence. He is the Wells professor at Indiana University for 2004. He writes and broadcasts regularly on international security topics. He became Lord Garden in June 2004 as a Liberal Democrat peer.

Dr **Karin von Hippel** is a Senior Research Fellow at the Centre for Defence Studies, King's College London. Her areas of academic interest include root causes of terrorism, and nation-building. In 2002, she directed a project on

European counter-terrorist reforms, funded by the MacArthur Foundation, and edited the volume, *Europe Confronts Terror*. She also advised the OECD on what development co-operation can do to get at the root causes of terrorism, and has been a member of Project Unicorn, a counter-terrorism police advisory panel in London. Her publications include, 'Terrorism as a Problem of International Cooperation', in Thomas Weiss and Jane Boulden, eds, *Terrorism and the UN: Problems and Prospects* (forthcoming); 'Définir les origines du terrorisme: un débat transatlantique?' in *La revue internationale et stratégique* (no. 51, autumn 2003); 'The Roots of Terrorism: Probing the Myths', in Lawrence Freedman, ed., *Superterrorism: Policy Responses* (Blackwell, 2002); and *Democracy by Force* (Cambridge, 2000), which was short-listed for the Westminster Medal in Military History. She also spent three years working for the European Commission and the UN in Somalia, and the UN in Kosovo.

Joanna Kidd read Modern History at the University of Oxford and International Relations at the London School of Economics. She served in the Royal Navy as a warfare officer on a variety of ships. Her last appointment was to the aircraft carrier, HMS *Illustrious*, which deployed to the Arabian Gulf in 1998. On leaving the Navy, she worked for four years as a Defence Analyst (Navy) at the International Institute for Strategic Studies, London, publishing and broadcasting frequently on naval and maritime matters. She is now a Research Fellow at the International Policy Institute, King's College London.

Dr **Susan B. Martin** is currently a Lecturer in the Department of War Studies at King's College London, where she is helping to develop a new programme in Science and Security. She received her BA in Political Science from Yale University and her MA and PhD in Political Science from the University of California, Berkeley. She was a Post-Doctoral Fellow at the Christopher H. Browne Center for the Study of International Politics at the University of Pennsylvania, and has also taught at Wesleyan University and Florida Atlantic University. She specialises in international relations theory and security studies, and her current research focuses on chemical, biological and nuclear weapons. Her work has appeared in the *Journal of Strategic Studies* and *International Security*.

Alison Pargeter is a Research Fellow at the International Policy Institute at King's College London. She works primarily on security issues in North Africa, with a particular focus on Libya. She has undertaken a number of projects on Libyan foreign policy, as well as following domestic developments there. Her other research interests include North African immigrant communities in Europe and their links to political violence and she is currently working on a project funded by the Economic and Social Research Council looking at this issue in the UK. She is also working on the role of the Muslim Brotherhood in Europe. Prior to joining King's College, she worked for the BBC as a World Affairs Researcher and freelance writer.

Bill Park is a Senior Lecturer with the Defence Studies Department of the War Studies Group, King's College, London, and Research Associate at the Centre for Defence Studies. He has published on Turkish foreign and security policy in journals such as *World Today*, *Jane's Intelligence Review*, *Defence Analysis*, *Mediterranean Politics*, and *Middle East Review of International Affairs*. He has given oral and written testimony on Turkey to committees of both Houses of Parliament, been used in advisory capacities by British and non-British government departments, and has broadcast and lectured widely on Turkish affairs. He is currently writing an *Adelphi Paper* on Turkish–US–northern Iraq issues and relationships for the International Institute of Strategic Studies.

Dr **Domitilla Sagramoso** is a Research Fellow at the Centre for Defence Studies, King's College London, where she is working on military and security issues affecting Russia, Central Asia and the Caucasus. She is also conducting research on Russia's relations with the West after September 11, with particular emphasis on the war on terrorism. She obtained a PhD at the School of Slavonic and East European Studies, University College London in 1999. Her thesis focused on Russia's economic and military policies towards the former Soviet states during the Yeltsin era. Her publication, *The Proliferation of Illegal Small Arms and Light Weapons in and around the European Union: Instability, Organised Crime, and Terrorist Groups* (Saferworld, 2001), was published to coincide with the UN Conference 'Illicit Trade in Small Arms and Light Weapons in All its Aspects'.

Laura Sandys has worked on issues relating to Iraq for over ten years. She has built and sold two companies specialising in political and international relations consulting, and has been interested in the Middle East for many years. She recently completed a Master's dissertation at Cambridge on the period of the Mandate in Iraq 1919–32, comparing the issues facing the British and those confronting the Coalition today. Currently she is working on energy pipeline projects in the Caspian and Caucasus and also has some commercial interests in Iraq. She is a Trustee of the Open University and a Senior Research Associate at the Centre for Defence Studies, King's College London.

Jane M.O. Sharp is a Senior Research Fellow at the Centre for Defence Studies, King's College, London. From 1999 to 2003 she was a member of the UN Secretary General's Advisory Board on Disarmament Matters and a member of the Board of the UN Institute for Disarmament Research (UNIDIR) in Geneva. She currently serves as a Trustee of the Institute for War and Peace Reporting (IWPR) in London and Washington D.C. and is on the editorial board of *Prospect* magazine (London). She has published widely on all aspects of international arms control and alliance politics, and on the impact on European security of NATO enlargement and the collapse of both the USSR and Yugoslavia. She has in press a book on the CFE treaty and is currently working on a manuscript for the US Institute of Peace (USIP) on 'Russia, the West and the Balkans'.

Guglielmo Verdirame is a Lecturer in Law at the University of Cambridge, a Fellow of Corpus Christi College and of the Lauterpacht Research Centre for International Law. He writes on a wide range of issues in international law, including: the United Nations and international institutional law; refugees and human rights; the use of force and security issues; international criminal justice; and the use of international law by domestic courts. Before moving to Cambridge he was a Fellow of Merton College, Oxford and a member of the Oxford Law Faculty. With Barbara Harrell-Bond, he is the author of *Rights in Exile: Janus-Faced Humanitarianism* (Berghahn Books, 2004). Another book, *UN Accountability for Human Rights Violations*, is forthcoming with Cambridge University Press.

Philip Wilkinson OBE, MRSAWS, M.Phil, MCGLI was commissioned from RMA Sandhurst in 1969 into the Royal Artillery. He served with commando, parachute and Special Forces, and commanded the artillery regiment in the UK Airmobile Brigade. He had six years of operational experience in the Far East, Middle East, Balkans, Falklands and a further six years in Northern Ireland, where he was made an MBE. In 1993, he was posted to the newly formed HQ Doctrine and Training with responsibility for peacekeeping doctrine and training, and developed a new concept for robust peacekeeping called Peace Support Operations (PSO), for which he was made an OBE. His final appointment in the Army was Assistant Director of the Joint Doctrine and Concepts Centre, where he was the principal author of NATO doctrine for operations other than war and achieved an M.Phil. He has written PSO doctrine for the UK, NATO, Sweden, the Republic of South Africa and since leaving the Army has co-authored the new *UN Handbook for the Conduct of Complex Peacekeeping Operations*. On leaving the Army, he joined the Centre for Defence Studies at King's College, London and switched the focus of his work to security and defence policy issues. This has included the provision of policy, doctrine and training support to a wide range of countries including Rwanda, Bosnia and Herzegovina and Sri Lanka. In November 2002 he was appointed a Member of the Royal Swedish Academy of War Sciences.

Introduction

Paul Cornish

History's judgement on the armed conflict which broke out in Iraq in March 2003 can only be guessed at. And there is no shortage of guesses. For many critics, the invasion of Iraq will prove to have been an irresponsible, if not idiotic miscalculation by western leaders, particularly President George Bush of the United States and Prime Minister Tony Blair of the United Kingdom. As a result of their blunder, these critics argue, the United States, Europe, the Middle East and perhaps even the whole world are much less secure now than they were before March 2003. Any idea that the attack on Iraq was a justifiable act of revenge for the terrorist mass murders which took place in New York and Washington in September 2001, is in these critics' view fatally undermined by the failure to establish an explicit link between those attacks and Saddam Hussein's regime. And the consequences of this fundamental error will, in any case, be disastrous as even more murder and mayhem is unleashed on western governments and societies. As for those who argued that the invasion of Iraq was an appropriate means to pre-empt the threat of Iraqi proliferation and use of so-called weapons of mass destruction (nuclear, biological and chemical), the critics point to the failure to discover WMD arsenals (however much proof there might be of WMD *programmes*) as, at best, an embarrassment for the American and British governments. For some, the intervention was a flagrant breach of international law; an unwarranted aggression against a sovereign state which not only resulted in the death of thousands of innocent Iraqis, but which was embarked upon before all other, non-military means to resolve the conflict with Iraq had been exhausted. Others would have it that all this discussion of security, terrorism, weapons of mass destruction and international law misses the point. For them, history will show a sinister, neo-imperialist conspiracy to have been at work, one which sought not only to secure access for the United States to the world's dwindling natural resources (particularly oil), but which also sought to remake the world according to an American political, economic and social template. In the name of this conspiracy, western electorates and legislatures were deceived into supporting an unjustified war, based on intelligence reports and other evidence which was proved to be false or corrupt.

Barely audible among the vigorous denunciations of Bush, Blair and their allies, there are others for whom the intervention against Iraq was necessary and will be shown to have been noble and enlightened. Some argue that the real scandal is that it took so long to deal with Saddam Hussein; his regime was not destroyed when it should have been, in 1991, and a decade's worth of UN Security Council resolutions demonstrated only the international community's capacity to contain itself, rather than a miscreant and dangerous government. By this view, the invasion of Iraq was not a breach of international law, but an expression of the spirit of that body of law; the regime of Saddam Hussein (under which hundreds of thousands of innocent Iraqis had been killed) had long since shown international law to be tattered and impotent, and the intervention represented an important opportunity, which could not be overlooked, to re-establish international norms against WMD proliferation. Some supporters of the intervention have focused on the humanitarian dimension; for them, the intervention was an enlightened, liberal act, and an historical turning point which finally laid to rest the shibboleth that a government (or tyrant) can do whatever it likes to its people, while remaining under the protection of the discredited international code of sovereignty and non-intervention. By this argument, history will show a new understanding of international rights and duties to have taken hold, one in which sovereignty is regarded less as an absolute right than as a privilege, conditional upon the humane and reasonable treatment of those very people in whom the sovereignty of the state ought to reside. Others, finally, appear to have taken a more pragmatic line, forming the view that Saddam Hussein was enough of a problem in enough areas – his predatory attitude to neighbouring states; his proliferation and use of WMD; his state sponsorship of terrorism; and his humanitarian record – that it would be better for all in Iraq and in the Middle East, and for all concerned with the Middle East, simply to do away with his regime once and for all. By this view, the verdict of history might simply be that history itself triumphed, with the people of Iraq allowed to recover their past and set out their future.

The context, conduct and consequences of the intervention in Iraq have, plainly, given rise to vigorous and wide-ranging discussion, touching on complex issues of politics and diplomacy, religion, military strategy, economics, and international and domestic law. *Conflict in Iraq* aims to contribute to this often heated debate by assembling the work of established experts in the field of international security and defence, all of whom are in one way or another associated with the Centre for Defence Studies (CDS) at King's College London. The 16 chapters which follow represent the views of independent analysts, with expertise in one or more areas of the debate. There has been no attempt to present a consolidated overall view of the intervention, or to reach consensus on any detailed aspect of the debate. Instead, we have sought precisely the opposite; *Conflict in Iraq* aims to map out the complexity and diversity of both issues and opinions.

In Part One we examine the historical background to the conflict, and the political, diplomatic and military context in which long-running disagreements with Iraq broke down into violent confrontation. Laura Sandys argues that the British role as occupying power and Mandate authority in Iraq between 1914 and 1932 offers striking parallels with the current American experience, and suggests that important lessons are there to be learned. She notes that the British began their involvement in Iraq motivated by the highest ideals, but left hastily in the face of mounting opposition, having constructed political and social institutions which proved inadequate to the task of long-term stability, security and national cohesion. Michael Clarke examines the more recent diplomatic record, focusing on the policies (and errors) of Baghdad, Washington and London, and on the difficulty of building and maintaining international consensus on the question of Saddam Hussein and Iraq. The major participants in the Iraq crisis of 2003 have, in Clarke's view, all been deeply damaged, and it remains to be seen how quickly and effectively that damage can be repaired. For Jane Sharp, it is the twists and turns in the so-called 'special relationship' between the United States and the United Kingdom which are of most interest. In Sharp's view, the Blair government demeaned itself in its dogged determination to remain alongside the Bush Administration, and gained little or nothing from its 'slavish devotion' to Washington. As the only western power – and NATO member – sharing a border with Iraq, Turkey occupied a particular, and particularly difficult, position in the approach to war. In Bill Park's assessment, the disagreement between Turkey and the United States over access to northern Iraq was much more than a politico-military spat; it exposed profound differences of opinion between the two governments on the matter of security and stability in the region. In Ankara's view, the Bush Administration showed itself unable or unwilling to take seriously Turkey's particular security concerns. The result of all this could be a fundamental shift in Turkey's alliance policy; dissatisfied and frustrated by its dutiful alliance with the United States in NATO, Turkey might now, suggests Park, redouble its efforts to move closer to the European Union. Finally in Part One, Guglielmo Verdirame accounts for the international legal context to the conflict and takes issue with the idea of democratisation by force; the notion that radical political change and social and cultural improvement in the Middle East or elsewhere can be achieved by – and can justify – intervention and the organised use of armed force.

The conduct of the campaign is analysed in Part Two. In the first of their jointly written chapters, Philip Wilkinson and Tim Garden describe the Coalition's concept of operations and the significance of key technological/doctrinal principles; network-centric warfare, mission command, manoeuvrism, and joint vision and planning. In their second chapter, Wilkinson and Garden analyse the balance of Iraqi and Coalition forces, describing the equipment and tactics of both sides, and offer a blow-by-blow account of the ground and air campaign. Analysis of the maritime campaign is provided by Joanna Kidd. Although Coalition naval and maritime forces performed effectively and efficiently during the campaign, Kidd asks whether the West's naval forces – particularly the United States Navy – have transformed themselves adequately in recent years to meet evolving threats and dangers. The much-vaunted transformation of American armed forces is also taken up by Andrew Dorman, who examines the background, conduct and consequences of the campaign from a United States perspective. Dorman's central conclusion is that more conceptual and practical preparation is required for the United States to be in a better position to meet the twin challenges of low-level insurgency and post-conflict reconstruction. Insurgency operations and so-called 'asymmetric warfare' are the focus of Wyn Bowen's chapter. Bowen argues that, for a variety of reasons, Saddam Hussein's asymmetric counter-strategy against the Coalition was not the success many imagined it would be. Ironically, however, a more successful asymmetric strategy has been fought by Saddam's supporters and other forces since the collapse of the regime. Final analysis of the asymmetric dimensions of the conflict in Iraq are therefore, suggests Bowen, uncomfortably incomplete.

In the final part of the book we look to the consequences of the conflict. Susan Martin unpacks the debate on 'weapons of mass destruction' – a misleading term – and argues that although the UN's inspection and disarmament programme would probably not have eliminated Iraq's chemical, biological and nuclear (CBN) potential, the threat posed by a CBN-armed Iraq to regional and international security did not require or justify preventive military intervention. Looking to the future, Martin argues that important lessons must be learned about the value of coercive disarmament and preventive attack. At the heart of both policies is a simple paradox; the assumption seems to be that the threat or use of military force can be an incentive to abandon CBN weapons. But it can often be that coercive diplomacy and the threat of overwhelming western military power can create a perverse disincentive to comply, with CBN weapons seen as a valuable way to compensate for any conventional military disadvantage. Karin von Hippel focuses on the problem of post-conflict reconstruction, mainly over the first six months after the end of the military campaign. With so much experience of post-conflict reconstruction having been gained since the end of the Cold War, von Hippel asks which of the major lessons were applied, and which were ignored. She finds, disappointingly, that the Bush Administration was not inclined to consult and draw upon the vast body of practical experience and sophisticated advice contained in the many studies by policy makers and analysts, from both sides of the political divide and on both sides of the Atlantic. Alison Pargeter's chapter assesses Arab responses to the 2003 conflict, from governments and at the popular level, and looks closely at the way Arab intellectuals and the Arab media responded to the crisis. Acknowledging that predictions of widespread Arab opposition to the intervention against Iraq were in the end unfounded, Pargeter argues that even in their worst-case analysis, western governments got it wrong, misunderstanding both the nature of the regimes in the region, and the reactions of the Arab masses. The economic consequences of the conflict – for the world economy as a whole, for the United States and Europe and for countries in the Middle East, as well as for the international oil market – are the subject of Domitilla Sagramoso's chapter. Once again, in spite of some predictions the conflict did not cause a global recession, and the macroeconomic consequences of the conflict could prove to be negligible. Yet while the situation in Iraq remains volatile, macroeconomic predictions are best read with some caution. John Garnett is also cautious about the consequences of the conflict, sensing that Iraq might neither develop into the stable democratic state foreseen by some optimists, nor meet the gloomier predictions of civil war and breakdown. Instead, the result might be an Iraqi central government which looks the part but which is so weak that it proves unable to ensure the stability essential for further investment and economic growth. It would probably be unfair to describe such a scenario as a failure, but it would certainly not be possible to view it as a success. Finally, in the concluding chapter Paul Cornish focuses on the politico-military aspects of the conflict and its consequences, examining the significance and implications of the conflict for strategic thinking and practice in the early twenty-first century. Cornish's concern is that western governments did not simply sponsor the high-technology, rapid warfare seen in Iraq; they also subscribed to the erroneous and dangerous idea that where western armed force leads, an appropriate political environment will follow. In the process, these governments have paradoxically undermined their own capacity to control the resort to, and use of armed force, and to manage the consequences. The unfortunate outcome could be that western governments will have lost still more of the initiative to terrorists, proliferators and other adversaries, and to tyrants and humanitarian abusers.

Part One
Context

1
British and US Coalition Approaches to State-Building and Reconstruction in Iraq: Legacies and Lessons from the British Occupation and Mandate (1914–32)

Laura Sandys

Introduction

Analysts divide between those who regard history as a bank of information, experience and lessons to be drawn upon in changed and changing circumstances, and those for whom history is simply the record of what has been, rather than a guide to the present or future. The contention of this chapter is that there are striking and valuable parallels to be drawn between the recent experience of the US-led Coalition in Iraq, and the policies of the British during the period of occupation and Mandate, 1914–32. Important similarities in intention and behaviour can be discerned between those who, at different times, have occupied and taken on the challenges of nation-building in Iraq. The goal of establishing a modern, western-facing liberal democracy in Iraq is, certainly, an ambitious one, and the hurdles facing the coalition are great. But the experience of the British does shed some light on the pitfalls and challenges – both domestic and external – that any foreign occupying power must confront in Iraq. There are also, importantly, similarities to record in the reaction of the Iraqis to occupation, in the aspirations of the Kurds, and in the goals of the Shia.

Britain's greatest legacy was, plainly, the creation of Iraq as a legal, geopolitical entity. But Iraq's borders were defined in the context of broken promises and the British established a cleft country that, even if territorial integrity were to be sustained into the future, would always be challenging to those whose aim was to lead Iraq. Britain's historical policies towards, and relations with Iraq's different religious and ethnic communities still resonate powerfully today. Many commentators would agree with David Gardner's assessment of the situation in contemporary Iraq: 'The outcome of this fascinatingly risky attempt to refashion the Middle East will depend on whether the US is able to work with the Shia.'[1] The parallels between the British approach to the Shia and the challenges facing the Coalition today are indeed compelling. Britain, a western secularising foreign power, built a dysfunctional relationship with the Shia, based on a lack of understanding and a fear of both the Shia spiritual tradition and their numerical superiority. Of course, the Coalition will not exclude the Shia from positions of political authority in the new Iraq. But it does appear that some of the prejudices and preconceptions that drove British policy in the 1920s and that eroded trust between the occupiers and the Shia, might also have taken hold within the Coalition today.

Just like the British, the Coalition and its successor administrations also face the matter of the tribal factor. The Coalition inherited a re-energised tribal power structure in Iraq. Promoted by Saddam during the last ten years of his regime, in a bid to secure his increasingly precarious grasp on power, these primordial, localised and anarchic power bases have been in the ascendancy across the rural outlands of Iraq. The consequences of tribal power were well illustrated during the British period of Mandate. Basic lack of security on the ground, combined with the persistence of the British belief in hierarchy, meant the authority of tribal lords was steadily strengthened. The tribal structures acted as a break on the modernising project. They developed into a series of parallel structures of governance, and undermined the ambitions for a centralised Iraq, a homogeneous legal and institutional state. While the Coalition might not have championed the tribal leaders with too much enthusiasm, they have nevertheless relied upon them for security and stability. Dependence upon these anti-modernising factions may once again – as with the British – undermine the modernising and stabilising project that the Coalition has embarked upon.

The lessons to be drawn from the British occupation and Mandate are manifold. The British administration suffered from internal divisions over the vision for Iraq. The British underestimated the cost of occupation, and misjudged the practical and political difficulties of occupation. Then, in the face of significant nationalist insurgency in Iraq – the Iraq Revolt – and increasing political and economic domestic pressures, Britain chose an early escape from its responsibilities to Iraq. Thus, what was arguably a noble quest to introduce a western-styled Middle Eastern government was defeated by expense, domestic pressures and Iraqi resistance. But this chapter begins with an assessment of the Kurdish issue; a distinctive feature of the British legacy, and a problem that is as important and complex today as it was in the early 1920s.

The Kurdish issue – the British legacy

The most significant legacy of the British presence was the drawing of Iraq's borders in ways that continued to 'represent a sign of fragility and a source of apprehension'.[2] By creating a cleft country, with its significant Kurdish population, Iraq has had three major dilemmas that have not eased over time: sustaining territorial integrity in the face of Kurdish nationalism; building an Iraqi identity that goes beyond Arab ethnicity; and reaching an effective agreement on the Kurdish issue with its nervous neighbours.

As in many other former dependent territories and colonies, the political boundaries established by the British have created significant problems for Iraq since the 1920s, and remain contentious today. The borders of Iraq were drawn, as in other cases, according to British imperial interests; interests which proved inflexible, unsustainable and indefensible over time. But for the Kurds, the legacy of the British period was still more profound. In the Kurdish view, British involvement in their fate meant losing the potential to form and sustain their own nation, as well as betrayal by the international community. Today, if the violent narrative between the Kurds and the Arab Iraqis is not to be perpetuated, the Coalition may need to ensure that it does not leave Iraq before resolving the tensions between Kurdish and Arab identities, and forging a level of common interest between the two major Iraqi ethnicities.[3] This challenge is significant and similar to that faced by the British; balancing Kurdish autonomy and independence, while binding the future of the Iraqi Kurds into the potential of Iraq itself.

At the Treaty of Sèvres in 1920, between the allies and Turkey, there was a promise of an autonomous Kurdish region, which would be allowed to apply for admission to the League of Nations within a year.[4] This was a significant mark and commitment to an independent Kurdistan spanning Turkey, Iraq and Iran. Independence was not just on the agenda but had been agreed formally. However, by the time of the Treaty of Lausanne 1923, Britain's strategic interests had shifted and were now better served by improving relations with Turkey. Othman, a Kurdish historian, notes that 'Churchill maintained that peace with Turkey was of utmost importance both for the introduction of the intended reduction in the cost of British administration in Iraq and the British effort to contain Russia's southward advance towards the Persian Gulf.'[5] The Kurdish issue became the basis of a compromise that kept Turkey on Britain's side. While Turkey would not regain northern Iraq, its worse fear – that of Kurdish independence – was calmed convincingly by the British. The Lausanne Treaty, while accommodating aspects of both the British and Turkish agendas, in the eyes of many Kurds showed 'how they were used as pawns during the Lausanne negotiations, how their lands were forcibly incorporated into Iraq and Turkey, and finally how the Lausanne negotiations affected British policy towards the Kurds in northern Iraq'.[6] Promises made and broken on grounds of imperial strategic interests provide stark lessons that are not lost on today's Kurds. In an effort to compensate the Kurds for what they perceived to be their lost independence, the British attempted to establish what Marr describes as 'autonomous provinces in the Kurdish areas of the Mosul *vilayet* that could be loosely attached to their Arab administration in the plains'.[7] However, this autonomous model also failed, and the cycle of uprising, violence, intrigue and broken deals that has plagued relations between the Arabs and Kurds of Iraq, started in earnest.

Kurdish nationalism and desire for independence, while in existence prior to the British occupation, never had a better chance of success than under the British. This sense of a missed opportunity has been at the core of Kurdish identity ever since. While Kurdish Iraq was formally integrated as part of Iraq, incorporation heralded a period of Kurdish resentment towards the state itself and left a legacy of unfulfilled ambitions. The British were neither able nor particularly interested in coming to a settlement with the Kurds. In the first place, the British traded the Kurds' hope for independence for their own strategic goals (in particular peace with Turkey and the development of new oil interests in Kirkuk and Mosul), disingenuously offering forms of autonomy to the Kurdish region while at the same time crushing them if their aspirations went beyond the desires of the British. On withdrawal, the British provided palliative reassurances for Kurdish well-being in the face of an Arab nationalist government that the British themselves had installed.

Today the challenge for the Coalition and transitional administrations, and for the new leaders of Iraq, is to secure a long-term and sustainable settlement with the Kurds, stopping short of independence; an elaborate compromise that eluded the British. There are few commentators who would dismiss the complexities of Kurdish nationalism. Even so, while a settlement was never reached under the British, calls for Kurdish independence are in the ascendant once again. Stansfield argues that the overthrow of Saddam may even prove to have been a double-edged sword for the Kurds, with the pressure for greater integration coming at a time when they have been enjoying the fruits, many of them financial, of their autonomous status.

By some accounts, Kurdish independence may be an option once again, given 'an increasingly virulent Kurdish nationalism'[8] that may not be containable. Certainly, the scope for unifying modern Iraq under one identity, one cultural and historical narrative and one central administration is limited by the fact that northern Iraq has enjoyed over ten years of autonomy under the protection of the international community. In the north, the Kurds have had their own parliament, have normalised elections and have ring-fenced funding from the UN Oil for Food programme. The education curriculum is in Kurdish and the teaching of Arabic is not compulsory, which may further drive an identity split. While the Kurds have stated their commitment to federalism and to sustaining their place within Iraq, if there is any hint of a reduction of their current power base, the US may face a reaction similar to that experienced by the British in the first Kurdish uprising in 1919. Some Kurds quietly and cautiously admit that independence is their true aim,[9] but others are more explicit in demanding a referendum on an independent Kurdistan.[10] As Laipson notes, 'the reintegration of the Kurdish north is not a given'.[11]

There is a growing debate in the United States about Iraq's territorial integrity that may add more fuel to the demands of Kurdish nationalism. Leslie Gelb is one of those commentators who have joined a broader discussion about the possibility of a 'three state solution'. While he admits that this has been 'unthinkable in Washington for decades', the *de facto* independence of Kurdistan for many years may make reintegration impossible, and concessions to greater autonomy might in any case avoid a civil war.[12] However, other analysts are more optimistic and have more faith in the idea of Iraq as an established country. Patrick Clawson, for example, argues that a very important factor for cohesion in Iraq is oil, making for 'powerful glue'.[13]

The Kurds appear well aware of historical comparisons with the 1920s and their perceived betrayal at the hands of a foreign 'benefactor'. There are many references in Kurdish papers and by Kurdish commentators to the period of the Mandate, with wistful acknowledgement of the opportunities missed in gaining independence. While in public, independence is being talked down by the Kurdish Democratic party (KDP) and Patriotic Union of Kurdistan (PUK); it could be argued plausibly that these parties are merely waiting to judge the outcome of the next few years before fully declaring their hand.[14]

The nature of this 'bastardised' geography has not only plagued the Kurds. Throughout its history, the development of an Iraqi political and ethnic identity has been challenged by the existence of a non-Arab minority representing as much as 15 per cent of the population. Without the Kurdish territories Iraq would be an Arab country, based on the longer historical common narrative of Basra and Baghdad. Throughout its history, integrationist initiatives attempted by Iraq's leaders have frequently been thwarted by both the Kurdish desire for political inclusion in terms of power, and their insistence on ethnic exclusivism symbolised by political autonomy and cultural differentiation. The constant need to consider first the demands of the Iraqi state and then the demands of the Kurds has resulted in a series of 'push-me pull-you' policies ranging from extreme state repression to attempts to provide the Kurds with some level of autonomy. Once again, as Wimmer shows, this problem – and the response to it – has an historical pedigree:

The new regime [of the 1920s] envisioned the compulsory assimilation of the different minorities into the mainstream of Arabism which was regarded as the centrepiece of the nation's cultural heritage and its foremost contribution to world history ... The more the regime tried to enforce its vision of society, the fiercer the resistance became, giving rise to ever higher levels of repression and domination.[15]

With eight major revolts in northern Iraq from 1919 to 1958, the Kurds had a reputation of 'exploit[ing] any perceived weakness of central power to assert their own autonomy'.[16] These actions did nothing to reassure Arab Iraqis that the Kurds' intention was benign as far as the fledgling Iraqi state was concerned. This duality of identity and opportunism has been a theme throughout Kurdish politics, leaving successive Iraqi leaders with the impression that the Kurds' ultimate aim is nothing short of independence.

On the other hand, British exceptionalism was not without its difficulties. It appeared to the British that every time they offered greater autonomy, the Kurds pushed further for independence or were unable to agree on a mechanism within their own community. The British attempts at accommodation during the Mandate merely raised expectations, exposed the frustrations of the Lausanne Treaty, and fuelled the independence movement in northern Iraq. To compound the problem, the region of Kirkuk with its rich oil reserves 'has proved to be an insurmountable obstacle for the Kurds and the Iraqi government to reach mutually acceptable agreement on'.[17] The inclusion of Kirkuk from the time of the creation of Iraq has been the fault line for independence. With Kirkuk, Kurdistan has economic viability and strategic power, without Kirkuk, Kurdistan would always be dependent either on other states or international handouts.

While the repression and violence meted out to the Kurds throughout the history of Iraq cannot be justified, it should be acknowledged that those at the centre of the Iraqi nation-building project have frequently been frustrated in their goals by a 15 per cent minority of the population that at best resents the existence of the nation, and at worst aspires to secede. The need to articulate a national identity that could accommodate ethnic diversity was a challenge that defeated the first custodians of Iraq, and it is still a significant challenge today.

Finally, the geographical spread of the Kurds between Iraq, Iran, Turkey and Syria has made into an international cause a problem that a unified Iraqi state might have hoped could be contained and managed as a domestic issue. This has further undermined the capacity for Iraq's central government to arrive at durable domestic solutions in relation to the Kurds. The involvement of both Turkey and Iran in Iraq's affairs was evident in the 1920s, and it is evident today. Any resolution of the Iraqi Kurdish issue will certainly continue to attract the attention and concern (and, perhaps, direct involvement) of these two neighbours. During the Mandate, the Turks restated their claim over Mosul and launched some incursions into the Kurdish regions, creating a highly charged situation that was and still is a regular feature of Iraqi-Turkish relations. Even in 2002 the Turkish Defence Minster reasserted Turkey's claim over the region. As reported in the *Daily Star* in August 2002, the 'Turkish

Defence Minister Sabahattin Cakmakoglu, characterised the Mosul and Kirkuk districts of Iraq as parts of Turkey that were forcibly taken away from it after World War I, and northern Iraq in its entirety is a "trust" under Turkey's "safekeeping," which it will do its utmost to retain.'[18]

It might be, as a result, that any settlement arranged with the Iraqi Kurds will need at least the 'tacit approval'[19] or resigned acceptance by the Turks – still an important NATO ally. Without reaching a level of regional understanding the shadow of intervention may plague the relationship between Baghdad and the Kurds. In addition, this territorial fragility may again offer the excuse for a sovereign Iraq to build a substantial army, that may not only destabilise Iraq internally, but would also concern the Iranians who fear 'the remilitarisation of Iraq'.[20]

If the violent narrative between Kurd and Arab Iraqis is not to be perpetuated in the new, post-Saddam Iraq, the challenge for the Coalition is to ensure that it does not leave Iraq before resolving the tensions between Kurdish and Arab communities, and forging a level of common interest between the two major Iraqi ethnicities: 'As part of the founding principles of a new Iraq, the Arab majority will need to offer the Kurds a pact safeguarding their socio-political and cultural rights.'[21] If the Coalition fails, repeating the performance of the British before it, then the unwelcome prospect is of the destructive narrative between Baghdad and the Kurds repeating itself, with the evolving Iraqi state becoming destabilised internally, regionally and internationally.[22]

The Shia

It seems unlikely that the Coalition will repeat the British error of excluding the Shia majority from the levers of power. However, there are some issues confronting the United States and its allies that could, in the longer term, erode trust between the Shia majority and the Coalition. Some commentators, for example, voice the concern that the Coalition might emulate Britain's mistakes by seeking to understand the Shia and their aspirations 'through the distorted shorthand supplied by the dominant cultural stereotypes of the day'.[23] When the British began their Iraq campaign in 1914, they were initially welcomed by the Shia as liberators from the Sunni dominance of the Ottoman Empire. However, by the end of the Mandate, the Shia had almost entirely withdrawn from political involvement under the British and the appointed Sunni elite. Precisely why the Shia were left out of the British nation-building 'project' in the 1920s throws light on some of the issues facing the Coalition today. The British experience reveals that it has been all too easy to classify, isolate and then discriminate against the Shia in the project of nation-building in Iraq, in the main due to a lack of understanding of Shiism, distrust, and fear of its aspirations.

Fellows sums up the British concerns by stating that the 'Shi'is were noticeably absent from most government offices, partly because of their lack of administrative experience, partly because of anti-Shi'i attitudes among Sunni Arab Notables in Baghdad, but mostly because of British wariness of Shi'i clericalism'.[24] In the first place, the British did not recognise the cultural and confessional diversity of Shiism, ranging from secular merchants to Iranian clerics. The British perceived a more monolithic identity with the clerics at its head, failing to comprehend that, as today, 'internal Shia politics are complex and riven with rivalries'.[25] Gardner comments on the category error made by the British in assuming a common hierarchical frame of reference: 'Where the Sunni hierarchy tends to be uniform and conformist, if not always monolithic, the markedly distinct Shia approach tends to create multiple centres of competing influence.'[26] Translating these aspirations into a political context, Sami Zubaida has argued that 'Its [Shiism's] politics are far from uniform communal solidarity, but consist of many combinations of interest, ideology and movement, which often transcend communal boundaries.'[27]

These various groups had diverse opinions regarding the role of the nation state. The 'divines had long been equivocal about the new Iraqi state ... they refused to accept the Mandate because it meant that [Faisal's] administration would be under the influence of a non-Muslim power'.[28] The Shia intelligentsia, on the other hand, were eager to engage with the new state, although throughout the Mandate they were excluded from office and authority for a variety of nebulous reasons, often promulgated by the Sunni elites.[29] At the same time, Shia landlords and tribal heads felt that the state provided protection for their lands, and were often relied upon – and rewarded – maintaining law and order at the local level.

However, having characterised the Shia in terms of their most radical voice, the British instead chose leaders for Iraq from the Sunni community, who in their minds reflected more closely the British ideal of nation building. The lesson is obvious enough: however vocal and populist the radical clerics in contemporary Iraq might appear, it is essential that Coalition policies and attitudes towards the Shia community reflect the diverse nature of Shiism, rather than perpetuate the British misconception of a 'theocratic monolith'.

The British were also concerned that the Shia clerics were under the influence of Iran. Following the Islamic Iranian Revolution of 1905 the region saw the emergence of more theocratic states. With 80,000 Persians in Iraq (in Najaf and Karbala), the British felt far from comfortable providing a power base for this majority community. However, in the words of one commentator, 'Iraqi Shi'ism is radically different from its Iranian counterpart, not in its formal doctrine but in the way it has interacted with politics, and the economy.'[30] Many others have argued that, as more recent converts, it is the Arab culture and traditions that hold more sway over the Iraqi Shia, rather than their confessional relationship with Iran.

Influenced by their Sunni surrogates, the British were also persuaded that the Shia community had little or no experience of government and administration. This offered a seemingly unarguable, bureaucratic rationale with which to exclude the Shia from working with the British in the design and development of a new state. But the alleged lack of political experience was unfounded. Gertrude Bell described a Shia ecclesiastical leadership which was both complex and administratively well developed: 'their functions are not only religious; they excise a very strong suasion and are a power which the Turks have had occasion to regard with dislike and distrust'.[31] And Nakash records that by 1920

> the Shi'i religious establishment could compete with any government in Iraq over the influence and mobilisation of the local population. The existence of such a highly autonomous and politically active religious establishment posed a danger to the authority of the nascent Iraqi state.[32]

The marginalisation of the Shia on the grounds of political inexperience was in the main merely a reflection of Britain's interpretation of politics – formal, institutionalised and homogeneous – and rooted in distrust. The British did not appreciate the politics of the Shia, nor did they find in Shia political structures mechanisms that resonated with liberal western values. As a result, the new Iraqi state and its structures were associated with a minority vision of statehood, one that has dominated Iraqi politics ever since. Plainly, the Coalition should be concerned that misunderstandings and prejudices held by the British in the 1920s are not allowed to repeat themselves.

But the errors of the past do seem prone to repetition. After years of oppression, and a resurgence of religious fervour particularly in the last ten years, Nakash writes of the possibility of a 'big gap' between the American vision for Iraq and that of the dominant Shia.[33] A liberal, secular democratic structure in the image of America may be unacceptable to many Shia, and indeed to many Sunni. Many in Iraq have warned the Coalition not to impose political and social structures that privilege western values at the expense of Iraq's historical, religious and cultural traditions. Western liberalism as projected by the British in the 1920s never became embedded in Iraqi society, and may be even less likely to be accepted today.

The Shia have suffered over the last 80 years from governments who have proposed the ideologies of both democracy and socialism. Both have been seen to fail in Iraq and have been misused as tools of repression. For that reason, indigenous Islamic solutions are widely seen to represent 'a search for a new and effective social formula that might stand a better chance of being authentic'.[34] While the Coalition have both engaged with and recognised the importance of the Shia, taking their majority position within Iraq and on the Governing Council, some believe that once a fuller Iraqi debate on the political future of Iraq takes its natural course, that trust may erode.[35]

By some accounts, this breakdown in trust had begun to emerge by summer 2003, with accusations that some local elections in Najaf were cancelled by Coalition authorities concerned that the outcome might not have been to their liking.[36]

Furthermore, Iranian influence in Iraq may be perceived as threatening to the Americans, in light of their current relationship with one of the targeted 'axis of evil'. While not articulated in Iraq, Donald Rumsfeld has been explicit in his rejection of an Iranian political model migrating to Iraq. Nevertheless, in spite of the fact that the Iranian Shia tradition is different to that of the Iraqis, a common confessional, in a predominantly Sunni region, may well ensure closer relationships between Iraq and Iran in the future.

A period during which confidence and trust can be built with the Shia could well prove crucial to the future stability of Iraq. But there are very high political expectations at stake, with many leading Shia believing that their time has come. Managing these expectations through a period of transition, with competing agendas amongst Iraqis as a whole and within the Shia community itself, will be demanding. In June 2003 Ayatollah Bahr al-Ulum, a Shia cleric from Najaf widely respected as a religious scholar of liberal inclination, warned the Americans, 'we are trying to educate the people in peaceful [political] means, but we must have a positive response [from the Coalition] or we won't be able to hold the line'.[37] Trust and respect lie at the heart of the relationship between the Coalition and the Shia. While the British did not apply themselves to either understanding or appreciating the Shia, the Coalition will not be able to ignore or dismiss a strong and determined majority who believe that their time for power has arrived. As Gardner observes, 'The Iraqi Shia intend to claim their political entitlement after a century of struggle as a downtrodden majority.'[38]

The Sunni community

In one respect at least, the Coalition faces challenges significantly different from those which confronted the British; the relationship of the occupying authority with the Sunni community. The Coalition will need to secure the Sunnis a role within the Iraqi political arena. In other words, the challenge is to ensure that Britain's exclusion of the Shia is an example not followed, otherwise one disenfranchised group in Iraq will merely have been exchanged for another. That said, mutual animosity is perpetuated by constant insurgency. By some accounts, the Americans have already alienated a significant proportion of the Sunnis through 'heavy handed counter insurgency tactics'.[39] Furthermore, in the context of de-Ba'athification, the Coalition have found it difficult to identify Sunni leaders who are both representative and not associated with the previous regime. If the ethnic and confessional divisions within Iraq are not to be perpetuated, the challenge for the Coalition is to ensure that the Sunnis do not retreat from political life as the Shia did in the 1920s.

The social structure of Iraq is as complex today as it has been historically. Marr has argued for a broader, more inclusive understanding of this structure: 'To these ethnic and sectarian divisions must be added a third social dichotomy ... the division between town and tribe.'[40] During the Occupation and Mandate period the British engaged with the tribal leaders actively and gave them greater prominence than had the Ottomans. The British approach, a combination of calculated pragmatism and romanticism, ensured that tribal leaders were involved in the governance of Iraq as something akin to a 'rural aristocracy' made responsible for 'establishing and holding the balance between state and society'.[41] Sections of the British establishment held a well developed, romantic attachment to the image of the tribal leader, and to the idea of the tribe as central to Arab and oriental society. But the tribal organisation also offered a more prosaic path to the effective exercise of authority in Iraq. The British relied on tribal leaders to control parts of the country that their limited troop resources were unable to secure; a device that had been much used elsewhere in the British Empire. This established the tribal leaders at the core of rural law and order, a position that was made still more secure at the end of the First World War.

The British created a two-tiered political structure, one which undermined the central nation-building project, and possibly placed a brake upon economic and social modernising programmes through their tribal policies. The British reliance on the tribal structures was self-imposed and was initially stimulated by their concern for security and the lack of sufficient military and policing resources on the ground. As Michael Eisenstadt has noted, the US should be wary of being lured by 'The Tribal Temptation'.[42] In modern Iraq, as in the 1920s, security is a priority for the Coalition. The parallel with the British experience comes closer still, given that many consider the Coalition's levels of deployment to be inadequate to secure law and order in Iraq. The tribal problem is made more complex for the Coalition by Saddam's recent promotion of the tribal structures. While the British reinvigorated the tribes themselves, the Coalition is inheriting an existing and empowered primordial political structure.[43] The dilemma for the Coalition is that it may require compliance and support from the tribal leaders in the short term for security purposes, in order to install a political system, that ultimately aims to marginalise them. In addition, by engaging with the Sheikhs, the Coalition will give them and their structures credence. For one analyst, the situation is urgent:

if the US is serious about promoting democracy in Iraq, strategies to ensure its establishment have to be implemented quickly, but carefully, before localised groups become firmly entrenched, and the Iraqi state undergoes a process of deconstruction which may prove impossible to reverse.[44]

Clearly, as far as the ethnic divide, the confessional tensions and the parallel tribal power bases are concerned, the Coalition has much to learn from the British experience. The structural challenges of managing such a heterogeneous society, whose components have either monopolised the power of the state or have been subjugated by it, are significant:

> While the British colonial project clearly drew on Western models of political institutions and social practices, ... British rule was highly dependent on the application of distinctions founded on religion, ethnicity, and other categories to establish its dominance.[45]

The dilemma for the Coalition is the need to ensure representation for all ethnic and religious groups within the new Iraq, while not institutionalising these divisions in a way that may come to inhibit the development of a common Iraqi identity. From an Iraqi perspective, Kanan Makiya proposes that Iraq needs 'a re-design of the Iraqi state as a non-ethnically based federal and democratic entity'.[46]

The Iraqi state has always attracted 'resistance, indifference, or acceptance',[47] and since the period of the Mandate has used patronage, coercion and violence to secure its aims. The future of Iraq may therefore depend on the extent to which institutions and common norms can be developed which gain the confidence of these diverse sections of Iraqi society, and do not alienate them more deeply from the Iraqi state. In Marr's view, the challenge for the Coalition is that 'to recapture a sense of nationhood, Iraq's ethnic and sectarian communities, its tribal and clan groups, and its once vigorous urban middle class must rekindle a sense of common purpose and destiny'.[48]

The Coalition – its role in the new Iraq

Gertrude Bell summarised succinctly the invidious position any foreign occupying power faces in Iraq:

> To carry on civil government in an occupied country is a task which presents special difficulties. The Administrator is hampered by the proximity of hostile influences, by divided allegiances, and by the uncertainty of his own position.[49]

Quite apart from the management of the immediate post-conflict situation in Iraq, and the transition to a provisional Iraqi government, the role adopted by the Coalition in the coming few years will certainly be influential in the development of the new Iraqi state. For some, the issue reduces further still: 'the nature of and reaction to an American presence in Iraq over the next decade will, to a larger degree, determine the type of state that emerges'.[50] In this respect the British legacy has not been judged positively; while the

British involvement in Iraq did not precondition the emergence of a dictator such as Saddam Hussein, the choices made by the British certainly created the environment in which such a leader might emerge.[51] Of course, there are important distinctions to be drawn between the two experiences. But Britain's reaction to Iraqi nationalism and the increasing unpopularity of the occupation of Iraq, the inappropriateness of the western political structures the British sought nevertheless to place in Iraq, and the long-term relationship between the occupier and the occupied, are all areas where the Coalition can learn important lessons.

The British faced both internal and external challenges that may appear similar to those facing the Coalition. In the first place, the British administration was divided on the policy they would adopt in managing Iraq once the war was over. Second, the British underestimated the cost of occupation. Furthermore, they misjudged the difficulties of occupation. Then, in the face of a significant nationalist insurgency in Iraq – the Iraq Revolt – and growing political and economic domestic pressures, Britain chose an early withdrawal from its responsibilities to Iraq. In choosing an early exit the British found themselves turning hastily to a group within Iraq that reflected a British vision of the governance of this new state. In doing so, they imposed a non-Iraqi monarch leading a government dominated by a Sunni minority as the best means to ensure a quick withdrawal from the difficulties and cost of Mandate.

Yet, just like the Coalition in 2003, the British began with lofty goals for Iraq, pursuing the vision of a modern liberal democratic structure to the standards of the 1920s: 'for perhaps the first time in history, a major world power willingly attempted to transform a territory it had occupied into a sovereign state based on democratic principles'.[52] But it was not long before the British recognised that the democratic project in Iraq was particularly elusive and that their presence was turning an already unstable situation into something even worse. So, in the face of the Iraq Revolt in 1920, the British beat the retreat.

There were various reasons for the Iraq Revolt, but essentially it illustrated the stresses of a new administrative order imposed from outside. The Revolt was driven from various quarters: by those whose previous position of authority under the Ottomans had been eroded; those whose local power base had been undermined by a central administration; and those who were angered by taxation measures. By 1920 British policies had managed to alienate much of Iraqi society – both those who had lost power due to the British and those who had optimistically hoped for power under the British.[53] This constellation of the disaffected became a seminal point in Iraqi history not least because 6000 Iraqis lay dead as a result, but also because it represented 'a manifestation of both religious and incipient nationalist feeling'.[54] The Revolt has become 'part of the founding myth of Iraqi Nationalism'[55] with its significance not lost on future leaders of Iraq.

If the Revolt can be described as the result of a distant, disconnected foreign ruling group stimulating a disparate oppositionist movement united in 'opposition to colonial domination',[56] then there might be lessons – and concerns – for the future of Iraq. The quandary faced by the British in the 1920s may resonate today: 'How, under intense international scrutiny, could [the British] control a well armed society that had become increasingly resentful about the occupation of their country?'[57] As a result of the Revolt, together with rising costs and lack of public support for the occupation in Britain, from 1920 onwards Britain's primary goal was 'to unburden itself of its international responsibilities towards Iraq as quickly as possible'.[58] However, in its rush to leave, Britain handed over political power to a comparatively competent yet markedly unrepresentative Sunni elite. The British established some ostensibly respectable but weak and non-indigenous institutions, and further compromised these by insisting that the government of Iraq served Britain's strategic, economic and political interests.

In an internal Colonial Office memorandum, Winston Churchill, then Colonial Secretary, made the point plainly enough:

> we are letting ourselves in for all the work and costs, and excluding ourselves from any chance of return. If things go well there ought to be some returns both indirect and direct ... it would certainly be a pity faithfully to receive all the kicks and to reject any of the halfpence when at last they arrive.[59]

The rewards came in time: by 1932, through a series of treaties, the Iraqi government delivered to the British significant oil concessions, a strategic presence in relation to trading with India, and air bases. But every Iraqi government since 1932 has derived significant popularity from its eviction of these British assets, from Faisal I himself through to the nationalisation of all oil assets held by the British by Saddam in the 1970s.

Conclusion

The British began their involvement in Iraq motivated by high ideals. But they miscalculated the economic and political difficulties they would face. In the end, the British withdrew hastily, having constructed weak institutions that were dependent on a minority ruling elite. Further, by securing economic and strategic assets in Iraq as a reward for its efforts, the British institutionalised anti-foreign and anti-western sentiment.[60] The Coalition's commitment to the restructuring of Iraq is similarly high-minded, but the task is likely to be no less complex and fraught with risk than that faced by the British: 'The main challenge for the United States will be remaining in Iraq long enough to achieve significant and lasting benefits without overstaying its welcome and stoking anti-American sentiment.'[61] Even without an insurgency on the scale and scope of the Iraq Revolt, the Coalition is already feeling the strains of occupation, and it seems that their intent is to withdraw sooner than first expected.

Initially the US appeared inclined to resist pressures for a quick handover despite international public opinion, domestic economic pressures, and the views of some key figures on the Governing Council, all pressing for an Iraqi administration as quickly as possible.

However, in November 2003, with a significantly rising US death toll, searching questions in the US Congress on the expense of the occupation, and an American public beginning to question the Bush Administration's policy for Iraq, there appeared to be a change of direction in US policy.

The Coalition abandoned their seven-point transitional plan and instead imposed a deadline of six months to hand over to a Transitional Government,[62] promptly inviting the criticism that the Coalition was planning to exit too rapidly, just as the British had done, in the face of insurgency in Iraq and anxiety at home.[63] Indeed, the prospect of an early exit causes many in Iraq concern, among them Ayatollah Sistani. These anxieties are not a reflection of Iraqis' desire for sustained occupation, but are related to their fear that the transitional process proposed might place disproportionate levels of authority and power in the hands of those who are already close to the Coalition.[64] With a Transitional Government in place for eight months before full democratic elections, the concern is that the incumbents will seek to model the new constitution to their advantage, and that of the Coalition. Their particular concern, for example, is the constitutional position of the returning Iraqi diaspora, and especially those who have been associated with the Iraqi National Congress (INC) and the Iraqi National Accord (INA). It will be crucial, therefore, both that the new Iraqi constitution will be seen to be indigenous, and that the Coalition does not open itself to the charge that it has repeated Britain's mistake by building institutions that were 'less a system of government than a means of control'.[65]

The new, interim structures may face the same dilemma as that which undermined the King in the Mandate period; the need to show independence from the Coalition, while at the same time relying upon the Coalition's presence to ensure their own, and national security. On this basis, it had been proposed that the Transitional Government will 'invite' the Americans to stay on after the June transition as 'allies', under some form of status of forces agreement.[66] This policy might, however, cause tension and conflict between the new sovereign government of Iraq and the Coalition, as it remains unclear whether the Americans will bide by the wishes of the new government, or promote their own vision for the new Iraq.

The Coalition will also, finally, need to consider the legacy of the British in securing and sustaining interests in Iraq after their withdrawal. While American expertise may offer Iraq necessary skills, it remains the case that ownership or preferential rights over Iraqi assets may have to be legitimised by the people of Iraq, not simply by their leadership. Iraqi history reveals a strong tradition of anti-colonialism and antagonism towards foreign interests, and there might well be particular resentment towards any long-term US military bases established in Iraq.[67]

The challenges for the Coalition are thus extremely complex, and in some ways contradictory. The Coalition needs to secure the rights of all ethnic, religious and tribal groups, without at the same time embedding and institutionalising these divisions. The Coalition needs to support the development of a new indigenous political structure in Iraq, yet must do so without setting out to model the new structure in its own image, or too obviously along western lines. The Coalition needs to support a new democratic government, yet must refrain from exercising any sanction or leverage over the new government's strategy. And the United States must also, finally, be circumspect in the pursuit of its own interests in Iraq and the broader region, so as not to undermine the structures it aims to promote.

The experience of the British serves, at the very least, to identify some of the dilemmas facing the Coalition. If the British Occupation and the Mandate can provide lessons for today, it might be what the British did *not* achieve that could be most instructive for the Coalition. But there are doubts that the Coalition is even concerned to analyse the comparisons; 'The United States in Iraq today must understand that it is both living with the consequences of [British] failure and is in danger of repeating it.'[68] As Gertrude Bell warned in 1920, 'Well we are in for it and I think we shall need every scrap of personal influence and every hour of friendly intercourse we've ever had here in order to keep this country from falling into chaos.'[69]

Notes

1. D. Gardner, 'Time of the Shia', *Financial Times Magazine*, 30 August 2003, p. 18.
2. N. Ayubi, *Over-stating the Arab State, Politics and Society in the Middle East*, New York, I.B. Tauris, 2001, p. 112.
3. Y. Nakash, 'The Shi'ites and the Future of Iraq', *Foreign Affairs*, Vol. 82, No. 4, July/August 2003, p. 23.
4. P. Marr, *The Modern History of Iraq*, Oxford, Westview Press, 2003, p. 28.
5. A. Othman, 'The Kurds and the Lausanne Peace Negotiations 1922–23', *Middle East Studies*, Vol. 33, No. 3, July 1997, p. 521.
6. Ibid.
7. Marr, *The Modern History of Iraq*, p. 29.
8. G. Stansfield, Institute of Arab and Islamic Studies, University of Exeter, personal communication, 4 December 2003.
9. T. Judah, 'In Iraqi Kurdistan', in M. Sifry and C. Cerf (eds), *The Iraqi War Reader: History, Documents, Opinions*, New York, Touchstone, 2003, p. 579.
10. Dr N. Talabany, Open Letter to the Coalition Provisional Authority on a Referendum in Kurdistan, 6 August 2003: www.kurdweb.humanrights.de.
11. E. Laipson, 'Assessing the Long-term Challenges', in P. Clawson (ed.), *How to Build a New Iraq*, Washington, DC, The Washington Institute for Near East Policy, 2002, p. 13.

12. L. Gelb, 'The three-state solution', *New York Times*, 25 November 2003.
13. P. Clawson, 'Introduction', in Clawson, *How to Build a New Iraq*, p. 1.
14. Stansfield, personal communication, 4 December 2003.
15. A. Wimmer, *Nationalist Exclusion and Ethnic Conflict: Shadows of Modernity*, Cambridge, Cambridge University Press, 2002, p. 175.
16. C. Tripp, *A History of Iraq*, Cambridge, Cambridge University Press, 2002, p. 34.
17. Stansfield, personal communication, 4 December 2003.
18. See L. Sandys, 'A Game of Shadow Boxing: Iraq between Past and Future', www.opendemocracy.net, March 2003.
19. Nakash, 'The Shi'ites and the Future of Iraq', p. 23.
20. R.R. Francke, 'The Shape of a New Government', in Clawson, *How to Build a New Iraq*, p. 21.
21. Nakash, 'The Shi'ites and the Future of Iraq', p. 23.
22. Judah, 'In Iraqi Kurdistan', p. 570.
23. T. Dodge, *Inventing Iraq*, London, Hurst and Co., 2003, p. xi.
24. J. Yaphe, 'The Challenge of Nation Building in Iraq', in M. Eisenstadt and E. Mathewson, *Lessons from the British Experience*, Washington, DC, Washington Institute for Near East Studies, 2003, p. 47.
25. 'Salvaging Iraq', *The Economist*, 6 December 2003.
26. Gardner, 'Time of the Shia', p. 19.
27. S. Zubaida, Foreword, in F. Jabar, *The Shi'ite Movement in Iraq*, London, Saqi Books, 2003, p.13.
28. A. Kelidar, 'Iraqi National Integration under the British', in Eisenstadt and Mathewson, *Lessons from the British Experience*, p. 33.
29. S. Zubaida, *Islam, the People and the State*, New York, I.B. Tauris, 1995, p. 91.
30. Y. Nakash, *The Shi'is of Iraq*, Princeton, Princeton University Press, 2003, p. xviii.
31. P. Rich (ed.), *Arab War Lords and Iraqi Star Gazers: Gertrude Bell's 'The Arab of Mesopotamia'*, Lincoln, NE, Authors Choice Press, 2001, p. 68.
32. Nakash, *The Shi'is of Iraq*, p. 72.
33. Nakash, 'The Shi'ites and the Future of Iraq', p. 24.
34. N. Ayubi, *Over-stating the Arab State*, p. 51.
35. Stansfield, personal communication, 4 December 2003.
36. Gardner, 'Time of the Shia', p. 21.
37. Ibid.
38. Ibid., p. 16.
39. In personal communication with the author.
40. Marr, *The Modern History of Iraq*, p. 18.
41. Dodge, *Inventing Iraq*, p. 61.
42. M. Eisenstadt, 'Lessons for US Policymakers', in Eisenstadt and Mathewson, *Lessons from the British Experience*, p. 73.
43. Dodge, *Inventing Iraq*, p. 159.
44. Stansfield, personal communication, 4 December 2003.
45. S. Haj, *The Making of Iraq 1900–1963: Capital, Power and Ideology*, New York, State University of New York Press, 1997, p. 146.
46. K. Makiya, 'Our hopes betrayed: How a US blueprint for Post-Saddam Government quashed the hopes of Democratic Iraqis', *Observer*, 16 February 2003.
47. Tripp, *A History of Iraq*, p. 7.
48. Marr, *The Modern History of Iraq*, p. 307.
49. Rich, *Arab War Lords*, p. 52.
50. Dodge, *Inventing Iraq*, p. xix.

51. Ibid., p. 170.
52. E. Mathewson, 'Assessing the British Military Occupation', in Eisenstadt and Mathewson, *Lessons from the British Experience*, p. 64.
53. O. Bengio, 'Pitfall of Instant Democracy', in Eisenstadt and Mathewson, *Lessons from the British Experience*, p. 16.
54. Eisenstadt, 'Lessons for US Policymakers', p. 69.
55. Tripp, *The History of Iraq*, p. 44.
56. Yaphe, 'The Challenge of Nation Building in Iraq', p. 47.
57. Dodge, *Inventing Iraq*, p. x.
58. Ibid., p. 9.
59. Winston Churchill Internal Colonial Office memo, 7 May 1923. Sir Winston Churchill Archive Trust, Churchill College Cambridge. CHAR 2 126/25.
60. Marr, *The Modern History of Iraq*, p. 309.
61. Eisenstadt, 'Lessons for US Policymakers', p. 70.
62. See www.cpa-iraq.org/government/AgreementNov15.pdf.
63. M. Danner, 'Delusions in Baghdad', *New York Review of Books*, 18 December 2003.
64. 'Salvaging Iraq', *The Economist*, 6 December 2003.
65. Marr, *The Modern History of Iraq*, p. 29.
66. 'Salvaging Iraq', *The Economist*, 6 December 2003.
67. Nakash, 'The Shi'ites and the Future of Iraq', p. 25.
68. Dodge, *Inventing Iraq*, p. xii.
69. Gertrude Bell Archives. Newcastle University, for 14 March 1920, the time of the Iraq Revolt. See www.gerty.ncl.ac.uk/letters/l1343.htm.

2
The Diplomacy that Led to War in Iraq

Michael Clarke

There can be few precedents in recent history where leading western powers send their forces abroad to fight a brilliantly successful military campaign, remove a manifestly evil dictator, and yet have to live with continuing domestic hostility and cynicism towards the whole enterprise. Arguments over the motives, rightness, and the legitimacy of the Second Gulf War will not lie down.[1] The whole operation remains controversial. Perhaps the war is part of America's drive towards a 'compulsive empire'; perhaps a symptom of transatlantic breakdown; or perhaps it is merely a traditional example of a great power's reactions in the face of a manifest threat.[2]

It may turn out to be all of these things, but a simpler explanation from the present standpoint is that it was a crisis in which all of the significant actors overplayed their respective diplomatic hands to the point that a crisis inherently capable of resolution became an increasingly unavoidable war. This was not an accidental conflict: clearly there were major clashes of interests driving it along. But in a dispute in which there were so many diplomatic trade-offs to be made – so many entry points for diplomatic solutions – war was perceived as the worst outcome for all the players, save the United States, and even Washington was deeply ambiguous over what benefits a successful military operation would bring. Yet a long, relatively simple, crisis ended in war. Saddam Hussein repeatedly defied the international community, assuming that he could manipulate the situation to survive, and was then brought to his final defeat after 24 years of absolute power. The Europeans – chiefly France, Germany and Britain – dreaded a US war against Iraq, since this was easily the most divisive issue in transatlantic relations, yet in the event their own diplomacy did much to bring it about. Russia had something to gain as a diplomatic broker between the US and its adversary, as it had been in successive Balkan crises in the 1990s, yet ended up compounding European failures without strengthening its strategic partnership with the US. The

United Nations and NATO were at the heart, respectively, of the diplomatic road and the road to war, and yet both failed to represent more than the sum of their parts and were instrumental in presenting war eventually as an inevitable outcome to the crisis. The United States, according to most popular arguments, was the only actor who got what it wanted: a spectacular and successful war against an evil tyrant. But even this is an overstatement. The President and his close circle of advisers were determined to confront Saddam Hussein. They were prepared to engineer a decisive 'regime change' in Iraq, peacefully if possible, by war if necessary. Others in Washington were not so sure about the real objectives. And even the President did not want 'regime change through war' to be at the price of prolonged 'nation-building' in the very heart of an unstable international neighbourhood, still less one that hung about his neck in an election year. For President Bush, confronting Saddam through coercive diplomacy would be the most efficient solution to the crisis: to prepare for war but to succeed without having to go through with it.

The political outcome of the Second Gulf War is still in question. President Bush declared the 'military phase' to be concluded on 1 May 2003, though many have argued that this may come to be seen merely as the opening campaign rather than the war itself. Whether history comes to judge this event as a five-week war, or a two (or more)-year war, the fact remains that the diplomacy leading up to it did not reflect good statesmanship on the part of any of the main players in the drama. Everyone overplayed their hand.

Saddam Hussein and Iraq

The actor whose overplayed hand is simplest to explain is Saddam Hussein himself. Like so many tyrannical dictators he was a cunning and skilful tactician but a very poor strategist, who failed to appreciate how much the international world had changed since the 1990s and how vulnerable he had become as a result. Saddam Hussein was a quintessential crisis leader. He was a highly influential vice president in the al-Bakr Ba'athist government from 1968 and assumed total power in 1979 when he persuaded al-Bakr to step down and immediately had 66 rivals shot in a sudden leadership purge. He consolidated his power in this literal way by pretending that there was a crisis with Syria which necessitated such a purge. Thereafter, he sought to strengthen his power through a series of crises, some of which he created, others that were visited on him.

In 1980 Saddam launched an invasion of Iran, partly to capitalise on its weakness after the Iranian revolution, partly to prevent Iranian intervention among Iraqi Shia which threatened to destabilise his government. This unsuccessful eight-year war killed between 800,000 and 1 million people, costing Iraq around $200 billion in debts and immediate reconstruction costs and leaving it a major debtor during the 1980s. Debts left the country in control of less than half its oil revenues. In 1987 Saddam was confronted by a nascent Kurdish revolt in the north of Iraq and suppressed it in the brutal 'Anfal' campaign, which involved the use of chemical weapons at Halabja in 1988. In August 1990, only two years after his disastrous war he sought to escape from the economic and political problems facing him by invading Kuwait. His forces were ejected from it in February 1991 by a unanimous and unprecedented international coalition that included all the Arab nations in one way or another.[3] For the next decade he was subject to international sanctions and forced to cooperate with UN arms inspectors, who dismantled much of Iraq's missile arsenal and its nuclear programme.[4] In the summer of 1991 both the Kurds in the north and the Marsh Arabs in the south rose in revolt and were immediately suppressed. In response, the allies imposed no-fly zones in the north and south of the country to prevent Saddam using his air power for further repression and intervened in the north to provide 'safe havens' for the displaced Kurds. Originally the no-fly zones were policed by aircraft from the US, Britain and France. France subsequently withdrew from the operation and the two remaining allies fought a low-level war of aerial attrition for the next twelve years which involved five outright western air offensives against his installations and served to dismantle, piece by piece, Iraq's air defence system. In 1992 and again in 1993 Saddam faced Iraqi army plots to kill him. In 1995 he faced a major internal power battle when his two sons-in-law defected to Jordan. He lured them back in February 1996 with promises of safety and dialogue but killed them immediately. Only four months later he thwarted the biggest coup yet in the army. Later that year his son Uday survived an assassination attempt. In autumn 1998 he forced a crisis with the UN arms inspectors of UNSCOM which resulted in their withdrawal from the country. In response, the US and Britain launched the biggest air campaign of this period against Iraq in Operation Desert Fox which was another, fairly unsuccessful, attempt to coerce Saddam into cooperation or perhaps into exile. Each international crisis gave him the opportunity again to shore up his domestic power-base, to the point where serious contenders simply no longer existed by the time al-Qaeda mounted its spectacular attack against the United States in 2001.

As he confronted the post '9/11' world, where he knew he was again in the US spotlight, not least because of his public support for the attack, Saddam had good reason to believe he was a natural survivor.[5] He clearly had faith in his tactical instincts in a crisis: indeed, he was at his best in such situations. International sanctions had weighed heavily on the Iraqi economy but Saddam had manipulated them to his political advantage. Massive smuggling operations run by his eldest son brought billions of dollars to the leadership and the opportunity to offer trade contracts to members of the UN Security Council. He blamed sanctions for the parlous state of the economy, which his regime had largely neglected since the early 1980s. He had manipulated the aerial war over the no-fly zones to pose as a victim of US and British aggression, while setting traps to lure coalition aircraft into killing boxes. He trumpeted his defiance of the US and of the 16 United Nations resolutions the US claimed to be upholding, while working to split the international community in dialogues, notably with Russia and France. Within Iraq, he successfully played on tribal tensions to maintain control, keeping both the clerical and secular oppositions disunited, though latterly he tried to disguise inherently secular Ba'athism in a cloak of Islam.

Almost certainly, Saddam Hussein calculated that he could weather the coming storm by finding enough room for manoeuvre in the way the United Nations would pursue the arms inspections – the 'cheat and retreat' strategy that so enraged US presidents – and continue to work to split the allies diplomatically. Having not engaged in any new diplomatic adventures since the expulsion of the UN arms inspectors in 1998, he was in a more favourable position than in previous crises; he was not provoking a response, and was essentially passive in the face of new US allegations in respect to weapons of mass destruction. If the US President was coming after him, he may even have calculated that there might be some new opportunities in the situation beyond mere survival.

Between September 2001 and March 2003, however, Saddam seemed to be largely unaware of the major weaknesses of his position. First, he had always overestimated his status as a torch-bearer of the Nasserite revolution in the Middle East. Like most Ba'athists, he wanted to further the revolution that had begun in Egypt in 1952 . But he also had 'vaulting ambitions' beyond Ba'athism, to dominate the region and be arbiter of the politics of the Gulf, using Iraq's oil reserves and a modern military machine, not excluding nuclear weapons.[6] The Nasserite revolution had long since run out of steam, however, and its torch-bearers were the marginalised of the region – the Palestinians, Syria and Iraq – while Arab politics have been increasingly dominated by different forces that the Iranian revolution released after 1979. Saddam basked in the admiration of many of the dispossessed Palestinians, since he was their loudest champion, and won grudging respect from many in the 'Arab street', if not from their governments, for his repeated defiance of the United States. He appears to have confused grudging respect, however, for real political support and an ability to galvanise popular feeling within Arab nations. In reality, he had very little of either.

Second, Saddam appears to have completely under-estimated the change in US attitudes to the world after 1998. The 'Desert Fox' campaign was a turning point in US behaviour that he simply failed to recognise. Even under the presidency of democrat Bill Clinton, the United States was turning decisively unilateralist in its view of international order by 1998. Successive crises in the Balkans had not shown the UN or the international community in a favourable light. The Dayton Agreement on Bosnia in 1995 had been effectively a unilateral US initiative that had taken diplomacy out of the hands of most of the other actors, and after Dayton it was being enforced by NATO with the US driving it along. In August 1998 the US embassies in Kenya and Tanzania were struck by al-Qaeda terrorists, killing 224 people. The US unilaterally responded twelve days later with Tomahawk missile strikes on Kabul and Khartoum where it claimed Al-Qaeda had facilities. As Saddam played cat and mouse with the UNSCOM inspectors during September and October, Clinton caved in to congressional pressure to sign the Iraq Liberation Act to fund and train Iraqi opposition groups. And as the 'Desert Fox' crisis unfolded between October and December the US, backed by Britain, decided on unilateral military action without a new UN resolution, in the face of European disquiet – tepid support from Germany, nothing from Italy, and outright hostility from France.

The US, in other words, was already at a turning point before 9/11. But the events of 2001 added great emotional power and domestic consensus to the US approach to security. Saddam's view that democracies were inherently weak simply did not take account of the fact that the US now saw itself as at war with its adversaries; that it was no longer 'casualty averse'; that it would no longer be restrained by a lack of international consensus; even that it would prepare for a costly war with a presidential election looming. Saddam's erstwhile tactics of 'cheat and retreat', playing for time, working to split the UN Security Council, and so on, were henceforth largely irrelevant. The fact that his tactics appeared to have any diplomatic leverage at all during the six months leading up to the Second Gulf War was not due to lack of resolve on the part of the US to 'deal with Iraq' one way or another. It was mainly a concession to their British allies to attempt to achieve US objectives by the most legitimate means possible.

Not least, it is apparent that Saddam not only failed to grasp the real lessons of the 1998 crisis but actually learned the wrong ones from it. Senior Iraqi leaders and military officers debriefed by the US since the war confirmed that Saddam was convinced war could be avoided, or that at most, it would resemble the limited bombing campaign of 'Desert Fox' which Iraq would again withstand.[7] As in 1990, he assumed that intense diplomatic activity in the West was a sign of weakness rather than resolve and that the US only had the stomach for Clintonesque gestures rather than Bush Administration single-mindedness. In making such judgements he was underestimating both the changes that the Clinton Administration went through in its later years as well as the liberating effects the 9/11 shock had on its successor.

These major strategic miscalculations, over his level of support and the nature of the adversary he faced this time round, led Saddam to attempt to bluff it out in two quite self-defeating ways, where even his tactics on this occasion were overblown. He gave the international community every reason to believe that he had a great deal to hide and that he was manifestly in breach of UN Security Council Resolution 687 of April 1991 – which required his WMD disarmament after the First Gulf War, and Resolution 1441 of November 2002 – which left no doubt that Iraq remained 'in material breach' of previous resolutions requiring full cooperation with the UN inspection regime.[8] The regime could not satisfactorily explain what had happened to some 360 tonnes of bulk chemical warfare agent, around 3000 tonnes of precursor chemicals, and some 30,000 special munitions for chemical or biological delivery. It gave every indication of trying to frustrate the UNMOVIC (UN Monitoring, Verification and Inspection Commission) inspectors who went into Iraq in November 2002 to resume the work that UNSCOM (UN Special Commission) had abandoned in 1998. UNSCR 1441 included the tough requirement that Iraq provide an accurate, full and complete declaration of all its WMD and related programmes within 30 days. When it arrived, the declaration was almost casual in its inadequacy, and was evidently little more than an attempt to buy more time.

Saddam himself might have felt that he was maintaining credibility with the Arab street in refusing to kowtow to such intrusive international demands. It is quite likely that he felt there was both respect and useful fear to be generated in making patently unconvincing denials that he had mature WMD programmes.[9] If he believed that a full-scale invasion was unlikely, it may have appeared that there was much to be gained by bluffing that he had a large WMD stockpile at his disposal.[10] The truth about Iraqi WMD is still a matter of investigation, but the most likely explanation remains that they were originally developed primarily to hold off the 'human waves' of Iranian soldiers in the 1980–88 war; during this time Iraqi scientists discovered that the chemical and biological agents were insufficiently pure to be stored for long periods prior to weaponisation; after 1991 the UNSCOM inspectors tracked down most of Iraq's nuclear and missile programmes, leaving it with un-weaponised, unstable chemical and biological agents that were of little military use. In these circumstances, and under UNSCOM surveillance from 1991 to 1998, the Iraqi leadership concentrated not on building up stockpiles but rather on keeping the knowledge alive so that the quality of the chemical and biological agents, and the skill in weaponising them, could be improved for some future use.[11] Yet Saddam's elaborate deceptions, denials and evasions built all this into a credible, and immediate, WMD threat in the minds of most international observers – even those opposed to war as a solution to the 'problem'.[12] It is also possible that he may have thought his WMD programmes were more mature than they actually were. Like most brutal dictators, there is evidence that he was lied to by subordinates who dared not tell him the truth. Members of his inner circle 'routinely lied to him and each other about Iraqi military capacities', and within a shaky regime, governments which inspire so much fear among their officials and officers frequently create their own reality.[13] There is growing evidence that Iraqi sector commanders genuinely believed that battlefield chemical weapons were in the arsenal: never in their own sector, but always in the sector next door.[14] Perhaps the failure to find convincing evidence of weapons of mass destruction in Iraq since the end of the war is as much a surprise to Saddam as to the rest of the world.

The second tactical miscalculation also resulted from a collision between Saddam's leadership and reality, in the way he deployed his available military forces. He could rely on the absolute loyalty of very few of his 750,000-strong army. Even the Republican Guard divisions were not allowed inside Baghdad after the attempted coup in 1996; the city was defended by the Special Republican Guard. Army units were variously deployed around the country partly to keep internal order, partly to oversee each other, and partly to defend against attacks from Iran – however unlikely that eventuality had become by 2003. No discernible redeployment took place to guard against an invading force launched from Kuwait, despite the self-evident nature of the military scenario that was unfolding by January 2003. Post-war intelligence even suggests that the Iraqi leadership may have anticipated the main thrust of an attack coming from Jordan, in the west.[15] Saddam's only strategy appeared to be to strengthen the influence of Ba'athist party loyalists at local levels throughout the country, and disperse significant arms stocks so that a guerrilla war could be waged against invading forces. It was a strategy that assumed either that invasion was unlikely, or that a full-scale American invasion – if it did occur – could be countered by inflicting marginal casualties on the invaders and playing the victim before a global audience. Perhaps this was simple strategic paralysis on his part: an inability to make decisions at all in the face of the pressure. There is certainly evidence of extensive treachery and confusion within the Iraqi forces in the weeks leading up to the war.[16] If it constituted a deliberate military strategy, however, it was self-defeating. Having effectively confirmed everyone's opinion that he had WMD stocks which he was prepared to use, Saddam then overplayed his military hand by assuming that he could hold off an invasion or bog it down long enough to let world opinion work on the fear of WMD use, and so somehow force a diplomatic solution that would save him. But he vastly underestimated US resolve to carry the business through, he added to that resolve with his own bluffing tactics, and in creating such a fear of WMD use, he gave the Americans a clear military objective – to hit the Iraqi infrastructure hard, race to Baghdad and topple the regime so fast that Saddam would not be able to use his WMD to any effect.

Saddam had played – overplayed – a full part in creating the momentum towards war, as much by what he did not do as by what he did. He made few public statements himself, beyond bellicose defiance at the prospects of war, and Iraq's diplomatic machine was relatively quiescent as the crisis reached its climax. It was the sheer continuity of Iraq's diplomatic approach that sealed the fate of the regime. By relying on the old tactics of 'cheat and retreat'; by refusing to believe that the US was really serious; by bluff and inference, pan-Arab bravado and military sclerosis, Saddam wasted the various strengths of his position and consigned himself to a reactive role in the crisis, believing as erroneously as he did in 1991, that the United States would not, in the end, embark on war.[17]

The determination of the United States

On 20 March 2003 the United States proved that it would indeed embark on this war against Iraq, claiming to be in coalition with some 44 other countries.[18] It was a hollow claim. On the political front, Washington's 'coalition of the willing' effectively consisted of the US, Britain and Spain; on the military front, of the US, Britain and Australia.[19] The reality was that for the first time since Vietnam the United States went to war without the support, or even the acquiescence, of most of its important allies. Cynics have claimed that if the US could not lead a major coalition war against Iraq as it did in the First Gulf War of 1991, it nevertheless regarded an essentially unilateral war as a good second-best. The war occurred, it is often said, 'for one pre-eminent reason – because the United States wanted it'.[20] But the diplomatic story is not so simple. The United States found itself propelled forward towards the war it threatened but did not necessarily want, in a highly volatile region, for rationales that were strong but nevertheless confused, and in political circumstances that became progressively less – not more – favourable as the conflict approached. Not least, the United States paid, and continues to pay, a political and economic price for the war that greatly exceeds most of its initial expectations.[21] This is all in sharp contrast to the diplomacy of 1991, where the United States played a strong diplomatic hand for all it was worth and set its military action in terms of a 'new world order' after the Cold War. In 2003, by contrast, it played a strong diplomatic hand badly and fought a war in far less favourable circumstances, and with more unfavourable outcomes, than its interests and position would have suggested after the 9/11 attacks.

The significance and consequence of this degree of diplomatic ineptitude remains a matter of vigorous debate. Its explanation, however, lies in a combination of short- and long-term policy perceptions within the Administration in Washington which had the effect of dominating US perceptions and dictating an approach to war which made a deteriorating diplomatic position worse.

American policy was changing in some important ways before the attacks of 9/11. More assertive US attitudes to immediate crises that affected it, such as the attacks on the World Trade Center in 1993 and then on US embassies in Africa, the problems involved in the collapse of Yugoslavia and in dealing with the former Soviet satellites – were all underpinned by a growing realisation that the US no longer need feel constrained in pursuing what it perceived to be its national interests. And though as the 'sole remaining superpower' the United States was aware of its growing physical capabilities, it also felt increasingly vulnerable and challenged by terrorism, by what it characterised as 'rogue states', by fallout from the collapse of the Soviet Union and empire, even by doubts over the commitment of its erstwhile allies. Containment policies – which had been the bedrock of US thinking about most international issues in the previous era, not just in relations with the Soviet Union – were seen as inadequate to deal with modern threats.[22] And why should an unconstrained superpower choose the half measures and frustrations of containment if it now had the chance to confront its challenges directly? A new Washington policy elite grew into power during the 1990s who did not see why the US should refrain from flexing its diplomatic muscles to address those aspects of the global environment that were not favourable to America: all other states did, when they could.[23] As the 1990s went on, the argument went further: an assertive, even imperial, United States would still be a more benevolent force in the world than were the dominant powers of the imperial age: a US empire would be an 'empire of liberty'. With the inauguration of George W. Bush in 2001, the new policy elite, and a quite new approach to world politics, had arrived at the centre of power.[24]

This coincided with a new approach to military policy. The 'revolution in military affairs' was becoming a reality for the Bush Republicans now in Washington. The holy grail for military commanders has always been the ability to 'see' the battle clearly and be capable of acting decisively on that knowledge. Information technologies, satellite-based surveillance and communication, together with dramatic increases in precision targeting, all began to come together in the late 1990s to offer US military planners realistic prospects of fighting a new type of war with small, lethal, and precise forces that could take on guerrilla armies as successfully as they could dispose of old-style Cold War forces. The revolution in military affairs would, in the words of President Clinton's Defense Secretary in 1999, 'achieve decisive military results in fundamentally new ways'.[25] The Kosovo air campaign in that year, controversial as it was, went down in US military thinking as the first fruits of this technical revolution: it vanquished enemy forces cheaply, and it left even America's closest allies struggling to keep up with US technical prowess.[26]

Thus it was that the 9/11 attacks both shocked, and stimulated, an intellectually formidable political and military elite around the new President. 'The neo-conservative agenda and the hawkish, traditional agenda intersected', as one seasoned observer put it.[27] Those who became prominent included Condoleezza Rice, the National Security Adviser, and Paul Wolfowitz, the Deputy Secretary for Defense. Douglas Feith, Stephen Cambone and Abram Shulsky in the Pentagon, John Bolton in the State Department, John Hannah and Lewis Libby in the Vice President's office; all represented shades of more strident opinion than hitherto about how the US should react to the new challenges posed by the 9/11 attack. Longer-term intellectual backing for such approaches can be traced as far back as Leo Strauss who died in 1973 but whose influence still flowed through luminaries such as William Kristol, Norman Podhoretz and Richard Perle. Above all, Dick Cheney, the Vice President, and Donald Rumsfeld, the Secretary for Defense, emerged in the Bush Administration as the two toughest, most experienced and effective Washington operators of the whole presidential team: a dual *éminence grise* of the neo-conservative presence in the White House. Both had served as Defense Secretary before, both had lived through the frustrations of earlier Iraqi crises, and shortly after assuming his role of Defense Secretary, Rumsfeld found himself inside the Pentagon building on the day that al-Qaeda struck it.

All these elements came together in a 'National Security Strategy' presented to Congress in September 2002. In January of that year President Bush had cast Iraq, Iran and North Korea 'and their terrorist allies' as an 'axis of evil'.[28] Now he spoke to Congress about 'our enemies' efforts to acquire dangerous technologies ... America will act against such threats before they are fully formed'.[29] In June of that year he had spoken at West Point of fighting for – and then extending – 'a peace that favors liberty'.[30] Now he presented Congress with 'this moment of opportunity to extend the benefits of freedom across the globe'.[31] And barely a week earlier the President had presented to the United Nations 'Saddam Hussein's support for international terrorism'.[32] Now he made clear to Congress that 'the allies of terror are the enemies of civilisation' and 'America will hold [them] to account'.[33] Not least, the National Security Strategy named Iraq explicitly as a 'rogue state' in the same section which argued that the US would 'if necessary, act preemptively' using its revolutionised military forces 'to conduct rapid and precise operations'.[34]

In one sense, this may all appear to constitute a consistent grand strategic approach to the Iraq issue, however controversially it departed from past practice. The 9/11 attacks, by common consent, had cast all the elements of US security in a new light. Rumsfeld and Wolfowitz both stated that the shock of 9/11 changed the threshold of evidence they felt was necessary before initiating action. 'The lesson of September 11', said Wolfowitz in a series of TV interviews, 'is that you can't wait until proof after the fact.'[35] The logic is certainly plausible. A new policy elite saw the world differently to its predecessors. The 9/11 attacks had shown how dangerous a reactive – containing – policy could be. The 9/11 attacks could have been even worse if they had involved elements of WMD and showed how a new breed of terrorism would be prepared to use such elements if it could. So 'new terrorism', 'rogue states', and access to WMD were a new and deadly combination. Rogue states not only provided havens and succour for terrorists; they could also give them, or help them obtain, WMD. Afghanistan was the most obvious case of a broken-backed state that had been effectively hijacked by Islamicists and terrorists and was an immediate target of US policy within four weeks of 9/11. But Iraq was a more important target in the longer term – not broken-backed, more effective than the Taliban's Afghanistan, and much more capable of dispersing WMD through terrorist actions. No wonder that Washington's gaze, at once angry and fearful, fell increasingly on Iraq. Saddam Hussein did nothing to dispel the plausibility of this logic. Iraq became 'part of the insecurity we now feel', said Rice in 2002.[36]

There was, however, far less consistency in this line of logic than first appears. The problem of dealing with Saddam Hussein represented unfinished business for a number of the new policy elite in Washington, though not noticeably for George W. Bush himself.[37] The Bush team had inherited an inconclusive war of attrition against Iraq that involved failing sanctions, the no-fly zones and occasional air offensives which achieved very little. Condoleezza Rice had raised her concerns to 'deal' with Iraq when first signed up to the Bush election campaign in 2000, and in early 2002 was anxious to get the world to shift focus away from Afghanistan and back onto Iraq.[38] Cheney, Rumsfeld and Wolfowitz had arrived in the Administration also focused – by some accounts 'incessantly' – on somehow dealing with Iraq.[39] There was much discussion about links between Saddam Hussein's Iraq and al-Qaeda in the aftermath of 9/11, though it is clear that real linkages were tenuous, at best.[40] It was impossible to link Saddam directly to the 9/11 shock. The National Security Strategy therefore relied on a juxtaposition of current threats – terrorists, rogue states and WMD – to construct a precautionary principle, that such potential *combinations* of threats had to be met as early and as far from the US as possible.[41] 'Iraq', said George Bush, 'gathers the most serious dangers of our age in one place … we have every reason to assume the worst.'[42]

The idea that Iraq somehow represented the next most obvious problem after chasing the Taliban out of Afghanistan was, however, controversial even in Washington. Colin Powell had endorsed the continuation of containment against Iraq in 2000 and appeared to be unhappy at the prospect of a more offensive policy even after 9/11. Senior members of the first Bush Administration such as Brent Scowcroft and James Baker were sharply critical of the Administration's new approach to Iraq and were backed by influential journalists and observers, who saw the case against Iraq as strong but still largely circumstantial. The critics pointed out that the Administration's rationale seemed fuzzy and distracting: if the problem was WMD proliferation then North Korea or even Iran were manifestly more dangerous, if it was al-Qaeda, then they were dealing with a non-state actor *par excellence*. And if this was all part of some grand new deal to reshape and democratise the Middle East and the Gulf, then its effects on Israel, Syria, Turkey, let alone Iran, Saudi Arabia and the Emirates, would raise major problems for other aspects of US policy and plunge it deep into some of the world's most volatile politics.[43] There was also some significant bureaucratic infighting over the policy. The Defense Department, through its newly created Office of Special Plans, was handling all the most influential information, providing interpretations, and feeding material directly into the Office of the Vice President. Colin Powell and the State Department were increasingly sidelined since Bush's closest colleagues on this issue were undoubtedly Cheney and Rumsfeld.[44] Following the victory in Afghanistan, the Pentagon increasingly ran the political, as well as the military, campaign against Iraq.

The weakness that ran through all US diplomacy leading up to the war was established at this point, early in 2002. Long- and short-term objectives, the identification of the 'Iraq problem' with the 'war on terror', the need to create some policy consensus around the assertive 'neo-cons' close to the President, all came down to a single overwhelming policy issue: Iraq's failure to surrender its weapons of mass destruction after the 1991 war in defiance of successive UN resolutions. Paul Wolfowitz was very clear about the role of this argument in moving such a controversial policy forward; '... for reasons that have a lot to do with the US Government bureaucracy, we settled on the one issue that everyone could agree on: weapons of mass destruction'.[45] It was also the issue that directly invoked Iraq's successive failures to observe no fewer than 16 United Nations Security Council resolutions since 1990. Acting to uphold the authority of the UN was part of a strategy to keep many of the Washington critics onside and seemed likely to appeal to world opinion. In the spring of 2002 this element looked relatively uncontroversial.

The US thus set itself on a course 'to deal with' Saddam Hussein once and for all, peacefully if possible; by war if necessary. It was coercive diplomacy and the Bush Administration, unlike its predecessor, was not bluffing.[46] As one of the most senior British officials later expressed it, 'It is very clear to us that the initial objective was for military capability to be used for coercive purposes and only if the diplomatic track failed was it for military action.'[47] The US would carry a military operation through if it could not remove, or browbeat, Saddam by other means. As part of this approach Washington showed a genuine interest in having a renewed United Nations disarmament team inside Iraq, conducting inspections 'aggressively' either to disarm Saddam officially, or prove, just as officially, his evident perfidy.[48]

In April 2002 at his ranch in Crawford, Texas, President Bush outlined this coercive strategy clearly to Tony Blair, and received his support. From then onwards US policy was effectively on tramlines. By May 2002 the Pentagon was engaged in 'no foreigners' planning for military operations in Iraq. In June the design was sufficiently specific for the US to invite the UK and Australia into the planning cycle on a 'no commitment' basis.[49] The UN track had been rejuvenated in response to America's growing impatience, stimulating fresh meetings between UNMOVIC and the Iraqis in May and July. By mid September it was evident that Iraq's Foreign Minister, Naji Sabri, was sufficiently alarmed to look for ways to engage with UNMOVIC to try to derail US policy.[50] On 8 November the US could feel great satisfaction that it had persuaded the UN Security Council to adopt – unanimously – Resolution 1441 which gave Iraq 'one last opportunity' to provide 'immediate, unconditional and active' cooperation with the UNMOVIC weapons inspectors and to make a 'currently accurate, full and complete' declaration of all its WMD and related programmes within 30 days.[51] Saddam would now have either to succumb or defy the international community as the leading elements of US forces began to arrive at their Gulf bases.

Throughout this year, however, the US diplomatic stance remained an uneasy compromise between mixed motives, domestic opposition and the urge to garner international support. As the flurry of diplomatic activity increased in autumn 2002, its diplomatic position began to weaken even as its deployed military in the region gained in strength. Resolution 1441 turned out to be more ambiguous than the US had assumed. 'Material breaches' of the resolution on Iraq's part would only trigger a reconsideration by the Security Council of 'serious consequences' and most members considered that only the UN inspectors' reports could declare such a breach. The US would be dependent on the inspectors to expose Iraqi perfidy and would probably need a second resolution to authorise force explicitly. The 'WMD rationale' rapidly became a double-edged weapon for the US. If the objective was primarily to disarm Iraq then US military pressure and UNMOVIC inspections had to go hand in hand and be given sufficient time to expose the weapon stocks Iraq was assumed to be hiding. Then a second UN resolution could bring the matter to a denouement. But this gave Iraq more opportunities to 'cheat and retreat', impose delays, and leave the US in a military limbo and short of campaigning time from May as temperatures in Iraq climbed above 40° C. Those in the US Administration who had never favoured the UN route, especially Vice President Cheney, made no secret of their 'contempt' for the organisation: Rumsfeld repeatedly stated that things in Iraq 'were found by defectors, not by inspectors'.[52] As the arguments went back and forth from November to January, US impatience created a growing impression that it was interested in the UN process only if it could *expose* Iraq, rather than recreate the reasonably effective UN disarmament process of a decade earlier. In contrast to 1991, the US was losing support after November as it appeared to be using the organisation rather than upholding it. On 20 January the French Foreign Minister, Dominique de Villepin, ambushed Colin Powell in a ministerial meeting of the UN Security Council convened ostensibly to discuss terrorism: Powell was pressured on Iraq and after the meeting de Villepin publicly condemned the US 'rush to war'.[53] After this the US effectively gave up on the UN process and was frankly uninterested in all UN discussions during February.

Support for the US position was also becoming scant outside the UN. A major rift developed in Europe that affected American relations with both the European Union and NATO. Pentagon decision makers may not have been surprised at some equivocation within the EU but they seriously overestimated the unifying force of NATO as a mechanism to back their military strategy. At the political level there was a widespread assumption in the Pentagon that whether or not the European allies in NATO offered meaningful military forces to the US, they would, at least, offer moral support. President Bush believed he had a private assurance from the German Chancellor to this effect.[54] At the military level plans for the invasion of Iraq assumed a two-pronged invasion, with the 4th Infantry Division, along with British forces, creating a northern front through Turkey while other forces entered Iraq from Kuwait in the south. All this was assumed by US planners when they expected to get a UN consensus for decisive action. But as the consensus evaporated in November, it left US military plans well advanced and critically exposed to the most rumbustuous political debates NATO had ever witnessed.

Having failed to consult Turkey at an early stage about the northern pincer movement through its territory and with the equipment for the 4th Infantry Division already at sea, the US sought, in mid February, to sweeten the message to Ankara by having NATO commit itself to bolstering Turkish defences. It was a political gesture to a fellow alliance member with little real military significance. But France, Germany and Belgium blocked it: to Washington's astonishment and fury. In January, Wolfowitz had visited Ankara and declared that 'Turkish support is assured'.[55] At the end of February the new Turkish government had been won round to the US strategy – helped by a $6 billion aid package – but on 1 March the Turkish parliament repudiated the deal. NATO was in manifest crisis, the military plan had to be reworked less than three weeks before the offensive was due to begin, and the crack 4th Infantry Division was left, literally, all at sea for the duration of the war.[56]

More to the point, five weeks of diplomacy, from early February to mid March, all had the effect of deepening the crisis among the western allies and within the UN, rather than in bolstering the legal and political consensus around the US. There was to be no second UN resolution authorising force against Iraq. By the time Bush, Blair and Aznar met in the Azores on Sunday 16 March for what was regarded as a final council of war, the communiqué was not directed at Saddam so much as the UN Security Council. The message was clear: support the action or be bypassed. It was a far cry from the hopes and expectations of April 2002 when the US had assumed that a 'UN route' was a natural adjunct to a coercive military policy; and a world away from the wave of sympathy that had flowed to America the day after 9/11.

The ambitions of Britain

The five weeks of diplomatic failure leading up to the Azores summit were exasperating for the US but close to disastrous for Britain. For it marked the failure of an overplayed British diplomatic hand that eventually brought the country into a war it had always believed was avoidable, in conditions that saw Prime Minister Blair fail to deliver on all important aspects of an ambitious diplomatic design he had laid down almost a year earlier.

For Britain, this crisis posed dangerous, but relatively simple, questions. The Labour government had certainly not been averse to using armed force and had already fought four offensive campaigns in three years – in 'Desert Fox' with the US against Iraq in 1998, in Kosovo with the US and NATO allies in 1999, in Sierra Leone to bail out the UN in 2000, and in Afghanistan with the US in 2001. From these campaigns Tony Blair could feel with some justification that he had strengthened greatly the security relationship between Washington and London in both the Clinton and Bush Administrations. And like Washington, he was personally horrified by the events of 9/11. He always claimed to be exercised about the growing issue of WMD proliferation throughout 2000 and 2001 and had also spoken of the possibilities of massive terrorist attacks just prior to 9/11.[57] Now, like the Administration, he put those possibilities together and decided instinctively that such threats should be addressed sooner rather than later. He was convinced, too, that the US would never be the same after 9/11 and that America's allies would have to adjust to what he insisted were the 'new realities'.[58] There was no question, therefore, that in the aftermath Britain would support the US in Afghanistan: indeed, there was some exasperation that British forces could not do more.

The British had long since concluded, however, that there was no meaningful linkage between al-Qaeda and Iraq, and that troublesome as Saddam was, Iraq was not a sensible part of a 'war on terror'. In the US State Department's 'Overview of State Sponsored Terrorism' of May 2002, half a dozen claims were made to link Iraq to international terrorism.[59] But in Britain, Cabinet papers circulating among ministers in June 2002 listed all the transgressions the intelligence community could pin on Saddam's regime in a 44-page document and never once made a specific connections between Iraq and international terrorism.[60] It was a separate problem. The best that British officials could come up with was, according to one source, just 'bits and pieces'.[61] But President Bush's 'axis of evil' speech in January 2002 indicated how far the US view was hardening on Iraq, and in March Dick Cheney was in Downing Street leaving the Prime Minister and his staff in no doubt as to how closely the Bush team made the linkage.

Tony Blair made a non-decision that Britain would stand foursquare with the United States in all this – a non-decision in that the prospects of not doing so were never seriously entertained. Others have argued that there were alternatives for the British in all this, but for Tony Blair there was no sensible alternative but support for the United States.[62] 'We must steer close to America', he told the Cabinet in March.[63] The question was rather how far the US was prepared to push the military option. Blair received his answer at the Crawford meeting with Bush in April. There was henceforth no doubt about US determination and Blair sought to square this particular circle with a characteristically ambitious approach that made Britain a linchpin of the whole diplomatic effort.

Allying himself with Colin Powell and the 'multilateralists' in Washington, Blair helped persuade the President over that summer to embark seriously on the UN diplomatic route. As a result, Britain undertook a vigorous round of politics and diplomacy that sought to deliver on several difficult objectives simultaneously. First, the UN route highlighted the WMD argument, and this was doubly important to Tony Blair given that President Bush was such an unpopular figure in Europe. Standing 'foursquare' with the US cut little ice for its own sake among European allies, still less with their publics. So Blair had to sell the WMD argument on behalf of the US a lot harder than the US did itself. Washington could thrive on the ambiguity that there was little difference between Iraq and the 'war on terror', but Europe could not. Equally important, if he could sell a distinctive argument in the UN context, then Blair was creating legitimacy for the coercive approach.

Second, Britain assumed that it could act as a diplomatic bridge across the Atlantic. Russia and America would make their own deal, and there was every confidence that President Putin would huff and puff about the use of coercion but would eventually follow his best interests by falling into line behind the US. Beneath this bilateral level, it was assumed, Britain would deliver a neat diplomatic package; the Europeans upholding US strategy, while the US upheld the authority of the UN.

Third, it was clear to both London and the State Department in Washington that progress on the Palestine issue would be a prerequisite if the UN route was to command international legitimacy. The Prime Minister used his personal influence with both the Palestinian leadership and the Israeli government to try to reawaken some peace process in the light of the ongoing *intifada*. In truth, he knew that Britain and the Europeans counted for relatively little in the conflict compared to the US, but both the Foreign Office and the Prime Minister's personal envoy, Michael Levy, were busy throughout 2002 in seeking to compensate for President Bush's evident leaning towards Israeli Prime Minister Sharon and his growing antipathy to Yasser Arafat. Britain tried to use its own influence and that of Europe as a whole to 'balance' the overall approach of the western powers. In June President Bush unveiled the US 'road map' for peace between the Palestinians and Israel, which drew the US, the EU, the UN and Russia into a schedule for creating an independent Palestinian state by 2006. This, at least, gave Britain something on which to bite.[64] Henceforth, Tony Blair and the Foreign Office tried to convince the rest of the world that the Iraq crisis was all part of a new approach – maybe even a 'new deal' – for the Middle East. Again, Britain committed itself to a package that would convince the world that President Bush was sincere and capable of delivering on the road map once Iraq had been dealt with, while using its longstanding skills at the UN to build broader support for the US strategy.

Fourth, this was an exercise in coercive diplomacy, not a predetermined war, and the British hoped and believed until almost the brink of hostilities that war could be avoided if the western allies stood together to reinstitute active inspections and/or lever Saddam out of power. Jack Straw, the Foreign Secretary, was saying publicly in early January 2003 that war was by no means inevitable and that the odds still favoured a peaceful solution.[65] Diplomats knew that the issue would likely go down to the wire. Britain's most senior defence official, Sir Kevin Tebbit, is in no doubt that war might have been avoided if the international community had united on a second UN resolution even as late as March 7. The military die, at least for Britain, was not cast until after that time.[66] For Britain, coercive diplomacy required serious preparations for war as a device to try to avoid it.

Not least, the British government had to develop a strategy that could command general support from a public that was becoming increasingly sceptical about US policy in the 'war on terror' and who rated George Bush as a very poor world leader. A YouGov poll in the summer of 2002 showed roughly the same number of respondents (around a third) who judged George Bush the greatest threat to world peace, as opposed to those who named Saddam Hussein, and as the war neared, almost half of respondents (47 per cent) regarded Saddam as a major threat to world peace while fully three-quarters (75 per cent) had 'not much' or 'no' confidence in George Bush's leadership of the crisis.[67] As a Labour government, it also had to fashion a diplomatic package that would not create a revolt among a party that was growing restive about 'Blair's wars' and which did not leave the government open to the charge of 'poodlism' in its relations with the US.

This ambitious programme swung into gear after Blair met Bush at Camp David on 7 September. Powell had done all the spadework on which Blair was able to capitalise and Bush committed the US firmly at this meeting to the UN route. From then until the French 'ambushed' the US in the Security Council on 20 January, Britain was taking on these hefty challenges with both vigour and optimism.

Britain had credibility with the US since it was by then engaged in more detailed military planning at Central Command in Tampa. It used its credibility at the UN to push the initiative that resulted in the toughly worded Resolution 1441 of 8 November. If its terms were still more ambiguous than the US expected, Britain could nevertheless take comfort from its unanimity and the close support it had received from France in crafting the process. Officials were reasonably confident that they could get a second resolution, authorising force, if and when Saddam was revealed to be in flagrant breach of 1441. Military planning dictated an overall timetable that would have run its diplomatic course by April at the latest and this added an urgency to the diplomatic offensive.

By mid December, however, these neat package deals were looking increasingly doubtful. The Iraqis delivered their obligatory declaration to the UN, as they were required to do by Resolution 1441, on 8 December. It was a 12,000-page mishmash of a document; effectively an insult to the Security Council and its resolutions. This was a turning point for the US which convinced the White House that Saddam had taken a strategic decision not to cooperate. For Bush, military invasion was now inevitable and the UN route would only be useful insofar as it nailed Saddam's perfidy before the world community. This turning point within the Administration communicated itself to the outside world as a growing scepticism for the work of UNMOVIC, and barely disguised official contempt for Hans Blix who was lampooned in the US press as 'a cross between Mr Magoo and Inspector Clouseau'.[68] Allies of the US were becoming alarmed at the military momentum. US military preparations were not interpreted by other UN members as nuanced 'coercive diplomacy' as London would have liked, though Britain was careful in its own military preparations not to appear to add to the drumbeat of war.[69] Nor did London appear to appreciate the full significance of a growing tripartite coalition in Europe who opposed coercive diplomacy being pursued in this breathless way.[70] The increasing reservations of France and Germany were ascribed mainly to the demands of electioneering in both countries, and the involvement of Russia was seen as a bit of opportunistic fun on Putin's part before he fell in line behind his new 'global partner'.

From feeling that they were 'managing' the UN process to engineer a diplomatic coup, the British increasingly found themselves trapped by it. After December, the US was prepared to go ahead with or without a second UN resolution. But it became apparent in January that a second resolution was the only way Britain could keep the allies on board and claim undisputed legitimacy for any subsequent action. By the time the Security Council arrived at its most critical assessment meeting on 14 February – effectively the moment when the Council had to decide 'what next?' after 1441 – the US regarded a second resolution as an optional extra; for Britain it would be a diplomatic lifeline. The 14 February meeting was the most dramatic Security Council meeting for years. Foreign ministers debated publicly and extemporised as the arguments flowed back and forth. It was clear there would be no automatic second resolution arising from it, so the British switched tack and tried to craft a resolution that would demonstrate a 'change of heart' on Saddam's part. London became keen on the idea of setting six agreed 'benchmarks' for Iraqi compliance that would keep open a second resolution. The US was reluctant to draw the process out further and regarded any proposal that extended the matter beyond mid April as unacceptable.[71]

British officials continued to work hard right up to the March meetings of the Security Council to keep the process alive, trying to push the benchmarks initiative, targeting their diplomacy first on the African nations and then the South American nations on the Security Council. But the emphasis was now shifting inexorably to ascribing responsibility for the impending diplomatic failure. National positions were being shored up. Britain and Spain had been quietly promoting the notion of a European declaration of support for the US, but at the end of January it got out of hand and resulted in the 'Letter of Eight' published in the *Wall Street Journal*.[72] It had been a conspiratorial process, even within Whitehall; the French, the Germans, no one in the EU, knew anything about it until the open letter appeared. Within days it was followed by a public statement from ten central and eastern European countries who also wanted to be identified with it.[73] This simply guilded the split between 'old Europe', characterised by the Paris–Berlin axis, and 'new Europe' characterised by the Blair approach to link incoming countries explicitly to the US. Paris and Bonn were predictably furious and made it clear at the NATO meeting on 10 February. President Chirac declared that the 'ten' 'had missed a good opportunity to shut up'.[74] It was all a curious piece of British diplomacy for a country that considers itself good at building international consensus, and hardly an auspicious background to the critical debates in the UN at that time. Downing Street billed the long-scheduled Anglo-French meeting at Le Touquet as an opportunity to mend some fences, and played up the importance of all the other European defence issues on which they anticipated progress, but there could be no disguising the fact that Tony Blair was simply making no headway with Jacques Chirac. In February the German Foreign Minister, Joschka Fischer, had publicly confronted Rumsfeld in a meeting in Munich and gave every indication that he could not be convinced by any new arguments the US cared to put. On 10 March President Chirac offered Britain a propaganda gift when he declared that 'whatever the circumstances, France will vote "no"'.[75] Notwithstanding any fading hopes Britain had for a second UN resolution, these outbursts were played heavily by Downing Street as indications that the responsibility for failure was not down to the American-British strategy.

Finally, this impending diplomatic impasse was played out on a domestic scene where the government's ambitions were also failing. For both a domestic and international audience the government published two dossiers of intelligence-based evidence to outline the case against Iraq. The first appeared on 24 September 2002, the second on 3 February 2003.[76] The first of these documents subsequently took on immense importance in the context of domestic political controversy after the war that resulted in the Hutton Inquiry which reported in January 2004.[77] At the time, however, the dossier aroused little controversy. It was a strong, but still circumstantial, case against Iraq on the WMD issue at the beginning of the British diplomatic offensive and it did not have any noticeable impact on an already divided public opinion in Britain, or in the rest of Europe. Cabinet papers now published show that this view was shared in Downing Street – 'The document is good and convincing for those who are prepared to be convinced.'[78] But the WMD argument, even bolstered by accounts of Saddam's human rights abuses, had not eased the government's task. The second document of February is all the more revealing of how little headway the argument had made in the meantime. The initiative for it came directly from Downing Street, it offered no significant new intelligence material – the September dossier 'had been our best shot', as intelligence officials put it – and this dossier used, without attribution, large sections from an American student's PhD thesis. The document was immediately discredited, damaging the government's case. Robin Cook described it as 'a glorious, spectacular own goal';[79] all the more so when it was followed within ten days by major 'stop the war' demonstrations in British cities. Far from convincing its critics, the second dossier made the government look as if it was squirming on a WMD argument it really could not prove. At the end of February the government weathered a major revolt of 121 of its backbench MPs in Parliament. On the eve of war, 18 March, the number of rebels rose to 139 in the final House of Commons debate that authorised British action. The government survived, but only with a deeply divided party and the support of the main Opposition. It was not a healthy national frame of mind on which to embark on a major campaign.

Like the US Administration, Downing Street, if not UK officials themselves, went through the diplomacy of late February and early March with a growing sense of the inevitability of war. The UN route was failing. NATO was in disarray, and the Franco-German-Russian opposition to war turned out to be significant after all. No matter how often they repeated it, the 'WMD rationale' was failing to sway anyone not persuaded already. The Prime Minister was reduced to a whirlwind diplomatic tour in February and a series of public debates at home, all designed to convince the world that at least he was sincere. He appreciated that people had principled objections to his course of action, but was very anxious that no one should doubt the integrity of his reasoning. As the days ticked down to the start of military operations, Robin Cook, two other ministers and six parliamentary aides resigned from the government in protest.[80]

When Tony Blair went to the Azores for that final meeting before the attack on Iraq, he knew that the US had persisted with the UN route longer than it wanted to, in order to help him resolve some of the problems his support involved for the British. Perhaps he felt they had not given him enough support, or enough time, genuinely to make the UN route work. But the ambitious British approach was now in tatters. Other than some residual hope that the Iraq war might eventually become part of a rejuvenated Middle East peace process, the British had nothing to show for their instinctive support for US policy – beyond the oft-stated conviction that it was essentially right in itself.

The drift within the European allies

There had been many occasions in the past when the transatlantic alliance had been strained, and with Britain closing on the US, European unity had suffered. But this crisis was the worst for a generation.[81] Now Britain visibly lost influence over US policy and the major European powers found themselves all competing for the moral high ground. For George Bush and Tony Blair, the high ground meant dealing with manifest threats resolutely. For Spain's Prime Minister Aznar, it meant showing strength and courage among the traditionally marginalised states of Europe. For President Chirac of France and Chancellor Schroeder of Germany, the high ground meant holding out against any 'automaticity' that would trigger war in the absence of clear evidence. And for Russia's President Putin, the moral high ground was to avoid war under any conditions. If the dispute was over such objectives, then

European disunity on this scale might not be surprising. The fact remains, however, that these are the positions the Europeans eventually reached by March 2003. They did not begin from there, and the dynamics of diplomacy, especially for France and Germany, contributed to the momentum which drove the US forward, with or without further UN authority. Like most others in this crisis, they too overplayed their hand.

The early positions of France and Germany were heavily influenced by domestic electoral concerns. Leaderships and public opinion in both countries were instinctively cautious at the prospects of another Gulf war. In the French presidential elections of May and June 2002 Jacques Chirac won an overwhelming majority, was able to dispense with the restraints of *cohabitation*, and could then shape French foreign policy more firmly than he had ever been able in the past. Chirac responded to a strong mood of public scepticism at the prospects of military action, though feared that he could find himself isolated in Europe if he overplayed it. Nevertheless, France had a large economic stake in Iraq and the crisis seemed to highlight increasing differences of perspective between the US and the Europeans.[82] Chirac was not in a mood to be steamrollered: '... there will essentially be two poles,' he said in a subsequent justification of his position, 'Europe and the US, who share common values'. But 'the US is less and less interested in Europe. Since the fall of the Berlin Wall this trend was masked by events in Yugoslavia and the Balkans conflict.'[83] During the summer of 2002 he kept his position open, preparing contingency plans for military contributions to some sort of allied military expedition. At the time, French planners anticipated sending around 15,000 troops, perhaps more, to Iraq as part of a joint force, and as late as December senior French officers were liaising with US forces in Central Command HQ at Tampa.[84] Even in February 2003, seasoned US observers assumed from all this that 'Paris has made clear both that Iraq must be disarmed and that France will fight if war does come.'[85]

The German elections of September 2002, however, had by then exerted a major effect on Chirac's choices. Far less politically secure than Chirac, and reflecting a similarly sceptical public mood in Germany, Chancellor Schroeder took a strong electoral stance against US military action in Iraq, referring to it as a 'military adventure'. His Foreign Minister and coalition partner, Joschka Fischer of the Greens, performed strongly in the campaign and cemented his position as a respected voice in German foreign policy. Up to September, none of this alarmed Washington or London, though it did sour the atmosphere. President Bush had believed since May that he had a personal assurance from Chancellor Schroeder that the Iraq issue would not be hostage to electioneering. Britain continued to reassure the US that this was all part of the electoral dynamic. Schroeder duly scraped home in the elections of 22 September but the German position did not become less strident as a result. In power, Schroeder was trapped by his election rhetoric. By October there was a distinct hardening of the French stance as it became clear to Chirac that he would not necessarily be isolated in opposing military action. This growing community of outlook between Paris and Berlin was reinforced by vigorous work behind the scenes which stitched up a farming policy agreement at the EU summit in October without Britain's knowledge, and worked to make the 30th anniversary celebrations of the Elysee Treaty in January 2003 an important summit in itself, where they subsequently declared explicitly that they would oppose the US over Iraq.

Both allies were papering over some of the more objective cracks in the old Paris–Berlin axis. The Iraqi crisis had the effect of making a rapprochement appear more solid than it was, since the security interests of the two countries within Europe both tended to diverge. In truth, the erstwhile axis had been in trouble for some time; Chirac and Schroeder did not share the political chemistry to consolidate it, but the Iraqi crisis made the old axis look suddenly crucial for the Atlantic community.[86] If the rhetoric was strong, however, the diplomatic messages to the US were still mixed. Though Germany would not commit any troops to an operation, it indicated in November that German bases could be used for strikes against Iraq, and that it would send military aid to help protect Turkey. And it was keen to demonstrate its NATO credentials by agreeing to lead the alliance's peacekeeping force in Afghanistan.[87] In December Schroeder told Blair at Chequers that even if Germany could not be part of an operation it could still offer moral support.[88] If all this was an attempt to demonstrate discriminating policy, its subtle nuances were lost on the White House.

What was clear to the US, to the dismay of Downing Street, was that by the end of the year differences between the allies had become personalised in a series of 'grandstanding' performances by both Americans and Europeans which overshadowed much of the professional diplomacy that took place in the background. Schroeder was running with an issue that also bolstered his thin, and waning, domestic support; in Fischer's case, his thin, and growing, domestic support. Chirac was running with an issue that not only gave him unique cross-party support in France for almost the only time in his career – and on a principled stance – but showed him pointing the way for the other Europeans. And Dominique de Villepin, his Foreign Minister, argued his case to an admiring gallery in both Paris and New York in ways that provoked some of the worst Pentagon grandstanding in response. More than anyone else, de Villepin cleverly turned the debate about Resolution 1441 upside down. Any success that UNMOVIC was seen to have, he made clear, would be evidence that it should be given *more* time, not less, to disarm Iraq successfully. This was precisely the UN quagmire the US had feared after November.

In retrospect it is clear how much the personalities mattered and how the initial balancing of national positions was overtaken by the way in which competing arguments were put. Too much of the diplomacy between leaders was conducted via competing media interviews. French and German leaders appeared instinctively anti-American; American leaders instinctively aggressive. Ahead of President Bush's big speech to the UN General Assembly on 12 September, President Chirac opened up the 'no automaticity' argument and the need for a second UN resolution, not in the New York corridors of the organisation but in the *New York Times*.[89] Rumsfeld was already on record calling Europe 'a piece of real estate' too fragmented to be effective, but capable of 'injecting instability' into NATO.[90] Now, US politicians and officials frequently referred to NATO as a 'toolbox' of capabilities for the war on terror – not quite what the original Washington Treaty envisaged for the great collective alliance, nor how the Europeans viewed it.[91] There was frequent resort to full ministerial meetings of the UN Security Council which brought all the glare of world publicity down on a single, dramatic meeting. De Villepin, as chairman of the Security Council on 20 January, had Colin Powell in front of him to discuss terrorism in a relatively normal atmosphere. But de Villepin then convened the post-meeting press conference, without Powell present, and denounced the US 'rush to war'.[92] In the dramatic Security Council meeting of 14 February, de Villepin drew laughter and applause for his impassioned, extemporised statement (the first time anyone could remember that reaction in the Security Council): a feat Jack Straw managed to emulate in the Security Council on 7 March.[93] The infamous 'Letter of Eight' in February disclosed a major series of European disagreements in the pages of world newspapers rather than behind closed doors – a curious initiative for governments to support which owed much to the lobbying, on behalf of the White House, of the *Wall Street Journal* and Bruce Jackson, an unofficial US envoy in Europe.[94] This issue pitted the central and east European countries against the Paris–Berlin axis; a competition that Donald Rumsfeld insultingly characterised as between 'old' and 'new' Europe. A week later on 8 February 'old Europe' bit back when Fischer publicly confronted Rumsfeld at the Wehrkunde meeting in Munich and made clear that the US had simply not convinced the European democracies – with heavy emphasis on 'democracy' – of the US case.

Old Europe was coming together in a way that positively gratified President Chirac. Russia was clearly playing a wider game than merely seeking assurances from the US that its economic interests in Iraq would be protected. But President Putin was also concerned at US unilateralism and anxious to undermine criticism from his nationalist and communist opponents. In addition, there were a number of wider Russian interests with Europe and the Middle East to safeguard.[95] Putin was increasingly convinced that he would join a European anti-war coalition if one came together. But Russia, too, sent mixed signals to the US. Right through 2002 Russian diplomats in Washington played the economic arguments very hard. After all, Russia was estimated to have done $52 billion worth of trade with Iraq under the sanctions regime and was now owed at least $8 billion by Baghdad. The US was convinced that it was only a matter of negotiating the right price for Moscow's support.[96] Putin, however, watched events without committing himself. He had Igor Ivanov, his Foreign Minister, make most of the anti-war statements. He himself remained notably silent and then played his most dramatic cards late.[97] In early February 2003 he visited Berlin and Paris and assessed the backbone of the anti-US stance of 'old Europe'. On 10 February President Chirac abruptly reversed French opposition – which had been vehement – to Russian actions in Chechnya and praised Mr Putin's initiative for a referendum on the territory. He convinced the Russian leader that the Paris–Berlin axis represented mainstream diplomatic opinion on Iraq. With that the split within European capitals was complete and probably irretrievable, whatever subsequently happened at the UN in the 14 February meeting and thereafter. Two of the five Permanent Members of the Security Council, and Germany as a rotating member, were opposed to the policy of two other Permanent Members. Either the US, Britain (and Spain) would now have to bow to the authority of the UN over initiating military action, or they would have to confront the possibility of acting without it.

The clearest indication of this depth of breakdown among the European allies was the extent to which they rushed to shore up their arguments and allocate blame well before the Azores summit. Germany, France and Russia insisted at the UN that the organisation continue with a pointless plan to extend UNMOVIC's work when it was clear there was no possibility of it ever operating.[98] The most important damage had all been done well before then. On 22 January, France, Germany and Belgium had blocked the NATO attempt to vote more military assistance to Turkey; the same day that Chirac and Schroeder had celebrated the anniversary of the Elysee Treaty in what was made into an overt anti-war occasion. Chirac used the ceremony to declare that 'war is always an admission of defeat': a comment that drew the American Rush Limbaugh to snipe that 'in the case of France that's true'.

The international institutions: insufficient to prevent a war

The United Nations, NATO, and to a lesser extent the European Union, also played a part in the mismanagement of this crisis. Though international institutions can only reflect the politics of their membership, there is also a diplomatic momentum in such institutions which takes on a life of its own. In this case, where there was a dynamic towards diplomatic breakdown and war, there was nothing in the institutional setting that might have prevented it. All three institutions served to magnify and formalise a diplomatic drift that was slipping out of control from early on, and their procedures stimulated, rather than dampened, the antagonisms of their members.

The UN offered a road – the only road – towards a peaceful or a stable solution. It could have legitimised coercive pressure and forced either a regime change on Iraq or, more likely, a major climb-down by Saddam that would have allowed an enhanced, long-term UN inspection operation back into the country. If a peaceful solution was simply impossible, then a second UN resolution to back up Resolution 1441 would at least have legitimised military action and given the whole crisis, the subsequent war and the reconstruction efforts, a completely different complexion. Any of these courses of action would have been preferable to the outcomes that actually occurred, and though the UN as an organisation cannot be blamed for the behaviour of its members, its methods of reflecting that behaviour appear to have contributed to the final messy outcome.

The US had long been sceptical about the UN and certainly did not want a repeat of the episode in February 1998 when Kofi Annan's mission to Baghdad defused a threatened US attack with yet another deal that allowed Saddam to 'cheat and retreat'. According to Hans Blix, the Executive Chairman of UNMOVIC, Cheney, Rumsfeld and 'the leadership in the US Department of Defense' made no secret of their determination to ignore or even frustrate the will of the organisation.[99] It is not the case, however, that the US did not want the UN to succeed in this crisis, but it did want it to succeed in a particular way. It wanted unanimity and resolve from the UN, and up to Resolution 1441 in mid November, most in the US Administration thought they had got it. This was all part of the general strategy of coercive diplomacy that Bush had resolved upon in early 2002, whatever some of his staff privately thought about the UN.

Resolution 1441, however, turned out to be the high water mark of UN diplomacy in this crisis and the organisation was not able to exploit the unexpected degree of unanimity displayed in that resolution to keep everyone on board. UNMOVIC was not deployed quickly or powerfully enough following the resolution to give the impression that the UN was really serious about Iraqi disarmament. Notwithstanding later doubts about what there was for UNMOVIC to find, a widespread consensus existed at the time that as long as the inspectors could go about their work they should be able to uncover clear evidence of WMD programmes, and probably WMD stockpiles themselves. But for an organisation that seemed to hold the key to avoid a war, UNMOVIC was poorly resourced and did little to gain the trust of the more hawkish delegations at the UN. Its level of technical expertise was generally acknowledged to be lower than UNSCOM that it replaced, and unlike that more controversial organisation under the aggressive leaderships of Rolf Ekeus, David Kay and Richard Butler, UNMOVIC increasingly gave the impression that it was low on competence and confidence as it went about its work. Han Blix's crucial reports to the Security Council on UNMOVIC's progress on 27 January, 14 February and 7 March were indecisive accounts which confirmed the pre-existing views of UN members, rather than serving to move the issue forward in any direction. After the war, the US deployed around 1500 people – about ten times the number in UNMOVIC – to examine Iraqi WMD programmes and was determined not to let UNMOVIC back into Iraq.[100] It is frequently forgotten, however, that in the course of its work UNMOVIC destroyed more than 70 Iraqi al Samoud missiles which had been found to exceed permissible ranges laid down in 1991. This was a substantial measure of genuine and relevant disarmament that might have been used cannily by the UN, but instead the al Samoud issue made little international impression and was swept into the shoal of red herrings that included debate on Iraq's possession of aluminium tubes and yellowcake from Niger.

The UN had not risen to the occasion to provide a dynamic arena that identified new diplomatic avenues. Though its Security Council debates were the most dramatic for some years, there was too frequently a resort to full ministerial meetings of the Council, where full national positions were aired, and the US resorted to buying Security Council votes more explicitly than in the past. As a former adviser to the Secretary-General pointed out, the Security Council was proceeding by 'ugly means' which did not reflect true preferences, and the result would only harm UN legitimacy.[101] The UN staff were never able to stamp experience and authority on the diplomatic agenda; and once Resolution 1441 was found to be less unambiguous than it had at first appeared, the UN became the forum for the members' self-justification rather than creative diplomacy. The debates leading to the aborted second resolution in February and March were particularly damaging to the image of the organisation. 'The spectacle of the US Government begging [Guinea, as one of the members of the Security Council] for permission to sacrifice American blood and treasure to save the world from Saddam Hussein exposes the farce that the UN Security Council's Iraq debate has become', said the *Wall Street Journal*.[102] Little wonder that even UK parliamentarians should issue a call to 'restore the effective functioning of the UN Security Council' almost immediately after the war.[103]

If it was any comfort to UN officials, NATO was even more shocked and damaged by the turn of the crisis. After the 9/11 attacks NATO had been effectively sidelined by the United States. George Robertson, the NATO Secretary-General, had acted immediately on 12 September to invoke the famous Article 5 of the Washington Treaty which effectively sent the alliance to war on behalf of the US. Article 5 had never been invoked before and it was enacted in less than 90 minutes at an emergency meeting of the North Atlantic Council (NAC). In response, the US was grateful but unimpressed and went ahead more or less unilaterally with its operations in Afghanistan – getting more effective help against the Taliban from Russia than any of its NATO allies. In November 2002 the Prague Summit – which should have marked a new era with agreement to a dramatic NATO enlargement – was a low-key affair overshadowed by the looming conflict in Iraq. Certainly, there was an initial expectation at Prague that NATO would somehow be involved either in an initial attack on Iraq, or else in subsequent operations.[104] The alliance, however, merely declared itself 'united in the commitment to take effective action' to support the UN over Iraq, but did not elaborate any further and left the US to deal bilaterally with its key allies. The NATO Secretary-General nevertheless worked hard to reinforce the value of the alliance both for the

US and its other members and was inclined to offer firm leadership within the NAC to keep it moving.[105]

As military deployments began in December 2002 he was determined to maintain some momentum and persuaded the Pentagon to build legitimacy for its actions by invoking NATO support for some of the peripheral aspects of the action. Berlin had agreed that it would deploy troops to help defend US bases in Germany if American forces were launched from them. It was logical that NATO would also offer security assistance to Turkey, as a fellow member, if US forces also launched attacks from Turkish bases and crossed the Iraqi frontier from the north. The US had no need to offer Turkey such protection through NATO – or even at all, save in a symbolic capacity. But Robertson persuaded US planners that some useful fences could be mended by having NATO make the gesture.

Up until this time the growing political disarray among the allies had been generally expressed in public bilateral dialogues among the allies and, to an extent, within the European Union. In the EU France took a more active part in security discussions and matters of broad orientation, rather than military detail, were at issue. It was in EU summits in October and December that the antagonisms between Blair and Chirac found personal expression. The EU was also in the midst of enlargement negotiations with the Nice Treaty and yet found that most of its ten prospective members were now part of the 'new' – pro-American – Europe that was being distinguished from the 'old' axis of power. In February President Chirac used the EU's specially convened summit on Iraq to threaten the new prospective members with, in effect, a French veto on their accession if their 'un-European manners' did not improve. The stark fact was that the EU simply had no Common Foreign and Security Policy over Iraq. The transatlantic rift not only hijacked the EU's ability to act on such an important issue; it spilled over into the enlargement process – the most fundamental issue the EU had faced for a generation.[106] This was depressing, if perhaps not surprising.

NATO, however, now contrived for itself the nastiest surprise for years. Assuming that EU disarray would not effect NATO's more functional military planning, the Secretary-General pushed ahead in early February with plans for the alliance to offer military assistance to Turkey. But the political fallout from the crisis had already seeped into the North Atlantic Council. France, Germany and Belgium all indicated that they were not happy to support a military assistance initiative for Turkey. The Secretary-General resorted to the 'silent minute' procedure – which had worked before under his assertive chairmanship – whereby the Secretary-General took it upon himself to record a decision and left it open for members explicitly to object within a limited time. The dissenters called his bluff and renounced the silent minute. The alliance was subjected to the spectacle of the NAC refusing to endorse military help to a member under pressure. Turkey immediately invoked Article 4 of the Washington Treaty which declared a NATO state at risk, and in response, Robertson pushed an assistance agreement instead through the Defence Planning Committee, on which France does not sit, to create at least the appearance of collective action. The French were furious, the US disgusted, the Turks offended.

In part, that offence came home to roost two weeks later in the culmination of protracted negotiations between Turkey and the US/British coalition over the passage of forces through Turkish territory. In November 2002 Turkey had elected an inexperienced, Islamic party government, and public feeling against US policy was running high. On the other hand, Turkey wanted to be able to exert military influence in the Kurdish areas of northern Iraq if there was any prospect of post-war realignments. They had little time since the military build-up was pressing on. As 30 ships carrying the equipment for 62,000 coalition troops stood off Iskenderun, both the Turkish government and its military tied themselves in unseemly knots that exacted aid packages totalling $26 billion to allow the US to use its territory in return for a commitment that no more than 40,000 Turkish troops would penetrate no further than 60 kilometres into Iraq. Then in an unaccustomed flourish of democracy, the Turkish parliament voted on 1 March against the plan and the whole US strategy had to be hastily reshaped. Turkish airspace was made available to allied aircraft but not ports or land transit routes. The British had decided it was a lost cause in late January and by then had already diverted their forces to Kuwait.[107]

The prospective new members of NATO and the EU must have wondered what they had been so anxious to join. For an organisation that was trying to adapt itself to the post-Cold War world, NATO appeared to have fallen into simple self-destruction. For an organisation that strove to move Europe towards a new destiny, the European Union looked absurdly ambitious. And for the premier political arena in the world that sought to provide legitimacy and diplomacy, the United Nations gave an impression of low competence, and sometimes incompetence.

In truth, these characterisations are harsh on some of the professionals who worked to push this crisis in different directions. Iraq was, after all, one of the worst issues in recent times on which to build and maintain an international consensus. But by the beginning of the war it was generally acknowledged throughout the diplomatic communities of the world that once the fighting stopped there would have to be some major efforts at fence-mending, repair and reform within our major institutions as well as in our various bilateral relations. The crisis had been deeply damaging to all the major participants. Few can regret the defeat and removal of Saddam Hussein. But many will regret the diplomatic mechanics that brought it about in the circumstances of March 2003.

Notes

1. In western circles the 2003 conflict is now generally referred to as the 'Second Gulf War', though in reality it is the third, since the first war in the Gulf was the far more destructive one between Iraq and Iran during 1980–88 which killed at least 800,000 people.
2. For examples of such explanations, see R. Jervis, 'The Compulsive Empire', *Foreign Policy*, July/August, 2003; R. Kagan, *Of Paradise and Power: America and Europe in the New World Order*, New York, Alfred A. Knopf, 2003; Charles Krauthammer, 'The Unipolar Moment Revisited', *The National Interest*, Winter 2002/03.
3. On Iraqi policy leading to the 1990 war, see L. Freedman and E. Karsh, *The Gulf Conflict, 1990–1991*, London, Faber, 1993, pp. 19–63.
4. On the successes and limitations of UNSCOM's disarmament activities in Iraq, see S. Feldman and Y. Shapir, eds, *The Middle East Military Balance, 2000–2001*, Cambridge, MA, MIT Press, 2001, pp. 47–50. Arms Control Association, Special Report, *Iraq: A Chronology of UN Inspections and an Assessment of Their Accomplishments, 1990–2002*, Washington, ACA, 2002.
5. Con Coughlin, *Saddam: The Secret Life*, London, Pan Books, 2002, p. xxxi.
6. David Blair writing on the capture of Saddam Hussein in the *Daily Telegraph*, 15 December 2003.
7. Joint Forces Command, 'Iraqi Perspectives on OIF [Operation Iraqi Freedom]. Major Combat Operations', classified, but reported in outline in the *New York Times*, 12 February 2004, p. 1.
8. See the statement of the Solicitor-General to Parliament for the formal case of Iraqi breaches of its UN obligations. House of Commons Debates, 17 March 2003, written answer, c.515.
9. This is certainly the view of Hans Blix, see his *Disarming Iraq: The Search for Weapons of Mass Destruction*, London, Bloomsbury, 2004, pp. 265–6.
10. See, for example, one summary of the UNSCOM assessments in Richard Butler, *Saddam Defiant: The Threat of Mass Destruction and the Crisis of Global Security*, London, Weidenfeld and Nicolson, 2000.
11. This argument is best summed up by Rolf Ekeus, Executive Chairman of UNSCOM 1991–97, excerpted in the *Sunday Times*, 3 August 2003, Review, p. 8. See also a later assessment in Rolf Ekeus, 'Reassessment: The IISS Strategic Dossier on Iraq's Weapons of Mass Destruction', *Survival*, 46(2), 2004, pp. 73–87.
12. See, for example, a leading US opponent of the war and former National Security Adviser, Brent Scowcroft, 'Don't Attack Saddam', *The Wall Street Journal*, 15 August 2002, where Saddam's WMD programmes and his menace to the world and US interests are taken as a given.
13. Joint Forces Command, 'Iraqi Perspectives on OIF', p. 1.
14. Personal interviews with US officials, March 2004.
15. One Iraqi intelligence report fed back to Baghdad two days after the beginning of the war apparently placed 20,000 Israeli troops in the western desert of Iraq. No documents recovered since the end of the war show any anticipation on Saddam's part that Iraq might be overrun by coalition troops. See 'Spy files show Saddam's delusions', *The Times*, 18 March 2004.
16. *Sunday Times*, News Review, 11 January 2004, pp. 1–2.
17. *The Times*, 18 March 2004, p. 4.
18. Washington File 21.03.03, 'White House releases list of more than 40 coalition members', Embassy of the United States, 21 March 2003.

19. On the involvement of Australia in the operation, see Australian Ministry of Defence, *The War in Iraq: ADF Operations in the Middle East in 2003*, Canberra, February 2004.
20. Martin Kettle, 'America wanted war', *Guardian*, 16 July 2003, p. 19.
21. See a very good summary of initial cost estimates in William D. Nordhaus, 'Iraq: The Economic Consequences of War', *New York Review*, 5 December 2002, pp. 9–12. See also Carl Keysen, et al., *War with Iraq – Costs, Consequences and Alternatives*, Cambridge, MA, AAAS, 2002.
22. See, for example, John Hillen, 'US Policy Towards Iraq: Statement Before the Committee on Armed Services of the US House of Representatives', 10 March 1999.
23. See a seminal article that centred on the evolution in thinking of Condoleezza Rice at this time: Nicholas Lehmann, 'The Next World Order', *The New Yorker*, 1 April 2002.
24. See Edward Rhodes, 'The Imperial Logic of Bush's Liberal Agenda', *Survival*, 45(1), 2003, pp. 131–54.
25. Secretary of Defense, William S. Cohen, *Annual Report to the President and the Congress*, Washington, US Government Printing Office, 1999, p. 122.
26. See Benjamin S. Lambeth, *NATO's Air War for Kosovo*, Santa Monica, RAND, 2001, pp. 219–22.
27. Charles Kupchan of the Brookings Institution, reported in the *Financial Times*, 8 April 2004, p. 8.
28. State of the Union Address, President Bush to Congress, 29 January 2002.
29. The National Security Strategy of the United States of America, 17 September 2002.
30. Presidential Speech, West Point, New York, 1 June 2002.
31. The National Security Strategy of the United States of America, 17 September 2002.
32. US Government, Background Paper, 'A Decade of Deception and Defiance: Saddam Hussein's Defiance of the United Nations', 12 September 2002, p. 18.
33. The National Security Strategy of the United States of America, 17 September 2002.
34. Ibid., pp. 14–16.
35. *Daily Telegraph*, 28 July 2003, p. 10; *Daily Telegraph*, 10 July 2003, p. 16.
36. Quoted in David Sanger, 'Debate over attacking Iraq heats up', *New York Times*, 1 September 2002, p. 1.
37. Bob Woodward, *Bush at War*, New York, Simon and Schuster, 2002, p. 25.
38. On her attitude in 2000, see John Kampfner, *Blair's Wars*, London, Simon and Schuster, 2003, pp. 154–5. On her 2002 attitude, see Hans Blix, *Disarming Iraq*, p. 58.
39. The most controversial account of this 'incessant' concern with Iraq is in Richard Clarke, *Against All Enemies*, New York, The Free Press, 2004, pp. 241–6. A more considered account is to be found in Daniel Benjamin and Steven Simon, *The Age of Sacred Terror*, New York, Random House, 2002, pp. 219–55. Also Bob Woodward, *Bush at War*. The charge comes from across the political spectrum, however, from Madeleine Albright of the Clinton Administration to Paul O'Neill, a Bush Treasury Secretary.
40. Jeffrey Record, 'Threat Confusion and its Penalties', *Survival*, 46(2), 2004, pp. 51–71.
41. A polemical view of this whole trend of thinking is provided by Bob Woodward, *Plan of Attack*, New York, Simon and Schuster, 2004, especially pp. 20–2.

42. 'President Bush outlines Iraqi threat', Office of the Press Secretary, 7 October 2002.

43. On a grand design for the Middle East, see William Kristol and Lawrence Kaplan, *The War in Iraq: Saddam's Tyranny and America's Mission*, New York, Politico's Publishing, 2003. But see also Woodward, *Plan of Attack*, Mark Mazower, 'How US hawks hijacked Mideast policy', *Financial Times*, 4 November 2003, p. 19; John Donnelly and Anthony Shadid, 'Iraq war hawks have plan to reshape entire Mideast', *Boston Globe*, 9 October 2002, p. 1.

44. Kampfner, *Blair's Wars*, pp. 162–3.

45. Originally quoted in an interview with Sam Tanenhaus in *Vanity Fair*, July 2002. See also unedited transcript of the interview excerpted in *The Times*, *T2*, 20 June 2003, p. 21.

46. See Lawrence Freedman, 'War in Iraq: Selling the Threat', *Survival*, 46(2), 2004, p. 11.

47. House of Commons Defence Committee (HCDC-1), *Lessons of Iraq, Vol. 1*, HC57–1, London, The Stationery Office, March 2004, paragraph 24.

48. Blix, *Disarming Iraq*, pp. 12–13.

49. HCDC-1, *Lessons of Iraq*, paragraphs 28–9.

50. Blix, *Disarming Iraq*, p. 74.

51. United Nations Security Council Resolution 1441; Press Release SC/7564, 8 November 2002.

52. Blix, *Disarming Iraq*, pp. 70–71, 261.

53. *Financial Times*, 27 May 2003, p. 8. 'Military intervention', said de Villepin, 'would be the worst possible solution.'

54. Ibid.

55. Kampfner, *Blair's Wars*, p. 280.

56. HCDC-1, *Lessons of Iraq*, paragraphs 62–6.

57. Freedman, 'War in Iraq', p. 17; Kampfner, *Blair's Wars*, p. 155.

58. Kampfner, *Blair's Wars*, pp. 159, 164, 173.

59. US State Department, *Patterns of Global Terrorism 2001: Overview of State-Sponsored Terrorism*, 21 May 2002, Government Printing Office, Washington DC.

60. CAB/33/0005. Published in *Report of the Inquiry into the Circumstances Surrounding the Death of Dr. David Kelly C.M.G.* (The Hutton Report) 28 January 2004, HC 247, London, TSO, 2004, pp. 365–409.

61. Private source quoted in Coughlin, *Saddam*, p. 32.

62. On the notion that there were clear alternatives, see David Coates and Joel Krieger, *Blair's War*, Cambridge, Polity Press, 2004.

63. Robin Cook, *Point of Departure*, New York, Simon and Schuster, 2003.

64. David Frum, *The Right Man: The Surprise Presidency of George W. Bush*, London, Weidenfeld and Nicolson, 2003.

65. Radio 4, *Today* programme, 13 January 2003.

66. House of Commons Defence Committee (HCDC-3), *Lessons of Iraq, Vol. 3, Oral and Written Evidence*, HC57–3, Q.1702, Q.1708.

67. See, YouGov polling, available at http://www.YouGov.com. These figures were drawn from a poll conducted on 28–29 February 2003.

68. Ian McIntyre, 'Blix Bombshell Proves a Damp Squib', *The Times*, Review, 13 March 2004, p. 13.

69. HCDC-1, *Lessons of Iraq*, paragraphs 24–5.

70. Kampfner, *Blair's Wars*, pp. 289.

71. Blix, *Disarming Iraq*, p. 184.

72. *Wall Street Journal*, Opinion, 30 January 2003.

73. This became known as the declaration of the 'Vilnius 10'. See *Financial Times*, 28 May 2003, p. 19.
74. Ibid.
75. Interview on French TV, 10 May 2003. His words were, 'quelles que soient les circonstances'.
76. *Iraq's Weapons of Mass Destruction: The Assessment of the British Government*, 24 September 2002, London, TSO, 2002.
77. Hutton Report.
78. CAB/11/0069. Published in the Hutton Report, p. 657.
79. House of Commons Foreign Affairs Committee, *The Decision to go to War in Iraq, Vol. 1*, HC 813–1, London, The Stationery Office, 2003, paragraph 134. See also Woodward, *Plan of Attack*, pp. 247–50 on the 'best shot' US intelligence also had.
80. Cook, *Point of Departure*.
81. A good account is provided in Philip H. Gordon and Jeremy Shapiro, *Allies at War: America, Europe and the Crisis over Iraq*, New York, McGraw-Hill, 2004.
82. Christopher Layne, 'The European Counterweight', *Aspenia* 19/20, 2003, p. 65.
83. Interview with *Financial Times*, 26 May 2003, p. 15.
84. *Financial Times*, 27 May 2003, p. 15.
85. Robert Hunter, 'How Deep an Ocean?', *Newsday*, 23 February 2003.
86. Robert Graham, 'The Fragile Franco-German Core', *Aspenia* 19/20, 2003.
87. Reported in *Financial Times, Special Report*, 25 November 2002, p. iv.
88. Kampfner, *Blair's Wars*, p. 289.
89. *New York Times*, 8 September 2002, p. 1.
90. Interview with CNN, 15 June 2001.
91. *Financial Times*, 20 May 2003, p. 17.
92. To be fair to Villepin, this statement was in answer to an aggressive question at the press conference.
93. Blix, *Disarming Iraq*, pp. 181, 212.
94. *Financial Times*, 28 May 2003, p. 19.
95. Yevgeny M. Primakov, *A World Challenged*, Washington DC., Brookings Institution Press, 2004, pp. 130–5.
96. See, for example, Angela Stent and Lilia Shevtsova, 'America, Russia and Europe: A Realignment?', *Survival*, 44(4), 2002–3, pp. 121–34; Strobe Talbot, *The Russia Hand: A Memoir of Presidential Diplomacy*, New York, Random House, 2002.
97. Grigory Yavlinsky, 'Russia should join a cold war on Iraq', *Financial Times*, 7 March 2003, p. 19.
98. Blix, *Disarming Iraq*, pp. 249–50.
99. Ibid., p. 261; also pp. 13, 58, 220, 271.
100. House of Commons Foreign Affairs Committee, *The Decision to go to War in Iraq, Vol. 1*, HC 813–1, London, TSO, 2003, paragraphs 173–80.
101. The adviser was John Ruggie. *Financial Times*, 11 March 2003, p. 13.
102. *Wall Street Journal*, 12 March 2003, p. 12.
103. House of Commons Foreign Affairs Committee, *Foreign Policy Aspects of the War Against Terrorism*, HC 405, London, TSO, 2003, paragraph 235.
104. *Financial Times*, 15 November 2002, p. 12.
105. NATO Press Office, '11 September – One Year On. NATO's Contribution to the Fight against Terrorism.' Fact Sheet. 10 September 2002.
106. International Institute of Strategic Studies, *Strategic Survey 2002/3*, London, Oxford University Press, 2003, pp. 109–10.
107. HCDC-1, *Lessons of Iraq*, paragraph 63.

3

The US-UK 'Special Relationship' after Iraq

Jane M. O. Sharp

Introduction

British policy makers have long deluded themselves that they enjoy a special relationship with their counterparts in the United States. For scholars and practitioners of international relations this delusion does not usually survive any length of time in Washington DC where the idea of a special relationship is risible. British forces who serve in coalition operations with the US realise they are 'special' only in the sense that Washington takes them for granted when planning military operations, much as Britain relies on the Ghurkas. Intelligence officers sometimes claim they have privileged access to US sources, but soon understand that any sharing is on a strict 'need to know' basis.

Some political observers in Britain claim that the myth of a special relationship is imposed on new prime ministers by the Foreign and Commonwealth Office, to ensure that Britain continues to punch above her weight. But some prime ministers have certainly rebelled against it. In the 1960s for example, Harold Wilson refused to support the United States in Vietnam despite bullying by President Johnson. And in the 1970s, Edward Heath was much more interested in developing a special relationship with Europe than with the USA.

Tony Blair, however, is a firm believer in the myth of a special relationship. He also claims that Britain serves as a bridge between the United States and Europe, which implies that Britain should never have to choose between the two. In 2002–3, however, by supporting George Bush's preventive war against Iraq, Blair chose allegiance to Washington at the expense of relations with his major EU allies. This war, undertaken without UN authorisation, was deeply unpopular in Britain because although Saddam was a ruthless dictator, Iraq posed no threat to Europe, to the United States or to any of Iraq's Gulf neighbours.[1]

In one sense Blair was following the example of Margaret Thatcher who, in August 1990 in Aspen, Colorado, famously urged George Bush senior 'not to wobble' as the President was contemplating how to respond to Saddam's invasion of Kuwait. Thatcher was out of office by November 1990, but her successor, John Major, was an enthusiastic partner in the UN-authorised Coalition that fought the 1991 Gulf War to liberate Kuwait from Iraqi occupation (Operation Desert Storm).[2] Major and Bush senior also worked together to support the Kurds in Northern Iraq and to contain Iraq with air strikes (in addition to UN sanctions) in the early 1990s.

This chapter addresses British participation in the Iraq war which began in March 2003, in the context of the special relationship. It begins with a brief account of Blair's relationship with President Clinton when a policy of containing Saddam Hussein was deemed appropriate. The second section explores Blair's relationship with President Bush, when war was judged necessary. The third section assesses Blair's case for war as presented to the British people – the threat from Saddam's weapons of mass destruction – which most Britons found unconvincing including two of Blair's Cabinet. The final section weighs the costs and benefits to Britain, and to Blair personally, of the Iraq war.

Blair and Clinton on Iraq: containment

In 1997–2000 Blair forged a close working relationship with Clinton, especially on the Balkans and the Northern Ireland peace process. Blair was also proactive in European affairs, even to the point of proposing a defence identity for the EU in 1998. Indeed, despite Blair's decision in June 1997 not to join the euro immediately, other European leaders found francophone Blair the most articulate and congenial British Prime Minister they had ever known.[3]

The Iraq issue came to the fore in Washington in this period because Clinton had to deal not only with a Republican controlled House and Senate, but also with a new right-wing pressure group, the Project for the New American Century, under the chairmanship of William Kristol. This group included several neo-conservatives (including Paul Wolfowitz, Donald Rumsfeld and John Bolton) who would later serve in the Administration of George W. Bush. They lobbied very effectively for regime change in Iraq and a permanent US military presence in the Gulf region. One result was the Iraq Liberation Act passed in 1998 which committed the United States to regime change in Iraq and also required the Clinton Administration to finance several Iraqi opposition groups.[4]

Regime change in Iraq was not popular in the US in the late 1990s, however. Several senior military figures testified to Congress against financial aid to Iraqi exile groups.[5] Clinton's senior military advisers advised against a new war with Saddam, believing the costs would be prohibitive. The CIA judged the Iraqi opposition in exile feckless and disconnected from events on the ground, and stopped funding Ahmad Chalabi's Iraqi National Congress because of less than transparent accounting. Moreover, the regional neighbours who would have had to serve as bases for US troops were far from enthusiastic, and the European allies – preoccupied with peace support operations in the Balkans – were not interested in another Gulf war.[6] The policy agreed by Blair and Clinton was thus to contain Saddam Hussein, not to make war.

Nevertheless during both his presidential terms Clinton continued to enforce the no-fly zone which the US and the UK imposed over Iraq after the 1991 Gulf War. When Saddam ceased to cooperate with the UN inspection team (UNSCOM) in 1998, Blair backed Clinton's decision to retaliate with four days of intensive US and UK air and missile attacks (Operation Desert Fox) on selected targets in Iraq.[7]

Blair and Bush on Iraq: preventive war

When George W. Bush was inaugurated as President in January 2001, Clinton advised Blair to stay close to the White House, but few observers on either side of the Atlantic anticipated a close relationship between Bush and Blair. It was the shock of September 11, 2001 which cemented the bond. More than most Europeans, Blair understood the impact of 9/11 on the psyche of the American people and shared Bush's vision of the need to defuse the threat from fundamentalist Islam by imposing democracy throughout the middle east. Blair left no doubt after 9/11 that he was with Bush all the way in the fight against terrorism, but precisely when Blair signed up for the war against Iraq is not clear. US Secretary of Defense Donald Rumsfeld, and his deputy, Paul Wolfowitz, wanted to oust Saddam as soon as possible after Bush took office, but after 9/11 both Blair and Powell persuaded Bush to focus first on al-Qaeda and the Taliban.[8]

Once the US-led Coalition had defeated the Taliban regime in Afghanistan in late 2001, Bush re-focused on Iraq.[9] In March 2002 Bush curtailed several anti-terrorist programmes in Afghanistan and Pakistan, and ordered US Special Operations Command to move scarce linguists and Special Operations people from there to the Gulf.[10] This severely depleted the military assets available to continue the campaign against al-Qaeda and the Taliban, as well as the effort to stabilise Afghanistan. As Richard Clarke, the former US counter-terrorism czar, has noted: 'America did not eliminate the al Qaeda movement, which morphed into a distributed and elusive threat ... instead we launched the counterproductive Iraq fiasco.'[11]

After Bush designated Iraq, Iran and North Korea as the 'axis of evil' in his State of the Union address to Congress in January 2002, in London Prime Minister Blair asked his intelligence chiefs for an assessment of Iraq. The Joint Intelligence Committee (JIC) submitted a paper to the Prime Minister's office in March which showed little evidence of any WMD activity since the UN inspectors left Iraq in 1998.[12] Nevertheless, senior UK government officials told John Kampfner that Blair committed himself to regime change in Iraq as early as April 2002. Visiting Bush in Crawford, Texas, Blair noted that 'a brutal regime like Saddam's cannot be allowed to develop WMD', suggesting that Saddam did not have WMD, but might develop a capability if left unchecked.[13] Only later, when his legal advisers told him that regime change was not an acceptable legal rationale for war, did Blair make Saddam's WMD capability his *casus belli*. By June 2002, Britain was a full partner in Operation Southern Focus, in which US and UK air forces dropped 606 bombs on 391 selected targets, including the network of fibre-optic cable used to transmit military communications, as well as key command centres and radars. General T. Michael Mosely told Michael Gordon of the *New York Times* that this operation was designed to lay the foundations for the forthcoming military campaign against Iraq.[14]

Unlike Blair and the US neo-conservatives, counter-terrorism experts in Washington, as well as senior advisers from the former Bush Administration (1989–92), opposed a new war against Saddam. In August 2002, Brent Scowcroft (former National Security Adviser) warned George W. Bush that

> any campaign against Iraq whatever the strategy, cost and risk, is certain to divert us for some indefinite period from our war on terrorism. Worse, there is a virtual consensus in the world against an attack on Iraq at this time. So long as that sentiment persists, it would require the US to pursue a virtual go-it-alone strategy against Iraq, making any military operations correspondingly more difficult and expensive. The most serious cost, however, would be to the war on terrorism. Ignoring that clear sentiment would result in a serious degradation in international cooperation with us against terrorism. And make no mistake, we simply cannot win that war without enthusiastic international cooperation, especially on intelligence.[15]

Scowcroft also thought a new war against Iraq would enrage the Middle East by not focusing first on settling the Israel-Palestine conflict:

> there would be an explosion of outrage against us. We would be seen as ignoring a key interest of the Muslim world in order to satisfy a narrow American interest. Even without Israeli involvement the results could well destabilize Arab regimes in the region, ironically facilitating one of Saddam's strategic objectives.[16]

Scowcroft's views were widely shared in Britain, especially among the armed forces which were sorely stretched in the Balkans and Afghanistan.

Blair would clearly have preferred to go to war against Iraq as part of a broad coalition. During the summer of 2002, Blair and his Foreign Secretary, Jack Straw, expressed concern about the prospect of unilateral US action in Iraq to Colin Powell, who was himself urging his President to take the case for disarming Saddam to the United Nations. Bush did so on 12 September 2002. Five days after his speech to the UN, in a less conciliatory mood, George Bush released his National Security Strategy document, which outlined a new doctrine of preventive war.[17] This went further than pre-empting an imminent threat, which has several precedents in international law, to permit going to war to remove any regime that might conceivably pose a threat sometime in the future. As one international lawyer noted, such a doctrine 'stands the (UN) Charter on its head' and if applied universally would result in global anarchy.[18] Implementing such a doctrine against Iraq would be difficult unless the Administration could prove that Iraq was an imminent threat to the United States. But in September 2002 the intelligence agencies in Washington were cautious about claiming that Iraq posed any kind of threat, not least because since the UNSCOM inspectors left in 1998, there had been no reliable information.

Blair's WMD dossiers

Tony Blair came to Bush's rescue in late September by publishing the first UK dossier on Iraq. The JIC assessment of March 2002 was not published because there was insufficient evidence of a credible threat from Iraqi WMD. Through the spring and summer of 2002, however, as the Bush Administration grew more and more impatient to initiate military operations against Iraq, the document went through a number of drafts at meetings chaired by Alastair Campbell, the Prime Minister's director of communications. Campbell's participation suggested that, far from a balanced objective assessment of the available intelligence, the dossier was to be a public relations document to support Britain's participation in Bush's war. Jonathan Powell, Blair's Chief of Staff, warned Campbell by email on 17 September that the JIC draft did not justify claiming that Iraq posed a threat to anyone, least of all Britain. But the dossier published on 24 September 2002 did just that, claiming that Iraqi WMD posed a 'current and serious' threat to Britain.[19] The timing of publication, soon after Blair's trip to Camp David, suggested that the dossier was also intended (in tandem with the 17 September National Security Strategy document) to persuade American legislators to authorise Bush to use force in Iraq. In early September several US senators complained that they did not yet have enough reliable evidence on which to base a vote.[20] After the publication of the UK dossier on 24 September in London, in early October, the CIA released its 2002 National Intelligence Estimate (NIE) which also claimed a serious threat from Iraqi WMD, although when the entire draft of the NIE was published in July 2003 it was found to be heavily caveated by various intelligence agencies who found most of the claims unreliable.[21] On

11 October 2002, however, the impact of the UK dossier and the uncaveated NIE generated a Senate vote of 77–23 to give Bush carte blanche to use force against Saddam.

UN Security Council Resolution 1441

Blair convinced Bush that he must follow up his 12 September speech at the UN with a Security Council resolution which would either persuade Saddam to disarm or permit a multilateral coalition to force disarmament. There was no talk at the UN of regime change. Achieving Security Council consensus on the language for the resolution was not easy. Eventually on 8 November 2002, all 15 members of the Security Council approved UNSCR 1441 calling on Saddam to accept new UN inspectors, and fully comply with earlier resolutions banning possession of WMD, or face serious consequences. UN inspectors (UNMOVIC) entered Iraq on 27 November.

In late 2002, knowing that war was inevitable, but still hoping it might be fought by a multilateral coalition under UN authorisation, Blair and Straw tried, but failed, to persuade Bush to focus on post-war stabilisation of Iraq, specifically that the UN play the key role in post-war reconstruction. Blair's staff in London, and the British mission to the UN in New York, were appalled when in January 2003 Bush assigned full responsibility for post-war administration of Iraq to Donald Rumsfeld and the Department of Defense.[22] Rumsfeld appointed a retired general, Jay Garner, to establish the Office of Reconstruction and Humanitarian Assistance (ORHA) and explicitly forbade him to use any of the material in the US State Department Study, *The Future of Iraq*, which Secretary of State Powell and his staff had been working on since April 2002. For Tony Blair – in order to nurture the special relationship – to commit British forces to a war for which he knew there was no serious post-war planning, must rank as one of the most irresponsible policy decisions of his premiership.

'The dodgy dossier' of February 2003

In late 2002 and early 2003 senior officers in the intelligence agencies in London and Washington raised a number of doubts about WMD claims by Bush and Blair.[23] Blair's response was yet another dossier in early February. Unlike the September 2002 dossier, this one did not directly involve the intelligence services, but was cobbled together by the Coalition Information Centre (CIC) in the Foreign Office (under the direction of Alastair Campbell) to present to journalists travelling to Washington with the Prime Minister. It was not fact-checked and became the object of ridicule as it was a mixture of unattributed excerpts from a ten-year-old PhD thesis, and open-source journal articles in which the language had been changed to hype the supposed threat from Iraq. Known as 'the dodgy dossier', it was a source of acute embarrassment to Jack Straw, who was never consulted about it, but had to suffer the consequences. He would later describe it as 'a real Horlicks'.[24]

Although Blair and Straw continued to imply through January and February 2003 that war could be averted if Saddam cooperated with the UN inspectors, it now seems clear that Bush and Blair had already decided, regardless of any progress made by UNMOVIC, and without any consultation with France or Germany, that the inspections would be judged a failure, and that this failure would be the rationale for Washington and London to go to war.[25] The debate on Resolution 1441 revealed that most UN Security Council members judged that another resolution would be required to justify military action against Iraq. Accordingly, in early March, Bush, Blair and Prime Minister Anzar of Spain drafted another resolution, but only one other Security Council member (Bulgaria) supported it.

France, Russia and Germany all stated that they could not support a war on Iraq and hinted they would veto a second resolution.[26] The French position was emphasised by President Chirac on 10 March on French television:

My position is that regardless of the circumstances, France will vote No because it considers this evening that there are no grounds for waging war in order to achieve the goal we have set ourselves – to disarm Iraq.[27]

In London, Blair feigned shock and horror at Chirac's intransigence, but was probably delighted, as he was then able to exhort his Cabinet to blame France for his failure to get another resolution. Chancellor Gordon Brown led the charge against France at the Cabinet meeting on 13 March.[28] Thereafter, loyal Blairite MPs and Cabinet members repeated anti-French statements ad nauseam in the next ten days leading up to the war, in a shameless stirring up of francophobia in Britain's Eurosceptic press.

On 14 March, Jeremy Greenstock, the UK Ambassador to the UN, told Blair that there were only four votes for a new UN resolution (USA, UK, Spain and Bulgaria), so it was withdrawn. With US troops already deployed in the sweltering heat of the Gulf, Bush was unwilling to wait any longer. Blair's willingness to go to war with neither 'international authority nor domestic support' triggered Robin Cook's resignation from the Cabinet on 17 March. In his resignation speech, Cook, who had had access to much of the same intelligence as Blair, said he doubted that Iraq had any deployable WMD.[29] Eight UK government ministers and parliamentary secretaries, in addition to Cook, resigned over the war.

Blair nevertheless achieved a House of Commons vote in favour of war on 18 March, but only after intensive lobbying based on two 'promises' from Bush which proved quite empty.[30] One was that the UN would play a vital role in post-war Iraq, the other was that the Bush Administration would pursue as a high priority the 'road map' to a settlement between Israel and Palestine.[31] As conditions in Iraq deteriorated in 2004, the Bush Administration became more interested in having the UN come to the rescue, but was unwilling to cede any real power. With respect to the Middle East, far from showing any initiative, Bush caved in to Ariel Sharon's aggressive policy towards Palestine, even to the point of ceding Israel control of 116 of their 120 illegal settlements in the West Bank.[32] Far from challenging this reversal of the 'road map' Blair also gave Sharon's proposal his blessing.[33]

An additional argument which Blair made to wavering legislators in March 2003 was that the Attorney-General, Lord Goldsmith, had advised the government that there was enough justification to disarm Iraq in UNSCR 678, the original UN authority for the First Gulf War. This was a highly controversial opinion and at least one international lawyer on Goldsmith's staff resigned in protest.[34]

Blair on the defensive

After George Bush declared the main combat phase of the war over on 1 May 2003, conditions in Iraq deteriorated into chaos, reflecting the lack of any serious post-war planning by coalition forces. Not only were Iraqi insurgents killing coalition troops every day and many Iraqis were complaining that conditions were far worse than under Saddam's regime, but none of the US-led inspection teams found any trace of WMD. This led those who had opposed the war on both sides of the Atlantic to question the basis on which Bush and Blair went to war, namely Saddam's possession of WMD. In the US, senior officials in the Bush Administration admitted that WMD had been the bureaucratic reason to go to war, but the real reason had been regime change. That option was not open to Tony Blair, however, who made his case for war to the British people solely on Iraqi WMD. Indeed, Blair maintained that Iraq had WMD long after these claims were denounced as unreliable by intelligence agencies in both the UK and the US. While it was common knowledge that Saddam acquired WMD in the 1980s, encouraged by the Reagan Administration which considered Saddam their ally against Iran at that time,[35] it was also clear that there had been no hard evidence about Iraqi WMD activity since UN inspectors dismantled all known nuclear activity in 1998.[36]

One problem in assessing raw intelligence in Washington was the number of agencies competing for the attention of policy makers. It appears that since September 11, 2001, the CIA, the Defense Intelligence Agency (DIA) and the State Department were completely outplayed in terms of access to the White House by a conservative cabal of policy analysts in the Pentagon's Office of Special Plans (OSP). Established by Paul Wolfowitz, Deputy Secretary of Defense, led by William Luti, a Deputy Undersecretary of Defense, and reporting directly to Douglas Feith, Undersecretary of Defense for Planning, the OSP had access to data from all the established agencies, but also relied heavily on information from Iraqi exiles.[37] In October 2002, Donald Rumsfeld expressed the hope that these exiles would discover things that 'might have been overlooked by the CIA'.[38]

Of the many claims about Iraqi WMD which have been discredited, four stand out. Two relate to Saddam's purported nuclear weapons programme. The first being his attempt to buy uranium oxide from Niger, and the second that he was importing aluminum tubing that had no other purpose except to enrich uranium to weapons-grade material. Third was that Saddam maintained a viable biological weapons programme as evidenced by a number of mobile laboratories and the retention of large stocks of anthrax. Fourth was Iraq's capability to threaten western democracies with long-range chemical weapons that could be deployed within 45 minutes of an order.

Was Iraq seeking uranium oxide (yellowcake) from Niger?

Rumours from Italy that Iraq was seeking uranium oxide from Niger surfaced in US intelligence circles in early 2001, but first appeared publicly in the UK dossier on Iraqi WMD released on 24 September 2002. In early 2001, the Italian Military Intelligence and Security Service (SISMI) dug up an old report about Wissam al-Zahawie, the Iraqi Ambassador to Rome, visiting Niger and several other African states in February 1999. The 1999 documents did not mention that al-Zahawie was trying to purchase uranium oxide. But when SISMI passed the 1999 report to the CIA in 2001, the Italians added a note speculating that this could be the purpose of the trip as Iraq had bought uranium oxide from Niger in the 1980s.[39]

Vice President Dick Cheney urged CIA Director George Tenet to investigate the SISMI report. Tenet sent former ambassador Joseph Wilson to Niger and Wilson reported back in late February that the claim was unreliable.[40] The evidence involved cutting and pasting old Niger government letterhead and forging the signature of a long retired government official. Moreover, all uranium exported from Niger was transmitted through a French company whose records were easy to check and showed no such transactions. Tenet distributed Wilson's findings to other Washington-based intelligence agencies on 9 March 2002. Meanwhile, the State Department's Bureau of Intelligence and Research (INR) had already informed Colin Powell (on 1 March 2002) that the claims regarding Iraqi attempts to purchase uranium from Niger were not credible and should not be publicised.[41]

When Jack Straw shared early drafts of the first UK dossier on Iraq with Colin Powell and the CIA in early September 2002, George Tenet cautioned Britain not to include any claim about Saddam trying to obtain uranium from Niger, but did not share with Straw the February 2002 report from Ambassador Wilson. In June 2003 the House of Commons Foreign Affairs Committee asked Jack Straw why the Blair government persisted in using demonstrably unreliable information in its dossiers. Straw's response, in a letter dated 12 July 2003, was that Britain had sources on Iraqi WMD that were independent of the United States. Straw claimed that the Americans gave no explanation or supporting documents for their doubts.[42] This hardly reflects US sensitivity to a 'special relationship' with the UK.

On 27 January 2003, Mohammed ElBaradei, Director-General of the International Atomic Energy Agency (IAEA) in Vienna, told the UN Security Council that he had seen no evidence to suggest that Iraq had revived its nuclear weapons programme since the elimination of that programme in the 1990s. Undaunted, President Bush repeated the claim about uranium from Niger in his State of the Union address to Congress on 28 January 2003; on this occasion laying the responsibility for the claim squarely on the British dossier of September 2002. Stephen Hadley (Condi Rice's deputy at the National Security Council) later acknowledged that this should not have happened as the CIA had warned the White House there was no reliable evidence to support such a claim.

Colin Powell was sceptical of the uranium claim and left it out of his speech to the UN Security Council on 5 February. On 9 March, Powell went further and acknowledged that the evidence on the uranium claim might be false. Condi Rice made a similar admission on 13 July 2003, claiming that all the President did in his State of the Union speech was report in good faith the intelligence from Britain, in the 24 September 2002 dossier, namely those now infamous 16 words: 'the British government has learned that Saddam Hussein recently sought significant quantities of uranium from Africa'.[43]

Thus, after doing Bush a favour by publishing the British dossier in time for the US Senate vote on Iraq, once the Niger story was acknowledged to be a forgery Bush implied in his State of the Union address that the unreliable source was Britain. Another example of the 'not-so-special relationship'.

Was Saddam importing aluminum tubes to enrich uranium?

Another piece of 'evidence' for Saddam's nuclear weapons programme touted by the OSP in Washington and by Blair in the September 2002 dossier was that Iraq was importing aluminium tubes that could only be used in centrifuges designed for enriching uranium. In early September, OSP leaked this story to Judith Miller and Michael Gordon of the *New York Times* who reported administration claims from Iraqi exiles that seeking nuclear weapons was a top priority for Saddam, but also noted that since there had been no UN inspectors on the ground in Iraq since 1998 it was difficult to claim anything about Iraqi WMD with any certainty. Bush Administration officials admitted to Gordon and Miller that in the absence of hard evidence they hoped to use a 'mosaic of disturbing news reports' to underscore their dire warnings about Iraq's WMD ambitions.[44]

Dick Cheney and Condi Rice hit the TV talk shows on Sunday 8 September 2002 with the aluminium tubes story. The following month George Tenet took one of the tubes to a closed Senate hearing as a kind of 'smoking gun'. The US Department of Energy (DOE) had their doubts because the tubes were the wrong size to be used to enrich uranium. The INR concurred and believed the tubes were designated for a multiple-rocket-launching system for which they had found an Iraqi purchase order on the internet. UN inspectors confirmed the INR conclusions. In Vienna the IAEA also concluded that there was no evidence to suggest that Iraq was planning to use the imported aluminium tubes for any other purpose than the reverse engineering of rockets.

Did Saddam have mobile biological weapons laboratories?

The purported evidence for a viable Iraqi biological weapons programme, mentioned in Colin Powell's speech to the UN Security Council on 5 February 2003, was the presence of two mobile laboratories which had been observed in satellite photographs of Iraq. The CIA and the DIA both repeated these claims in a joint report released 28 May 2003. Yet none of the various teams of inspectors in Iraq in 2002–3 found any trace of biological weapons in these trailers.[45] What they did find was equipment sold to Iraq by the British company Marconi, which earlier DIA engineering inspectors had already decided was to launch hydrogen balloons for the purpose of weather forecasting.[46]

In January 2004, David Kay, head of the Iraq Survey Group (ISG), told the Senate Armed Services Committee in Washington that not only had the ISG found no trace of WMD anywhere in Iraq, but that he did not expect there were any to be found because the intelligence was 'all wrong'.[47] This finding is consistent with earlier statements of the two Swedish directors of both UNSCOM and UNMOVIC. Rolf Ekeus, who led the UNSCOM team of UN inspectors from 1994 to 1998 said in September 2003 that he believed the Iraqi policy on biological weapons (BW) was always to build the capability to produce BW at some future date, but not to produce for storage and thereby create a problem of storage.[48] Hans Blix, Director of UNMOVIC, repeatedly said that he believed Iraq destroyed all its chemical and biological weapons in the 1990s, even though they did not fully report all their destruction procedures.

Despite (or perhaps because of) these consistently negative findings on Iraq's BW capability, Bush and Blair repeatedly rubbished the work of UNMOVIC.[49] In defiance of all the available evidence. Tony Blair also claimed, in a pre-Christmas 2003 broadcast to British troops serving in Iraq, that there was still 'massive evidence of clandestine laboratories' for BW. When asked to comment on Blair's claims, Paul Bremer, head of the US-led Coalition Provisional Authority (CPA) in Iraq, dismissed them as a 'red herring' and said specifically: 'That is not what David Kay has said.'[50] Another example of the Bush Administration choosing not to support Tony Blair's version of the facts.

In April 2004, Colin Powell finally admitted that he had been wrong about the mobile biological laboratories, but excused himself by saying he had received assurances from the CIA that the claim about the BW labs was 'multi-sourced and solid'.[51]

Ready to deploy chemical weapons?

From tentative suggestions of a future WMD capability in the JIC draft on Iraqi WMD in March 2002, the dossier that Blair published on 24 September asserted that Iraqi troops could threaten Britain with chemical shells within 45 minutes of an order to do so. As Robin Cook notes in his memoirs, the 45-minute claim was repeated four times in the dossier.[52]

On 29 May 2003 the BBC's *Today* programme broadcast an interview with a reporter who claimed that a UK intelligence officer suggested that the Prime Minister's dossier should not have emphasised the 45-minute claim, as it came from a single uncorroborated source. It should therefore not have been portrayed as a hard fact, and especially not in a statement purporting to deal with long-range WMD which could threaten Britain. At least two other journalists, who had spoken to the same government source as the *Today* reporter, made similar accusations. Tony Blair and his immediate staff were outraged by the accusations of bad faith and lashed out at the BBC. As the political storm intensified, Dr David Kelly, a highly respected government scientist and former UNSCOM inspector (who was scheduled to return to Iraq as part of the US-led Iraq Survey Group) told his Ministry of Defence (MoD) line manager that he had spoken to the journalists in question. Kelly's superiors promised him anonymity. Others, elsewhere in the MoD and in the Prime Minister's office, decided to deflect public attention from Tony Blair to Kelly and insisted that the MoD expose his name to journalists. Kelly was then subject to humiliating questioning by a parliamentary committee in early July. This ordeal unhinged Kelly, who committed suicide near his home on 18 July 2003.[53]

This tragedy triggered a judicial inquiry, headed by Lord Hutton, into the circumstances surrounding Kelly's death. The Hutton judgment, delivered on 28 January 2004, exonerated the Prime Minister from dishonesty in preparing the dossier, but chose not to comment on the wider issue of the reliability of the intelligence or on the rightness of Blair's decision to commit British troops to Bush's war. Because the inquiry was unusually transparent, however, the British people were able to come to their own conclusions about the integrity both of the Prime Minister and his staff, and of the intelligence services. Senior intelligence officers confirmed that speculation had been converted into hard fact to suggest a more imminent threat.[54] As Robin Cook claimed in his resignation speech on 17 March 2003, and as few in Britain now doubt, Tony Blair and his staff used intelligence not to guide policy, but to support a policy that the Prime Minister had already privately agreed with George Bush a year earlier.

Costs and benefits of the special relationship

Blair had little to show for his slavish devotion to the special relationship in general and George Bush's preventive war doctrine in particular. His Iraq policy diverted British assets from the more serious and time-urgent campaign against the al-Qaeda network, and undermined the international institutions on which the security of Britain rests: the United Nations, NATO and the European Union.

Blair's insistence, despite evidence to the contrary, that Iraqi WMD posed a serious threat made Britain the object of scorn and ridicule in Europe in particular and in the international community in general. Like Bush, Blair relied too much on Iraqi defectors with their own agendas who invoked outdated and inadequate information to justify going to war. He lowered Britain in the opinion of the rest of Europe and lost the trust of the British people at home.[55] Despite explicit warnings from his own intelligence chiefs, Blair chose to put British interests at greater risk, as evidenced by the bombing of the Consulate and British banks in Istanbul in November 2003. In the short term the war also undermined the security of the Iraqi people by sucking in a new generation of jihadists. The war also undermined the peace process in the Middle East. Far from promoting the quartet's 'road map', in April 2004, both Blair and Bush went out of their way to endorse Ariel Sharon's aggressive policy towards Palestine.

Although Bush showered praise on Blair, even inviting him to address a joint session of Congress, in general supporting Bush did not win Blair many favours or friends in the US. British nationals were still detained in Guantanamo Bay in 2004, for example. Just before the Iraq War, Secretary of Defense Rumsfeld brushed off Britain's likely military contribution as insignificant. Later, the National Security Council did not hesitate to make Britain the scapegoat for its own intelligence failures. Blair gained few friends in Washington because he failed to deliver on key promises: to bring France and Germany into the Coalition against Saddam and to obtain UN authorisation for military action. Former Foreign Secretary Douglas Hurd noted that Blair had about as much influence on Bush as the farthing wheel on a penny-farthing bicycle.[56]

While the downfall of Saddam was universally welcome, it brought little if any improvement in the security situation in Iraq, whereas the costs of the war were abundantly clear. In October 2003, Iraqi combatant and non-combatant deaths in the war were estimated in the region of 15,000 – a heavy price to pay, especially when there was no evidence that Iraq would emerge from war a more stable and democratic state than under Saddam.[57] In the spring of 2004, counterproductive US military tactics, which deployed helicopter gunships against Iraqi civilians in the cities of Fallujah and Najaf succeeded in uniting the Sunnis and Shias in opposition to the coalition forces, reminiscent of British mistakes in Iraq in the 1930s.[58]

Even more damaging to the reputation of coalition forces were revelations in the spring of 2004 that detainees in Iraq were subjected to the same kind of torture and abuse of human rights that the United States initiated for the interrogation of al-Qaeda suspects in Guantanamo Bay and Afghanistan.[59] Red

Cross reports in February 2004 also implicated British forces in the prisoner abuse scandal in both Afghanistan and Iraq.[60]

There is little evidence that Blair learned anything from the debacle in Iraq, but what about other European leaders? How likely are France and Germany to join a future coalition led by either the USA or the UK, not to mention the disillusioned Spanish and Polish governments who both paid a very high price in terms of their own casualties and their loss of support at home? After al-Qaeda attacks in Madrid on 11 March 2004, the government of Aznar was defeated at the polls and the new Socialist Prime Minister pulled Spanish forces out of Iraq. In the aftermath of the Madrid bombings, Polish President Kwasniewski complained that his country had been deceived by information on WMD and warned that Polish troops might also be withdrawn from Iraq.

Since Blair manifestly derived no benefit from his 'special relationship' with George Bush, allegiance to Washington does not appear to pay.[61] On the other hand, nor does defiance on the French model. The only influence EU leaders, like Blair, Chirac and Schroeder, could have in Washington would be to forge an EU policy consensus. On Iraq, Blair deliberately detached himself from his EU partners to support Bush in Iraq. This made Britain as much of a pariah in the international community as the United States. As another former Tory Foreign Minister said of Blair's relationship with Bush: 'That's enough grovelling PM.'[62]

Notes

1. Alan Bennett, 'A Shameful Year', *London Review of Books*, 8 January 2004, captures the feeling of many in the UK over Blair's Iraq policy.
2. The Desert Storm coalition included most of the western allies as well as the neighbouring Gulf states.
3. Though some found Blair arrogant. See Peter Riddell, *Hug Them Close*, London, Politico's, 2003, p. 77.
4. Iraqi opposition groups designated for US support by the Iraq Liberation Act include: Iraqi National Congress (INC); Iraqi National Accord (INA); Movement for a Constitutional Monarchy; Kurdistan Democratic Party (KDP); Patriotic Union of Kurdistan (PUK); Islamic Movement of Iraqi Kurdistan. Funds were offered to, but refused by, the Supreme Council for Islamic Revolution (SCIRI). See International Institute for Strategic Studies, *Strategic Survey 1998–1999*, London, IISS, 1999, at p. 173.
5. General Anthony Zinni, then US Commander in the Persian Gulf, testified to the Senate Armed Services Committee on 28 January 1999. Zinni opposed the plan to overthrow Saddam by force and argued that suport for Iraqi opposition was ill conceived and could destabilise the region. Ibid.
6. On Clinton's policy towards Iraq, see Madeleine Albright, 'Migraine Hussein', chapter 17 in *Madame Secretary: A Memoir*, New York, Mirimax Books, 2003, pp. 272–87; see also *Strategic Survey 2002–2003*, London, IISS, 2003, p. 146.
7. On Operation Desert Fox, see IISS, 'Iraq: Still Desperately Defiant', *Strategic Survey 1998–1999*, London, IISS, 1999, pp. 168–76.

8. On Blair persuading Bush to focus on al-Qaeda not Iraq in September 2001, see Riddell, *Hug Them Close*, pp. 155–60.

9. Bob Woodward, *Plan of Attack*, New York, Simon and Schuster, 2004.

10. Seymour M. Hersch, 'Stovepipe', *The New Yorker*, 27 October 2003, p. 80.

11. Richard A. Clarke, *Against All Enemies*, New York, Free Press, 2004, p. x.

12. HoC Foreign Affairs Committee, *Ninth Report: The Decision to Go to War in Iraq*, London, 7 July 2003, para. 23.

13. John Kampfner, 'Evil Axis', chapter 8 of *Blair's Wars*, London, Simon and Schuster, 2003, pp. 152–73. See also John Kampfner, 'The Year that Brought Blair to Book', *New Statesman*, 15 December 2003.

14. Michael R. Gordon, 'US air raids in '02 prepared for war in Iraq', *New York Times*, 20 July 2003.

15. Brent Scowcroft, 'Don't attack Saddam', *Wall Street Journal*, 15 August 2002.

16. Ibid.

17. *The National Security Strategy of the United States of America*, Washington DC, 17 September 2002 (www.whitehouse.gov/nsc/nss.pdf).

18. Thomas M. Franck, 'What Happens Now? The UN After Iraq', *American Journal of International Law*, Vol. 97, No. 3, July 2003, pp. 607–20.

19. *Iraq's Weapons of Mass Destruction: The Assessment of the British Government*, London, 24 September 2002, at pp. 6 and 25.

20. Eric Schmidt and Alison Mitchell, 'US lacks up to date review of Iraqi arms', *New York Times*, 11 September 2002.

21. For the NIE main judgements and caveats see, Joseph Cirincione et al., *WMD in Iraq: Evidence and Implications*, Carnegie Endowment for International Peace, January 2004, Appendix 1.

22. National Security Directive 24, January 2003.

23. For concern in the US, see Kenneth Pollack, 'How did we get it so wrong?' *Guardian G2*, pp. 1–5, 4 February 2004, and Michael Massing, 'Now They Tell Us', *New York Review of Books*, 26 February 2004, pp. 43–7; for concern in the UK see the Hutton Inquiry website: www.the-hutton-inquiry.org.uk.

24. FCO/CIC, *Iraq: Its Infrastructure of Concealment, Deception and Intimidation*, February 2003. On Straw's response to the 'dodgy dossier', see Kampfner, *Blair's Wars*, pp. 264–7

25. Hans Blix, *Disarming Iraq: The Search for Weapons of Mass Destruction*, London, Bloomsbury Press, 2004, p. 285.

26. Robert Graham, Krishna Guha and Guy Dinmore, 'War opponents vow to block new UN Resolution', *Financial Times*, 6 March 2003.

27. Chirac on 10 March 2003, cited by Patrick Wintour and Martin Kettle, 'Blair's road to war,' *Guardian*, 26 April 2003.

28. Robin Cook, *Point of Departure*, London, Simon and Schuster, at pp. 320–1.

29. Ibid., pp. 359–65 (resignation speech).

30. Blair speech on 18 March 2003, available at www.number-10.gov.uk.

31. The 'road map' had earlier been endorsed by the quartet of the UN, the EU, Russia and the USA.

32. Harvey Morris, Guy Dinmore and Christopher Adams, 'Bush backs Israeli Plan to hold on to land', *Financial Times*, 15 April 2004; Judy Dempsey and Heba Saleh, 'EU states condemn Bush over Israel plan', *Financial Times*, 16 April 2004.

33. Jonathan Freedman, 'Sharon's triumph is Blair's defeat', *Guardian*, 15 April 2004.

34. Goldsmith opinion in Hansard. 17 March 2003, column 515W in answer to a parliamentary question. During 2002–3 Goldsmith submitted at least four different legal opinions on the legality of military action against Iraq, each more pro-war than the one before. The last was in response to a request for clarification (that war would be legal) from Admiral Lord Boyce, Chief of the UK Defence Staff in March 2003. See Jean Eaglesham, 'Double blow to Blair's efforts to end war talk', *Financial Times*, 8 March 2004.

35. On declassified documents describing Donald Rumsfeld's missions to Iraq for the Reagan Administration in 1984, see Christopher Marquis, 'US courted Saddam despite use of poisons', *New York Times* and *International Herald Tribune*, 24 December 2003.

36. On the history of the UNSCOM inspections, see Frank Ronald Cleminson, 'What happened to Saddam's Weapons of Mass Destruction?' *Arms Control Today*, September 2003, pp. 3–6.

37. On the Office of Special Plans, see Seymour M. Hersch, 'Selective Intelligence', *The New Yorker*, 12 May 2003, pp. 44–51.

38. Rumsfeld cited in ibid.

39. Hersch, 'Stovepipe', p. 79.

40. Joseph Wilson later went public with a summary of his report in 'What I didn't find in Africa', *New York Times*, 6 July 2003.

41. For a detailed chronology of these communications, see Paul Kerr, 'Iraq Special', *Arms Control Today*, September 2003, pp. 17–21.

42. Straw's letter is cited by Kamal Ahmed, 'Blair ignored weapons warning', *Observer* (London), 13 July 2003.

43. On Bush Administration admissions that the claim about Uranium from Niger was false, see, David E. Sanger, 'US admits error on Iraqi uranium', *International Herald Tribune*, 9 July 2003; David Sanger and Judith Miller, 'Deputy of Bush accepts blame for faulty report', *IHT*, 24 July 2003; Edward Alden, Hubert Wetzel and James Harding, 'Bush under fire over Niger uranium connection', *Financial Times*, 9 July 2003.

44. Michael Gordon and Judith Miller, 'US says Hussein intensifies quest for A-bomb parts', *New York Times*, 8 September 2002. In late May 2004, the *New York Times* apologised to its readers for its irresponsible reporting before the war.

45. After the UN inspection team (UNMOVIC) was withdrawn from Iraq in March 2003, just prior to the war, the Bush Administration sent four additional sets of inspectors to hunt for WMD. The first was 'Force 20', a covert group that entered Iraq just before Operation Iraqi Freedom. The second was a group of Site Survey Teams that accompanied the initial invasion forces in mid March 2003. The third was the '75th Exploration Task Force' designed as a follow-up to the main invasion force. The fourth was the 'Iraq Survey Group' initially headed by Major General Keith W. Dayton, then by former UNSCOM and IAEA inspector, David Kay which went to Iraq in July 2003.

46. Douglas Jehl, 'Iraqi trailers said to make hydrogen, not biological arms', *New York Times*, 9 August 2003.

47. On David Kay's initial report, see Mark Hubbard, Marianne Brun-Rovet and James Harding, 'Iraq probe yet to find illegal weapons', *Financial Times*, 3 October 2003; on Kay's testimony to the US Senate Armed Services Committee, 28 January 2004, see *Transcript: David Kay at Senate hearing*, downloaded from www.cnn.com.

48. Ekeus interview with Jim Lehrer on Public Broadcasting Service *Newshour*, 22 September 2003.

49. Hans Blix, 'Bashing Blix and ElBaradei', chapter 10 of *Disarming Iraq*, pp. 215–36.
50. Luke Harding, 'Bush's man rejects Blair weapons claim', *Observer* (London), 28 December 2003; Jean Eaglesham, 'Blair faces fresh attack over weapons', *Financial Times*, 29 December 2003; Reuters, 'US official contradicts Blair on Iraq weapons labs', *International Herald Tribune*, 29 December 2003.
51. David Johnstone and Eric Schmitt, 'Powell claims CIA for error', *International Herald Tribune*, 5 April 2004.
52. Robin Cook, *Point of Departure*, p. 216.
53. For an excellent account of Kelly's ordeal, see John Cassidy, 'The David Kelly Affair', *The New Yorker*, 8 December 2003; see also the Hutton Inquiry website: www.the-hutton-inquiry.org.uk.
54. Hutton Inquiry website: Brian Jones (DIA) testimony on 13 September 2003 and Sir Richard Dearlove (SIS/MI6) testimony on 15 September 2003. See also Brian Jones, 'There was a lack of substantive evidence ... We were told there was intelligence we could not see', *Independent*, 4 February 2004.
55. Local elections in June 2004 placed Labour in third place behind the Conservative and Liberal Democratic Parties; a result most analysts attributed to widespread opposition to Blair's support of the Iraq War.
56. Douglas Hurd, 'The penny-farthing's little wheel', *Financial Times*, 16 April 2003.
57. Carl Conetta, *The Wages of War: Iraqi Combatant and Non Combatant Fatalities in the 2003 Conflict*, Cambridge, MA, Project for Defense Alternatives Research Monograph No. 8, October 2003.
58. Toby Dodge, 'Violence, incompetence, instability', *The World Today*, October 2003, pp. 5–7; see also his book about the British mandate in Iraq in the 1920s: *Inventing Iraq: The Failure of Nation Building and History Denied*, New York, Columbia University Press, 2003. See also Fareed Zakaria, 'Our last real chance', *Newsweek*, 19–26 April 2004, pp. 35–8.
59. Evidence of prisoner abuse came from the US government memoranda as well as from the International Committee of the Red Cross and Human Rights Watch. See, for example, Dana Priest and Jeffrey Smith, 'Memo offers justification for use of torture', *Washington Post*, 8 June 2004; Dana Priest and Mike Allen, 'Memo on torture draws focus to Bush', *ibid.*, 9 June 2004; and Dana Priest and Bradley Graham, 'Guantanamo list details approved interrogation methods', *ibid.*, 10 June 2004.
60. Patrick Tyler, 'Blair offers an apology for abuses by soldiers', *New York Times*, 10 May 2004, and 'British official says soldiers may soon face abuse charges', *ibid.*, 11 May 2004.
61. Elizabeth Pond, 'Post War Europe', in her *Friendly Fire: The Near-Death of the Atlantic Alliance*, Washington DC, Brookings Institution Press, 2003, pp. 75–96; see also William Pfaff, 'This could be the end of a beautiful friendship', *International Herald Tribune*, 15 January 2004.
62. Malcolm Rifkind, 'That's Enough Grovelling PM', *The Spectator*, 10 May 2003.

4
Turkey, the United States, and Northern Iraq

Bill Park

Introduction

The refusal by Ankara's National Assembly on 1 March 2003 to permit US troops to enter Turkish territory, from where they could launch a ground attack against northern Iraq, did more than complicate Washington's war plans. The tortuous and fraught negotiations leading to the vote left a bitter aftertaste, and deeply undermined US-Turkish relations. A pungent demonstration of the diplomatic breakdown was offered by Assistant US Defense Secretary Paul Wolfowitz, whose responsibility it had been to coax Ankara into supporting Washington's war plans. In an interview with CNN-Turkey in early May, Wolfowitz suggested that Turkey apologise for its mistake in refusing the entry of US troops, and chided Turkey's military leadership for failing to exercise leadership by lobbying more actively for a positive parliamentary vote.[1] Wolfowitz's comments caused uproar in Turkey,[2] and prompted Prime Minister Recep Erdogan to declare that 'Turkey, from the beginning, made no mistakes.'[3] Pointedly, and seemingly without irony, the Turkish military leadership itself queried whether a more assertive military role would have been compatible with Turkey's democratic processes.[4]

Inadvertently, Wolfowitz's comments, and the Turkish reaction to them, drew attention both to the disjunctions between American and Turkish strategic vision and national interests, and to the potential for conflict between global strategic perspectives and behaviour on the one hand, and local political processes and interests on the other. After all, the Turkish parliamentary vote faithfully reflected the strong anti-war preferences of Turkish public opinion, was unanimously supported by the Republican People's Party (CHP) parliamentary opposition, and was insufficiently troubling to the politically powerful Turkish General Staff (TGS) to encourage them to intervene more actively in a manner more to Washington's liking. In the light of these events, it remains at least an open question whether an intensification of direct US engagement in the affairs of the broader Middle East region would prove compatible with a close and harmonious US-Turkish strategic relationship. It similarly raises the question of whether a broader democratisation of Middle East politics would necessarily produce regional policies that are compatible with US interests.

Iraq's neighbour

Within weeks of 9/11 (if not before), the Bush Administration turned its attention to the unsettled score of Saddam Hussein's weapons of mass destruction (WMD) programme, and entertained the idea of 'regime change' in Baghdad. Wolfowitz's July 2002 visit left Ankara in little doubt that, in the event of war, US plans would involve ground attacks launched from Turkish territory.[5] As both a neighbour of Iraq and a strategic ally of Washington, Turkey found itself uncomfortably in the spotlight. Bulent Ecevit's coalition government warned Washington of Turkey's opposition to war, while urging Baghdad to comply with United Nations inspections and resolutions, which were now being revived with the unanimous passage of Resolution 1441 in November 2002. In the same month, Turkish elections brought the moderate Islamist Justice and Development Party (Adalet ve Kalkinma – AKP) to power. It was no less fervent than its predecessor in wishing to avoid war. The US, however, having been unwilling to put pressure on Ankara during Turkey's national elections, was fast losing patience, and Turkey's new government immediately found itself a target of Washington's diplomatic attentions.

Ankara's unease with Washington's approach derived in many respects from the same sources that fed the broader international opposition to US policy. However, Turkey also had reasons of its own for fearing a renewal of armed conflict with Iraq. As a consequence of both the 1990–91 war and the sanctions and isolation of Iraq that followed it, Turkey had lost major trading opportunities with a neighbour with which it had generally enjoyed close economic and political relations. This had been a serious blow to Turkey's weak economy. Furthermore, Turks were bitter that promises of financial compensation had failed to materialise. During the ensuing decade, Turkey's economy had become more fragile still, and Ankara feared that a renewal of conflict in the region could inflict a severe setback to its IMF-sponsored economic reform programme.

Turkey's domestic political context was also a factor. The AKP government achieved electoral victory on a platform of economic reform and rehabilitation. A related priority was the implementation of an ambitious programme of political, legal and administrative reforms to ready the country for hoped-for

EU accession negotiations. Furthermore, the AKP administration represents a constituency more sympathetic to Turkey's own Islamic character and to its Muslim neighbours. Abdullah Gul, acting Prime Minister as the crisis unfolded, was known to favour a tilt in Turkey's foreign policy towards the Islamic world. Otherwise, few of the mostly novice AKP deputies had much experience or interest in foreign affairs.[6]

As war approached, it became increasingly evident that there would be no regional groundswell of support for US-led action against Iraq. Arguably, this may have inflated Ankara's estimation of its indispensability to Washington. State Department spokesman Marc Grossman later conceded that Washington might not have done enough to disabuse Ankara of its overconfidence.[7] In any case, whatever the outcome of any war, Turkey would continue to inhabit the region, and would need to rebuild any fractured relationships with its neighbours, Arab and Iranian. In the wake of 9/11, the anti-Americanism so prevalent in much of the Islamic and especially Arab world appeared to become more influential around the region. Turkey was concerned about the implications for regional stability of any new war with Iraq, and of its own potential isolation in the region.

Kurdish ramifications

The potential ramifications for the Kurdish issue of any war with Iraq caused Ankara the greatest headache. Developments in Iraqi Kurdistan subsequent to the 1990–91 war constituted a major consideration for Ankara's policy makers.[8] The flood of around half a million Iraqi Kurds towards the Turkish border after the failed post-war uprising against Baghdad, and the international community's involvement in the consequent humanitarian crisis, had led, via safe havens, a 'no-fly-zone' policed from Incirlik in Turkey, and the withdrawal of Baghdad's forces from the area in October 1991, to the establishment of a self-governing Kurdistan Regional Government (KRG) zone nestling against the Turkish and Iranian borders. The zone, governed by an uneasy coalition of the Patriotic Union of Kurdistan (PUK) and the Kurdish Democratic Party (KDP), did not extend to the Mosul and Kirkuk oilfields, which nevertheless form part of what has been traditionally regarded as Iraqi Kurdistan. This experiment in self-government and democratisation created a tangible sense of well-being and freedom for the mainly Kurdish inhabitants of the area. They would have little reason to welcome the re-establishment of any overly intrusive rule from Baghdad, with or without Saddam.[9]

In Ankara's view, the Kurdish issue posed a threat both to regional stability and to Turkey's own territorial integrity. As such, it has long been seen as a core national security issue. Up to half of all ethnic Kurds, who straddle the Turkish, Iraqi, Iranian and Syrian borders, live in Turkey. Turkish security forces fought for almost 20 years in the southeast of the country against the separatist Kurdish Workers Party (PKK), at a cost of nearly 40,000 lives. Sporadic exchanges between Kurdish separatists and Turkish security forces have occurred inside Turkey even since the overthrow of Saddam. Over the years, Turkish troops launched substantial raids across the border – at times with the agreement of Baghdad, or the cooperation of Iraqi Kurds – in pursuit of PKK fighters. Ankara has maintained smaller forces in northern Iraq almost continuously since the 1980s, and conducted numerous air raids. Although the establishment of the KRG coincided with an intensification of PKK activity in southeastern Turkey, it also afforded Ankara considerable freedom of action in northern Iraq.[10] Since the 1999 arrest and subsequent incarceration of the PKK's leader, Abdullah Ocalan, it even appeared as if Ankara had finally 'won' its internal war against Kurdish separatism.

Nevertheless, Ankara has never acclimatised itself to the existence of the KRG. It fears it might serve as a pole of attraction, or a model, for Turkey's restive Kurds, or it might become emboldened enough to lend them direct support. It could garner international sympathy for the idea of wider Kurdish national self-determination leading ultimately to a sovereign Kurdish state. Ankara's reaction to the prospect of a war against Saddam was shaped by the suspicion that full independence is the ultimate goal of Kurds on both sides of the border, and that moves towards the establishment of an independent Kurdish state could have an unravelling effect across the region. The destruction of Saddam's regime threatened to bring such a prospect closer. In Turkey's view, any new war with Iraq could – whether by design, default or through opportunistic exploitation of chaos and uncertainty – raise the risk of an enlarged, oil-rich, and more autonomous if not fully independent Kurdish self-governing entity emerging in northern Iraqi territory. Ankara's doubts concerning Kurdish aspirations were reinforced by the draft KRG constitution drawn up in 2002, which envisaged that the oil-bearing Iraqi Kurdish provinces be incorporated into any future Kurdish self-governing zone within a loose Iraqi federal framework, that Kirkuk should be its capital, and that it should retain control over its own armed forces.[11] Ankara also entertained fears of a renewal of PKK activity in the chaos of war, and a replay of the refugee crisis of 1991.

National policy takes shape

Ankara's anti-war stance found expression partly through regionally based endeavours to find alternatives to war. Throughout the crisis, Turkey sought to preserve some kind of relationship with Baghdad. Ankara repeatedly pleaded with Baghdad to lance the tension by cooperating with UN inspectors, whilst for its part Baghdad repeatedly requested that Turkey desist from complying with US demands. As late as January 2003 the Turkish Trade Minister led a large delegation of businessmen to Baghdad, partly to drum up trade but also in order to deliver yet another message to Saddam Hussein imploring him to cooperate with the UN.[12]

In December 2002, Turkey's AKP government – apparently without first informing the foreign ministry or the military – announced it would explore the scope for a regional initiative aimed at resolving the issue of Iraqi arms programmes without recourse to war.[13] Although some interpreted this move as aimed at demonstrating to the AKP's domestic constituency that the government had done its best, it also reflected the government's sincere preference that war be avoided. To this end, Gul embarked on a tour of Middle East capitals in January, and secured agreement for a summit to be held in Istanbul later that month. Attended by Egypt, Syria, Jordan, Saudi Arabia and Iran, the outcome was an inconclusive discussion and a weak final communiqué. The communiqué did implore Saddam to cooperate with UN inspectors and to terminate any WMD programmes, but drew back from an earlier idea that he might be persuaded to go into exile.[14]

Ankara particularly sought to align its position with those of Iran and Syria, who in large measure shared Turkey's perspective on the Kurdish issue. Relations with Syria had improved in the wake of Assad's expulsion of Ocalan in 1998, and those with Iran had long demonstrated elements of cooperation as well as conflict, not least with respect to the Kurdish issue. These diplomatic efforts continued, even intensified, in the immediate aftermath of Saddam's removal and as Iraqi Kurdish forces appeared to be tightening their grip on northern Iraq. A flurry of diplomatic activity drew Washington's sting, as the US began turning its attention to the uncooperative and troubling behaviour of Turkey's other two Middle Eastern neighbours. Indeed, it stoked American suspicions – dismissed by Ankara – that the 1 March vote indicated a deeper realignment of Turkish foreign policy.[15] Washington's suspicious reaction again demonstrated both the continued ill feeling in the wake of the Turkish parliamentary vote, and the lack of a shared US-Turkish understanding of the region's affairs.

In the wake of Wolfowitz's July 2002 visit, the TGS concluded that it was unlikely that Washington would be dissuaded from its chosen path, and instead sought better to position itself to protect the national interest by drawing up plans to insert substantial Turkish forces into northern Iraq alongside US troops. In addition to the 5000 or so Turkish troops that had long been stationed inside Iraq and engaged in monitoring and countering PKK activity, in October Ankara began building up its forces on the Turkish side of the border, reaching up to 50,000 by December. Their purpose would be to monitor and deal with any PKK activity, manage the movement of refugees, and deter moves towards the establishment of an independent Kurdistan in Iraq. The TGS appeared to share with the AKP government a sense of the indispensability to the US of Turkish cooperation, and was content to go along with the hard bargaining between Ankara and Washington that intensified in the wake of the November election.[16] These negotiations focused on the economic compensation Ankara might extract from Washington, the terms under which Ankara might permit access to its territory by US and allied forces, and the arrangements for the introduction of a more substantial Turkish force into northern Iraq.

Ankara's negotiating approach was to interconnect these issues, using Washington's needs as a lever. To Washington's increasing irritation, Ankara sought to maximise the leverage it had as a consequence of its strategically vital location, or at least to minimise the damage to Turkey as a consequence of its location. Washington's preference for a two-front war, the relentlessness of its military build-up in the region, and the very imminence of conflict, appeared from Washington's perspective to be mercilessly exploited by Ankara. It seems though that both the TGS and the AKP government too anticipated that, after a decent interval, US troops would be permitted to mount ground attacks on Iraq from Turkish territory. It also appears, however, that the TGS believed that Turkish troops would be permitted to accompany them. Washington's failure to share Turkish perspectives on the Kurdish issue, and its desire to limit the scope for direct Turkish military engagement in northern Iraq, may go some way to explaining the TGS's passivity both before and after the 1 March National Assembly vote.

Washington enters the bazaar

Wolfowitz emerged from a December 2002 trip to Ankara declaring that 'Turkish support is assured'. Turkish comment was far more circumspect, however,[17] and in fact Wolfowitz had failed to obtain permission for US access to Turkish territory.[18] Although Ankara had been privy to US war planning since July, the Turks had thus far done little to accommodate them. Ankara instead seemed intent on trading off the number of US troops permitted to enter Turkey against Washington's acquiescence to a substantial Turkish move into northern Iraq.[19] It was reported that the US had agreed to consider a geographically limited deployment of Turkish troops across the border, with the proviso that they steer clear of Kurdish towns and cities. Not surprisingly, any introduction of a substantial Turkish military force was deeply upsetting to Iraq's Kurds, who threatened to physically resist the entry of Turkish troops into the KRG area.[20]

It was not until 6 February that a Turkish parliamentary vote permitted around 4000 US personnel to enter the country to commence the upgrade of facilities, at an estimated cost to the US of $300 million. Fifty AKP deputies along with the entire opposition voted against the measure.[21] Furthermore, the Turkish government accompanied the vote with the rider that it did not necessarily imply subsequent approval for the entry of US troops, which would also require parliamentary approval. The AKP government's repeated protestations that it could not guarantee to win over its own deputies unless Washington met Turkish demands was not simply a crude negotiating ploy – which is how many in the US saw it. Some government figures – not least Prime Minister Gul, but also the Speaker of the National Assembly and President Sezer – remained openly unenthusiastic about granting US military access to Turkish territory. Given that opinion polls suggested that over 90 per cent of the population were against a war with Iraq, and that many AKP deputies and the entire CHP opposition shared this view, parliamentary approval for the entry of US troops was indeed far from a foregone conclusion.[22] Nevertheless, Washington continued to base its military planning and build-up on the availability of Turkish bases – presumably because it anticipated that the all-powerful TGS would eventually pressure the politicians into line.

The Kurdish conundrum

The Iraqi Kurdish leaderships were also initially nervous about the prospect of US action against Saddam's regime. They feared that the considerable gains in autonomy that they had made over the previous decade would be put at risk by war in the region, and they suspected that, once again, Washington might abandon them to their fate – in the form of Turkish troops, or a new autocrat in Baghdad, or both – once Saddam had been removed.[23] With Ankara, however, the Kurds too recognised that they had to accommodate themselves to the likelihood of US military action in northern Iraq. It was nevertheless as clear to Iraqi Kurds as it was in Ankara that, although the US needed the support of both parties, Kurdish and Turkish interests were almost diametrically opposed.[24] Even so, the KRG appreciated that it was vital to reassure Ankara of its commitment to a unified Iraq[25] – not least as a consequence of Washington's desire that it do so. Such reassurances cut little ice in Turkey.

Ankara also sought to muddy the waters for any Kurdish enclave in a future federal Iraq by championing the cause of its Turkic kinsmen in the region.[26] The decision to champion the Turkmen cause appears to have been made by the TGS during the summer of 2002.[27] Backed by Ankara, the Turkmen – estimated to number between 500,000 and 3 million – claimed discrimination against them by the KRG, and that if Iraq's future was to be an ethnically based federation, then Turkmen too should enjoy the benefits of self-government. This argument has particular significance because of the concentration – according to Ankara and the Iraqi Turkmen Front (ITF) but to few others, a 60 per cent preponderance – of Turkmen in the Kirkuk oil-bearing region of northern Iraq.[28] The prospect of a Turkish-backed self-governing Turkmen entity centred on oil-rich Kirkuk[29] would of course greatly complicate arguments for an ethnically based Kurdish self-governing province in a federal Iraq, and offered a forewarning of the demographic squabbles and ethnic tensions in the region that followed the Coalition victory in April 2003. In the meantime, Washington found itself cornered into recognising the Turkmen cause in the face of KDP opposition when, in the autumn of 2002, the ITF was belatedly incorporated into the US's 1998 Iraqi Liberation Act and thus into meetings of the US-sponsored Iraqi opposition. This paved the way for the subsequent inclusion of an ITF representative on the Iraqi Governing Council (GC) established in the wake of Saddam's overthrow.

A more sinister twist to Turkey's approach to Iraqi Kurdistan was the occasional indication of irredentism. Turkish nationalism had often expressed resentment at the loss of Mosul and Kirkuk in the 1923 Lausanne Treaty. Thus Defence Minister Sabahattin Cakmakoglu, admittedly a member of the far right National Action Party (MHP), chose in August 2002 to remark that Iraqi Kurdistan had been 'forcibly separated' from Turkey (by the British) at the time of the Republic's foundation in 1923, and that Ankara retained a protective interest in the fate of the region.[30] During the Gulf War Ozal had similarly mused about Turkish claims to the region in the event of an Iraqi collapse.[31] In 1986, too, Ankara warned the US and Iran that it would demand the return of Mosul and Kirkuk in the event of disorder in Iraq as a consequence of the Iran–Iraq War.[32] On the eve of the recent conflict, the AKP government's Foreign Minister, Yasar Yakis, apparently sought legal clarification of the status of Mosul and Kirkuk,[33] and in the wake of Saddam's demise former Turkish President Suleyman Demirel openly expressed regret that Turkey had not been allowed to retain Mosul in the 1920s.[34] Some Turks have pointed out that Mosul and Kirkuk were ceded to Iraq, not to any Kurdish state that might subsequently emerge.[35]

Kurds, Turks and Americans

Washington now found itself involved in difficult three-way talks with Ankara and the Iraqi Kurds on arrangements for the northern front. Tension between Ankara and the Iraqi Kurds was particularly high over the fate of the northern Iraqi oilfields.[36] But Ankara was also worried about any suggestion that Kurdish forces might play a major part in the overthrow of the Iraqi regime.[37] Ankara became increasingly nervous about the US arming Kurdish fighters, particularly were it to involve heavy equipment, and insisted that any arms distributed to the Kurds be recovered at the earliest possible opportunity. Continued Turkish resistance to American suggestions that Turkish troops in northern Iraq be placed under US command, and attempts to negotiate downwards the number of US troops earmarked for the northern front intensified both American and Kurdish apprehension that Turkey might be prepared to act quite independently of the US.[38] Washington's negotiators found themselves obliged to offer reassurances to both sides – to Ankara that Washington was committed to Iraq's territorial integrity, and to the

Kurds that their aspirations for autonomy within a federal structure would be met. Washington agreed that it would fall to US troops to take Mosul and Kirkuk, thus denying to either Turkish or Kurdish forces the ability to determine the fate of the oil-bearing region.[39] During his December visit to Ankara, Wolfowitz was careful to insist that after Saddam, Iraqi oil resources would belong to the Iraqi state as a whole.[40] In an attempt to coordinate operations, a three-way US-Turkish-Iraqi Kurd committee was mooted at the very end of 2002, but it appears that Turkish uncertainty prevented it from becoming operational.

Coming to a head

In the wake of a National Security Council meeting on 31 January, the Turkish government finally agreed that on 18 February it would seek parliamentary approval for the entry of US troops into Turkey. The vote would be linked to approval for the despatch of Turkish troops to Iraq. However, the financial package, the number of US troops to be allowed in and the terms of Turkish entry into Iraq, had not yet been settled, and an increasingly impatient US was obliged to engage in frustrating and sometimes bizarre last-minute negotiations with Ankara over these issues.[41] Ankara resisted Washington's attempts to ensure that the terms of the substantially increased offer should fall within the IMF rescue package for Turkey, and also now began insisting on a written guarantee to offset any future congressional opposition to the deal.[42] Furthermore, as rumours circulated that Washington was making concessions to Ankara with respect to northern Iraq in order to secure agreement, so Iraqi Kurdish objections became ever more strident. In any case, with four or five US ships carrying tanks and other heavy equipment for the 4th Infantry Division sitting helpless off the Turkish coastline, and another 30 or so ships on their way, and against the dramatic backdrop of a raging diplomatic fallout in NATO over the despatch to Turkey of Patriot air defence systems, AWACS aircraft, and chemical and biological defence units, the Turkish government stalled on putting the issue to the vote, arguing that the National Assembly would not accept what was on offer.[43]

With a transparent lack of enthusiasm, and with concerns now being voiced by the Turkish President, Parliamentary Speaker and others over the legality of the procedure, on 26 February the government finally introduced a measure to parliament that would permit the entry of 62,000 US troops, 255 jet aircraft and 65 helicopters, for a period of six months. On 1 March, after more delay and in the wake of a National Security Council meeting at which the powerful Turkish military had remained mute, parliament rejected the measure by just three votes as a result of AKP abstentions. The entire opposition voted against the entry of US troops – although it supported a Turkish military incursion into northern Iraq.

Although US military and civilian officials sought to put a brave face on the outcome, US war planners were now left in something of a quandary, compounded by the absence of any plans to resubmit the bill to the Turkish parliament. The calendar now precluded a heavy infantry assault from Turkish soil. The aid package having been withdrawn, and amidst warnings to Turkey not to intervene into Iraq unilaterally, US thinking now shifted towards the possibility of mounting a lighter and smaller attack against northern Iraq with forces that might be flown directly to air bases there. In the event, of course, US forces were parachuted in. This, together with air attacks against Iraq, would also require Turkish parliamentary approval for US overflight rights. It took substantial pressure from Washington, and an intervention by the TGS, to encourage cooperation with the US, before the issue was put before the Turkish parliament. On 20 March, on the very day that the war commenced, overflight rights were granted in a vote in the Turkish parliament that also granted permission for the Turkish army to enter northern Iraq. US assault troops were still not to be allowed onto Turkish territory, however. Turkey was the last NATO ally to grant overflight.[44]

Conclusion

The extent and nature of the fallout from this saga will take time to become clear, but it seems likely that US-Turkish relations, Turkey's relations with Iraq, the Kurdish aspiration for self-determination, the future of Iraq, the stability of the region, and the strength of Turkish democracy, are all certain to have been affected to some degree. The incorporation of a $1 billion supplementary vote into the war budget sent to Congress by the Bush Administration, coupled with Secretary of State Colin Powell's 'kiss and make up' visit to Ankara in early April 2003, were early indications that all was not lost in US-Turkish relations. Powell's visit sealed Ankara's agreement that special and airborne troops that the US had deployed to northern Iraq could be supplied – though not with armaments and ammunition, for that would have required a parliamentary vote – from Turkish territory. Within weeks of the coalition victory, Turkey began standing down its troops on the border with Iraq,[45] and appeared ready to shift towards a more constructive engagement with Iraq's future – for example, by offering humanitarian assistance to Iraq.[46] A visit to Iraq by a Turkish foreign ministry delegation in May, during which discussions were held with KRG spokesmen, offered just one indication that the atmosphere could soften. At every opportunity both sides insisted on the enduring strength of US-Turkish relations.[47]

Yet Wolfowitz's comments in his 6 May 2003 interview with leading Turkish journalists conveyed the truer picture – of a frosty atmosphere in which some difficult questions were being asked. Although the cooling of US-Turkish relations can be traced back primarily to the 1 March National

Assembly vote, post-war relations were made more difficult still by the new situation in Iraq. Ankara continued to cultivate Iran and Syria in an endeavour to create a regional consensus against excessive Kurdish ambitions, and in January 2004 Syria's President Bashir Assad visited Turkey. And Ankara's warnings of the dire consequences of Kurdish over-ambition lost none of their stridency. However, during the months following Saddam's overthrow, Ankara continued to find itself on the outside looking in. Although Ankara offered to contribute, Turkey was not even invited to the meeting held in London in early May 2003 to assemble a multinational peacekeeping force for Iraq. To Ankara's dismay, it was agreed there that the force was to be put under the command of NATO newcomer Poland. Washington appeared similarly disinclined to indulge Turkey in the allocation of reconstruction contracts. Even worse, Ankara's offer to provide 10,000 troops to assist in the peacekeeping effort in Iraq had to be withdrawn in November 2003 in the face of fierce Iraqi Kurdish opposition.[48]

Thus the Kurdish issue continued to bedevil US-Turkish relations. Turkey's non-cooperation with Washington's war plans resulted in the ultimate irony that America's thinly spread and relatively lightly armed forces were left with no option but to rely on Iraqi Kurds as force generators, to a greater degree than either Ankara or Washington would ever have desired. The air drop of US forces into northern Iraq was as much a signal to Ankara not to intervene unilaterally as a manoeuvre in the fight against Saddam. Although Turkish forces remained in northern Iraq, Ankara had lost much influence there in the light of the US presence and the close relationship the US military established with the Iraqi Kurds. Although the Kurds were wise enough to hand nominal control of northern Iraq to US forces soon after its liberation, Ankara could but look on with alarm as the Kurdish political and administrative hold over the region inevitably tightened, US-Kurdish cooperation in northern Iraq intensified, and the rest of Iraq looked unlikely to transform into a viable political entity for some time to come. After all, Turkey's concerns had always been focused more on the aftermath of any war.

The election of a Kurd-dominated interim authority in Kirkuk,[49] and sporadic interethnic violence in the region between Kurds, Arabs and Turkmen, all served to keep the Turkmen issue alive and to highlight US-Turkish differences on the Kurdish issue. Ankara's determination to maintain its military presence in Iraq – notwithstanding KRG requests that they be withdrawn and a deal forged in late 2003 that US forces would tackle the PKK in northern Iraq – and to champion the Turkmen cause, survived the collapse of Saddam's regime. The potential for US-Turkish clashes was demonstrated by the furore surrounding the 4 July 2003 arrest by US forces of eleven Turkish Special Forces commandos and a number of Turkish and Turkmen civilians during a raid on a building in Sulaymaniyah in northern Iraq, on the basis of intelligence reports that the Turks were engaged in 'disturbing activities'. The establishment of a US-Turkish commission to investigate the incident did not prevent the TGS chief General Ozkok characterising the incident as heralding 'the biggest crisis of confidence' between the two sides. Ankara also made it clear it had no intention of withdrawing its forces from northern Iraq.[50]

In short, a still more serious clash between Ankara and Washington over the future of Iraqi Kurdistan remains a distinct possibility, both as a consequence of the situation on the ground, with Washington's Kurdish allies sharing with the US the responsibility for security in the area, and resenting the continued Turkish military presence there, but also as a consequence of negotiations over Iraq's future. The Iraqi Kurds appeared the most organised and representative of the Iraqi factions making up the US-sponsored Governing Council established in the wake of the war to develop a new governing system for the country. They will play a major part in determining Iraq's future. On the other hand, the Iraqi Arab opposition to the establishment of a Kurdish-Arab federation along lines proposed by the Kurds, as well as the unease felt by all regional states, including Turkey, at such a prospect, is at odds with the Kurdish insistence that the KRG retains the autonomy it has enjoyed for more than a decade, and territorially expands to incorporate all the provinces of Iraq traditionally regarded as Kurdish, including Kirkuk. Washington could yet be forced to obstruct the ambitions of its erstwhile Kurdish allies. This will be a difficult course to take. Washington might also struggle to prevent Iraq degenerating into chaos as the prospect of a viable political arrangement for post-Saddam Iraq recedes. The pieces of the jigsaw thrown up by US-led regime change in Baghdad are yet to hit the ground, and Washington might yet have to reap what it has sown in Kurdistan.

As the US finds itself drawn ever more towards the political and resource issues of the Middle East, Turkey will remain a strategically located NATO ally. Successful regime change in Iraq could intensify Turkey's own development as a major oil and gas transit route. The US will remain Ankara's most important strategic, economic and political sponsor. On the other hand, the Pentagon, hitherto Ankara's most ardent advocate in Washington, experienced the frustration of having its war plans in effect sabotaged by Turkey's behaviour, and may be loath to leave itself over-dependent on Turkish cooperation in the future. Although in early 2004 the US was granted permission to use Incirlik to rotate over 100,000 troops out of Iraq, that the agreement caused a political furore in Turkey suggested a lingering bitterness on both sides. The long-term future of the facility remains unclear.

It is reasonable to surmise that Turkey's domestic political ground may be shifting too. In the negotiations that preceded 1 March, Washington sometimes behaved as if the TGS was the main conduit to Turkish decision making. In the past this has been a well founded assumption. However, the TGS failed to make a stand at the NSC meeting called just days before the parliamentary vote, which in any case might have represented an attempt by the AKP leadership to shift responsibility to the TGS. Possibly the TGS believed the vote would pass, and sought to avoid too closely associating itself with what remained a deeply unpopular measure amongst the Turkish public. Possibly too, the unusually quiescent TGS Chief, General Ozkok, genuinely aspired to reduce the military's role in domestic Turkish politics, in line with the EU's accession requirements. The TGS was certainly disappointed with Washington's resistance to a substantial Turkish troop presence in northern Iraq, and as a consequence may have been prepared to live with whatever the Turkish National Assembly produced.

Of course there was an element of miscalculation on Ankara's part during the negotiations with the US. Both the government and the military believed that the US had no choice but to offer whatever Ankara asked for, and to wait until Ankara was ready. In failing to recognise that Washington would resort to a 'Plan B', both the military and civilian elements of the government overplayed their hand. At the same time, there was an element of defiance in the behaviour of the AKP deputies, and perhaps of the government and military too. The domestic and regional galleries were successfully played to in Ankara's resistance to US pressure. This expression of Turkish democracy may not have been wholly to the liking of either the TSG or the US.

But the whole saga also revealed a profound US-Turkish clash of perspectives. Turkey's post-Cold War value to Washington has been largely based on the US management of its confrontation with Iraq. From Ankara's perspective, that US regional perspectives may leave little room for Ankara's deepest security concerns has been made crystal clear. Already there are indications that the Turkish reaction to this realisation will be to indulge the prickly and proud nationalism, tinged as it is with a degree of anti-Americanism, that is never far from the surface, even in the TGS.[51] An additional consequence could be Turkish shifts towards closer regional alignments and towards the EU rather than the US. Furthermore, the US's need for Turkish acquiescence may be considerably reduced in the absence of Saddam's regime. Developments in post-Saddam Iraq will largely determine how far any US-Turkish disengagement is taken. What does seem likely is that future US-Turkish relations will be seriously affected by this clash of interests and mutual misperception on the part of two hitherto close allies.

Notes

1. For a transcript of the interview, see www.dod.gov/transcripts/2003/tr20030506-depsecdef0156.
2. 'Wolfowitz remarks draw ire in Turkey', *Turkish Daily News (TDN)*, 8 May 2003.
3. For a general discussion of issues raised by Wolfowitz and of the Turkish response, see Nicole Pope, 'Wolfowitz's Advice', *The Middle East*, No. 700, 16 May 2003, pp. 23–4.

4. As an example, see the interview given by Chief of the Turkish General Staff General Hilmi Ozkok, reproduced in full in *Turkish Probe*, 1 June 2003.
5. For early indications of US thinking on a war with Iraq, see 'US Plans for Massive Invasion of Iraq', *UPI Washington Politics and Policy Desk*, 10 July 2002; 'US plan for Iraq is said to include attack on 3 sides', *New York Times*, 4 July 2002.
6. For an early assessment of the AKP government, see 'Muslim Democrats in Turkey?', Gareth Jenkins, *Survival*, 45(1), Spring 2003, pp. 45–66.
7. For a transcript of his remarks, made on 6 May, see www.state.gov/p/20332. See also 'Missteps with Turkey prove costly', *Washington Post (WP)*, 28 March 2003, for an early American recognition of US diplomatic flaws in its approach to Turkey.
8. For a brief and useful account, see Philip Robins, *Suits and Uniforms: Turkish Foreign Policy since the Cold War*, London, Hurst, 2003, pp. 312–42.
9. For details on the KRG zone, see Tim Judah, 'In Iraqi Kurdistan', *Survival*, 44(4), Winter 2002–3, pp. 38–51; Carole A. O'Leary, 'The Kurds of Iraq: Recent History, Future Prospects', *Middle East Review of International Affairs*, 6(4), December 2002.
10. For general overviews of Turkey's Kurdish war, see Robert Olson, ed., *The Kurdish Nationalist Movement in the 1990s: Its Impact on Turkey and the Middle East*, Lexington, University of Kentucky Press, 1996; Kemal Kirisci and Gareth M. Winrow, *The Kurdish Question and Turkey: an Example of Trans-state Ethnic Conflict*, London, Frank Cass, 1997; Henri J. Barkey and Graham E. Fuller, *Turkey's Kurdish Question*, Oxford, Rowman and Littlefield, 1998.
11. Chris Kutschera, 'Iraqi Kurds Agree to Agree – for Now', *The Middle East*, no. 329, December 2002, pp. 25–7; see also by the same author, 'Federalism First', *The Middle East*, no. 335, June 2003, pp. 20–1.
12. 'Turkish trade delegation urges Iraq to avert war', *Financial Times (FT)*, 10 January 2003.
13. 'Turkey to drum up Arab support for war', *FT*, 19 December 2002.
14. For a text of the communiqué, and for a report on the proceedings, see *TDN*, 25 January 2003.
15. 'Turkey denies shift in foreign policy', *FT*, 8 April 2003.
16. For a consideration of the TGS's stance, see 'Turkey and the United States: Drifting Apart?', *Strategic Comments*, 9(3), London, International Institute for Strategic Studies, 2003.
17. 'US officials confident of Turkey's support', *WP*; 'US to Discuss Upgrading Turkish Bases "ahead of war"', *FT*, both 5 December 2002.
18. 'US: will Turkey tag the line on Iraq?', *TDN*; 'Turkey has conditions for support of War', *WP*, both 4 December 2002.
19. 'Turkey, US near accord on deployment', *WP*, 17 January 2003; 'Turks open borders to 20000 troops', *Daily Telegraph (DT)*, 28 January 2003.
20. See, for example, comments made by the KDP leader Massoud Barzani as reported in Nicole Pope, 'Cross Border Concerns', *Middle East International*, No. 683, 13 September 2002, pp. 11–12, and Jon Gorvett, 'A Hugely Unpopular War', *The Middle East*, No. 328, November 2002, pp. 10–11; also 'Americans in talks on Turkish troops', *International Herald Tribune (IHT)*, 7 February 2003; 'US troop deal alarms Kurds', *Guardian (G)*, 10 February 2003.
21. 'Turks say US can upgrade bases there', *WP*, 6 February 2003.
22. Gorvett, 'A Hugely Unpopular War'.

23. Roddy Scott, 'Kurds Nervous Over US Plans for Iraq', *Jane's Intelligence Review (JIR)*, April 2002, pp. 40–1; see also Gareth Stansfield, 'Dream On', *World Today*, 59(2), February 2002, pp. 9–11.

24. Jim Muir, 'Kurds Reconciled', *Middle East International*, No. 685, 11 October 2002, pp. 9–10; Pope, 'Cross Border Concerns'.

25. 'Turkey cannot stay impartial', *TDN*, 6 March 2002.

26. For a general consideration of the role of Turkmen in Ankara's foreign policy, see H. Tarik Oguzlu, 'The "Turcomans" as a factor in Turkish Foreign Policy', *Turkish Studies*, 3(2), Autumn 2002, pp. 139–48.

27. 'Turkey and the United States: Drifting Apart?', *Strategic Comments*, 9(3).

28. 'Iraqi Turcomans concerned about security', *TDN*, 18 March 2003; see also 'Turkey and the United States: Drifting Apart?', *Strategic Comments*, 9(3).

29. 'Ziya: Turkey won't give Kirkuk up, even if we do', *TDN*, 13 June 2002.

30. Pope, 'Cross Border Concerns', p. 11; Gorvett, 'A Hugely Unpopular War', p. 11; and Bill Park, 'Turkey and Iraq: Bridgehead or Bridge?', *World Today*, 58(10), October 2002, p. 8.

31. Hale, 'Turkey, the Middle East and the Gulf Crisis', p. 691.

32. Robert Rabil, 'The Iraqi Opposition's Evolution: From Conflict to Unity?', *Middle East Review of International Affairs*, 6(4), December 2002.

33. Nicole Pope, 'Eyes on Turkey', *Middle East International*, No. 691, 10 January 2003, pp. 14–15.

34. 'If Turkey had kept Mosul, there would be no N. Iraq issue, says Demirel', *TDN*, 19 December 2003.

35. Gunduz Aktan, 'If Iraq operation takes place', *TDN*, 20 November 2002.

36. 'Crucial US allies on Iraq fall out over oil', *G*, 1 November 2002.

37. 'Kurdish leader offers to help US with Iraq invasion', *G*, 15 August 2002.

38. 'Turkey deploys troops near Iraqi border' and 'Kurds deny US military build up', *TDN*, 17 December 2002; 'General Staff denies reports of extraordinary build up on Iraqi border', *TDN*, 19 December 2002; see also 'Turkey and the United States: Drifting Apart?', *Strategic Comments*, 9(3).

39. 'Americans may take over Kirkuk and Mosul to ease concern of Ankara', *TDN*, 17 September 2002.

40. 'US: will Turkey tag the line on Iraq?', *TDN*, 4 December 2002.

41. 'US prodding Turkey to be "more active"', *TDN*, 3 February 2003; 'Ankara urged to back "military measures"', *FT*, 3 February 2003; 'War on Two Fronts', *Newsweek*, 24 February 2003.

42. 'Yakis, Babacan return from Washington talks', *TDN*, 17 February 2003.

43. 'Turkey stalls approval for US troops', *G*, 18 February 2003.

44. 'Turkey lets US use airspace', *WP*; 'Parliament votes for overflight rights to US', *TDN*, both 21 March 2003.

45. Nicole Pope, 'Kirkuk Nerves', *Middle East International*, No. 699, 2 May 2003, pp. 10–11.

46. 'Turkey making amends for Iraq flop', *TDN*, 25 June 2003.

47. 'Turkey, US affirm strategic ties in Ziyal visit', *TDN*, 18 June 2002.

48. 'Blessings in disguise', *G*, 8 November 2003.

49. 'Local council elected in Kirkuk, draws protests', *TDN*, 26 May 2003.

50. 'US to return freed Turkish soldiers to north Iraq', *WP*, 6 July 2003; 'US resolves troop clash with Turkey', *WP*; 'Ozkok; biggest crisis of trust with US', *TDN*; 'US arrest of soldiers infuriates Turkey', *G*, all 8 July 2003.

51. For a powerful expression of such sentiments, see remarks made in May at a TGS-organised symposium on 'Globalisation and International Security', by Deputy Chief of the TSG General Yasar Buyukanit, published by the Strategic Research and Study Center (SAREM), Ankara (2003).

5
International Law and the Use of Force against Iraq

Guglielmo Verdirame

Introduction

This chapter examines the legality of the use of force against Iraq in March and April 2003. The UK and US argument that previous resolutions of the United Nations (UN) Security Council gave a legal basis for the intervention has been met with considerable resistance by other states and by many international lawyers. Other claims, such as those based on the doctrine of pre-emptive self-defence, appear even more problematic. Although it might be far-fetched to proclaim the end of the UN Charter-based system that regulates the use of force,[1] the Iraq crisis has deeply divided the international community, including allies within the North Atlantic Treaty Organisation (NATO), like few issues before. In the aftermath of the war, questions on the justification offered by the UK and US have not been dispelled, as the search for the weapons of mass destruction (WMD) has failed to yield clear and convincing results.

Use of force under the UN Charter

The general prohibition on the use of force is rightly considered one of the great achievements of international law in the twentieth century, and the *sine qua non* for strengthening the rule of law in international relations. Since its appearance in the Briand-Kellog pact, the prohibition has been included in the UN Charter at Article 2(4), which provides for only two exceptions: self-defence (Art. 51) and the use of force by the members of the UN collectively when authorised by the Security Council.[2]

The regulation of the use of force is thus, at first sight, uncomplicated: one general rule and two exceptions. However, a number of factors complicate it. Firstly, there are significant differences in the interpretation of the scope of the 'inherent right' to self-defence and of the extent, if any, to which states can lawfully use force in anticipation of an attack.

Secondly, the system of collective security has not come to existence in the terms originally envisaged by the framers of the Charter, although, as is so often the case in international law, the practice has intervened to remedy this limit. Collective enforcement has thus been delegated to member states acting under the authority of the Security Council.[3] This evolution can be viewed as evidence of the fact that the regulation of the use of force is susceptible to change and adaptation to new circumstances, provided that prohibition remains the presumption.

Thirdly, states have at times invoked exceptions to the prohibition that do not feature in the Charter, arguing that they are customary. The most notable example is the right to use force on humanitarian grounds. Writers take different views on its status under current international law: some maintain that such an exception is already part of international law;[4] others, probably the majority, argue that a rule to this effect might at best be in the process of being formed;[5] and, finally, some deny its legality outright.[6]

The US-UK reason for intervention

Despite much talk about the new Bush doctrine of pre-emptive self-defence,[7] the key statements by the UK and US to the Security Council made no mention of it. The reason that the UK and the US offered for the intervention was that previous Security Council resolutions on Iraq authorised it.[8] In particular, three resolutions – two dating back to the First Gulf War, and the third one adopted in the context of the recent crisis – were believed to afford sufficient legal basis to justify the use of force. These resolutions had all been adopted under Chapter VII of the Charter, which empowers the Security Council to authorise various measures, including the use of force, when it determines 'the existence of any threat to the peace, breach of the peace, or act of aggression' (Art. 39).

Of these resolutions, resolution 678 adopted on 29 November 1990 authorised member states to use 'all necessary means to uphold and implement resolution 660 (1990) and all subsequent relevant resolutions and to restore international peace and security in the area'. Resolution 678 provided the basis for the use of force against Iraq in order to liberate Kuwait, although the military intervention would have been lawful even without it, because the US-led coalition could have justified it as collective self-defence, that is, the right to intervene in defence of the state victim of an aggression. This resolution has been invoked by Britain and the US in the recent crisis, and its broad wording could favour their legal position, especially in the light of the subsequent practice of the Security Council, in which narrowly defined formulations were generally adopted to identify the scope of an authorisation to use force.[9] For example, Resolution 836 (1993) on Bosnia limited both the means that the states could use and the objective they were pursuing, by authorising them 'to take all necessary measures, under the authority of the Security Council, through the use of air power, to support UNPROFOR in the performance of its mandate'. Resolutions 814 and 837 (1993) on Somalia, and Resolution 940 (1994) on Haiti were also narrowly worded.

The other resolution on which the Anglo-American case rested was Resolution 687 (1991), which was adopted at the end of the 1991 Gulf War and laid down the conditions for the ceasefire. This resolution made it clear that international peace and security had not yet been restored, despite the liberation of Kuwait. Indeed, the Security Council 'affirmed' its previous resolutions in the first paragraph of the operative section. The Council imposed a variety of measures on Iraq, which included the acceptance of the inviolability of the Iraq–Kuwait border; the 'destruction, removal, or rendering harmless, under international supervision' of all biological and chemical weapons – including the components necessary for their manufacture – and of ballistic missiles with a range beyond 150 kilometres; the obligation not to acquire or develop nuclear weapons of any kind; and Iraq's liability for various categories of war damages and the institution of the UN Compensation Commission to deal with claims related to such liability.

The most recent resolution that was used by Britain and the US to justify the war was the much-debated Resolution 1441, adopted by the Security Council on 8 November 2002. The preamble of the resolution recalled Resolutions 678 and 687, lending another textual element in support of the view that the authorisation to use force had not somehow withered away. The Council also affirmed that Iraq 'has been and remains in material breach of its obligations' under previous resolutions, and decided to accord it 'a final opportunity to comply with its disarmament obligations'. Iraq was then required to submit a 'currently full, accurate and complete declaration of all aspects of its programmes to develop chemical, biological, and nuclear weapons, ballistic missiles, and other delivery systems'. The Council concluded by warning Iraq of 'serious consequences' if it continued to violate its obligations.

Resolution 1441 was the result of intense negotiations at the UN. One of the most contentious points was whether it contained an automatic authorisation to use force in case of non-compliance by Iraq. There is little doubt that countries like France and Russia would not have voted in favour of the resolution, had they understood it to allow such automatism. Authorisations to use force need to be explicit, and the text of Resolution 1441 alone, as well as the circumstances surrounding its adoption, would be hard-stretched to support the view that it conferred a *prima facie* legal mandate to use force. But the US and UK argument did not rest exclusively on Resolution 1441, as we have seen, and the two governments insisted that this latest pronouncement of the Security Council ought to be read in conjunction with the ones that had preceded it.

Where does this leave us in terms of the assessment of the strength of the legal case for military intervention? At some level, there would appear to be a plain logic to the American and British argument: the ceasefire had been broken by Iraq and 'fire' could start again, particularly since the Council had reiterated over the years the obligation to disarm. Resolution 1441 strengthens this argument with its talk of a 'final opportunity' to comply, the first step of which was the provision of an 'accurate, full and complete' declaration.

Nevertheless, the main problem with this legal argument for war is that it depends on an 'open-ended' reading of Resolution 678, which, even if textually sustainable, is ridden with constitutional difficulties. The Security Council can delegate enforcement to member states, but not the determination of whether enforcement should take place. It has indeed been argued that the 'purported delegation by the Council' of the power to determine if a breach of or threat to peace and stability existed was 'unlawful'.[10] Furthermore, the text of Resolution 686, adopted one month before Resolution 687, appears to make the continued validity of the authorisation to use force in Resolution 678 contingent upon Iraq's compliance with a series of demands that were all related to the invasion of Kuwait and did not include disarmament of Iraq itself.[11]

The argument for the legality of war, dubious as it was, appears to have been seriously undermined by the failure to find WMD in Iraq.[12] The little that has been found about Saddam Hussein's WMD programmes since the end of the conflict could at best support the conclusion that the Iraqi government's statement to the Security Council in December was 'full, accurate and complete', as Resolution 1441 had required. However, it would be disingenuous to suggest that this fact alone could have offered a sufficient legal – or, indeed, political – basis for the war. A deceitful statement is a very different thing from a threat. As for Saddam Hussein's reasons for adopting a conduct that encouraged rather than allayed suspicions, and eventually led to his demise, only time may be able to offer an explanation.

Post-conflict legal arrangements

Discussions on the post-conflict arrangements for Iraq hinged upon the role of the UN. Only four years before the UN Security Council had established a comprehensive mandate for an interim administration in Kosovo, regardless of the absence of UN authority for the military action that had preceded it. However, Iraq presented a rather different picture, as consensus in the Council remained difficult to obtain, and the US was, at least at first, ambivalent towards the involvement of the UN. Galvanised by the rapidity of the military success, the coalition was initially attracted by the prospect of administering Iraq without the UN, although the UK and the US had different views on this. The UN was torn between those (member states and UN officials) who, having opposed the military intervention, did not want to step in to offer any form of assistance to the coalition, and those who thought that a UN presence in Iraq would serve, amongst other things, to minimise the damage caused to the multilateral process in the previous months.

After weeks of stalemate, on 22 May 2003 the Security Council adopted Resolution 1483 which led to the appointment of Sergio Vieira de Mello as Special Representative of the Secretary-General in Iraq. The main task of the UN mission in Iraq was

> coordinating among United Nations and international agencies engaged in humanitarian assistance and reconstruction activities in Iraq, and, in coordination with the Authority, assisting the people of Iraq to co-ordinate the activities defined in the mandate of a UN administration.

Despite referring to the UN role in Iraq as 'vital' in the preamble, the responsibilities that this resolution conferred on the UN were rather limited, compared with previous post-conflict situations, such as Kosovo and East Timor. A UN Assistance Mission in Iraq, along the lines proposed in Resolution 1483, was finally instituted with Resolution 1500, adopted on 14 August 2003. Resolution 1500 was passed within a few days of the truck-bomb attack against the UN headquarters and the killing of Sergio Vieira de Mello and his colleagues, events that were to cast a long shadow on the future of the UN in Iraq.

The next most significant intervention of the Security Council came with the adoption of Resolution 1511 in October 2003. The resolution identified the Iraqi Governing Council and its ministers as

> the principal bodies of the Iraqi interim administration, which, without prejudice to its further evolution, embodies the sovereignty of the State of Iraq during the transitional period until an internationally recognized, representative government is established and assumes the responsibilities of the Authority.

The resolution stated that 'governing responsibilities and authorities' would 'return' to 'the people of Iraq as soon as practicable', but did not indicate a timeline for the transfer of power. Nor did Resolution 1511 contain a detailed indication of the responsibilities of the UN, although it referred to the strengthening of the role of the UN, particularly in the provision of humanitarian relief, in economic reconstruction and development, and in efforts to restore and establish national and local institutions for representative government.

In the case of Kosovo, it has been argued that the Security Council in establishing the post-conflict administration gave the NATO military intervention an *ex post facto* authorisation. A similar argument based on Resolution 1511 would be even more tenuous. Resolution 1511 contains no such express endorsement, and it even leaves out of its 'unequivocal condemnation' attacks against the coalition forces. One clear consequence of this resolution, however, is that it legalises the presence of the US and Britain in Iraq, by authorising

> a multinational force under unified command to take all necessary measures to contribute to the maintenance of security and stability in Iraq, including for the purpose of ensuring necessary conditions for the implementation of the timetable and programme as well as to contribute to the security of the United Nations Assistance Mission for Iraq, the Governing Council of Iraq and other institutions of the Iraqi interim administration, and key humanitarian and economic infrastructure.

The US, on behalf of the multinational force, is placed under an obligation to report to the Council every six months on its discharge of the mandate.

Fears about the sidelining of the UN in the aftermath of the swift military victory of the coalition forces were in part allayed by Resolution 1511, but the optimism was short-lived. In practice, continued insecurity meant that, despite the resolution, the UN presence on the ground remained very limited, and the UN played, at best, a chiefly political role through the Special Adviser to the Secretary-General, Lakhdar Brahimi. The Coalition Provisional Authority has thus remained the main administrative body, although functions have been slowly transferred to fledgling Iraqi authorities.

On 8 June 2004, the Security Council adopted another resolution on Iraq. Like its predecessor ten months before, Resolution 1546 has been adopted under Chapter VII and has been hailed as a milestone. The resolution's main aim was to give international support to the transfer of power to the Iraqi authorities on 30 June 2004. In this respect, its political significance should not be underestimated. The formation of an interim Iraqi government was 'endorsed' by the Security Council, and the new government should not encounter any problem in receiving international recognition. The resolution 'reaffirms' the authorisation for the multinational force established under Resolution 1511, but only after noting that the presence of the force is 'at the request of the incoming Interim Government'. The role that Resolution 1546 envisages for the UN is one of assistance and advice – not a repeat, therefore, of the experiences in Kosovo, East Timor or Bosnia where the UN was entrusted with the exercise of far wider administrative responsibilities. Perhaps the most significant element to emerge out of the negotiations that preceded the adoption of Resolution 1546 is that UN officials, in particular the Secretary-General and his adviser on Iraq, have again played an important political role, mediating between competing claims and interests, and seeking to elaborate proposals that could muster broad consensus.

Assessing the case for war with hindsight

Unless a significant new discovery is made – and the likelihood of such a revelation diminishes as time goes by – the most persuasive conclusion to be drawn is that, although the Saddam Hussein regime had extensive WMD programmes in place in the 1990s, very little of these programmes was active or likely to be in use at the outbreak of hostilities in March 2003. What, therefore, was the war all about? And how is the argument offered for its legality affected by these developments?

A possibility that cannot be ruled out is that the Iraqi regime transferred some WMD either to terrorist groups or to neighbouring countries as the conflict approached. This scenario would signify a strategic failure for the US-led coalition, to the extent that the objectives of the conflict – disarmament and non-proliferation – would not have been met. From the point of view of the legality of the intervention, however, this factual scenario would support the argument that Iraq was in fact in breach of the resolutions of the Security Council.

It is also possible that WMD have not been found in Iraq – nor will they be – because they did not exist in 2003. The regime had destroyed nearly all its stockpiles, and the policy of containment adopted in the aftermath of the 1990 Gulf War had been effective. The most benign extension of this argument is that the intelligence services mistakenly believed that Iraq still possessed significant quantities of WMD, and advised their governments accordingly. Such an eventuality would, at the very least, signify a colossal failure of intelligence on the part of the western services, and cast further doubts on the legality, let alone the appropriateness, of the intervention. In this case, the intervention would have resulted from an error of fact, which led to the conclusion that Iraq was in breach of the resolutions of the Security Council and that it continued to constitute a threat to peace and security. However, errors of fact are not excusing factors in international law: a wrongful act remains such, even if its perpetrator believed in good faith that a certain factual circumstance obtained that, if true, could have made the act lawful.[13]

Another possibility is that WMD were not what the war was about. While Iraqi possession of WMD was offered as the reason, the motive for the war lay elsewhere. The intelligence services had evidence of biological and chemical programmes in the 1990s, but were divided on the extent of the threat posed by Iraq when the war broke out. On this basis, it might be argued that the decision to intervene was part of a different plan: a 'root cause' approach to Middle Eastern terrorism. By this view, the removal of Saddam Hussein was seen as indispensable for stabilising the Middle East, and the stabilisation of the Middle East, in turn, necessary to undermine terrorism. The gamble would have been to use war as an instrument of rapid social and political change with a perfectly pacified Middle East as the ultimate objective – to use war, in the words of Karl Marx, as the 'midwife that expedites the birth of a new order'. The philosophy behind it could be termed 'democratic messianism', the belief that the spread of democracy will usher in an era of perpetual peace amongst nations, and that the promotion of democracy through all means, including force, can only be for the better.[14] While it is axiomatic that war is an instrument of change, its use in this way by states would amount to a departure from the Enlightenment idea that constitutes the premise of the current international legal system: the notion that the 'scourge' of war is the greatest evil.[15]

Another important consideration is that, when they had to articulate a legal justification for war, both the UK and the US chose to rely on an argument that did not refer to the contentious doctrine of pre-emption. As explained, the official argument of the US-led coalition was based on the enforcement of the resolutions of the Security Council. Pre-emption might have been the real motive for the intervention, while the resolutions of the Council were used as a mantle of legality. But the distinction between reasons and motives has important consequences. In fact, a rule of customary international law is formed when the objective element of state practice is combined with the subjective element of *opinio juris* (or the belief that the practice is legally binding). State practice is a broad notion, which includes both what states do and what states say they do; it does not, however, cover 'what states think', that is their motives. As such, motives, although relevant to political and strategic analyses, are legally irrelevant, as they are not susceptible of being 'translated into a norm with legal force'.[16] It is therefore decisive that the legal articulation of the case for war did not invoke pre-emption. Some authors have missed the importance of this fact, and have somewhat prematurely imputed a reason to the US and the UK, where perhaps there was still little more than a motive.[17]

The US did, in truth, attempt to articulate pre-emption as a legal doctrine in its well-known National Security document.[18] The 'New Chapter' supplement to the UK's 1997 Strategic Defence Review, however, only contained a brief and rather vague statement.[19] On the basis of those two documents alone it would still have been difficult to assert that a cohesive legal articulation of pre-emption had been formulated. At the critical time when pre-emption could have been crystallised in their state practice by expressly relying on it as the justification for war, the US and the UK chose to revert to a traditional legal approach. Had the UK and the US relied instead on pre-emption, we would have faced a systemic challenge to the legal regime on the use of force and on collective security.

This is not to say that pre-emption should be completely disregarded. Despite its slim chances of ever becoming part of international law, pre-emption reflects a strategic necessity, as recognised in 1959 by Henry Kissinger. As long as the risk of a surprise attack with massively destructive weapons continues, the 'powerful incentive to anticipate ... by launching a pre-emptive attack' will be part of the system.[20] In the bipolar context in which Kissinger was writing, the most powerful device to defuse this incentive proved to be an intellectual creation: the doctrine of deterrence and its corollary, Mutually Assured Destruction.[21] The contribution of international law was to complement this system, on the one hand by putting the surprise attacker squarely outside the boundaries of legality, and, on the other, by developing a regime of arms control.

With the proliferation of nuclear, chemical and biological technologies and the collapse of the bipolar order, international lawyers and national security strategists have in front of them another intellectual challenge, namely to devise legal and institutional mechanisms for dealing with WMD proliferation and terrorism that are as effective as pre-emption could hypothetically be, but not as destabilising.[22] This challenge is particularly timely now that the Iraqi crisis has shown the pre-emptive doctrine to be a political liability for the US, since it did not afford a legal basis for its actions in Iraq that even the US was prepared to rely upon, and exposed the US to a barrage of criticism from all quarters.[23]

A solution might be offered by strengthening the non-proliferation regime through the introduction of a new explicit exception to the general prohibition on the use of force in order to permit forcible measures in the most dangerous instances of WMD proliferation.[24] Forcible counter-proliferation would not solve all the security problems of our era, but it would constitute another important instrument in the global security toolkit. At present, the main non-proliferation agreements – the Nuclear Non-Proliferation Treaty (NPT), the Biological Weapons Convention (BWC) and the Chemical Weapons Convention (CWC)[25] – are beset by the lack of adequate enforcement mechanisms. Mechanisms for monitoring compliance exist, at least under the NTP and the CWC, but there is very limited room for effective action in case of non-compliance. Moreover, these treaties contain almost identical provisions allowing state parties to withdraw if the 'supreme interests' of the country have been jeopardised by extraordinary events.[26] It was this rule in the NPT that North Korea invoked to justify its withdrawal in January 2003.[27]

Outside the counter-proliferation regime, there is the possibility, at least in principle, for the Security Council to act under Chapter VII, if it finds that systematic non-compliance amounts to a threat to peace and security. However, the Council's record in the counter-proliferation area is all but encouraging. In addition, as the main target of a non-conventional terrorist attack, it would simply be unreasonable to expect US administrations, with all the military might they possess, to delegate the most pressing issue on their national security agenda to the Security Council with its history of indecisiveness, division and ineptitude. As the UN Secretary-General himself admitted, the international community cannot be viewed as 'a suicide pact': if rules and mechanisms do not exist or if they do not operate effectively, 'states will resort to other means to reduce or eliminate threats to their way of life – or to their very existence'.[28] These comments have been echoed by the Director-General of the International Atomic Energy Agency who has warned that the threat of nuclear proliferation is so great that 'if the world does not change course, we risk self-destruction'.[29]

Conclusion

The use of force is the fundamental testing ground for international law, since the preservation of peace remains the main value and objective of the international legal system. The fissure in the Security Council on Iraq was bound to cause some damage, but it would now seem that this damage has to some extent been contained. Firstly, while there can be no absolute guarantee that the collective security system will play a central role in the next major international crisis, it should not be forgotten that the marginal role of the Security Council in such crises has historically been the exception rather than the rule. One cannot dismiss the importance of the fact that, throughout the crisis, the Security Council was the main forum where the Iraqi question was discussed and decisions were announced. Secondly, after some uncertainty at the beginning, the model for the post-conflict arrangements in Iraq does not depart from the practice of the 1990s and assigns a central role to the UN.

The issue that still needs to be addressed in international law regarding the use of force is the proliferation of WMD, in the light of the fact that terrorist groups that have made no secret of their plans to get hold of such weapons. With hindsight, it is indeed possible to view the military intervention in Iraq as the result of a jittery US Administration that, in the aftermath of 9/11, saw the prevention of a non-conventional attack on its soil as the key national security objective. The international legal system and the multilateral security process have not yet found a way of reassuring the US; for example, by embracing the principle that force could be used against states that are prepared to provide terrorist groups with WMD technology.[30] As long as the US remains under a clear threat, instability will persist. International lawyers cannot realistically hope to play the same role in decisions to use force that the Archbishop of Canterbury plays in Shakespeare's *Henry V* (Act I, Scene 2), where the Archbishop's opinion on the legality of war is determinative of Henry V's decision to go to war. But they can come up with the intellectual solutions that can help the international community deal with the current crisis. Neither the dogmatic defence of the normative and institutional status quo, nor the obstinate denial of the security challenge faced by the US is of any practical or intellectual merit.

However, if the real reason for the war was to foist radical change upon the Middle East in the belief that terrorism would not be defeated without wide-reaching political change, then the assessment has to change. While the combined strategic challenge of WMD and terrorism can be met through an effective legal counter-proliferation system, there is not a basis in international law for using force as a strategic tool to improve an imperfect peace; nor should there be, as the moral and pragmatic reasons behind the current position are ponderous. Faced with such a trend, international lawyers can only reiterate the principle that an imperfect peace in the present is always to be preferred to a perfect peace in the future.

Notes

1. This would probably be Michael Glennon's view: 'Why the Security Council Failed', *Foreign Affairs*, 82, 2003, p. 16.
2. There is a vast literature on the use of force in international law. Some of the most recent and interesting additions are C. Gray, *International Law and the Use of Force*, Oxford, Oxford University Press, 2000; T. Franck, *Recourse to Force*, Cambridge, Cambridge University Press, 2002.
3. On this point, see D. Sarooshi, *The United Nations and the Development of Collective Security*, Oxford, Oxford University Press, 1998.
4. C. Greenwood, 'Is there a Right of Humanitarian Intervention?', *World Today*, 49(2), 1993, p. 34 and, by the same author, 'International Law and the NATO Intervention in Kosovo', *International and Comparative Law Quarterly*, 49, 2000, p. 926.
5. A. Cassese, 'Ex *inuria jus oritur*: Are We Moving towards International Legitimation of Forcible Humanitarian Countermeasures in the World Community?', *European Journal of International Law*, 10, 1999, p. 23; C. Chinkin, 'The Legality of NATO's Actions in the Former Republic of Yugoslavia under International Law', *International and Comparative Law Quarterly*, 49, 2000, p. 910.
6. See, for example: I. Brownlie and C.J. Apperley, 'Kosovo Crisis Inquiry: Memorandum on the International Law Aspects', *International and Comparative Law Quarterly*, 49, 2000, p. 878.
7. See, for example, the contributions to the symposium on the 'Implications of the Iraq Conflict' in the *American Journal of International Law*, 97(3), 2003, as well as other comments on pre-emption referred to below. Pre-emptive self-defence is not a locution with a precise legal meaning. It is here used in the sense in which the US Administration used it in the National Strategy document. The notion of 'anticipatory self-defence', which does have a longer history in international law, is different from pre-emptive self-defence. In the 1837 *Caroline* case (29 *British and Foreign State Papers* 1137), the American and British governments agreed that for a self-defensive action to be lawful there had to be 'a necessity of self-defence, instant, overwhelming, leaving no choice of means, and no moment for deliberation'. The US doctrine of pre-emptive self-defence purports to adapt this concept, and in particular the underlying notion of imminence, to the realities of today's world and to the technological advances that have made a surprise attack potentially more devastating than ever in the past. Pre-emption cannot, however, be viewed as a corollary of the rigorously defined anticipatory self-defence; it 'anticipates' the moment for the self-defensive action so radically that it gives rise to an altogether new legal concept.
8. US Mission at the United Nations, Press Release No. 40 (03) of 27 March 2003, available at www.un.int/usa. See also S.D. Murphy, 'Contemporary Practice of the United States Related to International Law', *American Journal of International Law*, 97, 2003, p. 427, and W. Taft IV and T.F. Buckwald 'Preemption, Iraq and

International Law', *American Journal of International Law*, 97, 2003, p. 557. On the UK practice, see the statement of the UK representative, Jeremy Greenstock, on 19 March 2003 (www.ukun.org), and the advice of the Attorney-General (Lord Goldsmith, 'Legal Basis for Use of Force Against Iraq', 17 March 2003, available at www.labour.org.uk/legalbasis).

9. This view is taken by C. Greenwood, 'New World Order or Old? The Invasion of Kuwait and the Rule of Law', *Modern Law Review*, 55, 1992, 153 at 169. On the debate on Resolution 678, see Sarooshi, *The United Nations*, p. 174ff.

10. Sarooshi, *The United Nations*, p. 179.

11. The legal advisers to the Russian government placed great emphasis on Resolution 686 (see *International and Comparative Law Quarterly*, 52, 2003, p. 1059). A similar position is adopted by V. Lowe, 'The Iraq Crisis: What Now?', *International and Comparative Law Quarterly*, 52, 2003, 859 at 865. It is noteworthy, however, that the first paragraph of Resolution 686 affirms that 'all twelve resolutions noted above continue to have full force and effect'. Moreover, Resolution 686 could be viewed as a provisional statement of the terms of the ceasefire that Resolution 687, adopted a month later, spelled out in detail. It should not be overlooked that the first operative paragraph of Resolution 687 affirms all the previous resolutions, 'except as expressly changed below to achieve the goals of the present resolution'.

12. The interim report of the Iraq Survey Group (available online at http://news.bbc.co.uk/1/hi/world/middle_east/3160270.stm), released in the autumn of 2003, referred to 'dozens of WMD-related programme activities and significant amounts of equipment that Iraq concealed from the United Nations during the inspections that began in late 2002', but did not contain the much-awaited evidence of actual WMD. In January 2004, David Kay, who had been the head of the Survey Group, told a Senate hearing that it was 'highly unlikely that there were large stockpiles of deployed militarised chemical and biological weapons' in Iraq (S. Jeffrey, 'We were all wrong says ex-weapons inspector', *Guardian*, 29 January 2004).

13. It is only if the error of fact can be proven to originate from an irresistible force or an unforeseen event (*force majeure*) that it can become a circumstance precluding wrongfulness (Article 23, International Law Commission's Article on State Responsibility, UN GA Res. 56/83, 12 December 2001).

14. The 'democratic peace' has a long tradition in western thinking, and is at present particularly popular amongst foreign policy makers in the US. Although currently associated with neo-conservative thinkers, Democrats have not been alien to this idea (see, for example, S. Talbott, 'Democracy and the National Interest', *Foreign Affairs*, 75, 1996, p. 6). See J.L. Ray, 'Does Democracy Cause Peace?', *Annual Review of Political Science*, 1, 1998, p. 27; B. Bueno de Mesquita, J.D. Morrow, R.M. Siverson, and A. Smith, 'An Institutional Explanation of the Democratic Peace', *American Political Science Review*, 93(4) December 1999, p. 791.

15. See M. Howard, *The Invention of Peace and the Reinvention of War*, London, Profile Books, 2001.

16. Lowe, 'The Iraqi Crisis'.

17. Most notably Michael Byers ('Preemptive Self-defense: Hegemony, Equality and Strategies of Legal Change', *Journal of Political Philosophy*, 11, 2003, p. 171) who seems to have persuaded himself about the existence of a conspiracy, on the part of the US, to change international law on the use of force. It is not clear how international law, especially customary law, could change through hidden conspiracies, given the well-known requirements of uniform and extensive state

practice and evidence of *opinio juris*. Conspiracy theories have a distinct lure because of their unfalsifiability; they seldom explain anything.

18. *The National Security Strategy of the United States of America*, Washington, 17 September 2002 (www.whitehouse.gov/nsc/nss.pdf).

19. UK Ministry of Defence, *The Strategic Defence Review: A New Chapter*, July 2002 (www.mod.uk/issues/sdr/newchapter.htm).

20. H. Kissinger, 'Arms Control, Inspection and Surprise Attack', *Foreign Affairs*, 38, 1959/60, p. 557.

21. P. Bobbit, *The Shield of Achilles: War, Peace and the Course of History*, London, Penguin Books, 2002, pp. 11–15.

22. Two attempts to answer these dilemmas are L. Feinstein and A-M. Slaughter, 'A Duty to Prevent', *Foreign Affairs*, January–February 2004, 83(1), 2004, p. 136; and my article 'The Case for Forcible Counter-Proliferation', *In the National Interest* 3(4), 2004 (available at www.inthenationalinterest.com/Articles/Vol3Issue4/Vol3Issue4Verdirame.html).

23. It could also be argued that proposing such a controversial notion has, in some ways, clouded debate on important issues and has fuelled perceptions of the US as bent on challenging the existing legal order.

24. I have expounded this argument in my article 'The Case for Forcible Counter-Proliferation'.

25. Treaty on the Non-Proliferation of Nuclear Weapons, *signed on* 1 July 1968 and *entered into force* on 5 March 1970; Convention on the Prohibition of the Development, Production and Stockpiling of Bacteriological (Biological) and Toxin Weapons and on Their Destruction, *signed on* 10 April 1972, *entered into force* 26 March 1975; Convention on the Prohibition of the Development, Production, Stockpiling and Use of Chemical Weapons and on Their Destruction, *signed on* 13 January 1993, *entered into force* on 29 April 1997.

26. Art. X, NPT; Art. XVI, CWC; Art. XIII(2), BWC.

27. Mohammed ElBaradei has suggested that the NPT be amended to remove the possibility of unilateral withdrawal ('Saving ourselves from self-destruction', *New York Times*, 12 February 2004).

28. UN Secretary-General, 'Implementation of the UN Millennium Declaration', Report of the Secretary General, 3 September 2003, UN Doc. A/58/323 at para. 21.

29. ElBaradei, 'Saving ourselves from self-destruction'.

30. The Security Council has adopted resolutions, under Chapter VII, that oblige all states to prevent the supply, direct or indirect, of technology and military equipment to al-Qaeda and affiliated groups. However, these resolutions do not allow states to use force against non-compliant states. See for example SCR 1526 (2004).

Part Two
Campaign

6
Military Concepts and Planning

Philip Wilkinson and Tim Garden

Introduction

The campaign launched against Iraq on 20 March 2003 came to an end just weeks later, with the symbolic toppling of a statue of Saddam Hussein in central Baghdad on 9 April, and the fall of Tikrit, Saddam's home town, on 14 April. On 1 May 2003 President Bush declared major combat operations – known as 'Operation Iraqi Freedom' in the United States, 'Operation Telic' in the United Kingdom and 'Operation Falconer' in Australia – to be complete, during a carefully staged visit to the aircraft carrier USS *Abraham Lincoln* off the coast of California.[1]

Focusing largely on ground and air forces, this chapter draws together some of the military implications of a campaign in which intensive operations lasted barely a month, and in which lower-scale military operations still continue to occupy Coalition forces. The chapter will offer judgements as to the strategic and tactical approaches of both Coalition and Iraqi forces, and will analyse the campaign against a doctrinal template of current western military thinking. The chapter begins with a brief review of the historical and diplomatic background to the war of 2003, assessing the legacy of the First Gulf War of 1990–91, and the military implications of the diplomatic activity that preceded the war of 2003.

Historical context and diplomatic constraints

When Iraq invaded Kuwait on 2 August 1990, the international community responded in near unison. The UN authorised military action for a clear breach of international law. Most of the states in the region became part of the US-led coalition. Saudi Arabia, sharing borders with both countries, became the main mounting base for the military operation. An extraordinary coalition of 34 nations[2] built up their air and ground forces over five months, before launching a major air campaign on 17 January 1991. Coalition air and missile attacks continued for nearly six weeks. Allied air supremacy was achieved, and the continual bombardment of Iraqi defensive positions set the conditions for a rout when major ground operations began on 24 February. With some 660,000 military personnel deployed for the operation, just 100 hours of land operations were needed to expel Iraqi forces from Kuwait. The conflict cost the coalition 340 deaths, of which one-quarter were caused by 'friendly fire'.[3]

From 1992 onwards, American, British and (until 1998) French military aircraft patrolled much of the skies of Iraq in the northern and southern no-fly zones. When the work of UN weapon inspectors became impossible in late 1998, they were withdrawn and Operation Desert Fox was mounted. American and British aircraft flew more than 650 strike and strike support sorties, while 415 cruise missiles were launched against key targets in Iraq. Over a period of 70 hours an intense air campaign was mounted to degrade Iraqi capabilities, which it was thought might be used to produce or deliver weapons of mass destruction.[4] Following 9/11, the US and a number of allies mounted a major offensive military operation against terrorist bases and the Taliban leadership in Afghanistan. Long-range air power from aircraft carriers and distant bases meant that this was a less intense bombardment than seen in previous campaigns. Nevertheless, using air attacks, Special Forces and local forces, it proved possible to remove the Taliban regime.

The Gulf War of 1990–91, followed by air operations against Iraq during the 1990s and then operations in Afghanistan after 9/11, all meant that by 20 March 2003, when the latest attack on Iraq began, US and allied forces had accumulated over a decade of what was to prove to be crucial operational experience in the use of precision weapons to shape the battlefield for effective land operations.

The scope and pace of diplomatic activity – at the United Nations, across the Middle East and in Europe – affected military preparation and the nature of the campaign plan. In 1990–91, the US-led coalition enjoyed not only a UN resolution authorising military action, but also the support of 34 nations. The consequent benefits of basing rights, host nation support, overflying rights and direct military assistance were very significant, as were the financial contributions from a number of governments. In 2003, in military terms at least, the US would have been able to conduct the campaign on its own. Nevertheless, George Bush claimed credit for having assembled a coalition of more than 40 nations.[5] The list of coalition members was curious in some respects; Turkey, in spite of its refusal to allow basing rights, was shown as a member, while Qatar, where the main military headquarters was located, was absent from the list. Furthermore, the military contribution of states such as Micronesia and the Solomon Islands could hardly have been significant. In terms of military forces, the main contributors were the UK with 45,000 troops, Australia with 2000, and a small number of Polish troops. By any objective measure, the 2003 operation was not militarily as well supported as that in 1990–91. What was far more important to the US effort was to find a suitable local mounting base. Kuwait provided that facility, with US Central Command (CENTCOM) headquarters being based in Qatar and thereby allowing some dispersion of forces. The unwillingness of Turkey to provide a second mounting base to the north was a major challenge to US planning. The number of forces immediately available was reduced, and military planners also had to take account of the historically and strategically complex relations between the Kurds, the Turks and the Iraqi regime. The absence of Turkish bases removed the option of invading from Turkey and thereby increased the overall risk to coalition forces.

The campaign was constrained in other, more immediate ways. It was clear from the outset, for example, that concerns over civilian casualties and damage to civilian infrastructure would narrow the scope of military activity. As a result, targeting decisions would be closely controlled to ensure that, as far as possible, tactical actions would not have an adverse effect on long-term political goals and post-conflict peace-building. The campaign would, in other words, be fought with the speed of the German Second World War blitzkrieg, but without its destructiveness. Furthermore, and in spite of the much-discussed aversion of western armed forces and their governments to battlefield casualties, it was understood that ground forces would probably have to accept more casualties than they would expect if a less discriminating targeting approach had been taken. The climate was another constraint on military planning. Before the start of the campaign in March, much was made of the debilitating effect upon personnel and matériel of operating in the Iraqi summer and consequently of the need to start operations before the end of April, at the very latest. Climatic considerations might well have been raised by the coalition's military commanders in order to speed the political decision making process and in order to create time for military units to be positioned and prepared to conduct operations.

Diplomatically, the need for UK Prime Minister Blair to be given time to show that United Nations diplomacy had run its course, and for him to persuade his own political party of the legality of the war, imposed considerable extra pressure on the Permanent Joint Headquarters (PJHQ) at Northwood and on the UK's liaison staff at CENTCOM in Tampa, Florida. While CENTCOM's planning staff were generally sympathetic to the need for their UK counterparts to delay deployment decisions for political reasons, delays imposed by the Prime Minister's office did cause some embarrassment for UK commanders.

Concept of operations

The concept developed at Tampa, Florida, by General Tommy Franks and the staff at CENTCOM was for a joint (maritime, land, air, space) campaign, initiated by an air-led assault – the 'shock and awe' campaign.[6] The land assault was planned to be from the north out of Turkey and the south from Kuwait. The northern front was to be led by the 4th Mechanised Infantry Division supported by Kurdish forces, and the southern attack on Baghdad was to be two-pronged, with the 3rd Mechanised Infantry Division taking the western axis along the River Euphrates (Najaf, Karbala, Hillah) and the major elements of the 1st US Marine Corps Expeditionary Force (1 MEF) taking the eastern axis to Baghdad along the general line of the River Tigris through al-Kut. The UK's major land component of 1st Armoured Division consisted of 3 Commando Brigade, 16 Air Assault Brigade and the 7th Armoured Brigade. 3 Commando Brigade was to seize the al-Faw peninsula, Umm Qasr and Abadan, and along with the 7th Armoured Brigade, Iraq's second city of Basra. The taking of Basra was designed to mask the right flank of the US main effort towards Baghdad. This masking manoeuvre was the principal task of the 7th Armoured Brigade and it was hoped that early successes in Basra would undermine the morale of the regime in Baghdad. Air assault forces of the US 101st and 82nd Airborne Divisions, and the UK's 16 Air Assault Brigade would be used to seize and hold strategic targets and oilfields, to act as a reserve, and to conduct a series of feints and deception operations designed to compound the confusion of the Iraqi high command.

The joint concept of operations required rapid establishment of air superiority in turn enabling large-scale, simultaneous precision attacks against the Iraqi regime infrastructure, military centres and communication systems. At the same time, a rapid advance on the ground from both the north and the south towards Baghdad would take advantage of the aerial disruption to the centre of power. Subsidiary actions to secure western Iraq to keep Israel out of the war, and to secure oil facilities against destruction would be mounted simultaneously by Special Forces.

The traditional insistence on achieving a three-to-one superiority over an enemy before beginning a campaign was put to one side. The coalition went to war with the minimum of ground troops – fewer than half those available for the relief of Kuwait in 1991 – and with only about one-third of the tanks that were considered necessary to drive the Iraqi army out of Kuwait in 1992. As a result, Iraq's tank force outnumbered that of the coalition by approximately 1500 to 320. Comparison might also be drawn with NATO's Kosovo operation in 1999. For an area equivalent to just 4 per cent of the territory of Iraq, and with only one-tenth of Iraq's population, NATO deployed on this peacekeeping (rather than combat) operation with approximately five brigades – roughly 40 per cent of the size of the coalition force sent into action on 20 March 2003.

The coalition concept of operations, and its subsequent execution, fuelled considerable debate between two schools of military thought. On one hand were those who advocated a heavy and cautious approach, and on the other, those who preferred a lighter and more manoeuvrist approach; what

General Wesley Clarke described as the advocates of 'a new kind of war' against the 'plodding old arm thinkers'.[7] To a considerable extent, the debate is a legacy of the Cold War. Those military officers who had been schooled in the armour-heavy and dimensionally limited culture of the Cold War were more comfortable with the 'Powell Doctrine' of overwhelming force, rather than the multidimensional, manoeuvrist approach favoured by the current generation of senior officers. The First Gulf War of 1991 had been a campaign of the Cold War genre, and perhaps the last of its kind; coalition forces confronted an opponent using mainly Soviet equipment and tactics, precisely the enemy they had prepared for over decades. But in 2003, US Secretary of Defense Donald Rumsfeld championed the multidimensional, manoeuvrist school in spite of the concerns of senior retired military officers that too few troops were being committed. Rumsfeld's novel 'light, lean and mean' doctrine – 'What will follow will not be a repeat of any other conflict. It will be of a force and scope and scale that has been beyond what has been seen before'[8] – certainly prevailed in the combat phase of the campaign, but the lack of so-called 'boots on the ground' limited the ability of the coalition to win the peace.

Style of operations

In several ways, coalition operations in Iraq demonstrated the style and sophistication of modern western military thinking and capability. The campaign in Iraq was driven by new thinking in a number of ways: manoeuvrism; mission command; network-centric warfare; campaign design, and joint vision and planning.

Manoeuvrism

The armed forces of America, Britain and Australia aspire to manoeuvrism in military operations; taking the indirect approach and applying strength against identified weakness, rather than attacking main forces and fighting a war of attrition. Hence the desire by General Franks to press on to Baghdad, perceived to be the Iraqi regime's centre of gravity, rather than destroy the Republican Guard forces and Iraqi regular army piecemeal en route. The campaign in Iraq, with its emphasis on psychological warfare, on the destruction of Saddam's command and control systems, and on the maintenance of operational tempo, has been a classic example of manoeuvre warfare. Manoeuvrism stresses the need to defeat and disrupt the enemy's will to fight, by taking the initiative, attacking from the least expected direction, and by applying constant and unacceptable pressure at the times and places the enemy least expects. Manoeuvrism calls for an attitude of mind in which doing the unexpected and seeking originality is combined with a ruthless determination to succeed. The demands of originality and unpredictability were certainly put to the test when Turkey refused access to US forces. The air and psychological warfare campaigns were designed to 'decapitate' the regime, and to set the conditions for the two-pronged mechanised attack from Kuwait. The attack would be led by the 3rd Mechanised Infantry Division and the 1st Marine Expeditionary Force, supported by the UK assault on Basra and a series of feints by the air assault forces and actions by Special Forces in the west to prevent Scud attacks upon Israel. Coordinated and synchronised, these various assaults, using different means, in different domains, were designed to attack, destroy, dislocate and disorientate Saddam's leadership, command and control infrastructure.

Manoeuvrist thinking lies at the heart of asymmetrical warfare, and is particularly attractive to a numerically inferior force; it should be noted that Iraqi combat forces outnumbered those of the coalition by a ratio of 3 to 1. However, the manoeuvrist approach does entail the risk that disruption of the enemy will not occur as predicted and hence can seem less predictable and reliable than the use of overwhelming force. This dilemma was at the heart of the debate between those who wanted more troops to be deployed and thereby reduce the risk of failure – the 'Powell Doctrine' of overwhelming force – and those who were prepared to risk Rumsfeld's light option. But the essence of manoeuvre warfare is that a certain level of casualties is inevitable and that reverses at the tactical level can be accepted if they are necessary for the maintenance of operational tempo and the achievement of operational goals. Those critics who argued that the coalition plan had stalled because Iraqi forces had been bypassed rather than being destroyed piecemeal, demonstrated an alarming ignorance of the well-publicised manoeuvrist approach. In practice, however, attritional and manoeuvrist forms of attack are not mutually exclusive styles of warfare, and any operational plan is likely to contain elements of both. The manoeuvrist approach would not, for example, exclude the use of attrition by coalition air forces at a decisive point to wear down Iraqi ground forces, or to gain maximum psychological effect. Hence the coalition's focus on the Republican Guard; their demise would have been a severe psychological blow to Saddam's regime as well as devastating his fighting capability. Manoeuvrism also, finally, attacks the enemy commander's decision making process by achieving a faster decision making cycle, often described as 'getting inside the enemy's OODA loop' ('Observation, Orientation, Decision, Action'). The enemy is challenged to make decisions at a rate faster than he can cope, so that he takes increasingly inappropriate action or none at all, thereby paralysing his ability to react. This is the essence of pre-emption and disruption, which are key to the manoeuvrist approach.

Mission command

Mission command is central to the manoeuvrist approach to operations and has four enduring themes: timely decision making; a clear expression of the commander's intention; an ability on the part of subordinates to fulfil the

Must also mention simultaneity

commander's intention; and the determination, at all levels of command, to see the plan through to a successful conclusion. All this requires a decentralised style of command that promotes freedom and speed of action and initiative, yet all within a clear understanding of the superior commander's intent and subject to his broad direction. Mission command gave American, British and Australian commanders the flexibility to test the defences in Basra and Baghdad by the use of armoured raids (reconnaissance in force) and then, on meeting minimum resistance, to exploit the situation to the full. Mission command delegates authority to the lowest level in order to give junior commanders the maximum flexibility to exploit a 'high-speed' battle space. The more traditional Cold War style of 'directive command' would have insisted that commanders in Iraq refer tactical decisions to the highest level, and as a consequence would have inhibited the ability of the commander of 3rd (US) Mechanised Infantry Division and the commander of 1st (UK) Armoured Division to develop innovative approaches to invest and capture Baghdad and Basra respectively. Tactics were developed *ad hoc*, at the tactical level, rather than relying upon a more traditional and cautious street-by-street, block-by-block approach that would have been both more destructive and expensive than the imaginative approaches that were employed. Within their area of responsibility, commanders were allowed to determine when, where and how to exploit the operational 'tipping point' when it became clear.

Network-centric warfare

'Network-centric warfare' was another obscure expression much used by the media and in public debate before, during and after the conflict. The ideas behind network-centric warfare are scarcely new; throughout history, reliable information and intelligence about enemy actions and intentions has been considered vital to military success. In the context of manoeuvrism, high-quality, timely information is key to the ability operate within the enemy's 'OODA loop'. What became clear in Iraq in 2003, however, was that the latest surveillance, processing, communications and weapons could give coalition forces a considerable manoeuvrist advantage. Network-centric warfare could speed up the coalition's OODA process by ensuring maximum connectivity and speed between target identification and attack. The linking of satellite information and real-time visual displays from drones (unmanned air vehicles (UAVs) such as Predator and Phoenix) with Special Forces reconnaissance and contact reports allowed for precision air strikes by orbiting aircraft within just minutes of target identification.

Campaign design

Within CENTCOM's campaign plan constructed at Tampa and then Qatar, several key indicators would have been defined precisely: the desired end-state, Iraq's centres of gravity, and the decisive points in the campaign. That said, the sequence of activities and the designation of the main effort or critical path would have remained entirely flexible in order to allow maximum exploitation of the situation as it unfolded around Basra and Baghdad. Seen in this way, a modern campaign plan can be viewed as a preconceived series, or matrix, of subordinate contingency plans that are structured along different lines of operation along which decision points will be identified when new paths can be taken for operational advantage. The campaign plan will be revised and refined as often as time allows. Although the coalition would have had a preferred path of action, campaign planners would have considered and anticipated innumerable contingencies. The planners would also, of course, have built in some level of redundancy in order to cope with the vagaries of warfare; the so-called 'fog of war'.

Joint vision and planning

The various doctrinal concepts and planning tools are all pulled together into what the American military refer to as the 'Joint Vision'. The US Joint Vision has the following features:

- Dominant awareness – see first, understand first
- Decision superiority: dominant manoeuvre – strategic, operational, tactical
- Precision engagement
- Full dimension protection
- Focused logistics
- Agile, adaptive force
- Technological edge
- Superior training
- Dynamic doctrine.[9]

In accordance with the precepts of the US Joint Vision, the plan for Operation Iraqi Freedom was conceived as a sequence of phased military objectives:

- Special operations and psychological preparation of the battlespace
- Distributed and parallel ground and air operations to:

  - paralyse the Iraqi leadership and command and control system
  - control key centre and assets (to include SCUD capabilities)
  - set the conditions to seize and sustain the initiative in the ground campaign
  - set the conditions for a viable post-war Iraq
  - ensure bearable Syrian, Iranian, and Kurdish impacts
  - protect the oilfields
  - prevent massive pollution of the Gulf
  - find and control WMD and facilities

- Rapid advance to fix the Republican Guards divisions
- Massive air attacks to further reduce the Guards divisions
- Enter Baghdad from several directions
- Occupy the rest of Iraq.

The role of Special Forces

Special Forces were much used before, during and after the campaign, among them the UK's Special Air Service (SAS), with its Australian and New Zealand sister organisations, the UK's Special Boat Service (SBS), and from the United States the Delta Force, and Sea Air Land (SEAL) teams.[10] Within 48 hours of the start of the campaign, the Iraqi airbases H2 and H3, near the border with Jordan, were captured by about 150 men from three SAS squadrons including 100 Australian SAS troopers. These airfields were subsequently held by Royal Marine Commandos and US Rangers so that the SAS could be deployed elsewhere against other high-value targets. The seizure of the airfields was the role for which Special Forces had originally been formed; the capture or destruction of high-value military objectives behind enemy lines.

Throughout the campaign Special Forces were deployed in their more traditional mode to attack headquarters and key communications nodes in the Iraqi fibre-optic communications network. Special Forces were also deployed to seize strategic oilfields by *coup de main* operations, and to search for and destroy weapons of mass destruction and Scud missiles in order to prevent their use. The majority of operations were successful, but not all. No weapons of mass destruction or Scud missiles were deployed and fired, but equally none were found. The only known disaster came near the northern city of Mosul when a patrol, reputedly from the UK SBS, was dropped too close to Iraqi troops and had to conduct an emergency extraction operation, leaving its vehicles and equipment behind. All patrol members were extracted safely but their vehicles and equipment were exhibited by the Iraqi authorities and provided them with one of their few public relations successes.

What was new in this campaign was the rapid transfer and management of human and signals intelligence from the Special Forces such that strategic targets could be attacked within minutes by air-delivered precision weapons. The attempts to attack and kill Saddam Hussein and his sons Qusay and Uday, as well as other key individuals, were classic examples of this shortened 'kill chain'. From the very first attack on the night of 19 March on the Dora Farm in Baghdad using cruise missiles and bunker-busting bombs, to the attack on the al-Saa restaurant in the affluent al-Mansour district of Baghdad on 7 April, to the attack against the Ba'ath party headquarters in Basra, it would appear that new techniques had been developed to shorten the reaction time between the acquisition of strategic information and its tactical exploitation.

The role of air power

During the the 1991 Gulf War, NATO's 1999 Kosovo operation and to some extent the campaign against the Taliban regime in Afghanistan after 9/11, the public became very aware of the aims, scale and impact of coalition air operations. The role of coalition air power in the 2003 campaign is as yet difficult to define precisely, although some lessons can be drawn. The role of Iraqi air forces is much easier to assess, since it appears that no Iraqi air operations were mounted throughout the operation.

Coalition offensive air operations were conducted by surface- and air-launched cruise missiles, air-delivered precision-guided bombs and free-fall ballistic bombs. One estimate of total bomb and missile expenditure is 29,199;[11] about the same number of munitions as used in the Kosovo air campaign, which lasted three times as long. Yet Iraq is 17 times the combined area of Serbia, Montenegro and Kosovo. Daily strike rates averaged around 1000,[12] which is of the same order of magnitude as in the 1991 Gulf War.[13] The significant difference for the 2003 operation was that the majority (68 per cent[14]) of weapons used were precision-guided.

The unplanned early start to operations is likely to have caused some difficulty in adjusting the Air Tasking Order rapidly. The normal cycle time of 72 hours is seen as a limitation on flexibility. According to USCENTAF, a special capability to find, fix, track, engage and assess the most important targets had to be developed. These were known as Time Sensitive Targets (TST) and comprised leadership, weapons of mass destruction and terrorism-related targets. Among more than 30,000 designated targets, only 156 were TSTs. It is not clear whether this ratio reflects lack of intelligence or capability, or that no more TSTs were needed.

The primary missions in the air campaign included the suppression and destruction of Iraqi air defence systems. These had been softened up before hostilities began through the intensified no-fly zone operations. The large-scale availability of precision weapons meant that it was also possible to target the regime leadership and communication nodes at the same time. The strategy was to disconnect the regime leadership from its military commanders, and those commanders from their fighting units. Air superiority was achieved from the start. However, the resistance initially offered during ground operations in the south meant that air-power effort had also to be directed to supporting the ground advance.

The integration of ground and air operations made it possible for offensive strike aircraft to be used at times in more direct support of ground forces. A particular worry was the Iraqi defence line to the south of Baghdad, where three Republican Guard divisions were deployed. In late March, while sandstorms prevented the rapid progress northwards of US forces and hampered normal close air-support missions, Iraqi defensive positions could nevertheless be attacked repeatedly with a range of munitions. One A10 squadron, for example, reported a higher than usual usage of cluster bombs during this period, even though pinpoint targets were obscured.

Once the weather cleared, Republican Guard defences could again become the focus of offensive air operations. The capture of Tallil airfield outside Nasiriyah provided a refuelling and rearming facility for close air-support operations. Strike aircraft with unused munitions from missions elsewhere were authorised to attack Republican Guard positions on their return flights. By 4 April, the Medina Division of the Republican Guard was estimated to be at less than 18 per cent of full strength, and the Hammurabi Division was rated as below 44 per cent.[15]

Throughout the campaign strategic attacks continued against selected targets in Baghdad. The use of penetration bombs to attack a telecommunications tower indicates that the communication nodes were a high priority. The apparent lack of cohesion in Iraqi defences may in part be attributable to a lack of communications from higher authority. Aversion to risking civilian casualties also limited some targeting, and in general the target selection process differed from the 1990–91 Iraq campaign. In 2003, bridges and major routes were not struck as coalition forces made rapid progress across the ground. Perhaps more surprisingly, the electricity facilities were largely left undamaged, either because of concerns about longer-term humanitarian problems, or in order to keep the administrative infrastructure in place to help post-conflict reconstruction.

Despite their relatively low public profile, air-power operations appear to have been the key to the rapid degradation of Iraqi defences, and hence to the relative ease with which coalition ground troops took over the country. The lack of any Iraqi air operations made little difference, as Iraqi aircraft would have been rapidly destroyed if they had attempted to fly. Over 1800 coalition aircraft were involved, 802 cruise missiles were fired, and enough fuel was transferred in the air to keep a 737 airliner flying for nearly twelve years.[16] It is not clear yet how important a role UAVs played, but it was the first time that Predator drones had been flown simultaneously in support of combat operations.[17]

Conclusion: Saddam's defeat

By the time coalition forces reached the outskirts of Baghdad, Saddam's fate was sealed. Operating with little or no central direction, the much-vaunted Republican Guard divisions were quickly pinned down and then destroyed piecemeal in coordinated attacks by coalition aircraft and ground forces. Arguably, the Gulf War of 2003 was a war Saddam Hussein should not have fought. His once powerful armed forces had not been able to make good the losses suffered in 1991.[18] Yet even at their best in 1991, his T72 tanks and his air force had proven no match for the tanks and aircraft of the United States and the United Kingdom. Saddam's defensive plan was seriously flawed, even though he had months to prepare. When it became clear that Turkey was unwilling to allow an allied attack from the north, Saddam should have redeployed his forces to confront the imminent attack from the south, the likelihood of which was clearly revealed by the positioning of the coalition's main forces in Kuwait. From an allied perspective, the southern option was high-risk; limited disembarkation facilities, few manoeuvre options, a narrow front, a distance of several hundred miles from the operation's start-line in Kuwait to Baghdad, and the Rivers Euphrates and Tigris as obstacles along the way. Yet other than to fire three missiles at coalition forces in Kuwait, Saddam did nothing to attack and disrupt coalition forces when they were concentrated and at their most vulnerable in Kuwait, by mining and sabotaging port facilities and demolishing key bridges over the Tigris and Euphrates. Most fatally, Saddam mis-oriented his forces. Saddam did not use well-known western casualty aversion to his advantage, by placing his main defences around Baghdad and by using a combination of minefields and other artificial and natural obstacles to slow down coalition forces and channel them into prepared killing zones. Instead of a fierce struggle against Saddam's six Republican Guard divisions in carefully prepared positions, coalition forces met Iraq's ineffective regular army, much of which simply melted away. Coalition forces were thus able to seize and maintain the initiative, and could embark on a relatively casualty-free run all the way to Baghdad. Given total air dominance by the coalition, the only options open to Iraqi forces were either to close with coalition forces or to operate from within urban areas and from behind the cover of the civilian population. But they did neither; only a few paramilitaries offered any meaningful resistance.

Notes

1. Presidential statement, US State Department transcript, 1 May 2003.
2. Afghanistan, Argentina, Australia, Bahrain, Bangladesh, Canada, Czechoslovakia, Denmark, Egypt, France, Germany, Greece, Honduras, Hungary, Italy, Kuwait, Morocco, Netherlands, Niger, Norway, Oman, Pakistan, Poland, Portugal, Qatar, Saudi Arabia, Senegal, South Korea, Spain, Syria, Turkey, United Arab Emirates, United Kingdom and United States.
3. A. Mason, *Air Power: A Centennial Appraisal*, London, Brassey's, 1994, p. 137.
4. Secretary of Defense William S. Cohen, Department of Defense news briefing, 19 December 1998.
5. President Bush, White House daily press conference, 20 March 2003. The list of 44 Coalition supporters given by the White House included Afghanistan, Albania, Angola, Australia, Azerbaijan, Bulgaria, Colombia, Czech Republic, Denmark, Dominican Republic, El Salvador, Eritrea, Estonia, Ethiopia, Georgia, Honduras, Hungary, Iceland, Italy, Japan, Kuwait, Latvia, Lithuania, Macedonia, Marshall Islands, Micronesia, Mongolia, Netherlands, Nicaragua, Philippines, Poland, Portugal, Romania, Rwanda, Singapore, Slovakia, Solomon Islands, South Korea, Spain, Turkey, Uganda, United Kingdom, United States and Uzbekistan.

6. The much-used expression 'shock and awe' originated in H.K. Ullman and J.P. Wade, *Shock and Awe: Achieving Rapid Dominance*, Washington DC, National Defense University Press, 1996.

7. General Wesley Clarke, 'Battle lines drawn at Pentagon over new kind of war', *The Times*, 20 March 2003.

8. Department of Defense daily brief, 20 March 2003: www.defenselink.mil/news/Mar2003/t03202003_t0320sd.html.

9. Presentation by General Larry D. Welch, USAF (ret) at King's College London, 20 May 2003.

10. It is believed that Polish Special Forces, known as GROM, were also operating in Iraq alongside the SAS, SBS and Delta teams.

11. USCENTAF, 'Operation Iraqi Freedom – By the Numbers', 30 April 2003, p. 11. USCENTAF also reported 16,901 20 mm rounds and 311,597 30 mm rounds being fired by coalition aircraft.

12. In the first eleven days, 700 cruise missiles and 9000 precision bombs were dropped, according to Secretary of Defense Donald Rumsfeld at his 1 April 2003 press briefing.

13. Dr Eliot A. Cohen, *Gulf War Air Power Survey. Volume II*, Washington DC, 1993, Part 2, p. 269, fig. 29.

14. Ibid., p. 11.

15. B. Graham and V. Loeb, 'An air war of might, coordination and risks', *Washington Post*, 27 April 2003.

16. USCENTAF, 'Operation Iraqi Freedom', p. 8.

17. Ibid., p. 7.

18. J. Keegan, 'Saddam was easily defeated – which is why the war goes on', *Daily Telegraph*, 4 June 2003.

7
Campaign Analysis: Ground and Air Forces

Philip Wilkinson and Tim Garden

Introduction

Announcements about troop deployments came at an increasing pace in the months leading up to hostilities. The UK had particular political sensitivities about appearing to make military deployments which might compromise diplomatic options. In a succession of announcements starting in December 2002, the Defence Secretary, Geoff Hoon, announced precautionary measures including booking sea transport and warning reservists, followed by deployment of advance parties, reserve call-ups, and the deployment of naval forces, and finally ground and air units. In the US, the build-up of forces continued in parallel. There were continuing air operations over the two no-fly zones. These had seen an increased use of offensive munitions by the US and UK since the middle of 2002. The targets that were attacked remained for the most part air defence related. But what was the condition of Iraqi forces waiting for the coalition forces as they prepared in Kuwait?

Iraqi forces

Force structure

At the beginning of the war, Iraqi forces numbered about 375,000, including 80,000 Republican Guard and 20–25,000 Special Republican Guard (in Baghdad), plus 650,000 reservists. Iraq's major serviceable equipment included 1500 main battle tanks (T55s and T72s), 2000 armoured personnel carriers (various), 2250 artillery pieces, about 100 missiles of relatively short range (Frog, Scud, al-Samoud), 100 attack helicopters and some 300 aircraft, both fighters and ground attack. Most equipment was a generation old, of dubious serviceability and no match for US and UK capabilities. Iraq's regular army consisted of 16 divisions, of which six were armoured or mechanised and distributed about the country.[1] These divisions did not materialise as formed units, though some individuals may have fought with the militia and Fedayeen (paramilitaries). It was rumoured that the 1st and 5th Iraqi army corps had been intended to defend the strategically important cities of Mosul and Kirkuk. The Republican Guard of 80,000 soldiers consisted of three armoured, one mechanised and two infantry divisions, the best known of which were the Nebuchadnezzar, Hammurabi and Medina Divisions. Since 1998, the Republican Guard had been placed under the direct command of the presidential palace and Saddam's son Qusay, rather than the Defence Ministry; reflecting its principal role hitherto as an instrument of internal repression. The military commander was General Ibrahim Abdal Satter Mohammad al-Tikriti, one of Saddam's inner circle from his home town of Tikrit. Many officers came from Tikrit and were mostly Sunni Muslims, but not all. Certainly by the standards of the Iraqi army, the Republican Guard was an elite. Its men were not conscripts, were better trained, better paid, lived in better quarters and were better disciplined than the regular army. The average guard earned 11,000 dinars per month – 4000 more than a conscript. However, even as a Special Force they were not completely trusted by Saddam. The Siriya was a small enforcement squad created by Saddam to be positioned behind the guards to make sure they did not run away.

The initial deployment of the Republican Guard saw three armoured divisions – the Medina, Hammurabi and al-Nida – placed south of Baghdad at Karbala. Each comprised about 10,000 soldiers, 150–200 tanks, about 250 armoured personnel carriers and 50–60 artillery pieces. Of the two infantry divisions, the Baghdad division was deployed at al-Kut, 100 miles southeast of Baghdad, with the Nebuchadnezzar Division originally dispersed around Kirkuk and Mosul in northern Iraq, but then redeployed to reinforce the Medina Division in the Karbala gap. The sole mechanised division, the Adnan Division, had some tanks but was mainly equipped with armoured personnel carriers and was based around Tikrit.[2]

The Special Republican Guard of 20–25,000 men consisted of four brigades and 14 battalions. It was a commando force armed mostly with light and medium weapons, but it also had two tank battalions, three artillery batteries and three air defence batteries. Its main job was to oversee the loyalty of the Republican Guard and to maintain Saddam's grip on the regime and Baghdad. They were reportedly trained in house-to-house fighting, with the task of inflicting losses that coalition commanders would find unacceptable. Finally, the Special Security Organisation consisted of several hundred officers who coordinated the close protection of Saddam and his family and various militia groups or Fedayeen. They also dealt with dissidents. Under the command of Saddam's younger son Qusay and General Abed al-Hamid, the Special Security Organisation was closely linked to the Ba'ath party, its militia and Fedayeen.

The strength and degree of control exercised by the Special Security Organisation over the people of Iraq appears to have been badly underestimated by coalition commanders. While this was not significant at the operational level, it did cause a number of tactical reverses when cities such as Basra did not immediately reject the Saddam regime in favour of the coalition.

Shortly before the invasion, Saddam seems to have ordered his commanders to reorganise Iraq into four military regions: northern, Baghdad, central and southern. Saddam's younger son and heir-apparent, Qusay, and General Mizban Khadr Hadi were given command of the central region. The elder son Uday was given command of the internal security forces, and along with his brother Qusay, the responsibility for the defence of Baghdad. The southern region, including the city of Basra, from which direction the invasion was expected to come, was given to Saddam's cousin, General Ali Hassan al-Majid, often known as 'Chemical Ali'. General Izzat Ibrahim Douri was given command of the northern region. Both al-Majid and Douri were wanted for war crimes against the Kurds in the north and the Marsh Arabs in the south, and for the invasion of Kuwait in 1990.

Equipment

Before the conflict Iraqi forces were of significant size, and were described as 'the most effective military power in the Gulf'.[3] But their equipment had been degraded by the years of sanctions. Although the Iraqi air force might have had 300 combat aircraft, it was not believed to have any effective combat capability against modern air forces. Of greater concern were the ground-based air defence systems with 850 missile launchers and 3000 anti-aircraft gun systems. The Iraqi navy had only nine small combat ships with an offensive mining capability. Chemical munitions were expected to be available to defending forces.[4] There was also a capability to mobilise significantly larger numbers. The reserve pool of 650,000 could theoretically have been supplemented from 3.4 million men of military service age.

Tactics

The use of paramilitary forces (Saddam's Fedayeen) in concert with civilian security and intelligence services resulted in a stiffer defensive force in the Shia southern area of the country that might have been expected. The defensive layers of Republican Guard divisions around Baghdad proved less resilient, and the expected hard resistance from elite units in the capital and in Tikrit never materialised. Although major routes to Bagdhad were mined at river crossings, no bridge was demolished by retreating Iraqi forces. This appears to have been a result of the destruction of command and control systems by coalition air power, and very rapid advances by US ground forces. The lack of any ability to operate in the air was a major drawback for Iraqi forces.

Five days after the war had started US General Wesley Clarke summed up Iraqi tactics in the following way: Saddam has shored up weak units with

Republican Guard detachments and Fedayeen. Some soldiers are hidden amongst the civilian population and using women and children as human shields. The Iraqis' advantages are knowledge of the terrain, willingness to take losses and their ability to blend with the population. They will have almost all the weapons they need to fight on an almost equal basis if they can close in on Coalition forces. They will use smoke and oil fires to obscure visibility and counter coalition air power. Their tanks, while no match for M1A1 Abrams or Challengers, are still formidable against troops and light vehicles. Their rocket-propelled grenades will penetrate light armoured vehicles. Their heavy machine guns are effective against helicopters and low flying aircraft. Their small arms are accurate and lay down a heavy rate of fire. The Iraqis will want to fight close and dirty, with Iraqi tanks darting in and out of garages and buildings; they will conduct small-scale offensive actions with dismounted soldiers supported by mortars. The fighting will be full of tricks we have already seen and more: ambushes, fake surrenders, soldiers dressed as women, attacks on rear areas and command posts. The Iraqis will be prepared to conduct high-risk missions of a kind we would not consider.

While generally overestimating Iraqi capabilities, this proved nevertheless to be a reasonable prediction of Iraqi tactics. That said, the bulk of Iraq's regular army appears to have decided to avoid battle, rather than confront the well-armed coalition. Although Iraq's regular army divisions simply left the battlefield, the Republican Guard divisions eventually made a stand, of sorts, outside Baghdad. But this resistance was soon worn down by coalition air power and defeated in detail by ground forces. The much-vaunted Special Republican Guard, like the regular army divisions, offered little substantial resistance.

Coalition forces

Operations in the north

On 2 March, the Turkish government postponed indefinitely a new vote on accepting 62,000 US troops after parliament's refusal to endorse the planned deployment. This surprise decision made planning 'more complicated', in the words of Ari Fleischer, the White House spokesman.[5] By 5 March no final decision had been made by the Turkish government. US Central Command (CENTCOM) was still hoping to use Turkish bases, but time was short and General Franks had to decide whether or not to reroute the 24 ships carrying the 4th Mechanised Infantry Division's heavy equipment south to Kuwait through the Suez Canal – a journey of seven to ten days. Whatever the final plan, the 15 Iraqi divisions, reportedly stationed in the north around the strategic cities of Mosul, Kirkuk and Tikrit, would need to be engaged, fixed and destroyed, and the Kirkuk oilfields seized before they could be set on fire.

The US inability to persuade Turkey to allow its bases to be used for an attack on Iraq and to open a northern front complicated CENTCOM's plans. The objectives of the northern advance were to take Mosul, Kirkuk and its oilfields, and Tikrit, and open the way to Baghdad. The capture of Mosul would have been a serious blow to the Iraqi government because it was the home of many senior army officers and officials. Kirkuk was, if anything considered even more essential. The province of Kirkuk is a major producer of oil, and securing Kirkuk swiftly was also considered important by policy makers because of its value to the Kurds. Military planners feared if the attack was delayed, Saddam might use the time to blow up the oilfields as he did in Kuwait in 1991. Thus with the closing of the northern option for the 4th Mechanised Infantry Division, the coalition had about 62,000 troops and 310 military aircraft in the wrong place.

With Turkey unavailable as a base, the northern option was limited to the deployment of air assault and Special Forces. Parachute and air assault forces could be inserted from the US 101st and 82nd Airborne Divisions and the UK's 16 Air Assault Brigade, with objectives limited to seizing key airfields at Dohuk, Arbil and Sulaymaniyah, and oil fields. These forces were not, however, considered sufficiently 'heavy' to fix and destroy the twelve Iraqi divisions reputed to be in the north. The US giant C17 Globemaster aircraft could be used to move battle tanks to the north, but only one at a time. It was always intended that air assault forces and Special Forces would be used to fight alongside Kurdish forces, but the fighting capacity of the Kurdish forces was, at the time, untested. In the end, Kurdish forces and Special Forces teams fought extremely successfully and went some way to offsetting the absence of the 4th Mechanised Infantry Division.

Kurdish forces

At the start of the war, the two western provinces of Iraqi Kurdistan, Dohuk and Arbil were ruled by the Kurdistan Democratic Party (KDP) led by Massoud Barzani. He claimed to have an army of 62,000, of whom 50,000 were combat troops, mainly infantry but with a few tanks and artillery pieces. They were originally a guerrilla force but had been upgrading into a more professional force. Many Kurdish officers who had served in the Iraqi army occupied senior positions in both Kurdish armies. In addition to the KDP forces, the Patriotic Union of Kurdistan was in control of Sulaymaniyah province in eastern Kurdistan. It claimed to have an army of about 40,000 men. The two parties, who had fought savage civil wars in the 1990s, had only recently established a joint military command. Both armies and the joint command had been receiving training support and specialist equipment from US Special Forces and CIA training teams from 1992 onwards. These teams remained 'embedded' when hostilities broke out, in order to perform liaison duties but more importantly to coordinate coalition air support.

Calendar of the campaign

The first shots of the war were fired on Tuesday 18 March in the mouth of the River Khawr al-Zubayr, south of the port of Umm Qasr, when a Kuwaiti gunboat challenged a flotilla of about 25 Iraqi dhows. The boats, suspected of laying mines, failed to respond when challenged. Hostilities proper began in the early hours of 20 March 2003, with the launch of a limited missile strike against targets close to Baghdad. Some 36 Tomahawk cruise missiles were launched from US ships in the Gulf and the Red Sea, against a building in which the Iraqi leadership was believed to be meeting.[6] The missile attack was followed up by air-delivered precision-guided bombs. The White House acknowledged that the start of the campaign had been initiated ahead of the main plan after intelligence information offered the possibility of a decapitation strike against the Iraqi regime.[7] In retaliation, Iraq fired three unsuccessful surface-to-surface missiles at Kuwait. One missile was launched at Kuwait City but was intercepted and destroyed, with two Chinese-made Seersucker anti-ship missiles landing in the desert without causing any casualties.

The main campaign began the following day with intense air attacks by cruise missiles and precision-guided bombs on key military and government targets in Baghdad and other regional centres. Simultaneously, advance elements of the 3rd (US) Mechanised Infantry Division pushed into Iraq towards Nasiriya, while the 1st (UK) Armoured Division and US Marines advanced towards Basra, and the oil terminal at Umm Qasr. Other air assault and Special Forces were tasked to seize and hold key strategic oil wells and airfields in the west.

The first week: 20–27 March

By nightfall on the first day of the war, coalition aircraft had flown over 1200 sorties, and 55 Tomahawk cruise missiles had been fired. There had been three unsuccessful Iraqi missile firings and an early exchange of artillery fire. At 5 p.m. the main coalition fire-plan commenced and pounded the closest Iraqi positions. At 7 p.m. marines launched their main offensives against al-Faw peninsula and Umm Qasr, flying in from HMS *Ocean* and HMS *Ark Royal*. At the same time, other marine units formed a blocking position to the north of al-Faw and seized a number of oil installations. The remainder of the 1st Armoured Division moved north to block any Iraqi counter-moves and to shield the right flank of the 3rd Mechanised Infantry Division and the remainder of the US Marine Expeditionary Force as they pushed north.

Throughout Day 2 fighting continued as the 7th Armoured Brigade (the 'Desert Rats') advanced north to Basra, and the US 3rd Mechanised Infantry Division advanced north towards Nasiriyah. In the south, the main fighting continued in and around the al-Faw peninsula and the harbour facilities at Umm Qasr. In the west, two Iraqi strategic airfields known as H2 and H3 were seized by Special Forces deploying from Jordan in Chinook helicopters.

Both airfields had been used in the past to store weapons of mass destruction (WMD). Seizing the air bases was also believed to be vital to prevent Saddam launching Scud missile attacks against Israel from the western Iraqi desert. Elements of the Royal Engineers, explosive ordnance clearance teams, and nuclear, chemical and biological teams and US combat forces seized and started to clear oilfields to the south and east of Basra. Seven oil wells had been set alight by Iraqi forces, but they were quickly extinguished.

US forces from the 3rd Mechanised Infantry Division, led by troops from 7th Cavalry Regiment continued to advance rapidly towards Baghdad, and within 48 hours had moved about 100 miles to Nasiriyah and the vital bridges on the River Euphrates. This advance constituted a 15-mile-long armoured column led by Apache attack helicopters with forward intelligence provided by JSTAR (joint surveillance and target attack radar system) aircraft and Predator unmanned air vehicles (UAVs). The Pentagon claimed that an Iraqi brigade of 8000 troops had surrendered to coalition forces near Basra. In Umm Qasr, the strategic old port fell, although isolated pockets of resistance remained. These were finally cleared on 24 March, after a three-day joint air–land operation.

By 24 March, just four days after the invasion had begun, Nasiriyah had been bypassed and the 3rd Mechanised Infantry Division had pushed on to Najaf, 100 miles south of Baghdad. International media were beginning to question the success of the coalition forces, even though coalition forces had at this stage advanced approximately 150 miles into Iraq, at the expense of twelve soldiers killed in combat, 19 killed in accidents and a further two deaths attributed to friendly fire. Umm Qasr had been declared safe and open, and US Marines had captured the bridges over the Euphrates in Nasiriyah to open another approach to Baghdad. Though isolated hit-and-run and mortar attacks against US Marines and coalition forces continued from the suburbs of the city for several more days, these were not of operational significance. Capturing the bridges over the Euphrates opened up two separate approaches to Baghdad: one to be exploited by the 3rd Mechanised Infantry Division in the west through Najaf to Karbala, and the other to the east by the 1st Marine Expeditionary Force (1 MEF).

On 26–27 March, there was inclement weather and sandstorms, slowing the allied advance short of the main Republican Guard defences around Baghdad. Air strikes continued, nevertheless, particularly against Republican Guard divisions surrounding Baghdad which were expected to be more difficult to break through than the defences in the south. Some elements of Iraqi forces to the north of Baghdad were deployed to reinforce the southern defences. At this stage, it appears that the Iraq military command was functioning well enough to redeploy forces at divisional level. However, air attacks on communications centres during this period may have been successful in breaking links between the military leadership and its troops.

It was during this period that the Republican Guard attempted a series of counter-moves, under cover of sandstorms, against the 7th Cavalry Regiment and other units of the US 5th Corps, and the 1 MEF as they advanced north towards Baghdad. Two columns, each of up to 1000 vehicles, including T72 tanks, counter-attacked at Najaf and at al-Kut. These may have been designated reserve forces from the Republican Guard forces. It is more likely, however, that they were an *ad hoc* force cobbled together at short notice and under extreme pressure from air attack. Presumably, the decision to counter-attack was taken under the mistaken assumption that the sandstorms and bad weather would mask movement from coalition surveillance and counter-strikes. This was the last semblance of any apparent coordination or central direction of Iraqi forces, and the order to counter-attack may have been the last order given by Saddam Hussein to his forces. There had been very little semblance of control to this point in the campaign, but thereafter, there was none, and Iraqi forces operated in a random and chaotic manner.

This point in the campaign was also critical from the coalition perspective. Resistance from the militia had interrupted the logistic tail and there had not been the mass surrender of Iraqi regular forces that military planners had hoped for. Coalition forces had been fighting for five to six days, and although not short of ammunition, they needed to be resupplied with food, water and fuel. The dilemma for CENTCOM was whether to consolidate the remarkable success that had been won thus far and give time for 4th Mechanised Infantry Division to marry up with its equipment in Kuwait and move north, or to press on against the Republican Guard in its prepared defences and attack Baghdad. Much would now depend on the effectiveness of 'shock and awe' and coalition air attacks to wear down the Republican Guard. At this point the Republican Guard divisions, presumably responding to higher orders to counter-attack and believing themselves covered by the storms, left their prepared defences and in doing so made themselves even more vulnerable to air attack. CENTCOM decided that the two-pronged attack on Baghdad by the 5th Corps and 1 MEF should continue.

At about the time of the attempted counter-attacks from Baghdad, British Challenger II tanks had a major meeting engagement with a column of 14 Iraqi T55 tanks, all of which they destroyed. As in the north, it would appear that the foggy weather had convinced the Iraqis that they could manoeuvre unobserved by British tanks. But this was not so, and after a troop of Royal Engineers had laid an over-bridge across a canal to allow the Challenger tanks to manoeuvre to a position of advantage, they were able to engage and kill the entire Iraqi force. This Iraqi move may have been part of a wider countrywide and coordinated counter-attack by Iraqi forces or simply a tactical redeployment.

At this stage, personnel from the 4th Mechanised Infantry Division began to arrive from the United States, just as their equipment was beginning to arrive in Kuwait. As a result, General Franks could open the northern front in order to confuse the Iraqi leadership and take the pressure off the southern approach to Baghdad. Some 1000 troops from the 173rd Airborne Brigade were parachuted into Kurdish-controlled northern Iraq to seize Harir airfield east of Kirkuk, working alongside Special Forces who had been in operation in the north for several months. Tanks and armoured vehicles were expected to follow, albeit slowly, to provide heavy support to the Kurdish Peshmerga as they attempted to gain control of the key towns of Mosul and Kirkuk.

The fact that the Iraqi army had not surrendered as a direct consequence of 'shock and awe' seems to have come as a surprise to some analysts, particularly those who had overestimated the effect of air power after the Kosovo air campaign. But for the military planners at CENTCOM that was only ever a 'best-case scenario'. The resistance by the 20–40,000 Fedayeen and their hold over the people, even the Shia Muslims in the south, had come as a surprise. Military planners had anticipated a major uprising by the Shia Muslims against Saddam in the south. The absence of such an uprising was, however, of tactical rather than operational consequence. The defeat of the Republican Guard counter-attacks around Baghdad and Basra was, arguably, the point at which the campaign tipped decisively in favour of the coalition. By this stage, Royal Marines had taken the al-Faw peninsula and US Marines had seized the strategically important oilfields of Rumaylah. The strategic port of Umm Qasr was in coalition hands within five days. Basra was surrounded but had not yet been captured. Two breakouts from Basra by Iraqi forces had been attacked and destroyed. The Iraqi leadership had been attacked in Baghdad and their command and control systems had been severely undermined. The counter-attacks by the Republican Guard were the last evidence of any central direction. The two prongs of the alliance push to Baghdad had made remarkable progress, coming within 70 miles of Baghdad. All key bridges were firmly in the control of coalition forces. The northern front had been opened by linking the 173rd Airborne Brigade with Kurdish and Special Forces, and in the west, US, UK and Australian Special Forces had seized key airfields. No Scud missiles had been fired at Israel. By 1 April, a battalion from the US 173rd Airborne Brigade had completed its deployment into northern Iraq.

The siege of Basra: 21 March to 7 April

As early as Day 2, the old strategic port of Umm Qasr had been secured and the 1st (UK) Armoured Division was able to switch its main effort westwards to encircle Basra. On 22 March, Basra airport was taken and bombing raids were subsequently conducted against regime targets in the city. On 24 March, British infantry attacked the Ba'ath party HQ in Zubayr, 15 miles west of Basra, while artillery began to engage Iraqi forces defending Basra. On the same day a column of up to 50 T55 tanks tried to break out of Basra but were engaged and halted.

The raid on the Ba'ath party HQ in al Zubayr was an early indication of the likely approach that would be used as the attack gathered momentum around

Basra and other major towns. Initial tactics were to surround the town or city and then attack headquarters, destroying Saddam's command and control arrangements and his ability to counter these raids, while conducting probing attacks to look for exploitable weaknesses elsewhere.

By 25 March, Basra was completely surrounded. On 26 March, there were reports of an uprising in Basra, with Iraqi civilians being attacked by the Fedayeen and Saddam's militia. On 27 March, 14 more Iraqi T55s were destroyed by British tanks as they tried to move towards al-Faw. During the following week British forces conducted various other engagements that allowed them to gain control of the Shatt al-Arab waterway and the suburbs of Basra, and to lay siege to Iraqi forces in the city centre.

On 28 March, the first substantial allied shipment of humanitarian aid to Iraq arrived at the docks of Umm Qasr. On 30 March, coalition air and ground forces captured the suburb of Abu al-Khasib after 15 hours of fighting. Once again, the assumption that Shia Muslims would rise up against Saddam's regime at the first opportunity had proven false. The coalition had underestimated the grip of fear that was still being exerted by the Ba'ath party and Saddam's militias. Instead, Basra was surrounded, and 16 Air Assault Brigade conducted a major engagement north of the oilfields at Rumaylah, destroying 17 Iraqi T55 tanks. A patrol from the UK Special Boat Service (SBS) attacked the Ba'ath party headquarters building containing up to 200 militia fighters, which was then destroyed in air strikes.

For a little over a week British forces watched, probed and waited, testing resistance in Basra. According to one assessment of the British position, British forces were by this stage doing

> what the British do best – wielding an iron fist in a velvet glove. Once it was realised that Basra would not come over to coalition forces, the British went into their standard 'urban mode' combining aggression against the bad guys, friendship with the majority and patience with everyone.[8]

On 7 April shortly after 5.50 a.m., having surrounded Basra for nearly two weeks, British tanks and armoured fighting vehicles mounted a three-pronged attack – Operation Sinbad – into the city centre. Three British soldiers were killed in the action, along with many Iraqis. The operation, based on intelligence gathered during the preceding two weeks, was driven by the judgement of the commander of the 1st (UK) Armoured Division to the effect that the situation had reached 'tipping point', with organised resistance about to collapse. Iraqi forces withdrew to their last stronghold, the district of Manawi Albashi, where they were defeated piecemeal.

The battle for Baghdad: 1–10 April

Ten days before the entry of main forces into Iraq, the UK's national contingent commander described Saddam's plans to suck coalition forces into street warfare in Baghdad, in the manner of the German siege of Stalingrad. According to intelligence reports, Saddam has constructed two concentric defensive lines around Baghdad, manned by five Republican Guard divisions of about 40,000 soldiers. Another defensive ring inside the city consisted of about 20,000 Special Republican Guards dedicated to protecting Saddam and his regime.

On 16 March, the *Sunday Times* reported 120,000 Iraqi troops deployed in three defensive circles around Baghdad.[9] These now included 50,000 Republican Guards equipped with 700 tanks, fighting alongside three units of Special Forces amounting to another 45,000 troops. A further 20,000 Special Republican Guards and several thousand bodyguards were reportedly assigned to protect Saddam and the regime's most sensitive targets. The Adnan Tulfah Mechanised Republican Guard division was reported to have moved from Mosul to Baghdad to be followed by the Baghdad division from al-Kut. A Republican Guard tank brigade was also reported to be moving in to reinforce the defences of Baghdad. The outermost of the three circles was about 30 miles out from the city centre and manned by three Republican Guard divisions – Medina to the west, Baghdad to the south and El Amarah to the northeast. This was reputedly the 'red line', where Iraqi commanders had been given authority to use chemical weapons. The middle line was reportedly manned by the remaining Republican Guards, while the inner circle, within the city, was the responsibility of the Special Republican Guard, the Special Security Organisation and Saddam's Fedayeen.[10]

More than 5 million people live in Baghdad and its environs and it was anticipated that the Republican Guard would make a bloody stand in the city and its suburbs. The coalition, however, did not intend to play Saddam at his own game, and would use its superior technology to identify and bypass Iraqi static defences. From the start of the war, Republican Guard positions in Baghdad, and the regime's key installations, had been subjected to continuous air attack and to armoured reconnaissance patrols. By 1 April, US forces had started to probe Iraqi positions around Baghdad while coalition aircraft continued regular bombing runs. With improvement in the weather around 29 March, battle damage assessments showed that Republican Guard divisions on the outer line of Baghdad's defences had been made virtually inoperable by coalition air and artillery attacks. However, considerable resistance was still being offered by the Medina, Nebuchadnezzar and Baghdad Divisions. After fierce exchanges of fire, several thousand Iraqis and fewer than ten US troops were killed. At this time the level of desertions began to increase, with Republican Guard troops surrendering to coalition forces or making their way individually or in small groups into Baghdad City.

By 2 and 3 April, 1 MEF, on the eastern approach to Baghdad, had seized the strategic town of al-Kut and routed the Baghdad division which 'folded without resistance'.[11] Having seized a vital bridge over the River Tigris, 1 MEF began manoeuvring to confront the al-Nida Division. On the western approach, the 3rd Mechanised Infantry Division, supported by elements of the 101st and 82nd Air Assault Divisions had encircled Karbala, defeated the Medina and Nebuchadnezzar Divisions, crossed to the eastern bank of the Euphrates and were also advancing to the outskirts of Baghdad. This effectively put US forces inside the Red Zone, which signals intercepts indicated had been declared a free-fire zone for Iraqi chemical weapons.

Nevertheless, with the defeat of the Republican Guard divisions on the outer ring of Saddam's defences, the way now lay open to assault Baghdad. Up to this point the Iraqi defence plan had been lamentable; even the major bridges on the Euphrates and Tigris rivers on the major approaches to Baghdad were only lightly defended. That said, the armoured approach to Baghdad by 1 MEF and the 3rd Mechanised Infantry Division, supported by coalition air power, was a remarkable demonstration of manoeuvre warfare. In the air, coalition sorties were proceeding apace, attacking strategic targets in and around Baghdad.

On 4 April, US forces attacked Baghdad airport. By 5 April, Baghdad airport had fallen to Special Forces and a major assault by 3rd Mechanised Infantry Division. CENTCOM in Qatar indicated they hoped to be able to land aircraft at the airport within 12–36 hours. With control of a strategically crucial airhead, the problem of extended supply routes was much reduced. Attack helicopters and close air support aircraft could henceforth respond in minutes. The resistance inside Baghdad continued but was incoherent and sporadic. Instead of the highly trained elite units that were expected, most firefights were with small elements of Saddam loyalist militias using hit-and-run tactics. By 6 April, Baghdad was surrounded by the 101st Airborne Division pushing in from the north, 1 MEF from the northeast and southeast, and 3rd Mechanised Infantry Division from the west and southwest. Having surrounded the city, the next stage, which was conducted without any pause so as to maintain operational tempo, was for US forces to begin armoured probes into the city centre by patrols of up to 30 M1A1 Abram tanks and armoured personnel carriers. Properly known as 'reconnaissance by force', these missions were quickly dubbed 'Thunder Runs'. Some Shia Muslims and even some Sunnis welcomed US forces into the city, and resistance to these armoured patrols was sporadic. At the same time, columns of civilian vehicles packed with civilians and probably military deserters were fleeing northwards out of the city towards Tikrit, expected to be Saddam's final bastion. The limited resistance encountered, however, fell far short of a coordinated, detailed and ferocious defence in the mould of Stalingrad.

As a result, the decision was taken to mount a major armoured push into the centre of the city, to finally tip the balance of the battle of Baghdad in the coalition's favour. In the words of one newspaper report,

This was to be no cautious, street-by-street nibbling away at the capital. It was an almighty sledgehammer blow. In an instant, General Blount [commanding the 3rd Mechanised Infantry Division] rendered obsolete decades of military wisdom on how to take a city.[12]

Able to respond quickly and decisively to the collapse of the Iraqi defences, the soldiers who took part in the battle for Baghdad nevertheless found it hard to believe it would be over so quickly and straightforwardly. The symbolic moment of victory was, of course, the destruction of the statue of Saddam Hussein in Firdos Square in the centre of Baghdad on 9 April 2003.

Fall of Kirkuk and Mosul

Within seven days of the start of the war, Kurdish Forces supported by US and British Special Forces and coalition air forces were closing in on Kirkuk. The front-line town of Qarah Anjir, the first in northern Iraq to fall, had been hastily abandoned by Iraqi troops as they fled south to more defendable positions. This opened the way for further US deployments into Harir airfield, which had earlier been occupied by one of the 173rd Airborne Brigade's battalions. However, it was not until 10 April that Kirkuk and Mosul fell to the Kurdish Peshmerga and coalition Special Forces. The Pentagon admitted that its troops were in Kirkuk, but declined to say that American forces controlled the city, although a Pentagon spokesman confirmed that elements of the 173rd Airborne Brigade would arrive in the city later. Responding to Turkish concerns and US pressure, Jalal Talabani, the Iraqi Kurdish leader, said his forces would hand over the city to US forces and withdraw within 24 hours.[13]

Fall of Tikrit – the last redoubt

By 13 April, US forces had pushed north from Baghdad with 250 armoured vehicles and were engaging Saddam's forces in the outskirts of Tikrit. A CENTCOM spokesman described fighting as 'spotty', but added: 'We are actively engaging any forces we need to. When we are engaged in a fire-fight it is always fierce.' With Iraqi resistance estimated at just 2500 troops, CENTCOM soon confirmed that the mass of the Adnan division of the Republican Guard, given responsibility for defending Tikrit, had evaporated.When US Marines in armoured vehicles, under air cover provided by Apache helicopters pushed into the city on 14 April, resistance melted away altogether and Saddam's last redoubt fell to US forces.

As US Marines captured the centre of Tikrit, the heart of the Ba'ath party and Saddam's home town, Brigadier General Vincent Brooks, speaking at CENTCOM in Qatar, indicated that decisive military operations were 'coming to a close'. Soon after, the Pentagon announced that two of the five aircraft carriers deployed in the region – USS *Kitty Hawk* and USS *Constellation* – were being recalled with their complements of aircraft.

Notes

1. 'Where are all Iraq's soldiers hiding?' *Daily Telegraph*, 4 April 2003.
2. 'War on Saddam', *Daily Telegraph*, 18 March 2003.
3. A.H. Cordesman, 'Iraqi Armed Forces on the Edge of War', Washington DC, CSIS, 7 February 2003.
4. UK MoD document expected some to be available at 45 minutes' notice. *Iraq's Weapons of Mass Destruction: The Assessment of the British Government*, Stationery Office, September 2002, p. 4.
5. The daily briefing can be found on the US government information website: http://usinfo.state.gov/xarchives/display.html?p=washfile-english&y=2003&m=march&x=20030321170034ifas03604242&t=xarchives/xarchitem.html.
6. 'How to watch the war', *New York Times*, 21 March 2003.
7. White House daily briefing by Ari Fleischer, 21 March 2003.
8. 'Basra: a very British siege', *Sunday Times*, 6 April 2003.
9. *Sunday Times*, 16 March 2003.
10. 'War on Saddam', *Daily Telegraph*, 18 March 2003.
11. Brigadier General Vincent Brooks, quoted in 'Allies 20 miles from Baghdad', *Daily Telegraph*, 3 April 2003.
12. Ibid.
13. *Daily Telegraph*, 9 April 2003.

8
Campaign Analysis: Maritime Forces
Joanna Kidd

The successful naval and maritime campaign against Iraq in 2003 was a more extensive and a more complicated one than that carried out in the First Gulf War of 1990–91. Although the naval threat from Iraq was much less significant than it had been in 1990–91, the additional demands made by the global war on terrorism and the lack of nearby land bases for conventional aircraft necessitated a very substantial and varied allied naval deployment. The naval and maritime forces, which took part in the campaign in support of allied land operations against Iraq, were to a very large extent from the United States. The United States Navy (USN) deployed over half of its active surface fleet to the Arabian Gulf and eastern Mediterranean, including five aircraft carriers (out of a total active number of twelve) and 21 amphibious ships (out of a total active number of 41). Evidence of overstretch in the USN was apparent as at one stage of the war 73 per cent of all USN active surface ships were at sea, a surprisingly high number given that Iraq is nearly a landlocked country. Furthermore, some shortcomings in the USN's current ability to carry out warfare in the littoral, as opposed to the Cold War environment of the open oceans, were apparent during the campaign. Despite the predominance of the USN the United Kingdom also undertook its largest naval deployment since the 1982 Falklands War, and Australia, Poland and Denmark also deployed naval vessels to the Arabian Gulf for the war.

Sea control

At the strategic level, the maritime campaign had one major aim, which was to support the allied land operations and land forces in Iraq. In order to achieve this aim, allied naval forces established and maintained sea control in the immediate theatre of operations in the northern Arabian Gulf (NAG) and also in the maritime approaches to it. Sea control is commonly defined as

134

the condition that exists when one has freedom of action to use an area of sea for one's own purposes for a period of time and, if necessary, deny its use to an opponent. Sea control includes the air-space above the surface and the water volume and seabed below.[1]

In the NAG, with the exception of the Iraqi coastline, sea control was not very difficult to achieve quickly as the conventional threat from Iraq was minimal. Almost all of the country's naval assets had been destroyed in the First Gulf War and had not since been replaced. The threat from the air was also minimal, as Rear Admiral Snelson, Deputy Coalition Maritime Joint Component Commander, said: 'He [Saddam] still has some missiles that he can fire from the land towards the sea but because we've got complete air cover over southern Iraq it's very difficult for him to move them.'[2]

However, the potential asymmetric threat from Iraq to allied naval forces was initially considered to be high. Admiral Snelson commented:

> Such attacks may range from cargo vessels or tankers being used as fire ships to explosive-laden small craft ramming coalition warships, or sabotage from divers ... Coalition warships are on high alert against suicide attacks after Iranian boats intercepted Iraqi speedboats packed with explosives on 26 March 2003.[3]

Despite such fears, there would appear to have been very few actual asymmetric attacks on allied naval forces from Iraqi forces. Therefore, as both the conventional and asymmetric threats in the NAG proved to be very slight, allied naval forces effectively had freedom of manoeuvre and were able to operate almost unhindered there.

The exception to this freedom of manoeuvre was in the immediate sea approaches to Iraq's coastline, which had been mined prior to the start of the war. Although Iraq's only port, Umm Qasr, had been seized on 21 March 2003[4] by UK and US Marines, shipping could not use the port immediately as the approaches to it had been mined. Coalition mine counter-measures (MCM) forces had already started to clear a channel up the mined Khawr Abd Allah approach to Umm Qasr and had begun to survey a route into the port in the earliest days of the war. Coalition MCM assets in theatre comprised the Royal Navy (RN) MCM vessels HMS *Bangor*, *Brocklesby*, *Blyth*, *Sandown*, *Ledbury*, *Grimsby* and Royal Fleet Auxiliary (RFA) *Sir Bedivere* (as MCM Tasking Authority), and the USN vessels USS *Cardinal*, *Dextrous*, *Raven* and *Ardent*. Other MCM elements comprised USN MCM helicopters, clearance diving teams from Australia and the UK and a USN Marine mammal detachment.[5] Iraqi forces were reported as proactively trying to thwart the clearance effort, and on 24 March 2003 several 'civilian vessels' were intercepted carrying mines into the area and were subsequently destroyed.[6] However, by 27 March 2003 the allied force had cleared a channel around 200 metres wide and

50 miles long up to the port.[7] Teams of divers had cleared a number of explosive charges from the docks and wharves.[8] In these mine-clearance operations the USN relied to quite a considerable extent on the RN MCM forces. Such dependence existed despite over a decade of discussion in naval circles that the USN should increase its MCM capabilities, as in the post-Cold War environment the navy was ever more likely to face such threats as its focus of operations shifted from the blue water of the oceans to the shallow water of the littoral. However, although the USN has recently begun to invest in new MCM technologies, it did not have sufficient MCM capabilities to cope by itself with the mine threat in the Iraqi littoral.

It should be noted that, in order to reach the NAG, all the allied naval forces had to transit the Strait of Hormuz, there being no other means of entry to the NAG by sea. At its narrowest point the Strait is only 23 nautical miles in width, and a substantial part of it is in Iran's territorial waters. It is possible to assume, therefore, that the allies must have established some form of agreement with Iran to enable the safe passage of allied shipping through the Strait; although the exact nature of the agreement and the extent of Iran's cooperation is not yet apparent in open sources.

Power projection

Having established sea control in the NAG, allied naval forces were able to support the allied land campaign in Iraq by means of power projection, defined as,

> in maritime terms ... the ability to project force from a maritime force into the territory of another state. It is any deployment of force ashore or the provision of fire to influence events ashore.[9]

Power projection was carried out chiefly by three major tactics: attacks on Iraqi targets by carrier-borne aircraft; Tomahawk missile attacks and amphibious operations. The USN accounted for all the operational aircraft carriers in theatre, having deployed five – *Harry S. Truman, Theodore Roosevelt, Abraham Lincoln, Constellation* and the *Kitty Hawk* – of its total number of twelve aircraft carriers to the region. The *Kitty Hawk* was used, however, not in the traditional carrier role but rather as a base for Special Forces operations. Each carrier (100,000 tonnes in displacement and with a crew of about 5000) was accompanied by a battle group generally composed of two Tomahawk land-attack cruise missile (TLAM)-armed nuclear-powered attack submarines and eight surface escorts (frigates, destroyers and cruisers). Although the UK did deploy its small aircraft carrier *Ark Royal* to the NAG, it was used as an amphibious platform. By mid April 2003[10] over 7000 individual power-projection strike sorties had been flown from the four USN carriers used in their conventional role, according to Vice Admiral Timothy Keating USN,

Naval Component Commander. As was the case with the ordnance launched by allied air forces, over 70 per cent of the ordnance launched from USN aircraft was precision guided, either by global positioning system or laser designator, whereas in the 1990–91 Gulf War minimal numbers of precision weapons were launched.[11] Carrier operations were at some times key to the overall air campaign, as allied air forces did not have access to bases in Saudi Arabia and on two occasions were prevented from flying due to poor weather. Having so ably demonstrated their ability to operate on a more flexible basis than land-based air forces, it seems likely that the case for aircraft carriers will have been strengthened in procurement debates in both the US and UK.

The second major means of allied naval power projection was the use of TLAMs, launched from surface escort ships and nuclear-powered submarines against Iraqi land targets. Over 800 TLAMs were launched by USN and RN by mid- April 2003,[12] with fewer than ten failing to reach their targets.[13] It should be noted that USN surface ships and submarines launched almost all the TLAMs, given that the RN had only two platforms (both submarines) in theatre which carried TLAMs. As so many TLAMs were used, it should now be apparent, as Vice Admiral Sir Jeremy Blackham notes, that they have secured a role as a tactical 'war-fighting weapon'.[14] Such a change in the role of TLAMs had been anticipated for several years, not least by their manufacturer Raytheon, which is producing the next generation TLAM, the tactical Tomahawk, at nearly half the price of its predecessor. However, TLAMs remain expensive tactical ordnance, and on that basis it appears likely that the USN's research into cheaper, long-range land-attack missiles will continue, perhaps with yet more urgency.

Amphibious and associated operations, such as naval gunfire support to allied land forces and the provision of afloat operating bases for Special Forces, was the third tactic used for power projection. The USN deployed 21 amphibious ships to the NAG, out of a total active number of 41 amphibious ships. These ships were deployed rapidly in four groups: two amphibious task groups of seven ships each (Amphibious Task Group East and Amphibious Task Group West), which deployed to the Gulf within two weeks' notice; and two amphibious ready groups of three ships each (led by the USS *Tarawa* and the USS *Iwo Jima*). One further ship was deployed independently of these groups. Such was the size of these deployments that Amphibious Task Group East was the most powerful amphibious force ever to leave the US East Coast. It carried approximately 8000 US Marines from the 2nd Marine Expeditionary Brigade and aircraft from the 2nd Marine Air Wing.[15] Amphibious Task Group West carried a similar number of marines; the two amphibious ready groups fewer marines. The primary mission of these amphibious units was to deliver the marines to the battle space and then support them ashore. The delivery of the marines to their disembarkation point in Kuwait was achieved successfully and with no opposition. Once in the battle space, the marines were supported by the amphibious ships' marine aviation (fixed-wing Harriers and a mix of rotary-wing aircraft) for close-air support sorties and combat resupply missions. Conversion of an aircraft carrier from its usual role to support land forces ashore was also carried out by the USN, which converted the *Kitty Hawk* into an afloat base for Special Forces.

An amphibious deployment was also carried out by the Royal Navy, which deployed two amphibious task groups; the first, led by HMS *Ocean*, consisted of four amphibious ships; and the second was centred on HMS *Ark Royal*, which carried Chinook helicopters, instead of its usual complement of fixed-wing aircraft, in order to support the Royal Marines of 3 Commando Brigade (Cdo Bde). Some of the RN escorting surface forces gave further support to Royal Marines ashore by providing naval gunfire support. On 20 March 2003, the frigates HMS *Chatham*, *Marlborough* and *Richmond*, together with HMAS *Anzac*, close in to the Iraqi coastline along the al-Faw peninsula, provided naval gunfire support to US and UK marines.[16] The USN's surface ships, due to their deep draught, would have had difficulty doing this, because of the extremely shallow water in the al-Faw peninsula.

Once 3 Cdo Bde, led by 40 Commando (and subsequently 42 Commando), was ashore, it took part in a combined operation with the US's 15th Marine Expeditionary Unit to capture the peninsula, key oil installations and the port of Umm Qasr.[17] The operation was achieved quickly and successfully. According to the UK Ministry of Defence,

> Although some oil wells had already been set alight, there was not the widespread sabotage that had been feared. Within 48 hours Umm Qasr had been captured and was being secured ...[18]

Such was the speed of the operation and the quickness and totality of the Iraqi forces' defeat that Colonel Stephen Fox, commanding officer of 3 Cdo Bde, became 'effectively the de facto mayor of Umm Qasr'.[19] The marines policed the town and ran the port, 'through 17 Port and Maritime Regiment – the first time UK forces have run a port in wartime since the Second World War'.[20] Further marine detachments patrolled the water approaches to Basra in small patrol craft; little resistance was met. Once the peninsula had been secured, most of 3 Cdo Bde advanced to Basra and took part in the successful assault and eventual taking of the city.

Sea lines of communication

Although allied naval forces had established sea control in the NAG and had access to it through the Strait of Hormuz, their approaches to it, otherwise called sea lines of communication, were not unthreatened. Sea lines of communication (SLOCs) are defined in British Maritime Doctrine as the sea routes that connect an operating military force with one or more bases of operations and along which supplies and reinforcements move. The expression is sometimes used more broadly in a strategic sense to include commercial shipping routes.[21]

In the case of the war against Iraq, the SLOCs extended from the eastern and, to a lesser extent, the western coasts of the US to the NAG, as almost all the allied naval vessels transited from the US. Securing these sea lines of communication was a complicated task due to the perceived threat of terrorist attack, and was one of the main causes of the USN's apparent overstretch. Al-Qaeda operatives had been assumed to be responsible for the 2000 attack on the USS *Cole* off the Yemeni coast, and also for attempted attacks on UK and US shipping in the Straits of Gibraltar in 2002. Fearing further al-Qaeda attacks, allied warships

> took several precautionary measures. Standing patrols of heavy machine gun-armed helicopters rotate on picket duty against surprise attacks and crew man stations with machine guns and night vision aids ...[22]

More importantly, almost all the heavy equipment and stores and supplies for the allied land forces was transported to theatre by sea. The transport of such logistics by sea was achieved more quickly than in the First Gulf War as the USN in the past decade has invested in large and fast sealift ships. Over 20 ships of this type (named the Watson and Bob Hope class) had been commissioned since the First Gulf War and this resulted in considerably faster transit times for logistics from the US to the NAG. However, the threat from al-Qaeda was felt to be so great that these transport ships, both military and commercial, were escorted (if coming from the eastern US), by allied naval ships from the Straits of Gibraltar, through the Mediterranean Sea, via the Suez Canal, the Red Sea, the Gulf of Oman and the Strait of Hormuz to the NAG. If coming from the US western coast, such ships were escorted through the Malacca Straits and then through the Strait of Hormuz. Allied high-value shipping (such as aircraft carriers and amphibious shipping) was also escorted along the same routes by naval surface ships.

Some countries not part of the war coalition had existing deployments in support of counter-terrorism operations to areas of particular vulnerability – for example, the German navy off Djibouti and the Indian navy in the Malacca Straits – and continued their deployments during the war. However, these deployments were small and did not take place in the Mediterranean, which meant that the USN's surface ships had to escort all allied shipping transiting there. As the USN's surface escort fleet has almost halved in size since the First Gulf War, the escorting task greatly stretched its resources. So great were the demands of escorting duties that in early March 2003 73 per cent of the USN surface fleet was at sea.[23] A large part of the USN's surface fleet is composed of Arleigh Burke destroyers, which are modern, large and very well armed ships. These ships are not necessarily the ideal ships to carry out escort duties as, although very capable of carrying out this task, their advanced weaponry and command and control systems are not needed for the task. Essentially, it was a waste of resources to task these ships for escort duties. However, the USN does not have many 'less sophisticated' surface ships in its order of battle. It does have 30 Oliver Hazard Perry frigates, which are smaller and less advanced than the Arleigh Burkes, but even these are perhaps too advanced for the task. Furthermore, despite being by far the largest navy in the world, the USN does not have the numbers of surface ships required to carry out such a large escort task without unduly burdening the surface fleet. The USN has been aware of this shortfall in its order of battle for a number of years and is intending to remedy it with the new 'littoral combat ship' (LCS), the plan for which was officially launched in November 2001. The LCS has been conceived as a new type of surface ship for the USN, small enough to be able to operate in the shallow waters of the littoral and armed so as to be able to counter the many and varied types of threat likely to be posed in the littoral, such as attacks from small, fast, attack craft, mines, diesel submarines, and so on. It is also intended that the LCS should be sufficiently cheap to design and build that it can be procured in large numbers, with a fleet of 56 currently proposed. Should this be the case, the overstretch in the USN's surface fleet should be eased considerably. However, to date, the design for the LCS has not yet been finalised; the size of the ship is still estimated to be between 600 and 4000 tonnes, which allows for significantly different designs of ship.

The task of escorting allied shipping through the Mediterranean was one which could have been carried out by the European Union (EU) as part of its evolving Common European Security and Defence Policy (CESDP), had there been political will to do so. Currently, the EU's proposed military Rapid Reaction Force has 17 destroyers/frigates and two corvettes committed to it by EU member states.[24] Although these ships are less sophisticated than their US counterparts, they would have been quite capable of carrying out the escort task. Furthermore, several EU member states' navies are experienced in operating together at a sub-NATO level, as the now-defunct Western European Union carried out maritime sanctions operations during the Bosnian crisis in the mid 1990s. Had the EU deployed this component of its Rapid Reaction Force, it could have carried out most of the escorting task in the Mediterranean and thereby relieved some of the burden from the USN's surface fleet. However, as there was clearly no political consensus within the EU about the war with Iraq, no such deployment was made. But it is perhaps instructive to note that this was a military task that the EU had the military capability to undertake.

Coastguard deployments

As already described, almost all the logistics for the allied land campaign were transported to the theatre of operations, or adjacent areas, by sea. Al-Qaeda was believed to pose a threat not only to these logistics when on board ships at sea, but also when alongside in port. Saudi Arabia's ports both in the Red Sea and the Arabian Gulf were understood to be under particular threat. Oil platforms in the Arabian Gulf were also believed to be highly vulnerable to al-Qaeda attack. The US and its allies did not consider that the Saudi Coastguard was able to counter this perceived threat by itself, mainly because of its small size (it has only four large craft[25]). Consequently, on 29 January 2003 the US Coast Guard deployed eight ships to the Saudi coast to protect the country's ports and also oil platforms from possible terrorist attack.[26] The deployment consisted of eight Island class patrol cutters and two port security units. An additional deployment was later made, consisting of the large Dallas class cutter and two further port security units. The latter is defined by the Coast Guard as 'a component of the U.S. Naval Warfare Command, [providing] waterborne and land-based protection for shipping and critical port facilities in support of U.S. and allied naval forces throughout the world'.[27] There were no successful attacks on Saudi ports or oil installations during the course of the war.

Diplomatic role

A further task carried out by the USN was the very traditional role of naval diplomacy. Mainly in order to give visible reassurance to Israel, the US deployed two nuclear-powered aircraft carriers, the *Harry S. Truman* and the *Theodore Roosevelt*, and their accompanying battle groups to the eastern Mediterranean for the duration of the campaign. There were other reasons for the battle groups' deployment, such as guarding the northern approaches to the entrance to the Suez Canal from possible terrorist attack, and providing visible means of support to the allied military installations and supplies on Cyprus. Furthermore, it was perhaps deemed prudent to have two of the five deployed USN aircraft carriers outside the NAG. The *Harry S. Truman* and the *Theodore Roosevelt* did, of course, launch aircraft for attacks on Iraqi targets. However, the deployment's main purpose was to demonstrate US political and military support, to Israel and the rest of the world, for Israel. Such diplomatic tasks are a very old use of naval assets, and a use that is particularly suited to naval forces.

Humanitarian operations

Probably the most important naval contribution to the alliance's humanitarian operations in Iraq was the opening of Iraq's sole deepwater port, Umm Qasr, and the clearance of the approaches to it. This achievement allowed supplies of food and other humanitarian aid to be brought directly to Iraq, rather than be transported by land from Kuwait. The first ship to arrive in Umm Qasr with supplies was the UK's Royal Fleet Auxiliary ship *Sir Galahad* on 28 March 2003, which carried with it about 300 tonnes of supplies. Further deliveries were made thereafter by military, or 'associated-military' shipping, including one by the Spanish navy's landing platform dock *Galicia*, which docked in Umm Qasr on 9 April 2003 and unloaded a field hospital and humanitarian aid to treat Iraqi casualties in country.[28] Commercial merchant shipping arrived in Umm Qasr, for the first time since war began, two days later on 11 April 2003. The first to dock was the UAE-registered *Manar*, which carried 700 tonnes of food, water and humanitarian aid.[29] Both merchant and military supply ships were escorted into the port by naval assets, as there was still believed to be a possible threat of attack from Ba'athist loyalists or al-Qaeda operatives.

The small tonnage of supplies carried by the initial ships to dock, illustrates the point that humanitarian supplies were slow to arrive in Iraq by sea. Deliveries of supply by air obviously are much quicker than those by sea; however, aircraft cannot transport the vast amounts of supplies that ships can. The apparent inadequacy of the response to the post-war humanitarian crisis in Iraq has led some commentators to call for the creation of a type of rapid reaction force of sealift ships in order to transport quickly large quantities of humanitarian aid to an area of need.[30]

Conclusion

The maritime aspect of the war against Iraq in 2003 was, in general, highly successful. No allied shipping, naval or merchant, was successfully attacked; considerable support was given to allied land forces; and no incident of maritime terrorism took place. Naval assets were able to be deployed to the theatre of operations rapidly, and as these assets were mainly from the USN, one can conclude that the fleet's readiness levels are good. Furthermore, the successful nature of the campaign must also demonstrate that the alliance's navies' personnel still retain a high degree of professionalism.

However, some shortcomings in the USN order of battle were evident. Despite nearly a decade of discussion about 'transformation' in US military circles, it would appear that the main way in which the US Navy has been transformed in that time is in size – the USN in 2003 is, in terms of numbers of ships and submarines, about 40 per cent smaller than it was at the time of the First Gulf War in 1991. Although some new capabilities, principally in the form of more precision-guided ordnance for carrier-borne aircraft and fast sealift ships, have been acquired in the last ten years, the USN's assets are still so-called 'legacy systems' most useful for fighting the Cold War, rather than al-Qaeda and littoral warfare against target states. As Admiral Vern Clark, Chief of US Navy Operations, said in August 2003,

What are the greatest and most pressing needs? It is the whole near-land scenario and undersea warfare and mine warfare and the surface threat that exists and sorting all of that out. You're going to need a set of tools to go in there that we need to develop for the future that we don't have in our Navy.[31]

In the 2003 war against Iraq, the USN was able to rely on its allies, in particular the UK Royal Navy, to provide it with some of these assets. Had there been political agreement in the EU on the war with Iraq, even the EU under the CESDP, could have helped the USN in its task of escorting allied shipping through the Mediterranean Sea and thereby ease the USN's overstretch. The USN intends to acquire most of these assets itself in a transformational acquisition package in the next decade. In Clark's words, from the same speech in August 2003:

So in 2004, I want to see the maturation of our investment streams into the combat capability of the future. I think that you all know what those programs are: DD(X) [new destroyer], CVN-21 [new design of aircraft carrier], LCS [littoral combat ship], EA-18G [new carrier-borne fighter aircraft], and Joint Strike Fighter.[32]

It remains to be seen whether the lessons learnt from the 2003 war against Iraq will be sufficiently strong to keep this transformational journey on track, and whether there will be much – or any – effect on European naval cooperation.

Notes

1. *British Maritime Doctrine*, 2nd edn, London, The Stationery Office, 1999, p. 232.
2. Guy Toremans, 'UK Naval Assets Play Major Role in Iraq Conflict', *Jane's Navy International*, 1 May 2003.
3. Ibid.
4. Nick Brown, 'Mine Countermeasures Operation Opens Up Iraq's Seaward Gateway', *Jane's Navy International*, 1 May 2003.
5. Ibid.
6. Ibid.
7. Ibid.
8. Ibid.
9. *British Maritime Doctrine*, p. 228.
10. Nick Brown, 'Naval Assets Crucial to Power Projection for Iraq Land Campaign', *Jane's Navy International*, 1 May 2003.
11. Ibid.
12. Ibid.
13. Ibid.
14. Vice Admiral Sir Jeremy Blackham, 'Early Lessons from Operation Telic', *Jane's Navy International*, 1 May 2003.

15. US Navy news, www.news.navy.mil/search/display.asp?story_id=8169.
16. Brown, 'Naval Assets Crucial'.
17. *Operations in Iraq: Lessons for the Future*, UK Ministry of Defence, 2003, chapter 3: 'Lessons from the Operation', www.mod.uk/publications/iraq_futurelessons/index. html.
18. Ibid.
19. Brown, 'Mine Countermeasures Operation'.
20. Ibid.
21. *British Maritime Doctrine*, p. 232.
22. Toremans, 'UK Naval Assets Play Major Role'.
23. US Navy, *Status of the Navy*, www.chinfo.navy.mil/navpalib/news/.www/status. html.
24. *The Military Balance 2002–2003*, Oxford, Oxford University Press for the International Institute for Strategic Studies, 2002, p. 219 'Selected Military High Readiness Forces' table.
25. Ibid., p. 117.
26. 'CG unites to deploy for Operation Enduring Freedom', *US Coast Guard News*, www.uscg.mil/d5/news/2003/r008-03.html.
27. Ibid.
28. Brown, 'Mine Countermeasures Operation'.
29. Ibid.
30. Blackham, 'Early Lessons from Operation Telic'.
31. Admiral Vern Clark, Edited Remarks, *Navy Times* Editorial Board, Springfield, VA, 13 August 2003.
32. Ibid.

9
The United States and the War on Iraq

Andrew Dorman[1]

Introduction

2003 proved to be a busy year for the United States Administration. In a comparatively short space of time it successfully led a conventional war against Saddam Hussein's regime. America now finds itself at odds with a number of its European and Arab allies and in dispute with the United Nations. This, in part, gave rise to some of President Bush's pessimistic comments in the 2004 State of the Union address.[2] This is in marked contrast to the euphoric message that President Bush gave in early May 2003 on board a US aircraft carrier sailing home from the Persian Gulf where he declared the war over. Since that time the United States has continued to sustain casualties at a far higher rate than that experienced during the 'war' phase. Moreover, despite widespread appeals for support and a significant political effort, the United States Administration finds itself with over 100,000 personnel still deployed in Iraq, hoping that the transfer of power to an interim Iraqi administration will work but with the prospect of the US deployment levels remaining at a significant level for some years to come.[3] With the ongoing commitment to the war against terrorism and support for the new government in Afghanistan, the US Administration has a level of military overstretch unprecedented in recent times and with little prospect of this changing in the foreseeable future.[4]

As a result there have been fears about further attacks in America, in line with the tragic experience of September 11, 2001, and the future does not look good. So far the issue of the war on Iraq has been less important domestically and there was considerable support for President Bush's decision to attack Iraq in 2003.[5] However, in this presidential election year (2004) this may well change. As a contender for the Democratic nomination, Howard Dean used his anti-war views to elicit support quite successfully. Perhaps more importantly, the failure to find weapons of mass destruction might yet have a dramatic impact upon President Bush's chances of re-election, and the resignation of his head of the search team in January 2004 was damaging.[6] The apparent intelligence failure that may have exaggerated the threat posed by such weapons is now subject to an inquiry and, if Tony Blair's experience is anything to go by, this may become a problem for the President that just will not go away. Moreover, unlike previous elections which have been fought on domestic issues, this election may well be fought on foreign policy.

Militarily, the war was also a fascinating experience, and many studies are now under way about the lessons that can be drawn. The planning and preparation for the war brought the US Defense Secretary, Donald Rumsfeld, into conflict with some of his senior commanders about how the war should be conducted. 'Effects-based warfare', 'shock and awe' and the 'Revolution in Military Affairs' are just a few of the terms bandied about by policy makers and analysts, and the war in Iraq may indeed herald a new level in warfare. Nevertheless, the Pentagon has also come in for a considerable amount of criticism for the manner in which it has run the post-hostilities phase of the conflict.

To place this war within the US context, the chapter has been divided into four parts. It will firstly consider the run-up to the war and examine the factors that led to US involvement. Secondly, the chapter will look at the how the war was conducted from a US perspective and consider the extent to which the war can be considered 'transformational'. Thirdly, it will consider how the United States has approached the issue of helping to rebuild Iraq and the problems it has had confronting various opposition groups. Finally, the chapter will reflect on the impact of the war for America.

The United States and the road to war

Virtually all decisions made within a political context are the result of a number of strands coming together, and it is rare that any can ever be seen to be without some degree of muddying of the waters. The controversy that surrounds the decision by the United States Administration to lead a coalition in the invasion of Iraq has divided world opinion and led to the most fundamental divisions between America and parts of Europe that we have seen since the end of the Second World War. France and Germany, in particular, were identified by the US Administration as the leaders against the US, and a division has emerged within the West about how the international system is evolving. Donald Rumsfeld hinted at this when he made reference to 'old and new Europe'.

There are a number of reasons for this. Firstly, for many there is a real concern about the reasoning behind the US decision to go to war. For some the view is that this war had been planned for a number of years and really was a legacy of the failures of the First Gulf War to deal with Saddam Hussein and the threat to Israel. They identify a particular narrow neo-conservative agenda trumpeted by a number within the Administration. This is certainly the argument put forward by Bush's former Treasury Secretary, who argued that Saddam's failure to fully comply with the UN weapons inspectors led by Hans Blix was merely a smokescreen. If this is the case then a number of America's allies, particularly the United Kingdom and Australia, have effectively been duped. Such an agenda, whilst it might have been held by a number, is insufficient to get the US to go to war and underplays the impact of other threads that came together to make the case for the war on Iraq overwhelming for America.

Firstly, the impact of the tragic events of 9/11 cannot be understated. In the space of a few hours the United States lost more people than it did during the Japanese attack on Pearl Harbor in December 1941. Moreover, the majority of those lost were civilians, unlike Pearl Harbor. For many in America there was a loss of innocence and a recognition that they were no longer safe at home. The attack also represented a challenge to the values identified with America. Summing up the situation just over a year after the attack, Bush stated:

> We must also never forget the most vivid events of recent history. On September 11th, 2001, America felt its vulnerability – even to threats that gather on the other side of the earth. We resolved then, and we are resolved today, to confront every threat, from any source, that could bring sudden terror and suffering to America.[7]

Horrific as the attack had been, subsequent investigation indicated that it could have been far worse. It was fortunate that the twin towers collapsed directly downwards. If they had fallen more to one side the casualties would have been far higher and involved far more buildings. Moreover, the fourth airliner that was lost in Pennsylvania never reached its intended target. In his 2004 State of the Union speech, Bush continued to emphasise the impact of 9/11 on policy makers and their thinking:

> Our greatest responsibility is the active defense of the American people. Twenty-eight months have passed since September 11th, 2001 – over two years without an attack on American soil. And it is tempting to believe that the danger is behind us. The hope is understandable, comforting – and false. The killing has continued in Bali, Jakarta, Casablanca, Riyadh, Mombassa, Jerusalem, Istanbul, and Baghdad. The terrorists continue to plot against America and the civilized world. And by our will and our courage, this danger will be defeated.[8]

Former Secretary of State Madeleine Albright has stressed the impact of the tragedy on President Bush. In a piece in *Foreign Affairs* she suggested that:

For President Bush, September 11 came as a revelation, leading him to the startled conclusion that the globe had changed in ways gravely hazardous to the security – indeed, the very survival – of the United States. This conclusion soon led Bush to a fateful decision: to depart, in fundamental ways, from the approach that has characterized US foreign policy for more than half a century. Soon, reliance on alliance had been replaced by redemption through preemption; the shock of force trumped the hard work of diplomacy, and long-term relationships were re-defined.[9]

Secondly, the Bush Administration, like its predecessors, has been concerned about the proliferation of weapons of mass destruction. In the 1993 attempted attack on the World Trade Center, which failed, there was evidence of an attempt to use chemical weapons. The Tokyo underground had been the scene of direct attack, and Iraq was believed to be developing a variety of weapons of mass destruction and had shown a willingness to use chemical weapons against its neighbour – Iran – and against its own people.[10]

In a speech in Cincinnati in the autumn of 2002, President Bush sought to make the case for the war on Iraq based on the fear that Iraq might share its programme with international terrorist groups:

> We know that Iraq and the al Qaeda terrorist network share a common enemy – the United States of America. We know that Iraq and al Qaeda have had high-level contacts that go back a decade. Some al Qaeda leaders who fled Afghanistan went to Iraq. These include one very senior al Qaeda leader who received medical treatment in Baghdad this year, and who has been associated with planning for chemical and biological attacks. We've learned that Iraq has trained al Qaeda members in bomb-making and poisons and deadly gases. And we know that after September 11th, Saddam Hussein's regime gleefully celebrated the terrorist attacks on America.[11]

Iraq could decide on any given day to provide a biological or chemical weapon to a terrorist group or individual terrorists. Alliance with terrorists could allow the Iraqi regime to attack America without leaving any fingerprints.

Finally, the ongoing commitment of US forces in the Middle East as a counter to Saddam Hussein has not been popular within the US Administration. The basing of forces in Saudi Arabia has galvanised Arabic opinion against the United States and in favour of Saddam Hussein, who was seen as the only Arab leader prepared to stand up to America. At the same time the maintenance of the no-fly zones over Northern and Southern Iraq were a drain on the US military and there was concern that at some point an aircraft would be shot down. Moreover, the sanctions policy was seen to be unfair, with the people of Iraq suffering whilst the Iraqi leadership was able to exert an even greater control over their country. The policy was also encouraging anti-American feelings in the region as pictures of the suffering of the Iraqi people were broadcast around the world.

In response to these new threats the US Administration has argued in favour of a policy of pre-emptive action. As Alan Dowd has argued:

> The Bush Doctrine's principle of preemption was tailor-made for Ba'athist Iraq – a country with growing ties to terror, an underground unconventional weapons programme, and the means and motives to mete out revenge on the United States.[12]

In other words there is confluence of elements: the need for the Administration to act before 9/11 is repeated, a concern about weapons of mass destruction, and a frustration over an ongoing commitment to the Middle East which was undermining America's position within the region. Supporting this analysis and running contrary to the right-wing conspiracy argument is the fact that, despite his desire to deal with Iraq, Bush bowed to international pressure, particularly from the United Kingdom, and went the UN route for a short time. However, when UN Security Council Resolution 1441 was perceived to have failed it led to the US commitment to use force against Iraq in March 2003. The Administration was prepared to compromise, but only to a certain degree, and in this Bush had the support of Congress and the American people. Moreover, from a military point of view there was concern about how far America was prepared to delay and then fight in the hottest part of the year.

America and the conduct of the war on Iraq

Planning for war and the conduct of the war can be viewed within two military contexts. Firstly, this war represented a significant change in approach to earlier wars and directly reflected some of the thinking associated with what has come to be known as the 'Revolution in Military Affairs' (RMA).[13] The approach taken was to focus on the desired strategic effect – the bringing down of the Iraqi regime and elimination of its weapons of mass destruction capability. This accorded with traditional Clausewitzian thinking. What had changed was the approach. This shifted away from the destruction of the opponent's military and economic infrastructure as the means of victory to one that looked to removing the regime by the coalition taking control of Baghdad.

Secondly, in comparison to the previous Gulf War, the war goals were different and most importantly involved the occupation of Iraq for a limited time. This dictated different requirements and, in particular, the need to preserve infrastructure for the rebuilding of Iraq mandated by international law. Moreover, this war was not going to be funded by others, so securing Iraq's oil wells and associated infrastructure undamaged was a requirement.

The plan that emerged followed on from a direct clash of view between Donald Rumsfeld, the Secretary of Defense, and the Joint Chiefs. The Bush Administration had come into office defining the new paradigm of warfare.[14] Rumsfeld wanted to fully embrace some of the new ideas encompassed within the RMA debate and fight a war with much smaller forces using speed and surprise to offset their numerical inferiority. The latter, whilst willing to accept this approach in terms of the use of superior technology and maximising their ability to conduct a war with increased tempo, still wanted a larger deployment of forces to minimise the risks involved. With these tensions in-built, the coalition commander, General Tommy Franks, had to play to the coalition's strengths. As a result, the Second Gulf War was significantly different from its predecessor. It involved simultaneous phases of operation rather than a sequential battle – we did not witness an air war consisting of a number of phases followed by a ground war, but in fact once the war officially began there were simultaneous land, air and sea phases with targeting based on achieving a rapid defeat but retaining a relatively intact Iraq.

At sea the coalition had a near monopoly of sea power. Iraq only had a small navy and the principal concerns for the coalition were the Iraqis' use of mines. The coalition were able to deploy sizeable forces at sea, including five US carrier task forces, two US amphibious task forces plus a UK one, together with supporting ships and submarines, a number of which were equipped with some 700 Tomahawk land-attack cruise missiles.

In the air, the size of the coalition force deployed was significantly smaller than for the First Gulf War and it was also more limited in the location of its air bases and the routing of its strike packages. However, there had been a marked capability improvement. There was a stark contrast between the first and second Gulf wars in terms of the number of smart munitions deployed. US forces alone fired 19,269 guided weapons.[15] Overall, 68 per cent of US ordnance deployed was precision-guided.[16]

The challenge for Franks lay in terms of the ground forces. At the start of the war, Iraq still had substantial armour and artillery. Indeed, in terms of troops their numbers were significantly larger. The original plan had been for coalition forces to attack southward from Turkey and northwards from Kuwait. When the Turkish government refused access for coalition forces, their plans were askew. With time running out, Franks intentionally left the equipment of the 4th Infantry Division in the Mediterranean because he knew that it could not be deployed into Kuwait in time for the land offensive, and it also tied up Iraqi forces in the northern part of the country.[17]

At the beginning of the campaign the US had already deployed V Corps to Kuwait, comprising 3rd US Infantry Division, a brigade of the 82nd Airborne Division and the 101st Air Assault Division, although the latter was not fully combat ready at the start of the battle. These were tasked to head straight for Baghdad and seize the city from the southwest. Franks also had the 1st Marine Expeditionary Force, which included the 1st Marine Division and 2nd Marine

Expeditionary Brigade:[18] these were tasked to approach Baghdad from the southeast and help in the seizure of the city. In the south, the British were given responsibility for securing the southern oilfields and making Iraq's second largest city, Basra, safe.

With forces approaching readiness, the exact timing of the operation was altered as a result of intelligence which indicated the location of the Iraqi leader, Saddam Hussein, and his sons. George Bush approved the attempt at a decapitating strike on the Iraqi leadership. The hope was that, if successful, the war could effectively be won before it began, and an air strike was undertaken on the night of 19–20 March with cruise missiles and F-117 aircraft. Unfortunately this was unsuccessful. Having authorised the strike, the planned two- to three-day air campaign of some 3000 precision strikes – 'shock and awe', as the press labelled it – had to be abandoned, and the ground campaign began before the air war as units moved in to seize key Iraqi oilfields before they could be sabotaged, thus safeguarding the future prosperity of the country.

The land campaign witnessed the rapid advance of US forces on Baghdad, bypassing the major urban areas on the way, where possible, to avoid being dragged into street fighting with the various Iraqi militias. There was considerable concern that the Iraqi regime might use weapons of mass destruction as US forces approached Baghdad, but this proved not to be the case. To maximise speed, Franks accepted that his lines of communication, along which his supplies would flow, would be vulnerable and there was evidence of this occurring with casualties incurred amongst these support troops. By 5 April, US forces were already on the outskirts of Baghdad despite heavy sandstorms which had slowed the advance. In the north, Kurdish forces were utilised to pin Iraqi troops down and the 173rd Airborne Brigade was flown into the area. To the west, the US used Special Forces to spread confusion and seize key airfields. With forces approaching Baghdad, a series of raids were undertaken, and when the opposition proved lighter than expected, US forces went into Baghdad and seized it. Forces were subsequently deployed to the north of Baghdad and the coalition had effective control far earlier than anyone had imagined.

The post-hostilities phase

At the beginning of May, George Bush confirmed in a speech made aboard a US aircraft carrier returning from Iraq that the war was officially over.[19] The assumption for many within the Bush Administration and, in particular, the Pentagon was that the hard work had been done. However, this has not proved to be the case and it is clear that winning the peace has proved to be far harder than winning the war. Nevertheless, the US Administration has stuck to the task, and the subsequent capture of Saddam Hussein appeared to lead to an overall reduction in the level of opposition to the US coalition. However, this has not been the case in some areas, particularly around Fallujah.

What the Iraq experience has shown is that the transition from war fighting to what was referred to as the post-hostilities phase is very challenging and that the new form of warfare which involves smaller dispersed forces is in many ways the exact opposite of what is required for the subsequent peace. According to John MacKinlay:

> The sudden role change dictates a commensurately sudden transfiguration of tactics, attitude and body language. The certainties of war fighting, the overwhelming use of firepower and the multiplying advantages of technology, air cover and area weapons are largely removed. Internal security tasks are manpower intensive and influenced by principles that are antithetical to war fighting.[20]

The mission therefore needed the same level of planning effort as that put into the war-fighting side, but this was not the case. This failure was the first of a series of mistakes made by the US Administration, and it failed to develop a co-coordinated cross-government approach to Iraq. Rumsfeld insisted that the Department of Defense be given responsibility for running Iraq, but they underestimated the scale of the reconstruction task. Iraq's infrastructure had been neglected for over 20 years, firstly as a result of the Iran–Iraq War, then the impact of the First Gulf War and the sanctions that followed. The US Administration had assumed that if the Ba'athist echelons of the Iraqi regime were removed from power in Iraq, then a new government could be formed by ordinary Iraqis. However, the Ba'ath party had been in control for some 40 years and had penetrated every aspect of society. The scale of change was therefore far greater. Institutions such as the army and police virtually disappeared overnight, and in the immediate aftermath of the removal of Saddam's regime there was widescale looting of the remaining infrastructure such as hospitals.[21]

The problems of fighting light and smart meant that there were too few people available following the fall of the Iraqi regime to provide basic security, and the widespread looting that followed caused further significant damage to the infrastructure, which now needs repairing. It is also worth noting that the problems were unevenly distributed and parts of the country were quite peaceful. The Americans took responsibility for the most challenging areas to the north of Baghdad where the Sunni minority was based. The situation in the south around Basra was easier because it largely consisted of Shia, who had been a repressed majority under Saddam. Equally, the Kurdish north was far quieter and less problematic.

More fundamentally, on the political side the development of new political structures for Iraq has been particularly challenging.[22] The dilemma for the US Administration is how to introduce democracy but ensure that the government that emerges is not anti-American. If the democratic system installed is based simply on a majority viewpoint, then Iraq would be dominated by the Shia majority and there is the possibility that they will insist on a Shia Islamic state similar to neighbouring Iran. This would inevitably result in a Sunni and Kurdish backlash and the opposition of the majority of neighbouring states. Moreover, any threat to the Christian minority would also be adverse to a US Administration domestically, which is more overtly Christian than many of its predecessors. The US Administration has therefore sought to develop a democratic model similar to its own, where majority and minority rights are preserved; in the case of America, through the rights of the individual (House of Representatives) and the rights of the state (Senate). This might work for Iraq for it would allow the Sunni and Kurdish minorities to counter the Shia majority and force them in theory to cooperate. However, the problem with such a system is that it looks very close to America's own system of government and therefore might be seen as an attempt by America to impose its own views on Iraq. Moreover, the Shia leaders are well aware of US aims and this is one of the reasons why they are insisting that the transitional government that creates the new constitution is democratically elected and thus subject to the Shia majority's viewpoint.[23] The Kurds are also opposed, arguing for their own independence and the division of Iraq. Such a solution would not be in the interests of Turkey, an important US ally, and the US has sought to keep Iraq intact. Time will tell how successful this is now that power has been transferred to the interim administration. If the security situation continues to deteriorate or the different groups divide, then civil war will result, with the US-led coalition stuck in the middle.

Although the level of opposition has diminished there is still a requirement for a considerable US military presence, and the US casualty figures continue to grow beyond those of the 'war'. Opponents to the coalition can be divided into four groupings, according to General John Abizaid:

1. 'The clear and most dangerous enemy to us at the present time are the former regime loyalists.'
2. 'The extremists are those that can fill a large number of different groupings. They represent religious extremists, they represent national extremists that may or may not have been associated with the Ba'athists, yet nevertheless desire to fight the coalition, and to ensure that no moderate Iraqi government emerges.'
3. 'There are a large number of criminals that are hired by the Ba'athists and the extremists to do their dirty work. As a matter of fact, in most of the cases of direct-fire engagements that our troops have, they find very young, out-of-work men that have been paid to attack our forces, and it is very important that as we progress militarily, we also progress politically and economically so as to get these young men, these angry young men off the streets.'

4. 'There are a small, yet important and well organized, group of foreign
   fighters, some of whom have been operating in Iraq for a long time, many
   of whom are infiltrating across various borders.'[24]

This has required the retention of a large military presence in Iraq and
necessitated rebuilding the Iraqi army, border and civilian police forces. This
has been a slow process and the US has looked for international support to
help reduce the US burden. Here it has been least successful, and the loss of
the Spanish contribution after the Madrid bombings was a real setback.[25]
In the southeast, the United Kingdom has taken responsibility for the Basra
region and a Polish-led multinational division has taken responsibility for
an area south of Baghdad and north of Basra. The US Administration has
sought additional allied contributions to take over a major area. The Indians,
Germans, French and South Koreans have all been approached to supply a
divisional headquarters, but their refusal has forced the US to retain force levels
greater than during the war.[26] As a result, by December 2003 the US military
were planning for a deployment of at least a further two years, but almost
certainly far longer, with 13 brigades earmarked, including reserve units.[27]
Despite these problems, the US has remained committed to the rebuilding
of Iraq. The scale of US financial support has been quite staggering. For
example, in September 2003 the US Administration requested $20.3 billion
from Congress to help rebuild Iraq.[28] This was just part of an $87 billion
supplement for the next fiscal year aimed at supporting the war on terrorism
in Iraq and Afghanistan. Senate finally approved an $87.5 billion package in
November.[29] How long the US will continue this given its own budget is a
matter of debate. The US budget is running a significant financial deficit, and
it is difficult to see US public opinion continuing to tolerate large expenditure
in Iraq whilst there are reductions in areas at home. The Bush Administration's
'mismanagement' of Iraq is one area that his Democrat opponents will seek
to exploit during the presidential election of 2004, although John Kerry, the
Democratic contender, has been very quiet on this issue to date. President
Bush is the first President since Herbert Hoover to see an overall drop in the
size of the workforce, and jobs rather than the economy are like to be the key
electoral issue. The continuation of expenditure on Iraq rather than jobs at
home may well determine the future presidency and Iraq policy.

Reflections on the American experience

For America the war on Iraq has been a sobering experience. As a result of
the decision to go to war, America finds itself more isolated within the world
than it has for some time. Traditional European allies such as France and
Germany found themselves at odds with the US viewpoint.[30] For the former
this has resulted in a long-term cooling of the US-French relationship. French
opposition to the war in Iraq and French opposition to the US dominance of

NATO have been linked and identified as a general anti-Americanism within the French political elite that can be traced back several decades. By way of contrast, the cooled relationship with Germany has been identified as a short-term one surrounding the current German administration. Many within the US government assume that the US-German relationship will be restored over time as Germany returns to a more transatlantic emphasis. What the opposition of the German and French governments has done is to encourage US support for the membership of both NATO and the European Union by the newly democratic states of central and eastern Europe who are generally in favour of the transatlantic relationship. The situation has not been helped by French and German calls for the development of an independent European military power projection capability through the European Union. To offset this, the Bush Administration has pushed for NATO transformation so that it may remain the key European security alliance.

At the same time, however, the size of the US commitment of military forces to both Afghanistan and Iraq has encouraged the US to seek a greater role in NATO. NATO has taken over responsibility for the International Security Assistance Force (ISAF) and with US encouragement is slowly expanding ISAF's remit beyond Kabul.[31] However, a significant US presence remains. For NATO's other members the issues of transformation and an enlarged Afghanistan commitment may be more than they are financially prepared to countenance.

The war has also had a detrimental impact on how America is viewed within the wider Arab world.[32] The war on Iraq appears to have stalled the US attempts to resolve the Israeli-Palestinian issue, and the current Administration has appeared more pro-Israeli than some of its predecessors. As a result, there has been much hostility to the US, and its influence has diminished as the leadership of its allies in the region seeks to be less publicly associated with it.

The experience in Iraq has also given further impetus to the review of US military deployments around the world.[33] Proponents of transformation are encouraging a lighter forward presence of forces and instead an increased ability to rapidly deploy from mainland America. This will undoubtedly impact upon Germany most of all, where the US currently deploys two of its ten divisions. The level of US withdrawal remains to be agreed, but it will undoubtedly be significant and it has been seen by some as part of the punishment for Germany's lack of support.

For America the war with Iraq has also raised important questions about the issue of military transformation. One commentator writing in the US Navy's journal *Proceedings* noted that 'we tend to defeat the enemy in battle, and we tend not to win the wars lately'.[34] The traditional Clausewitzian view that you defeat the enemy on the battlefield reflects wars of a previous era. Zinni, a former head of Central Command, went on:

The military traditionally is supposed to go out there and kill people and break things ... The military does a damn good job of killing people and breaking things. We can design a better rifle squad, build a better fighter, a better ship, a better tank. We are so far ahead of any potential enemy right now in those kinds of technological areas, in the areas of expertise of quality of leadership, and all the things that make military units great on the battlefield, that you wonder why we keep busting brain cells wondering how to do it better, or to transform into something else ... But that is not the problem nor has it been in the past.[35]

What is the role of the military beyond killing people and breaking things? The lessons being taken out of the Iraq experience by the Americans are twofold. Firstly, that transformation needs to continue, and secondly that counter-insurgency needs to be revisited and lessons learned from allied experience. Opponents are unlikely to play to America's military strengths – asymmetric warfare – which will most likely be the future face of conflict. Within this there are a number of other lessons that need to be drawn out. Firstly, parallel rather than sequential warfare is here to stay, with forces having to engage in a variety of different operations at the same time. This requires not only joint forces but also the different elements of government being brought together. You cannot run wars entirely from the Department of Defense alone; other government agencies need to be incorporated if the peace is to be won.

Secondly, whilst transformation may allow you to win wars with smaller, more technologically focused units, as Iraq showed, winning the peace requires far greater levels of personnel and this in part explains the calls for an expansion of the army.[36] Winning the peace may in fact require a larger ground force and this then needs to be sustained via a process of troop rotation. In other words, transformation is not just about equipment and military organisation for war. It is also about a change in the approach to war as a whole from initial diplomacy through to the reconstruction phase, to specialise in one element only is to court disaster.

Notes

1. The analysis, opinions and conclusions expressed or implied in this chapter are those of the author and do not necessarily represent the views of the JSCSC, the UK MoD or any other government agency. The research undertaken in support of this paper was funded by a grant from the Leverhulme Trust for a study on 'British Defence Adaptation in the post-Cold War World'.
2. President George W. Bush, State of the Union address, 2004, 20 January 2004, www.whitehouse.gov.
3. IISS, *The Military Balance, 2003–4*, Oxford, Oxford University Press for the IISS, 2003, p. 26.

4. 'What has U.S. Learned?', *Armed Forces Journal*, May 2003, p. 24; Stephen Farrell, 'The biggest US troop changeover since 1945 gets under way', *The Times*, 17 January 2004, p. 17.
5. 'What has U.S. Learned?', p. 24.
6. Catherine Philip, Stephen Farrell and Daniel McGary, 'Weapons chief delivers final blow as No.10 emerges from its trauma', *The Times*, 26 January 2004.
7. 'President Bush outlines Iraqi threat', Cincinnati, Ohio, 7 October 2002, www. whitehouse.gov/news/releases/2002/10/20021007-8.html.
8. State of the Union address, 2004.
9. Madeleine K. Albright, 'Bridges, Bombs or Bluster?', *Foreign Affairs*, September/ October 2003, p. 3.
10. 'President Bush outlines Iraqi threat'.
11. Ibid.
12. Alan W. Dowd, 'Thirteen Years: The Causes and Consequences of the War in Iraq', *Parameters*, Vol. XXXIII, No. 3, Autumn 2003, p. 48; see also George W. Bush, *The National Security Strategy of the United States of America*, Washington, DC, The White House, 20 September 2002, www.whitehouse.gov.
13. See, for example, Michael Russell Rip, *The Precision Revolution: GPS and the Future of Aerial Warfare*, Annapolis, MD, Naval Institute Press, 2002; Colonel John B. Alexander, *Winning the War: Advanced Weapons, Strategies, and Concepts for the post-9/11 World*, New York, St Martin's Press, 2003; Admiral Bill Owens with Ed Offley, *Lifting the Fog of War*, Baltimore, MD, Johns Hopkins University Press, 2001; Robert J. Bunker, ed., *Non-State Threats and Future Wars*, London, Frank Cass, 2003.
14. William P. Hawkins, 'Iraq: Heavy Forces and Decisive Warfare', *Parameters*, Vol. XXXIII, No. 3, Autumn 2003, p. 61.
15. Lt General T. Michael Mosley, 'Operation Iraqi Freedom – By the numbers', USCENTAF, Assessment and Analysis Division, 30 April 2003.
16. See ibid.
17. Anthony H. Cordesman, *The Iraq War: Strategy, Tactics and Military Lessons*, Westport, CT, Praeger, 2003, p. 59.
18. Ibid., pp. 37–8.
19. David E. Sanger, 'President says military phase in Iraq has ended', *New York Times*, 2 May 2003, p. 1.
20. John MacKinlay, 'Iraq Campaign Failed to Plan for Peacekeeping', *Jane's Intelligence Review*, June 2003, p. 37.
21. 'US scrambles to rebuild Iraqi Army. Decision to disband force seen by some as a major postwar mistake', *Washington Post*, 20 November 2003, p. 1.
22. Suzanne Goldenberg, 'White House rethinks Iraq plan', *Guardian*, 14 January 2004, p. 17.
23. Roland Watson and Richard Lloyd Parry, 'Bush forced to rethink plans for the transfer of power', *The Times*, 17 January 2004, p. 24.
24. General John Abizaid, DOD News Briefing, 13 November 2003.
25. Dana Milbank and Colum Lynch, 'Bush fails to gain pledges on troops or funds for Iraq. National Guard, reserve may plug holes', *Washington Post*, 25 September 2003.
26. 'US requests ROK troops to replace 101st Airborne', *Korea Times*, 3 October 2003.
27. 'US General: Forces will remain for couple of years', *USA Today*, 17 December 2003, p. 1.

28. Vernon Loeb, 'US tells how billions of dollars would rebuild Iraq. $4 million for area codes, $303 million for railroads, $240 million for road and bridge repairs', *Washington Post*, 25 September 2003.

29. 'Senate approves spending for Iraq: $87.5 Billion Package Set for Bush to Sign', *Washington Post*, 4 November 2003.

30. Barry Renfrew, 'Trans-Atlantic Alliance still shaken by Iraqi dispute', Associated Press, 22 December 2003, via NATO Enlargement Daily Brief, Tuesday 23 December 2003.

31. Judy Dempsey, 'NATO to reinforce ISAF', *Financial Times*, 2 December 2003.

32. 'What has U.S. Learned?'

33. 'US advances plan to redeploy forces in Europe', *Wall Street Journal*, 9 January 2004.

34. Anthony Zinni, 'Understanding What Victory Is', *Proceedings*, October 2003, p. 32.

35. Ibid., pp. 32–3.

36. William Matthews, 'Is the US Military too Small?', *Defense News*, 12 January 2004, pp. 4, 8.

10
Iraq's Asymmetric Counter-Strategy
Wyn Q. Bowen

... attacking an adversary's weaknesses with unexpected or innovative means while avoiding his strengths is as old as warfare itself.[1]

The concept of asymmetry revolves primarily around the significant and growing gap in conventional military capabilities between the United States and its allies, on one hand, and adversaries such as the Saddam regime and al-Qaeda, on the other. In short, developing states and terrorist organisations do not possess, and cannot afford, the capabilities to guarantee victory in a conventionally symmetrical conflict with the United States. Consequently, the only option is to seek to circumvent US superiority by avoiding direct force-on-force confrontations and to focus instead on key political and military weaknesses using unconventional, or 'asymmetric', strategies. A key political weakness is often said to be the West's sensitivity to casualties (friendly military, civilian and enemy military) especially in situations where less than vital interests are at stake. Examples of such strategies cited throughout the literature on asymmetry include: the threat and use of chemical, biological, radiological and nuclear weapons on the battlefield or against civilian targets; threats or acts of terrorism against military or civilian targets; irregular warfare in urban environments; the use of propaganda and disinformation to undermine support for military action and to complicate decision making; and information attacks against military and civilian computer systems and networks.

It should be noted that conflict can also be influenced by other asymmetries. A significant mismatch of interests at stake between adversaries can influence the resolve of all combatants to realise their objectives, whether stated or otherwise. However, the recent Iraq conflict did not appear to be characterised by a significant imbalance in this area between the Coalition and the regime. Fundamental differences can also exist between opponents in terms of their culture, mind-set and world-view. Differences here can result in divergent political and ethical constraints on what is perceived to be permissible in conflict. This was most certainly the case in the 2003 war in Iraq.[2]

This chapter examines the asymmetric strategy adopted by the Saddam Hussein regime against the Coalition prior to and during 'major combat operations' in Iraq.[3] The aim is not to present an in-depth analysis of Operation Iraqi Freedom/Telic, but rather to offer an initial assessment, based on open sources, of the political and military counter-strategy implemented by Iraq. The first section offers a brief definition of 'asymmetric warfare'. The chapter then assesses the pre-conflict stage of the Iraq crisis. The focus here is on the political and other approaches adopted by the Saddam regime in its failed attempt to avert a military conflict. The third section examines the asymmetric postures and methods adopted by the regime during major combat operations. The Coalition's pre-conflict concerns are highlighted and in each area their failure to fully materialise is examined. It is concluded that four principal factors explain the poor showing of Iraq's asymmetric counter-strategy:

- The Coalition succeeded in applying superior conventional military force to overwhelm a militarily ineffective and weak adversary
- The regime's counter-strategy during major combat operations lacked the necessary foundations, including popular support amongst the general Iraqi population, to put up a significant challenge. This is not to say the regime's long-term aim did not involve drawing the Coalition into a protracted and costly occupation of Iraq
- The Coalition fully appreciated the asymmetric challenges that the regime could potentially throw up and put in place the necessary preparations to deal with them both politically and militarily
- Iraq's asymmetric strategy was only workable if its opponent lacked the stomach to enforce regime change and to take some significant risks in the process. However, the regime failed to read correctly, chose to ignore, or was powerless to negate the solidity of the Bush Administration's post-9/11 resolve to address perceived threats through pre-emptive military action.

Pre-conflict

Baghdad's pre-conflict strategy aimed to avoid a military conflict by shaping the international debate over Iraq. By influencing this debate, the regime sought to convince Washington and London that the costs of military action would far outweigh the gains. The potential costs included a divided international community, a diplomatic crisis amongst the five Permanent Members (the P-5) of the UN Security Council, deep disagreements within NATO and the European Union, domestic political dissent, a messy and prolonged conflict, and wider instability in the Middle East and beyond. The potential gains included the removal of Saddam's regime as a destabilising influence in the region and the negation of Iraq's WMD capabilities.

A divided international community

The Saddam regime sought to generate a diplomatic crisis for the United States and the United Kingdom by playing on the lack of consensus amongst the major powers on how to deal with Iraq's disarmament. Although there was a general agreement that Baghdad was not fulfilling completely its disarmament obligations, serious differences of opinion existed on whether or not military force should be used. The US and the British governments believed that military action was a reasonable and necessary step on the escalation ladder to coerce the regime into fuller cooperation with the weapons inspectors, and ultimately to enforce disarmament through regime change if Baghdad continued to subvert the inspection process. This view emphasised the importance of building up a military presence for coercive purposes. In contrast, France, Russia, China and Germany wanted to resolve the issue without resort to war.

It appears the regime believed that Washington and London would not risk going to war without the backing of the UN Security Council. After the passage of UN Security Council Resolution 1441, Baghdad followed a strategy of partial and incremental cooperation with the UN inspectors. This was designed to split international opinion over the need for harsher action to be taken against the regime. The aim was to provide just enough cooperation to convince France, Russia, China and Germany that sufficient progress was being made to warrant a continuation of the diplomatic and UN disarmament process. Ultimately, this approach generated an unprecedented diplomatic crisis between the P-5 states over how to deal with Baghdad. On 5 March 2003, the diplomatic crisis reached its nadir when France, Russia and China made it clear they would not allow the passage of a new resolution that paved the way for war. Saddam Hussein's regime could not have hoped for a more favourable outcome in this respect.

Visions of mayhem and destruction

During the pre-conflict stage, the regime also sought to paint visions of mass casualties, mayhem and instability if the Coalition opted for military action. In part, the aim was to generate popular and political concern in the US, the UK and elsewhere over the potentially high casualty rate among both Coalition personnel and Iraq's civilian population. Before the war, Iraqi Vice-President Taha Yassin Ramadhan predicted that 'If US B-52s can kill 500 people at a time, operations by freedom fighters will be able to kill 5000 people.'[4] Moreover, Saddam's partial cooperation with the UN inspectors strongly suggested that the regime did have something to hide in the WMD field, especially given the materials highlighted by the UN inspectors that remained unaccounted for. The lack of WMD discoveries since the end of the war has led to speculation that the regime may have pretended to hand out chemical weapons to field commanders in an attempt to deter Coalition action through fear of the consequences of doing so.[5]

Prior to the war the regime also released from prison thousands of criminals.[6] Although this decision may have been taken to generate the image of a regime moderating its ways, in order to undermine international support for military action, it could also have been designed to feed perceptions of pending mayhem. Another approach may have been the regime's decision to pay compensation to the families of Palestinian suicide bombers in order to stir up the Israeli-Palestinian conflict.[7] The aim here may have been to distract international attention from Iraq to complicate US war planning. In short, it seems the regime sought to stir up instability in the wider Middle East in the hope that the Coalition would not risk an invasion for fear of alienating the Arab world.

Coalition resolve

Ultimately, of course, Saddam's pre-conflict strategy failed because war was not averted. The Bush Administration, and the Blair government, demonstrated sufficient resolve to launch a military campaign despite the lack of international support, the risk of generating political dissent at home, the prospect of a potentially messy and protracted conflict, and the prospect of a further destabilised Middle East.

After the war, US Secretary of Defense Donald Rumsfeld said the United States acted in Iraq because it saw the evidence of Iraq's WMD programmes and concealment 'in a new light – through the prism of our experience on 9/11'. According to Rumsfeld,

> On that day we saw thousands of innocent men, women and children, killed by terrorists. And that experience changed our appreciation of our vulnerability – and the risks the US faces from terrorist states and terrorist networks armed with weapons of mass murder.[8]

What this suggests is that the failure of Iraq's pre-conflict strategy was due to an important degree to the solidity of the Bush Administration's resolve to take preventive military action to counter perceived threats at source. Indeed, prior to 9/11, American policy on Iraq, and the issue of disarmament, appeared to favour continued containment together with greater use of 'smart' sanctions to target the regime rather than the Iraqi people. However, the loss of so many civilian lives on American soil radically altered the Bush Administration's threat perception and its resolve to tackle perceived threats. Along with destroying and disrupting al-Qaeda in Afghanistan and elsewhere, the perceived threat posed by Iraq and its WMD became a key focus of the Bush Administration from early 2002. The Administration's resolve was also bolstered by broad-based popular support for military action against the Saddam regime. So while Saddam succeeded in fracturing international opinion and dividing the Security Council, this was not sufficient to undermine US resolve to go to war and sustain a military campaign.

Could Saddam have avoided war?

It is possible that the Saddam regime could have averted war if the decision had been taken in February or March to cooperate much more fully with the UN inspectors. Such a decision would have pulled the carpet from underneath the Coalition's, and in particular Britain's, rationale for war. Why, then, did the regime not choose this approach? Did the regime misread the resolve of the Coalition to go to war without international support? Did the regime perceive that for reasons of internal and external security it could not be seen to give in completely on the WMD issue? Did Saddam perceive that the United States was going to attack Iraq and force regime change regardless of anything Baghdad did to demonstrate cooperation with the weapons inspectors? Did Saddam believe he could survive a military conflict that was aimed at toppling his regime? Did he believe that Iraq possessed the appropriate strategy and capabilities to avoid defeat or at least politically to outlast the Coalition in a prolonged and messy war? These are all key questions, yet they remain difficult if not impossible to answer without open access to the regime's key decision makers.

Major combat operations

As widely predicted beforehand, the war itself was not a conventional conflict because there was no direct force-on-force military confrontation. The vast disparity in conventional military power meant the Saddam regime had no choice other than to challenge the Coalition indirectly, or asymmetrically. Given the rapid conclusion of major combat operations, it is evident that the regime's asymmetric challenge proved to be largely ineffective. In July 2003, the UK MoD provided a succinct summary of the regime's efforts to fight the Coalition:

> Clearly, despite their numerical advantage, the Iraqis could not expect to match the coalition in regular combat. Even so, the failure of Saddam's regime to employ its conventional military capabilities to best effect was striking. This may reflect the undermining of its command and control mechanisms early in the coalition campaign, as well as the reluctance of regular forces to fight in defence of an unpopular regime.
> The Iraqi regular army put up stiff resistance in places, but mostly either surrendered or fled, abandoning their equipment and clothing. The greater threat to the coalition, particularly to lines of communication and rear areas, was from paramilitary and irregular forces closely associated with

the Saddam regime. Such forces were also probably responsible for much of the resistance encountered from regular army units that did fight, whose soldiers in some cases appeared to have been coerced by threats against themselves and their families.[9]

According to one commentator,

Iraqi strategy was largely inept, its forces used outdated and in many cases worn-out equipment, and air superiority was accomplished prior to the outbreak of hostilities. In Iraq our fiercest opponents were the Saddam Fedayeen and the foreign volunteers, who were both motivated by ideological factors.[10]

In July 2003, US Secretary of Defense Donald Rumsfeld told the Senate Armed Services Committee that several things the Coalition potentially expected to occur did not because of 'the speed and flexibility of the war plan'. Among other things, Rumsfeld noted: Iraq's neighbours were not hit with Scud missiles; the majority of Iraq's oilfields were not burned; there were no massive civilian casualties; there were no large masses of refugees fleeing across Iraq's borders; there was no large-scale collateral damage.[11]

Despite this poor showing, the Coalition certainly had some very specific concerns about the asymmetric options potentially available to the regime once major combat operations commenced. In part, these concerns were fed by the regime's attempts to paint a picture of doom if the Coalition opted for war. They were also influenced heavily by Coalition experiences of Iraqi counter-measures during the 1990–91 crisis and conflict.

WMD and theatre ballistic missiles

One of the Coalition's main concerns was that Iraq would use chemical weapons, biological weapons and theatre ballistic missiles against Coalition forces, Coalition allies (such as Kuwait and Saudi Arabia) and potentially Israel, along the lines of 1991. UN assessments of Iraq's unaccounted for WMD meant the regime's arsenal potentially included: chemical agents such as sulphur mustards, sarin, tabun and VX; biological agents such as anthrax and botulinum toxin; with delivery options including artillery shells/rockets, ballistic missile warheads, aerial bombs and mines.

The UK MoD noted in July 2003 that 'It was judged that the regime might use theatre ballistic missiles and possibly weapons of mass destruction if it could make the capabilities available for operational use and secure the obedience of subordinate commanders.'[12] Prior to the conflict, it is evident that British intelligence viewed chemical and biological use as a serious prospect in the event of the crisis developing into war. The 19 September 2002 draft of the British government's dossier on Iraq's WMD programmes noted that

... intelligence indicates that Saddam is prepared to use chemical and biological weapons if he believes his regime is under threat. We also know from intelligence that as part of Iraq's military planning, Saddam is willing to use chemical and biological weapons against an internal uprising by the Shia population. Intelligence indicates that the Iraqi military are able to deploy chemical or biological weapons within forty five minutes of an order to do so.[13]

Concerns about Iraq's chemical, biological and missile potential meant the Coalition had to put in place plans to prevent the use of, and to defend against, such weapons. For example, one of the air campaign tasks was 'to deter and counter the threat from theatre ballistic missiles, especially in the west of Iraq'. The prospect of chemical and biological use also vindicated the Coalition's emphasis on chemical, biological and nuclear (CBN) protection and training for deployed forces.[14]

During the conflict itself, Iraq responded to the decapitation strike of 20 March 2003 by launching five non-Scud missiles into Kuwait. More of these missiles were fired later and Coalition forces and civilians in Kuwait wore CBN protective clothing as a precaution. Aside from some limited missile attacks, the conflict did not witness the use of chemical and biological weapons and no Scud-derived missiles were launched against Israel, Turkey or Saudi Arabia. The lack of use could be explained in a number of ways.

The first possible explanation might be that Iraq no longer possessed chemical and biological weapons and Scud-type missiles. The failure so far of the Iraq Survey Group to uncover significant evidence of such capabilities since the end of the war seems to give credence to the argument that the regime destroyed these capabilities in line with UN demands either in the 1990s or following the return of inspectors between November 2002 and March 2003. In such a scenario it is possible that the regime opted not to offer evidence of destruction in order to keep the Coalition guessing about Iraq's WMD capabilities and thereby deter war.

A second explanation could be that the regime concealed its special weapons capabilities so deeply that it became too difficult to use them.[15] Indeed, British Prime Minister Tony Blair has noted that 'One advantage of this programme of concealment is that it places an inhibition on his [Saddam's] ability to use these weapons quickly.' The Prime Minister also noted that he did not have 'specific intelligence' on why Saddam did not use WMD, but added that 'he believed the dictator began a programme of concealment last September [2003]'.[16]

Another possible explanation might be that the regime was dissuaded from using these weapons. For example, the Coalition dropped 40 million leaflets into Iraq prior to and during the war, many of which urged Iraqi commanders not to use WMD. According to Vice Admiral Timothy Keating, head of US naval forces in the Gulf, the fact that Iraq did not launch any Scuds may have been directly attributable to this aspect of the campaign. Others have suggested that it may have been the persistence of coalition 'eyes and ears' in the air and on ground that deterred such action.[17]

While it is conceivable that Iraqi field commanders might have disobeyed orders to use chemical and biological weapons, it is unlikely that Saddam and his immediate entourage would have been deterred from issuing the orders. The inner circle had nothing to lose in this respect because the Coalition's aim was to remove the regime from power. Moreover, the regime had used chemical weapons and Scud-type missiles in past conflicts.

A fourth possible explanation could be that Iraqi command and control deteriorated so rapidly that this prevented the use of chemical and biological weapons. At least one commentator has argued that this explanation seems improbable.

> Although the victory of US and British forces was rapid, it wasn't that rapid. The war went on for three weeks, and Iraqi units mounted a credible resistance with conventional forces. Moreover, Baghdad had months to prepare for the US-led assault. That seems more than enough time to prepare attacks with unconventional weapons.[18]

Finally, there is the possibility that the regime gave some of its special weapons capabilities to a third party or parties. Recipients could have included terrorist organisations or countries like Syria. Indeed, there were reports of Israeli origin in the months running up to the war that Iraq's WMD had been evacuated to Syria and perhaps beyond.[19] Arguably, the likelihood of the regime providing terrorist groups with such capabilities could have increased when its survival was at stake and it had nothing left to lose.

Whatever the reason, or combination of reasons, for Iraq's non-use of WMD, the evidence issue raises the question of whether pre-war intelligence was faulty, or inflated to make the case for war. In this respect, the war is still being fought out in the political corridors of London and Washington.

Maritime environment

In the maritime environment the Coalition expected that Iraq might employ asymmetric methods such as 'random mining, suicide boats and surface-to-surface missiles'. Intelligence 'indicated that Iraq would try to repeat its tactic from the 1991 Gulf conflict of deploying hundreds of sea mines to deny freedom of manoeuvre to coalition forces in Iraqi and Kuwaiti coastal waters and rivers'.[20] The commander of the task group of Australian ships, Captain Peter Jones, noted that 'small boats on suicide missions' represented 'the most prevalent threat to ships in the Gulf'.[21] There were also concerns that 'Iraq might use aircraft or weapons of mass destruction' against Coalition naval forces in the Gulf. During the conflict, although the Coalition seized some 200 mines on two captured Iraqi tugs as well as six Iraqi patrol craft in Umm Qasr,[22] the worst-case projections did not materialise.

Iraqi pre-emption

The Coalition was concerned that the regime might launch 'pre-emptive strikes against Iraq's neighbours and/or coalition forces in the region'. The UK Ministry of Defence was particularly anxious that this might result from delays in the Coalition's military planning and preparation.[23] Again, this concern proved unfounded, possibly because the regime believed it could avert war by dividing the international community. Indeed, any attempt to pre-empt before Coalition forces had built up would have been undermined by this approach and strengthened the Coalition's hand.

Opportunist terrorist attacks

Beyond the asymmetric challenge posed by the regime itself, the Coalition was also concerned about the potential for terrorist organisations – such as those affiliated with al-Qaeda – to launch opportunistic attacks once major combat operations began. However, the Coalition did not suffer from any such attacks either in theatre or at home. This outcome led one commentator to remark:

> Not for the first time, western provocation has been met by great bravado – promises of terrible deeds and waves of volunteers surging against the imperialists. Yet the response has in fact been feeble and futile. The credibility of Islamic militancy has been undermined. It would be unwise to relax and assume the best; but any attack now would be to revenge military defeat rather than to aid victory.[24]

Western intelligence agencies had expected the worst because terrorist acts were threatened by Osama bin Laden. The Royal Navy certainly planned for potential terrorist attacks by committing 'significant resources' to protect 60 UK chartered merchant ships bringing in military equipment and 16 high-value Royal Naval and Royal Fleet Auxiliary vessels. Moreover, the Royal Navy allocated more than 50 per cent of the deployable fleet to escort duties 'in known threat areas and choke points',[25] such as the Strait of Hormuz at the base of the Gulf.

Protracted guerrilla and urban warfare

The prospect of a drawn-out campaign of urban warfare against Iraqi forces fighting street by street was also high on the list of Coalition concerns. Anxieties were probably exacerbated by Iraqi statements prior to the war about the prospect of thousands of casualties.[26] A preliminary assessment of Iraq's asymmetric counter-strategy suggests that the regime certainly sought to bog down the Coalition in urban warfare against a mix of regular and irregular forces, and to use cities as sanctuaries from which to launch attacks against the Coalition. The regime's aim appeared to be to prolong conflict in an attempt to outlast its adversary politically. However, a long-drawn-out war did not occur as some predicted it might.

The Coalition faced a relatively complex mix of forces in Iraq. This included: the Special Republican Guard, the Republican Guard, the regular Iraqi army, the various security and intelligence services, Ba'ath party loyalists, the Lions of Saddam and the Fedayeen. Asymmetric tactics employed against the Coalition included: the use of suicide bombers; dressing Iraqi forces in civilian clothing to blur the distinction between civilians and combatants; and showing the white flag when still harbouring intent to fire. As the UK MoD noted in July 2003,

> While such tactics did not have a significant impact, they showed a disregard for the provisions of the Geneva Convention, put the Iraqi population at risk, and presented the coalition with a challenge as to how to respond.[27]

Iraqi forces also targeted the Coalition's stretched and vulnerable supply lines which had resulted from the rapid advance on Baghdad. Indeed, 'The capacity in particular of Saddam Hussein's Fedayeen militia to harass these lines of supply emerged as one of the few Iraqi strategies to give the coalition real cause for concern.'[28] None of these activities altered the military outcome of the war. For example, the Coalition wisely bypassed the cities south of Baghdad and avoided the need to engage in urban warfare.

Understandably, the most significant resistance did not come from Iraqi regular forces but from those forces most loyal to Saddam and, therefore, who had the most to lose. In many respects this reflected the fundamental limits of a regime that did not enjoy popular backing when fighting for survival against an overwhelming military opponent.

In addition to the Coalition's vast conventional superiority, and its avoidance of urban warfare, at least two other factors contributed to the failure of the regime's strategy to drag American and British forces into a quagmire. First, it was evident that Iraq suffered from serious command and control failings.[29] Poor command and control meant that Iraqi organised resistance failed rapidly. According to the UK MoD,

> This left much of the determined, largely uncoordinated opposition in the hands of army remnants, irregular Feda'yeen, groups of foreign fighters and Ba'athist die-hards, with access to extensive stocks of locally held weapons and ammunition.[30]

Iraq's problems were probably also a result of the lack of popular support for the regime. Lawrence Freedman noted that it was evident that regime stalwarts could not rely on an acquiescent population to provide shelter, supplies and new recruits.[31] Moreover, there was little incentive to fight for a regime that was deeply unpopular and which looked doomed.

Environmental destruction and humanitarian crises

The risk that the regime would set alight Iraq's oilfields to generate an environmental disaster – similar to the burning of oil wells in Kuwait in 1991 – also caused anxiety. The Coalition was also wary about the regime's potential to create humanitarian crises to distract the Coalition away from its main task. US Secretary of Defense Donald Rumsfeld noted in July 2003 that the Coalition expected crises involving 'large masses of refugees fleeing across borders into the neighboring countries'.[32]

Although Iraqi forces did manage to set fire to some oilfields in the south of the country, the feared widespread sabotage did not occur. The Coalition had planned ahead in terms of dealing with this threat. For example, during the initial days of the campaign, British bomb disposal experts worked with specialist engineering teams to clear access to key areas of the Rumaylah oilfields so they could be returned to operating capability as soon as possible.[33] During the conflict there were no large-scale refugee flows of the kind seen in Kosovo in 1999.

Information campaign

During the war, Iraq's information ministry broadcasted propaganda and disinformation designed to manipulate both internal and external perceptions of the Coalition's progress. Prior to the Coalition's arrival in Baghdad, the ministry strictly controlled media access and images from inside and around the capital. Although the Information Minister appeared completely out of touch with reality from an external perspective, it is difficult to assess the impact of the regime's radio and TV broadcasts on the domestic audience in Iraq and in the wider Arab and Muslim world. It is likely that these broadcasts did have a significant influence on Iraqi and Arab perceptions, even though they were entirely ineffective as a means to avert the regime's defeat.

Coalition success as a key reason for lack of Iraqi effectiveness

In addition to Iraqi weakness and failings, it is important to give credit to the quality of the Coalition's vast superiority in technology and personnel. The Coalition's success was based on,

> the ability to direct lethal and precise artillery and aircraft fire on to any source of resistance, and the capacity to acquire high-quality intelligence and disrupt enemy communications to confuse and surprise, as well as basic professional training and tactical astuteness.[34]

Conclusion

The Iraq War of 2003 demonstrated the limits of asymmetric warfare when it is waged by a regime which is very unpopular at home, weak in conventional military terms and lacking a trump card, such as a deliverable nuclear weapon capability. Overall, the poor showing of the Saddam regime's asymmetric strategy during the 2002–3 crisis and conflict was the result of four key factors:

- The Coalition succeeded in applying superior conventional military force to overwhelm a militarily ineffective and weak adversary
- The regime's counter-strategy during major combat operations lacked the necessary foundations, including popular support amongst the general Iraqi population, to put up a significant challenge. This is not to say that the regime's long-term aim did not involve drawing the Coalition into a protracted and costly occupation of Iraq
- The Coalition fully appreciated the asymmetric challenges that the regime could potentially throw up and put in place the necessary preparations to deal with them both politically and militarily
- Iraq's asymmetric strategy was only workable if its opponent lacked the stomach to enforce regime change and to take some significant risks in the process. However, the regime failed to read correctly, chose to ignore, or was powerless to negate the solidity of the Bush administration's post-9/11 resolve to address perceived threats through pre-emptive military action.

As has been seen since 1 May 2003, remnants of the Saddam regime and other forces appear to have had much greater asymmetric success since the end of major combat operations than they achieved during the conflict. Discussion of the asymmetric dimension of the recent Gulf War seems uncomfortably incomplete when Coalition forces continue to be the target of an asymmetric warfare campaign several months after the toppling of Saddam. Indeed, the continuing terrorist attacks against Coalition targets, and the undiminished political controversy in the UK and US over the decision to go to war, suggest that the conflict is far from over, albeit in some non-traditional ways.

Notes

1. P.M. Hughes, Director US Defense Intelligence Agency, statement to the Senate Select Committee on Intelligence, 28 January 1998, 'Global Threats and Challenges: The Decade Ahead'.
2. For more on asymmetric warfare, see Lloyd J. Matthews ed., *Challenging the United States Symmetrically and Asymmetrically: Can America be Defeated*, Carlisle, PA, US Strategic Studies Institute, US Army War College, 1998; Ivan Arreguin-Toft, 'How the Weak Win Wars: A Theory of Asymmetric Conflict', *International Security*, Summer 2001, pp. 93–128; Steven Metz, 'Strategic Asymmetry', *Military Review*, July–August 2001, pp. 23–31; *National Strategy to Combat Weapons of Mass Destruction*, December 2002, www.whitehouse.gov/news/releases/2002/12/WMDStrategy.pdf;

John Parachini, 'Anthrax Attacks, Biological Terrorism and Preventive Responses', November 2001, RAND Testimony, www.rand.org/.

3. President Bush announced the end of major combat operations on 1 May 2003. 'Bush calls end to "major combat"', CNN, 2 May 2003, www.cnn.com/2003/WORLD/meast/05/01/sprj.irq.main/.

4. Andrew Newman, 'How to make human bombs', *Herald Sun* (Melbourne), 3 April 2003, p. 20 (Lexis-Nexis).

5. Ben Leapman, 'Saddam's WMD were a bluff', *Evening Standard* (London), 2 October 2003, p. 2.

6. Prepared Testimony by US Secretary of Defense Donald H. Rumsfeld, Senate Armed Services Committee, 9 July 2003, p. 5.

7. Newman, 'How to make human bombs', p. 20; Prepared Testimony by US Secretary of Defense Donald H. Rumsfeld, p. 7.

8. Prepared Testimony by US Secretary of Defense Donald H. Rumsfeld, pp. 5–6.

9. Ministry of Defence, *Operations in Iraq: First Reflections*, July 2003, p. 15.

10. Michael P. Noonan, 'The Military Lessons of Operation Iraqi Freedom', Foreign Policy Research Institute, Philadelphia, 1 May 2003, www.fpri.org.

11. Prepared Testimony by US Secretary of Defense Donald H. Rumsfeld, p. 3.

12. Ministry of Defence, *Operations in Iraq*, p. 15.

13. *Iraq's Programme for Weapons of Mass Destruction: The Assessment of the British Government*, Draft as of 19 September 2003, p. 19. See Draft dossier Iraqi WMD Programme, 19 September 2002, Document CAB/3/0022, The Hutton Inquiry, www.the-hutton-inquiry.org.uk/content/cab/cab_3_0022to0078.pdf.

14. Ministry of Defence, *Operations in Iraq*, pp. 5, 14, 26.

15. Lawrence Freedman, 'A strong incentive to acquire nuclear weapons', *Financial Times*, 9 April 2003, p. 21.

16. Philip Webster, 'Robust Blair set for shift over Saddam's arsenal', *The Times*, 9 July 2003, p. 13.

17. Kim Burger, Andrew Koch and Michael Sirak, 'What Went Right?', *Jane's Defence Weekly*, 30 April 2003, pp. 20–5.

18. Ted Galen Carpenter, 'Why Didn't Iraq Use Chemical and Biological Weapons Against U.S. Troops?', 2 June 2003, Cato Institute, www.cato.org/cgi-bin/scripts/printtech.cgi/dailys/06-02-03.html.

19. Ibid.

20. Ministry of Defence, *Operations in Iraq*, pp. 17, 23.

21. Newman, 'How to make human bombs', p. 20.

22. Ministry of Defence, *Operations in Iraq*, p. 17.

23. Ibid., p. 4.

24. Freedman, 'A strong incentive to acquire nuclear weapons', p. 21.

25. Ministry of Defence, *Operations in Iraq*, pp. 12, 33.

26. Newman, 'How to make human bombs', p. 20.

27. Ministry of Defence, *Operations in Iraq*, p. 12.

28. Burger et al., 'What Went Right?', pp. 20–5.

29. Freedman, 'A strong incentive to acquire nuclear weapons', p. 21.

30. Ministry of Defence, *Operations in Iraq*, p. 15.

31. Freedman, 'A strong incentive to acquire nuclear weapons', p. 21.

32. Prepared Testimony by US Secretary of Defense Donald H. Rumsfeld, p. 3.

33. Ministry of Defence, *Operations in Iraq*, pp. 11–12.

34. Freedman, 'A strong incentive to acquire nuclear weapons', p. 21.

Part Three
Consequences

11
CBN Weapons and Iraq: Lessons for Threat Assessment, Disarmament and Nonproliferation

Susan B. Martin

In the public debate leading up to the war, the analysis of the threat posed by chemical, biological and nuclear (CBN) weapons was often presented in a straightforward way: Iraqi possession of CBN weapons was unacceptable, because 'rogue' states like Saddam Hussein's Iraq could not be deterred and might pass these weapons on to terrorists.[1] Alternatives to preventive attack were summarily treated: the threat of CBN weapons was too great to rely on deterrence, and, it was asserted, the disarmament regime imposed by the UN had failed to eliminate Iraq's CBN capabilities.

This public discourse oversimplified the issues surrounding CBN weapons and Iraq in a variety of ways. First, no distinctions were made among the threats posed by chemical, biological, and nuclear weapons, and there was no analysis of the military utility of these weapons. Lessons from the Cold War and deterrence theory about how Iraq could use these weapons were almost entirely ignored. Second, important issues involved in CBN disarmament were brushed aside, with the difficulties of the disarmament process in Iraq attributed to the intransigence and deceptiveness of the Iraqi regime. And third, the possible negative effects of using preventive war as a nonproliferation tool were overlooked.

The first part of this chapter examines both the threat posed by a CBN-armed Iraq (what were Iraq's CBN capabilities, and what were the potential uses of any such weapons?) and the range of possible responses to that threat. The chapter then examines the United Nations' attempts at coercive disarmament of Iraq, and suggests that at least some of the problems encountered in disarming Iraq were due, not to Iraq *per se*, but to difficulties of the disarmament undertaking itself.[2] Finally, the chapter evaluates the strategy of preventive attack as a means of nonproliferation. While it is too early to determine the effect of the 2003 war in Iraq on the proliferation of CBN weapons, there are reasons to think that the impact will not be entirely beneficial.

The threat posed by Iraq's CBN weapons

Analysis of the threat posed by a CBN-armed Iraq must be driven by two considerations: Iraq's capabilities, and the ways in which Iraq could have used these weapons. While the debate before the war focused on the threat posed by 'weapons of mass destruction', it is important to distinguish among CBN weapons, because Iraqi capabilities in the chemical, biological and nuclear fields, and the potential uses of these weapons, are very different.

Iraqi capabilities

Information on Iraqi CBN capabilities comes primarily from two sources, studies of information gathered and released by UN inspectors, and information gathered and released by governments.[3] Neither of these sources are unproblematic; questions about the information released by American and British governments, as well as the intelligence on which it was based, have been raised in the wake of the war, and as the UN inspectors themselves acknowledge, their reports are based on information provided by the Iraqis, only parts of which they have been able to verify. Nonetheless, the UN reports are generally recognised as the most authoritative available, and they have been used as the primary source for the following discussion.[4]

Iraqi weapons programmes were most advanced in the chemical area and least advanced in the nuclear area, with the biological weapons (BW) programme falling somewhere in between. In the chemical area, Iraq had produced and successfully used in the Iran–Iraq War (1980–88) a variety of chemical agents, including tear gas, mustard gas, dusty mustard, and the nerve agents tabun, sarin and cyclosarin. They used a variety of munitions, including aerial bombs, mortars, rockets and artillery shells, and both fixed-wing aircraft and helicopters.[5] As declared to the UN Special Commission (UNSCOM), Iraq's chemical weapons (CW) programme had produced a total of 3859 tonnes of agent (mustard, tabun, sarin and a small amount of VX); 80 per cent of this was reportedly used in the Iran–Iraq War.[6] Iraq also declared possession of over 200,000 special munitions for CB warfare, including a chemical warhead for the al-Hussein missile; about 100,000 of these munitions were filled with chemical agents and were either used in the war or otherwise disposed of during 1982–88.[7] By the time of the First Gulf War (1991), Iraq was producing many of its CW munitions indigenously, including aerial bombs, rocket warheads and missile warheads; it was also producing some of the key chemical precursors for mustard and the nerve agents tabun (GA), sarin (GB), cyclosarin (GF), and VX.[8] Iraq was also researching other chemical warfare agents, including the hallucinogenic BZ and the nerve agent soman (GD), and was developing new delivery means, including other missile warheads, aerial bombs and real binary munitions.[9]

But the Iraqi chemical weapons programme was not without difficulties. For example, it is not clear that Iraq had succeeded in adding the stabilisers that increase shelf-life to its chemical agents, and its chemical munitions were often rather crude affairs that wasted much of the agent that they carried.[10] Despite these difficulties, based on their experience in the Iran–Iraq War, the Iraqis are believed to have seen chemical weapons as having great utility.[11]

Iraq also developed, produced and weaponised a variety of biological agents. While US intelligence suggested the existence of an Iraqi biological weapons programme before the First Gulf War, direct evidence of the programme was not discovered until 1995 – four years after UNSCOM inspections began.[12] The agents produced and weaponised by the Iraqis include anthrax; botulinum toxin; clostridium perfringens, which causes gas gangrene; and aflatoxin, which causes cancer.[13] Iraq also produced ricin, a toxin, and the plant agent wheat cover smut, although it is not clear that these agents were ever weaponised.[14] Iraq experimented with a variety of munitions, including missile warheads for the al-Hussein missile; aerial bombs; fixed-wing aircraft spray systems; a pilotless MiG 21; aerosol generators, including aerosol generators for delivery by drones; landmines; cluster bombs; 122 mm rocket warheads; artillery shells; and possibly projectiles for the Supergun project.[15] Iraq claims that many of these munitions were found to be ineffective for biological agents and work on them was discontinued; Iraq acknowledges filling only al-Hussein missile warheads and aerial bombs with various biological agents.[16] These munitions, too, suffered from problems; most of the biological agent they contained would have been destroyed by the explosive charge, and the agent that remained would not have been effectively dispersed.[17]

Iraq had not succeeded in making a nuclear weapon. Three components are necessary to have a usable nuclear weapon: weapons-grade fissile material, a workable nuclear device (for a implosion device, this includes a neutron generator to initiate a chain reaction, a high explosives package, and so on) and a delivery system that can carry the nuclear bomb to its target. Because of the size, technical sophistication and expense of the necessary facilities, as well as the controls on nuclear facilities monitored by the International Atomic Energy Agency, the production of the nuclear material is generally the largest obstacle to the development of nuclear weapons.[18] This was true for Iraq as well. The IAEA assessed in December 1998 that 'there were no indications that Iraq had produced more than a few grams of weapons-grade nuclear material through its indigenous processes [and] there were no indications that Iraq has otherwise clandestinely acquired weapons-usable material'.[19]

Before the First Gulf War in 1991, Iraq had not succeeded in designing and building a nuclear device.[20] It is also not clear that Iraq has the ability to develop a nuclear device that is small enough to be carried by its present missiles, in particular by the al-Hussein. According to the IISS, the IAEA judged that the crash programme initiated during the First Gulf War 'could have been able to cobble together a crude nuclear device by the end of 1991', although this is a judgement about what Iraq could have done, not about what it did.[21]

In this regard, it is important to remember that Iraq's weapons programmes did not always proceed along the lines that outsiders might have expected. Most analysts would argue that Iraq is capable of producing a radiological weapon, but Iraq's efforts to produce such a weapon were evidently a failure, because the Iraqi scientists involved chose an unsuitable radioactive material and an ineffective munition.[22]

The effect of sanctions and inspections on Iraq's capabilities

The UN regime of disarmament imposed on Iraq in the wake of the First Gulf War did make progress in disarming Iraq. Although Iraqi cooperation with the UN inspectors was at best grudging, UNSCOM accomplishments included the destruction of 48 long-range missiles, chemical and conventional missile warheads, 690 tonnes of chemical weapons agent, more than 3000 tonnes of precursor chemicals, and the main biological weapons production facility.[23] In the nuclear area, accomplishments included the removal of all known weapons-usable nuclear material and the physical capability for producing such material.[24] However, particularly in the area of chemical and biological (CB) weapons, there were materials that remained unaccounted for and discrepancies in the disclosures made to the UN.

As the failure by early 2004 to find CB weapons in Iraq after the war makes clear, the condition of Iraq's CBN weapons programmes in the months preceding the war is both controversial and opaque. But even if the arguments for the war were unfounded and the UN disarmament regime imposed under UN Security Council Resolution 687 had eliminated Iraq's current CBN capabilities, it is not at all clear that it could eliminate Iraq's *potential* capability, especially in the realm of CB weapons.

This is simply because an Iraq freed from the UN disarmament regime would have had the capacity and know-how to restart its chemical and biological weapons programmes. There is no way to remove from Iraq all knowledge of how to make these weapons, and since many of the required materials and facilities have both civilian and military applications, it is not clear that is even possible to eliminate the necessary physical capabilities.[25] In addition, Iraq was increasingly self-sufficient in the area of CB weapons. For example, it was producing some of the necessary precursors for chemical weapons.[26]

Iraq would have faced more difficulties in the nuclear area, because rebuilding its nuclear infrastructure would require imports of controlled materials and possibly foreign assistance. In addition, assuming that Iraq remained a party to the Nuclear Nonproliferation Treaty (NPT), standard IAEA safeguards would continue to apply to its nuclear facilities. However,

Iraq could have pursued nuclear weapons covertly, and, it must be assumed, would eventually have succeeded in acquiring nuclear weapons.[27] Thus even if the UN regime of inspections and sanctions did eliminate Iraq's current CBN capability, it could not have eliminated Iraq's CBN potential.[28]

This means that the coercive disarmament of Iraq necessarily entailed a long-term process. Indeed, the Security Council recognised that 'on-going monitoring and verification' of Iraqi disarmament would be required.[29] However, it is not at all clear that the Security Council, or the international community in general, would have had the political will to maintain the monitoring and verification regime over the long term.[30] The importance of this for Iraqi capabilities is that, unless one believed that the UN disarmament regime would remain in place for the foreseeable future, and that Iraq would continue to cooperate with it, the issue of a potential CBN-capable Iraq remained.

Potential uses of CBN weapons

The potential uses of chemical, biological and nuclear weapons vary widely. In general, three general categories of use can be identified: battlefield use, use as a strategic deterrent, and use as a terror weapon. Chemical weapons are generally battlefield weapons, most useful against troops that lack chemical protection equipment and who cannot retaliate in kind. Indeed, one of the reasons that Iraq's chemical weapons helped turn the tide in the Iran–Iraq War was the lack of Iranian preparation for both offensive and defensive chemical warfare.[31] The lack of offensive preparation meant that the Iranians did not have the ability to retaliate, so that Iraqi troops did not have to bear the burden of chemical warfare defences.[32] And the lack of defensive preparation meant that the Iraqi chemical attacks were more effective than they would have been otherwise.[33] Against troops that are prepared and trained for chemical warfare, chemical weapons are not decisive, and do not win wars. That said, the threat and/or use of chemical weapons can certainly slow down operations and increase the burden under which troops operate.

The decisiveness of chemical weapons against unprotected troops has also been questioned. For example, the use of chemical weapons in the Iran–Iraq War contributed not to the attainment of offensive military gains, but to a ceasefire that essentially re-established the pre-war status quo. And factors such as the purge that weakened the Iranian military and Iraqi dominance of the air may be more important than chemical weapons in explaining Iraq's ability to achieve a ceasefire.[34]

While chemical weapons do have some utility on the battlefield, they are unsuitable for use as a strategic deterrent because they lack the required destructive power. While chemically armed missiles fired at civilian populations would certainly inflict casualties and cause panic and fear, the level of destruction would not approach that required for strategic deterrence. This can be seen through a comparison of the destructive power of chemical versus nuclear weapons. Steve Fetter has estimated that an attack with a missile warhead carrying 300 kilograms of sarin nerve gas would kill between 200 and 3000 people and injure the same number again; the same missile carrying a 20 kiloton nuclear warhead would kill 40,000 and injure the same again.[35]

The final category of use is that of a terror weapon, and the ability of chemical weapons to cause panic and fear suggests that they could play this role. A crude chemical weapon aimed at producing panic and fear is within the grasp of many terrorist groups, although it would be more difficult for such groups to manufacture a sophisticated weapon that could cause mass deaths. While it is possible that state actors could pass sophisticated chemical (or biological or nuclear) weapons to terrorist groups, it is not clear why it would be in the interest of any state to do so. The operating hypothesis is that a state would use the terrorist group to carry out attacks that are in the state sponsor's interest, but that the state itself cannot risk carrying out on its own.

But the risks of using CBN weapons are great. For instance, the United States 'reserves the right to respond with overwhelming force – including through resort to all of [its] options – to the use of WMD against the United States, [its] forces abroad, and friends and allies'.[36] Since it is always possible that the weapons will be traced back to the state sponsor, it is not clear how the risks to the state are diminished by acting through a terrorist group. In fact, acting through a terrorist group is likely to expose the state to greater risks. Unless the state sponsor has direct control of the terrorist group, it is possible that the weapons it provides to the terrorist group will be used in ways contrary to the state's interests.[37] While state-sponsored terrorism does take place, the potential costs of providing CBN weapons to terrorist groups – devastating military retaliation and/or the overthrow of the sponsoring regime – make it unlikely that states will provide terrorists with CBN weapons.

Of course, a state may decide to use chemical weapons as a terror weapon itself. In this case, the state would attack another state with chemical weapons, not in support of a battlefield operation but in an attempt to coerce the target through the panic and destruction caused by the attack. But such an attack will not eliminate the ability of the targeted state or its allies to retaliate, and it is not clear what the attacking state could hope to gain that would be worth the risk.[38]

In contrast to chemical weapons, biological weapons have little utility on the battlefield.[39] They suffer from an inherent operational disadvantage. Because biological agents have to incubate within the body of the target before they begin to produce disease, biological weapons can never have an immediate effect.[40] Nevertheless, it is conceivable that biological weapons could still be used on the battlefield, especially in attacks on rear areas in an effort to disrupt logistical and support operations. Such attacks would increase the costs and complexity of the war for the targeted state, but it is doubtful that biological weapons would be 'war-winning' weapons if used in this way. The utility of this sort of strategy also depends on the length of time of the pre-war mobilisation and of the war itself. Although it was not adopted for this reason, the increased emphasis on mobility and long-range strikes in the new military doctrine of the United States serves to limit the utility of biological weapons on the battlefield even further.[41] Finally, the possible benefits of using biological weapons in this way have to be weighed against the potential costs. These include the possibility of a 'boomerang' effect, with disease spreading back to the user's own troops and population; international condemnation; and even nuclear retaliation.

While there is thus generally little incentive to use biological weapons on the battlefield, the destructive power of biological weapons, comparable to that of small nuclear weapons, suggests that they may serve as a strategic deterrent.[42] When a state faces a threat to its vital interests, the potential risks of using biological weapons may be less important than what it stands to lose if the threat goes undeterred.

To the extent that terrorists are interested primarily in producing panic and fear instead of mass death, biological weapons have also been described as the ultimate terrorist weapon, because the use of biological weapons by terrorists would produce a great deal of panic and fear, while killing very few people. This is because of the difficulties involved in weaponising a biological agent.[43] In particular, the technological hurdles involved in processing and dispersing the agent mean that it will be difficult for terrorists to carry out an attack that infects a large number of people.[44]

Since the attacks by the United States on Hiroshima and Nagasaki in 1945, nuclear weapons have been used to deter attack on the vital interests of the states that possess them. While states have made nuclear threats in crisis situations, nuclear weapons have not been used offensively in a world with more than one nuclear power.[45] Battlefield nuclear weapons have been developed and deployed, but they have never been used, because of the risk of escalation to strategic nuclear war. Indeed, during the Cold War, tactical nuclear weapons came to reinforce deterrence by serving as a potential tripwire, underlining the risk that even a small war could escalate to a strategic nuclear exchange.

Given that the production of the nuclear material required for a nuclear bomb is generally acknowledged to be beyond the means of terrorist groups, the potential for terrorist use of nuclear weapons depends on the likelihood of terrorist acquisition of nuclear material and/or a nuclear bomb through purchase, theft, or as a 'gift' from a nuclear weapons state. The reasons why such a sale or gift would not be in the interest of a nuclear state have been addressed above, in the discussion of state-sponsored terrorism.

I have argued that the military utility of CBN weapons is generally quite circumscribed. The largest threat posed by chemical weapons is on the battlefield, against unprotected troops who cannot retaliate, while the utility of biological and nuclear weapons is generally limited to their ability to serve as a strategic deterrent. Below I examine what this general argument about CBN weapons means about the threat posed by a CBN-armed Iraq.

The threat posed by a CBN-armed Iraq and ways to counter that threat

In some circumstances, chemical weapons do have great utility on the battlefield. This suggests that an Iraq armed with chemical weapons could indeed have posed a threat. However, it is not at all clear that the threat of a chemically armed Iraq required preventive attack and regime change. First, as argued above, chemical weapons are not war-winning weapons, especially against troops that are equipped and trained for chemical warfare. Second, there were other ways to counter the threat. For example, a credible commitment to provide chemical warfare defensive equipment and military aid to any state threatened or attacked by Iraqi chemical weapons would go a long way to eliminating any advantage that Iraq could gain from these weapons.[46] Thus the assistance and protection against chemical weapons provided to state parties of the Chemical Weapons Convention (CWC) acts as both an incentive for states to join the Convention and as a deterrent to the use of chemical weapons against CWC members.[47]

Arguments before the Second Gulf War in Iraq in 2003 made much of Iraq's willingness to use chemical weapons, implying that because Saddam Hussein had used these weapons before, he would use them again, perhaps indiscriminately.[48] There was little analysis, however, of the context in which Saddam Hussein had ordered the use of chemical weapons. Iraq did not use chemical weapons from the outset of the war with Iran, despite having the capability to do so.[49] David Segal argues that Iraq 'resorted to the use of chemical weapons to stave off defeat', and that its first use of lethal chemical agents was in response to Iranian human wave attacks with which it could not cope.[50] During most of the Iran–Iraq War chemical weapons were used defensively, although by the end of the war Iraq was also using them to support offensive operations.[51] Thus the use of chemical weapons during the Iran–Iraq War does not suggest that Saddam Hussein embarked on the war *because* he possessed these weapons, or that he was determined to use them from the outset. On the contrary, Iraq resorted to the use of chemical weapons only when it suffered major defeats.[52] While Iraq did make quite heavy use of chemical weapons by the end of the war, it is not at all clear that Saddam Hussein therefore concluded that chemical weapons would be an essential part of any future military operation.[53]

Iraqi troops did not carry chemical weapons with them as they invaded Kuwait. Saddam Hussein later ordered the deployment of chemical weapons in Kuwait, but later changed his mind and withdrew these munitions back into Iraq.[54] In the end, Iraq did not use its chemical (or biological) weapons during the First Gulf War. Indeed, it may have been deterred from doing so.

During the First Gulf War the United States was well prepared to defend itself against Iraqi chemical attack. The United States also issued deterrent threats, and had the ability to retaliate, either in kind with chemical weapons or with nuclear weapons.[55] In this situation, the Iraqis chose not to use the chemical (and biological) weapons they possessed.[56]

What about the possible use of chemical weapons as a terror weapon? One of the scenarios that was discussed before the Second Gulf War was that Saddam Hussein might order the firing of chemically armed missiles at Israel. But it is not clear how such an attack could be used to support an offensive Iraqi operation; any such strike would only trigger Israeli and/or American retaliation.[57] Such an attack is most plausible in the context of an attack upon Iraq, where the Iraqi aim would be to prompt Israeli retaliation and thereby cause dissent and conflict in the Middle East. Indeed, American intelligence analysis suggested in the months leading up to the Second Gulf War in Iraq that Saddam Hussein was most likely to resort to 'terrorist actions' in response to a threat to the existence of his regime.[58]

In short, a chemically armed Iraq may have posed a threat, but it was a threat that was manageable. Battlefield use of chemical weapons could have been deterred by and countered with defensive equipment and conventional support to the state so attacked, and the possible use of these weapons as terror weapons by Iraq or through sponsored terrorist groups could have been deterred by threats of retaliation.

An Iraq armed with biological and nuclear weapons is more problematic, although not for the reasons usually presented. The problem posed by a biological- or nuclear-capable Iraq lies not in any inherent offensive threat, but in the deterrent power that Iraq would gain. As argued above, in a world of two or more nuclear powers, nuclear weapons have not been used in support of aggression. Despite the intense conflict between the United States and the Soviet Union during the Cold War, neither state was able to figure out how to use nuclear weapons for offensive purposes without running the risk of destroying itself. A nuclear Iraq under Saddam Hussein would also have been limited to using nuclear weapons for deterrence, since Saddam Hussein had shown no interest in martyring himself or destroying his country.[59] Iraq's biological weapons would have served a similar purpose, once married to delivery systems that could target the vital interests of the state to be deterred. They would have had little utility on the battlefield, especially against prepared states. Indeed, William Patrick, who was head of product development for the US Army's former bioweapons programme, stated before the Second Gulf War began that Iraqi use of biological weapons on the battlefield would have no effect on the outcome of the war. He argued that the concentration of firepower that the United States could bring to bear meant that the war would be over before any troops became ill.[60]

Some have argued that Iraq's willingness to use chemical weapons means that Saddam Hussein would also have made use of any biological and nuclear weapons that he possessed.[61] There are two problems with this argument. First, as argued above, Saddam Hussein resorted to chemical weapons only in the face of serious defeat in the Iran–Iraq War. Second, it is not clear that Saddam Hussein's willingness to use chemical weapons tells us anything about his willingness to use biological or nuclear weapons. As discussed above, the destructive power and military utility of these weapons is very different, so it is not clear why Iraq's resort to chemical weapons should have any bearing on its willingness to use biological and/or nuclear weapons.

A CBN-capable Iraq has also been seen as unacceptable because of the risk that Iraq would pass these weapons to terrorist groups. It is true that there were connections between Saddam Hussein's regime and various terrorist groups, particularly Palestinian groups. And there is some evidence that the regime tried to coordinate (non-CBN) terrorist attacks during the First Gulf War.[62] But those efforts failed. It is not clear how Saddam Hussein could have gained by providing CBN weapons to terrorists; he was a tyrant motivated by the desire for power, rather than by ideological causes. If he had provided CBN weapons to terrorists, he risked provoking a retaliatory attack that would eliminate his regime, and above all else Saddam Hussein wanted to continue to rule Iraq. Finally, if Iraq was determined to give these weapons to terrorist groups, it could have done so long ago, having had chemical weapons since the early 1980s and biological weapons since the late 1980s.[63]

But was Saddam Hussein's Iraq susceptible to deterrence? Those who argued that a CBN-armed Iraq was strategically unacceptable asserted that it was not.[64] For example, the *National Security Strategy of the United States*, published in September 2002, declared that

> Given the goals of rogue states and terrorists, the United States can no longer solely rely on a reactive posture as we have in the past. The inability to deter a potential attacker ... do[es] not permit that option. We cannot let our enemies strike first.[65]

Arguments advanced in support of this position include the assertion that Saddam Hussein's past behaviour demonstrates that he was undeterrable.

For instance, Kenneth Pollack and others argue that Saddam Hussein's actions in the First Gulf War cast serious doubt on his susceptibility to deterrence.[66] Pollack acknowledges that some of the events in 1990–91, including the non-use of chemical and biological weapons in that war, suggest that 'Saddam has a crude understanding of deterrence logic and has been successfully deterred in the past'.[67] However, he argues that while President Bush threatened Iraq with 'the severest consequences' in response to terrorist action, use of CBN weapons, or the destruction of the Kuwaiti oilfields, Iraq only refrained from one of these, the use of CBN weapons.[68] Pollack argues that the destruction of the oilfields demonstrates that Saddam Hussein could not always be deterred. But to attribute the failure of deterrence in this case to the personality of

Saddam Hussein is to overlook the requirements for a credible deterrent threat. A deterrent threat has to be proportionate to the action to be deterred; generally, nuclear deterrence is seen as credible only in response to a threat to 'vital interests'. The threat of 'severest consequences' was thus a credible deterrent to the Iraqi use of chemical and biological weapons, because such use might have killed hundreds or thousands of American and allied troops as well as civilians. But it was not a credible deterrent to the destruction of oilfields. In the end, of course, the US bluff was called; the 'severest consequences' (regime change or an American use of nuclear weapons) were not unleashed in response to the burning of the oilfields.

A second set of arguments point to a set of individual and institutional factors (for example, Saddam Hussein was seen as aggressive, ignorant of the outside world, and a risk-taker, with no one in Iraq having the ability to challenge him without risking their life) that make it likely that Saddam Hussein would have miscalculated. As Pollack states, 'He takes actions that he does not realize to be suicidal when he takes them and often does not realize that they are suicidal until it is too late to avert disaster.'[69] This is seen as especially dangerous because backing down in the face of a threat would be taken as a sign of weakness that could threaten Saddam Hussein's control of Iraq.[70] The argument, then, is that Saddam Hussein could have blundered into a confrontation with the United States or Israel that risked nuclear retaliation, and that he then would have been too proud to back down. There are two problems with this thesis. The first is that it ignores the clarity of the costs that are attached to the use of nuclear weapons. As Kenneth Waltz has argued, in a conventional conflict, deterrent threats can be ineffective 'because the damage threatened is limited, distant and problematic', while in a nuclear world 'suffering may be unlimited'. In other words, miscalculation, easy in a conventional world, becomes much less likely when nuclear weapons are involved.[71] Then there is the issue of pride and prestige. Pollack argues that if or when Saddam Hussein had stumbled into a nuclear crisis, he may not have backed down because such 'weakness' could have threatened the survival of his regime.[72] The problem here is that a retaliatory nuclear strike is a direct threat to the survival of his regime, and, as Pollack himself argues, the 'survival of his regime in the short term is always [Saddam Hussein's] paramount concern'.[73] Arguably, backing down would have been less likely to lead to his elimination than a nuclear attack on Iraq.

This relates as well to a third set of arguments, which stated that Saddam Hussein would believe that his possession of nuclear weapons would deter the United States and/or Israel from responding to aggressive Iraqi actions in the region.[74] But it is not obvious that Iraqi possession of nuclear weapons would have decreased significantly the deterrent value of American and Israeli nuclear forces. While it can be argued that Iraqi possession of nuclear weapons would have decreased the likelihood that the US and Israel would resort to the use of nuclear weapons, it would not have eliminated that possibility.

And effective deterrence requires only the possibility, not the certainty, of retaliation.[75] Furthermore, even if deterrence had failed and a nuclear Iraq did launch a conventional war, the United States would still have been able to mount a conventional response, and Iraq would then have been faced with escalating to a nuclear exchange or backing down.[76] The costs of initiating a nuclear exchange with the United States – whose nuclear arsenal will remain quantitatively and qualitatively superior to any that Iraq can develop – would have been clear.

It would, then, have been possible to deter Iraq, even an Iraq armed with biological and/or nuclear (BN) weapons. This does not mean that a BN-capable Iraq did not pose a threat. While an Iraq armed with BN weapons was not likely to have used them in support of aggression or to supply them to terrorists, it would have been able to deter attacks on its vital interests – in particular, it would have been able to deter military intervention to overthrow the regime. This would have been a problem for plans to 'remake the Middle East', especially for those who saw the overthrow of Saddam Hussein as the prerequisite to the removal of US military forces from Saudi Arabia.[77] A nuclear Iraq would also have eliminated Israel's nuclear monopoly in the region. While the logic of deterrence suggests that this would not pose a threat to the existence of Israel, it would have changed the balance of power in the region and most likely have increased the prestige and influence of Saddam Hussein. In addition, Iraq would have been able to deter military intervention for humanitarian purposes. While the abuses of Saddam Hussein's regime, including the use of chemical weapons against civilians in Halabjah, were ignored by the West for many years, the West may at some point have decided that those abuses justified military intervention. Such intervention would not have been possible if Iraq acquired deterrent forces. But such forces only deter military intervention. The international community would still have been able to use non-military means to exercise influence over how Iraq treated its citizens, just as it does with China and as it did with the Soviet Union.

It may be, of course, that the wish to remake the Middle East, to preserve Israel's nuclear monopoly and/or to end the domestic abuses of Saddam Hussein's regime were in themselves good enough reasons to go to war. But this wider debate about the war is outside the scope of this chapter. The central argument of this chapter is simply this: the offensive and/or terrorist threat posed by Iraq's CBN weapons could have been met through a combination of defence and deterrence; the offensive threat posed by these weapons did not require a preventive war.

Coercive disarmament

The disarmament regime imposed upon Iraq by the United Nations was a consequence of Iraq's invasion of Kuwait on 2 August 1990. That same day, the UN Security Council passed Resolution 660, which condemned the invasion, demanded Iraq's withdrawal, and called for negotiations between Iraq and Kuwait to settle their differences.[78] International economic sanctions were imposed on Iraq in an attempt to pressure it to comply with Resolution 660 and withdraw from Kuwait.[79] However, Iraq did not withdraw, and under the authority of UN Security Council Resolution 678 (1990), which authorised the use of 'all necessary means' to implement Resolution 660, the First Gulf War began on 17 January 1991. After more than a month of air attacks on Iraqi targets, the ground war began on 2 February. Less than two days later, Saddam Hussein ordered Iraqi troops out of Kuwait, and Iraq formally accepted the terms of the ceasefire, as spelled out in UN Security Council Resolution 687 (1991), on 6 April 1991. According to Resolution 687, Iraq's CBN programmes as well as all ballistic missiles with a range greater than 150 kilometres were to be dismantled under international supervision. Iraq was to provide full details of its weapons programmes, and UNSCOM inspectors would verify those details and supervise the destruction of the prohibited items. Resolution 687 also mandated monitoring and verification programmes to ensure that Iraq did not reacquire or redevelop these weapons.[80] An arms embargo was imposed to further constrain Iraqi military power, and the sanctions originally imposed to compel Iraq to withdraw from Kuwait remained in place to help ensure that Iraq would comply with its disarmament obligations.[81]

The disarmament regime imposed upon Iraq was thus an effort at coercive disarmament. Coercive disarmament can be defined as an attempt to convince a state to disarm, through means short of a military attack to eliminate its weapons and/or overthrow its government. The concept of coercive disarmament thus draws on Thomas Schelling's distinction between brute force and coercion. A military attack to eliminate a country's CBN capabilities is an example of brute force; coercive disarmament, in contrast, seeks to influence a country's incentives to keep its CBN capabilities by raising the costs of doing so.[82] The United Nations wished to eliminate Iraq's CBN weapons, and it attempted to get Iraq to disarm through the terms of the ceasefire agreement. Other mechanisms such as sanctions were also used in an attempt to coerce Iraq to disarm. Coercive disarmament is a difficult business; the most prominent example of such an attempt – the regulation of Germany after the First World War – was not a resounding success.

The Iraqi case illustrates the difficulties involved in coercive disarmament. One such difficulty resides in the logic of coercive disarmament, while others have to do with coercive disarmament in practice. The logical difficulty is that it attempts to persuade a state to give up a means of security (its weapons) by threatening that security. 'Give me your gun or I'll shoot' is likely to be less persuasive than 'I'll put down my gun if you put down yours' or 'I'll help eliminate the need for your gun if you are willing to put it down.' This relates to drawbacks in the implementation of coercive disarmament in Iraq. The effort to disarm Iraq assumed that the weapons themselves were the problem.[83] It took place in a vacuum, with no attention paid to security concerns or regional dynamics that may have played a role in leading Iraq to pursue CBN capabilities in the first place. While the UN Security Council Resolution 687 (1991) does state that Iraqi disarmament would be a step 'towards the goal of establishing in the Middle East a zone free from weapons of mass destruction and all missiles for their delivery', no steps were taken towards creating such a zone.[84] This failure to address possible motivations for the pursuit of CBN weapons made it less likely that Iraq itself would come to see disarmament as in its interests, and helped to ensure that the disarmament process would remain coercive.

Other problems with the implementation of coercive disarmament in Iraq included the lack of a clear standard of success (what qualifies as disarmament), and questions about the political will to maintain the disarmament effort. It was not clear what standard would be used to judge when Iraq *was* disarmed, a difficult question given the importance of know-how and dual-use materials and facilities, especially in the production of CB weapons.[85] The issue of verification, and how much verification was sufficient, also needed to be addressed more fully. It has long been recognised that arms control and disarmament agreements cannot be 100 per cent verified. Instead, the goal of verification is to prevent a militarily significant violation, or a break-out capability, from going undetected. The judgement of how much verification is enough is essentially political, an issue that the UN inspectors made clear in their reports.[86] But it is not clear that the Security Council ever addressed this issue to the level of detail required. For example, were the 550 mustard-filled artillery shells that were missing militarily significant?

The Bush Administration indirectly addressed the question of standards – how to know whether disarmament was working in Iraq – when it suggested that South Africa provided an example that Iraq should emulate.[87] But it is not clear that the South African example is a good one. While the termination of South Africa's nuclear programme was verified by international inspectors, many questions about that programme remain, in part because South Africa destroyed all the relevant documents in 1993, prior to the arrival of IAEA inspectors.[88] And there has as yet been no verification of the termination of South Africa's chemical and biological weapons programme.[89] In short, the difference between Iraq and South Africa was not in what they claimed to have done, but in the willingness of the United States to believe them.[90]

Finally, because coercive disarmament relies on outside pressure to convince a state to disarm, instead of changing the state's situation so that it sees disarmament as in its own interests, coercive disarmament requires a long-term commitment to provide that outside pressure. But it is not clear that the international community can maintain the will and consensus essential to a long-term, coercive disarmament process. Indeed, the consensus on policy towards Iraq was weakening even before the issue of preventive war arose.[91]

Preventive attack as a nonproliferation tool

Preventive attack against states seeking CBN weapons is intended not only to eliminate the target state's CBN capabilities but to serve as a deterrent for other states. The hope is that a preventive attack on one state, for example Iraq, will deter other states from pursuing CBN weapons by making manifest the potential costs of such pursuit. Indeed, some see the Libyan disclosure and renunciation of its WMD programmes as a result of the war on Iraq.[92] But as with coercive disarmament, there is something paradoxical about the logic of preventive attack as a nonproliferation tool. Countries are supposed to be encouraged to forgo a potential means *of* security (CBN weapons) because of a military threat *to* their security. States that already feel insecure and are pursuing CBN weapons as a result are likely to perceive an increased threat from the new American doctrine of preventive attack. They are likely, in turn, to become even more determined to acquire CBN weapons. The incentive to acquire CBN weapons, and in particular BN deterrent forces, may also be reinforced by the contrast between the fates of Iraq and North Korea. While the North Korean crisis is still evolving, Washington's willingness to negotiate suggests that even a limited nuclear capability may deter the West from military action.[93]

The Second Gulf War may also put an end to the phenomenon of 'opaque proliferation', where states acquire a nuclear capability but keep it 'in the closet'.[94] If governments that pursue CBN weapons are threatened with preventive attack and regime change, they will have an incentive to acquire the most destructive weapons possible in as short a time as possible, and to declare clearly the existence of such a deterrent force as soon as they have it. Thus the threat of a preventive attack against states pursuing CBN weapons would make opaque proliferation much less attractive. The eagerness of North Korea to demonstrate its nuclear capabilities is suggestive in this regard.[95] Whether an end to opaque proliferation would be a positive or a negative development from the point of view of international stability and nonproliferation is not clear and may be context-dependent.[96] But it is certainly a question that deserves further analysis.

The Second Gulf War also offers one practical lesson about preventive attack as a nonproliferation tool, and that is that if one launches such an attack, it is important to have plans in place to assume control of weapons facilities in the target country. By early 2004, it appeared that the Second Gulf War may have done more to increase the risk of CBN proliferation, and in particular the possibility that Iraq's CBN materials and know-how could fall into the hands of the terrorists, than to eliminate those risks. The reported looting of Iraqi nuclear and missile factories suggests that whenever such a preventive attack is contemplated in the future, much more thought needs to be given to securing weapons materials and facilities.[97]

Conclusion

The conflict in Iraq offers important lessons about CBN weapons. First, the category of 'weapons of mass destruction' is misleading, and an accurate threat assessment requires a separate analysis of the threat posed by chemical, biological and nuclear weapons. Chemical weapons are most useful on the battlefield, while the utility of biological and nuclear weapons lies in their ability to serve as a strategic deterrent. Second, although the UN programme of coercive disarmament was unlikely to eliminate Iraq's CBN potential, the threat to regional and international security posed by an Iraq armed with CBN did not require or vindicate preventive war. The threat posed by Iraqi possession of chemical weapons could have been met with a combination of defence and deterrence, while a BN-armed Iraq could have been contained through deterrence. The conflict also offers some cautionary lessons about the role of coercive disarmament and preventive attack. The most important of these is that there is a paradox at the root of both of these policies. Both aim to use coercion or brute force as an incentive to get rid of weapons, yet weapons are often acquired in response to such threats. Given this paradox, the long-term effectiveness of these policies is in doubt.

Notes

1. The term 'chemical, biological and nuclear (CBN) weapons' is used deliberately in place of the more common 'weapons of mass destruction' (WMD). As I will argue below, 'weapons of mass destruction' is a poor analytic category and its use therefore muddies the issues raised by these weapons.
2. As explained in more detail below, the concept of 'coercive disarmament' draws on Thomas Schelling's distinction between coercion and brute force; it refers to an attempt to disarm a state by raising the costs of nondisarmament. See T.C. Schelling, *Arms and Influence*, New Haven, CT, Yale University Press, 1966.
3. Studies of Iraq's use of chemical weapons during the Iran–Iraq War also provide information on earlier phases of Iraq's chemical weapons programme.
4. In particular, the following discussion draws on 'UNSCOM's Comprehensive Review', especially Annex B, 'Status of the Verification of Iraq's Chemical Weapons Programme', available at http://cns.miis.edu/resdearch/iraq/ucreprots/dis_chem.htm (accessed 25 July 2003) and Annex C, 'Status of the Verification of Iraq's Biological Warfare Programme', available at http://cns.miis.edu/research/iraq/ucreport/dis_bio.htm (accessed 29 July 2003), and the 1997, 1998 and 1999 progress reports from the IAEA to the UN, S/1997/779, S/1998/927 and /S/1999/127 respectively, available at www.iaea.or.at/worldatom/Programmes/ActionTeam/reports2.html (accessed 11 August 2003).
5. See International Institute for Strategic Studies (IISS), *Iraq's Weapons of Mass Destruction: A Net Assessment*, London, IISS, 9 September 2002, pp. 43–8; A.H. Cordesman and A.R. Wagner, *The Lessons of Modern War, Volume II: The Iran–Iraq War*, Boulder, CO, Westview Press, 1990, Table 13.4 and pp. 511–12; Central Intelligence Agency, 'Iraqi Strategy and Tactics in the Use of Chemical Weapons during the Iran–Iraq War', 062596_cia_63704_63704.01.txt, released as part of the investigation

into Gulf War syndrome, available at www.fas.org/irp/gulf/cia/960626/63704_
01.htm (accessed 11 July 2003); 'Iraq–Kuwait: Chemical Warfare Dusty Agent
Threat', Serial: DSA 350–90, 10 October 1990, file: 970613_dsa350_90d_txt_0001.
txt, available at www.gulflink.osd.mil/declassdocs/dia/19970613/970613_dsa350_
90d_txt_0001.html (accessed 17 March 1999).

6. UNSCOM, 'Annex B: Status of the Verification of Iraq's Chemical Weapons
Programme', paras 12 and 13; see also IISS, *Iraq's Weapons of Mass Destruction*,
pp. 41–54. Note that the details of Iraq's VX programme are unclear. There
are reports that VX was used at the end of the Iran–Iraq War, although in its
declarations to UNSCOM Iraq declared that the production of VX was a failure.

7. UNSCOM, 'Annex B: Status of the Verification of Iraq's Chemical Weapons
Programme', para. 8.

8. Ibid., para. 11, Table 1; para. 22, Table 3 and para. 25; see also IISS, *Iraq's Weapons
of Mass Destruction*, p. 49.

9. UNSCOM, 'Annex B: Status of the Verification of Iraq's Chemical Weapons
Programme', para. 36. Binary munitions contain two relatively harmless chemical
agents which, when mixed in flight, combine to make a toxic agent. Iraq's early
'binary' munitions required manual mixing of the ingredients before launching
the weapon, and were thus not 'real' binary munitions.

10. See IISS, *Iraq's Weapons of Mass Destruction*, pp. 41–54.

11. See ibid., p. 41; CIA, 'Iraq's National Security Goals', December 1998, available
from http://www.gwu.edu/~nsarchiv/NSAEBB/NSAEBB80/wmd.02.pdf (accessed
2 June 2003); 'Iraq: Potential for Chemical Weapon Use', 25 January 1991,
file: 970613_dim37_91d_txt_0001.txt, available at: www.gulflink.osd.mil/
muhammadiyat/muhammidiyat_refs/n59en042/970613_dim37_91d_txt_0001.
html (accessed 11 August 2003); CIA, 'Iraqi CW and BW', file: 061896_
cia_62758_62758_01.txt, September 1990, available at www.gulflink.osd.
mil/decalssdocs/cia/19960618/061896_ciA_62758_62758_01.HTML (accessed 17
March 1999).

12. Examples of intelligence on Iraqi BW during the Persian Gulf War include 'Iraqi
BW capabilities', a report of the US Defense Intelligence Agency, 0628rpt.91, posted
at the Gulflink website, www.gulflink.osd.mil/declassdocs/dia/19961031/961031_
950901_0628rpt_91.htm and 'Assessment of threat at Salman Pak based upon most
current air campaign and BPA', 0093pgv.91p, dated 23 January 1991, available at
www.gulflink.osd.mil/decalssdocs/dia/199610311961031_950925_0093pgv_91p.
html; see also IISS, *Iraq's Weapons of Mass Destruction*, p. 37.

13. UNSCOM, 'Annex C: Status of the Verification of Iraq's Biological Warfare
Programme', para. 85.

14. Toxins are poisons produced by living organisms. Toxins act more like chemical
than like other biological agents.

15. The 350 mm calibre Supergun that UNSCOM destroyed had the potential to
hit targets up to range of 1000 km, although not with the accuracy required by
conventional armaments. See Federation of American Scientists, 'Project Babylon
Supergun/PC-2' available at www.fas.org/nuke/guide/iraq/other/supergun.htm
(accessed 27 January 2004).

16. UNSCOM, 'Annex C: Status of the Verification of Iraq's Biological Warfare
Programme', paras 38–66, para. 85. Note that Iraq states that it never tested the
warhead for the al-Hussein missile with a biological fill. See UNSCOM, 'Annex C:
Status of the Verification of Iraq's Biological Warfare Programme', para. 33; IISS,
Iraq's Weapons of Mass Destruction, p. 35.

17. IISS, *Iraq's Weapons of Mass Destruction*, pp. 35 and 40.
18. The IAEA monitors nuclear facilities declared by states who are members of the Nuclear Nonproliferation Treaty.
19. Iraq Nuclear Verification Office, 'Fact Sheet: Iraq's Nuclear Weapons Programme', available on the web at www.iaea.or.at/worldatom/Programmes/ActionTeam/nwp2.html (accessed 25 July 2003); see also IISS, *Iraq's Weapons of Mass Destruction* and the IAEA reports of 1997, 1998 and 1999 submitted to the UN Security Council as S/1997/779, S/1998/927 and S/1999/127.
20. See IISS, *Iraq's Weapons of Mass Destruction*, pp. 21–7. Iraq insisted that it had not finalised a nuclear weapons design at the time of the Gulf War, and the inspectors did not find evidence to the contrary. See Iraq Nuclear Verification Office, 'Fact Sheet: Iraq's Nuclear Weapon Programme' available at www.iaea.or.at/worldatom/Programmes/ActionTeam/nwp2.html (accessed 25 July 2003). But note that the IAEA report in 1997 stated that 'Iraqi programme documentation records substantial progress in many important areas of nuclear weapon development, making it prudent to assume that Iraq has developed the capability to design and fabricate a basic fission weapon based on implosion technology and fueled by highly enriched uranium.' S/1997/779, section 2.6, p. 59.
21. IISS, *Iraq's Weapons of Mass Destruction*, p. 21.
22. The IISS reports that 'tests with standard bomb casings modified to accommodate the radioactive payload did not result in significant dispersal of radioactive material.' Ibid., p. 20; see also W. Broad, 'Document reveals 1987 bomb tested by Iraq', *New York Times*, 29 April 2001.
23. See 'UNSCOM Main Achievements', available at www.un.org/Depts/unscom/Achievements/achievments.html (accessed 23 June 2003); see also S. Ritter, 'The Case for Iraq's Qualitative Disarmament', *Arms Control Today*, Vol. 30, No. 5 June 2000, available at www.armscontrol.org/act/2000_06/iraqjun.asp (accessed 15 August 2003).
24. See S/1998/927, 7 October 1998, para. 17; see also Iraq Nuclear Verification Office, 'Fact Sheet: Iraq's Nuclear Weapon Programme'.
25. Of course, the facilities to produce nuclear material are dual-use as well, since they also produce nuclear energy. But the characteristics of nuclear facilities (their scale, expense, the technology involved) makes them much easier to monitor.
26. For information on Iraq's indigenous production of precursors for chemical weapons, see UNSCOM Comprehensive Review, Table 3, para. 22 and para. 25; IISS, *Iraq's Weapons of Mass Destruction*, pp. 53–4; on its ability to restart its BW programme, see IISS, *Iraq's Weapons of Mass Destruction*, pp. 39–40.
27. The United States Department of Defense argued that it would take Iraq 'five or more years and key foreign assistance to rebuild the infrastructure to enrich enough material for a nuclear weapon'. United States Office of the Secretary of Defense, *Proliferation: Threat and Response, 2001*, Washington DC, US Department of Defense, January 2001, p. 40, available at www.defenselink.mil/pubs/ptr20010110.pdf (accessed 7 February 2004); see also IISS, *Iraq's Weapons of Mass Destruction*, p. 26.
28. There are, of course, disagreements about the extent to which the UN regime was able to eliminate Iraq's current capabilities. For example, much was made of the 550 mustard-filled shells for which the UN teams were unable to account.
29. The goal of ongoing monitoring and verification is clearly spelled out in UN Security Council Resolutions 687 (1990), 707 (1991), 715 (1991) and 1284 (1999).

30. For example, Iraq's economic potential created an incentive for states to soften or erode the constraints placed upon Iraq. See C. Hoyos and R. Khalaf, 'Trade becomes Iraq's strongest weapon', *Financial Times*, 10 September 2001 (accessed through Lexis-Nexis).

31. Iran did develop some chemical weapon capability during the Iran–Iraq War, and there have been some reports that it used chemical weapons. However, there are no well-documented cases of systemic use. The Iraqis did have some chemical casualties, though these may have been a result of Iraq's own use of chemical weapons; there are also reports of Iranian troops sending unexploded Iraqi chemical weapons back at Iraqi troops. One of the most notorious allegations of Iranian CW use is that Iran used CW against the town of Halabjah. These allegations stem mostly from US intelligence at the time of the Iran–Iraq War, a time at which the United States 'tilted' towards Iraq, partly as a result of the Iranian revolution. It is interesting to note that in the months leading up to the 2003 war in Iraq, Washington blamed the use of CW in Halabjah on Iraq. For a useful review of Iranian chemical warfare activities in the Iran–Iraq War, see J.P. Zanders, 'Allegations of Iranian Use of Chemical Weapons in the 1980–1988 Gulf War: A Research Note', Stockholm, Stockholm International Peace Research Institute, revision 29 March 2001. Other discussions of the use of chemical weapons by Iran include G.M. Burck and C. Cowerree, *International Handbook on Chemical Weapons Proliferation*, New York, Greenwood Press, 1991, pp. 237–66; A.H. Cordesman, *Weapons of Mass Destruction in the Middle East*, London, Brassey's, 1991, pp. 60–92; D. Segal, 'The Iran–Iraq War: A Military Analysis', *Foreign Affairs*, Summer, 1988; SIPRI Yearbooks 1988 (Table 5.3, p. 106) and 1999 (pp. 100–3); Cordesman and Wagner, *The Iran–Iraq War*, pp. 506–18; T. McNaugher, 'Ballistic Missiles and Chemical Weapons: The Legacy of the Iran–Iraq War', *International Security*, Vol. 15, No. 2, Fall 1990, pp. 5–34.

32. It makes sense for troops to use some chemical defensive gear even when they are employing chemical weapons against an enemy that is unable to respond in kind, because of the possibility of 'blow back'. The Iraqis seem to have suffered a significant number of casualties as a result of their own use of chemical weapons. See Central Intelligence Agency, 'CW Use in Iran–Iraq War: not finally evaluated intelligence'. File 062596_cia_63704_01.txt, available at www.fas.org/irp/gulf/cia/960626/63704_o1.htm (accessed 11 July 2002); see also Cordesman and Wagner, *The Iran–Iraq War*, p. 516.

33. For information on Iranian defences, see Zanders, 'Allegations of Iranian Use'. Iranian troops who kept their beards found that their facial hair limited the effectiveness of the masks that were available. See McNaugher, 'Ballistic Missiles', p. 20; Cordesman and Wagner, *The Iran–Iraq War*, p. 510.

34. See, for example, Segal, 'The Iran–Iraq War'; S.C. Pelletiere and D.V. Johnson II, *Lessons Learned: The Iran–Iraq War*, Carlisle Barracks, PA, Strategic Studies Institute, US Army War College, 1991; McNaugher, 'Ballistic Missiles', pp. 18, 21–2.

35. See S. Fetter, 'Table 6: A Comparison of the Casualties Produced by Nuclear, Chemical, Biological, and High-Explosive Warheads' from 'Ballistic Missiles and Weapons of Mass Destruction: What is the Threat? What Should Be Done?', *International Security*, Vol. 16, No. 1, September 1991, p. 27. He assumes 'a missile with a throwweight of one tonne aimed at a large city with an average population density of 30 per hectare'. The figures cited above are without civil defence. For a related discussion of the effect of missile attacks during the Iran–Iraq War, see McNaugher, 'Ballistic Missiles'.

36. See United States, *National Strategy to Combat Weapons of Mass Destruction*, December 2002, available at www.whitehouse.gov/news/releases/2002/12/WMDStrategy.pdf (accessed 11 August 2003).

37. The United States aid to opposition forces in Afghanistan was sponsorship of 'terrorism' from the Soviet perspective, and some of these forces later attacked the United States.

38. Chemical and biological weapons are not counter-force weapons because they do not cause physical destruction in the same way that conventional and nuclear weapons do. This means that these weapons cannot be used to eliminate the target's own weapons and thus its ability to retaliate. Even with nuclear weapons, it is unlikely that a counter-force attack would completely eliminate the target's ability to retaliate; in addition, retaliation may come from an ally of the target state.

39. For a more detailed discussion of the military utility of biological weapons, see S.B. Martin, 'The Role of Biological Weapons in International Politics: The Real Military Revolution', *Journal of Strategic Studies*, Vol. 25, No. 1, March 2002, pp. 63–98.

40. This is not true of toxins.

41. The Rumsfeld Doctrine has emphasised the use of light, fast and precise military forces, as opposed to the Powell Doctrine's emphasis on overwhelming force.

42. Fetter estimates that somewhere between 20,000 and 80,000 deaths could be caused by a single missile carrying 30 kg of anthrax spores. Again, this assumes no civil defence and 'a missile with a throwweight of one tonne aimed at a large city with an average population density of 30 per hectare'. Fetter, 'Ballistic Missiles and Weapons of Mass Destruction', Table 6, p. 27.

43. See J.P. Zanders, E. Karlson, L. Melin, E. Näslund, and L. Thaning, 'Appendix 9A: Risk Assessment of Terrorism with Chemical and Biological Weapons' in SIPRI, SIPRI Yearbook 2000, Oxford, Oxford University Press, 2000, pp. 537–59, available at http://projects.sipri.se/cbw/research/cbw-yb20009a.pdf (accessed 7 February 2004); J.B. Tucker, 'Chemical and Biological Terrorism: How Real a Threat?' *Current History*, Vol. 99, No. 636, April 2000, pp. 147–53; D.W. Siegrist, 'The Threat of Biological Attack: Why Concern Now?' *Emerging Infectious Diseases* [serial online] Vol. 5, No. 4, July–August 1999, pp. 505–8 available from www.cdc.gov/ncidod/EID/vol5n04/siegrist.htm (accessed 15 October 2002); D.C. Rapoport, 'Terrorism and Weapons of the Apocalypse', *National Security Studies Quarterly*, Vol. 5, No. 3, Summer 1999, pp. 49–67.

44. There seems to be little agreement on the degree of sophistication involved in producing the anthrax used in the 2001 letter attacks in the United States. See, for example, Scott Shane, 'Anthrax powder from attacks could have been made simply', *Baltimore Sun* 2 November 2002; Environmental News Service, 'Trained Technician Likely Launched Anthrax Attacks', 10 December 2002, http://ens-news.com/ens/dec2002/2002-12-10-09.asp#anchor3; Lawrence K. Altman, 'New tests confirm potency of anthrax in Senate Office', *New York Times*, 11 December 2001 (accessed through Lexis-Nexis). The attacks resulted in the deaths of five people, created a great deal of panic and fear, and imposed large economic costs.

45. As Richard Betts points out, the definition of 'offensive' or 'defensive' threats in crises can be difficult; it depends on the point in time one chooses to denote as the 'status quo' and the participants in a crisis may have quite different opinions about the offensive or defensive nature of a particular threat. See R.K. Betts, *Nuclear Blackmail and Nuclear Balance*, Washington, DC, Brookings, 1987, pp. 138–41. My point is more general: The 'nightmare scenario' of a nuclear power trying to use its nuclear capability to shield a conventional, offensive attack has not occurred.

46. Note that neither of these things happened in the Iran–Iraq War. Iran did not receive any great assistance with chemical warfare defence or any conventional military aid because it was the victim of chemical attack. Nor was Iraq ostracised because of its use of chemical weapons. If either or both of these things had happened, it is not clear that Iraq would have concluded that chemical weapons had great utility.

47. See Article X, 'Assistance and Protection against Chemical Weapons', of the Chemical Weapons Convention, available online at www.opcw.org/html/db/cwc/eng/cwc_article_X.html.

48. See, for example, E. Bumiller and J. Dao, 'Cheney says peril of a nuclear attack justifies an attack', *New York Times*, 27 August 2002, available from www.nytimes.com (accessed 27 August 2002); D.E. Sanger, 'First among evils? The debate over attacking Iraq heats up', *New York Times*, 1 September 2002, available at www.nytimes.com (accessed 31 August 2002); 'Full text: in Cheney's words', *New York Times*, 26 August 2002, available at www.nytimes.com (accessed 30 August 2002).

49. Iraq's chemical weapons programme began in the early to mid 1970s, and according to Cordesman and Wagner, Iraq 'weaponized mustard gas for use by mortars and artillery long before the Iran–Iraq War and to have had shells for at least 120-mm mortars and 130-mm artillery'. Cordesman and Wagner, *The Iran–Iraq War*, p. 507.

50. See Segal, 'The Iran–Iraq War'; McNaugher, 'Ballistic Missiles', p. 17; Cordesman and Wagner, *The Iran–Iraq War*, pp. 510, and 514.

51. See Segal, 'The Iran–Iraq War'; McNaugher, 'Ballistic Missiles', p. 18. Kenneth Pollack argues that 'by early 1984, Iraqi production was sufficient to allow Baghdad to employ chemical warfare in every major battle of the rest of the war and many minor ones – including skirmishes in Kurdistan that posed no threat to either the regime or the coherence of its defenses'. Kenneth M. Pollack, *The Threatening Storm: The Case for Invading Iraq*, New York, Random House, 2002, p. 259.

52. Saddam Hussein's regime also used chemical weapons against domestic opponents, particularly the Kurds. Human Rights Watch lists 39 known chemical attacks in Iraqi Kurdistan in 1987–88. See Human Rights Watch, *Iraq's Crime of Genocide: The Anfal Campaign against the Kurds*, New Haven, CT, Yale University Press, 1995, especially Appendix C, pp. 262–5.

53. Chemical weapons were also one of the means that Saddam Hussein used against internal opponents of the regime. While this has been justly condemned, the 2003 war was not justified on the basis of Saddam Hussein's tyranny and murder of his opponents, but on the threat to international security posed by his regime and its possession of CBN.

54. See Pollack, *The Threatening Storm*, p. 264.

55. While the United States did not explicitly threaten nuclear retaliation, it did state that any use of WMD would be met with 'overwhelming force'. The Chemical Weapons Convention was not opened for signature until 1993, and the United States reserved the right to retaliate with chemical weapons if so attacked in its reservation to the Geneva Protocol, so retaliation with chemical weapons would not have violated international law in 1991.

56. Pollack argues that the lack of chemical use by Iraq may have been due to a lack of preparation, rather than to deterrence. See *The Threatening Storm*, pp. 264–5. Even if Pollack is right, the lack of preparation suggests that Saddam Hussein did not see these weapons as essential or as weapons that should be automatically used.

See also 'Iraq's Chemical Warfare Capability: Lack of Use During the War', a CIA intelligence report that attributes Iraq's lack of use to fear of retaliation and Iraqi misjudgments about the course of the war. 'Iraq's Chemical Warfare Capability: Lack of Use During the War', file 970613_092496_ui_txt_0001.txt, available at www.gulflink.osd.mil/decalssdocs/cia/19970825/970613_092496_ui_txt_001.html (accessed 17 March 1999).

57. Israel would have a wide variety of ways to retaliate; in addition to its conventional strength, it is widely believed to have CBN weapons. (Israel has not joined either the Nuclear Nonproliferation Treaty or the Biological Weapons Convention, and has signed but not ratified the CWC.)

58. See 'Letter dated October 7 to Senator Bob Graham, Democrat of Florida and Chairman of the Intelligence Committee, by George J. Tenet, director of Central Intelligence, about decisions to declassify material related to the debate about Iraq', available at www.gwu.edu/~nsarchiv/NSAEBB/NSAEBB80/wmd13.pdf (accessed 17 December 2002); see also A. Mitchell and C. Hulse, 'CIA warns that a US attack may ignite terror', *New York Times*, 9 October 2002, available at www.nytimes.com (accessed 9 October 2002); M.R. Gordon, 'American aides split on assessment of Iraq's plans', *New York Times*, 10 October 2002, available at www.nytimes.com (accessed 10 October 2002).

59. The non-use of CB weapons in the 2003 war – whether due to Iraq's destruction of these weapons or a decision not to use existing weapons – supports this. Saddam Hussein had some chance of surviving a conventional attack on Iraq; indeed, he did survive and may have dreamed of re-establishing his regime until he was captured in December 2003. But the use of CB weapons risked provoking a nuclear response that would have killed him and/or destroyed the country he wished to rule.

60. D. Holt, 'Chemical, biological arms have major limitations', *Chicago Tribune*, 7 February 2003 (accessed through Lexis-Nexis).

61. See sources cited in note 44.

62. See Pollack, *The Threatening Storm*, p. 155; see also 'A Decade of Deception and Defiance: Saddam Hussein's Defiance of the United Nations', 12 September 2002, p. 18. This is a Bush Administration document that provides some examples of Saddam Hussein's involvement with international terrorism; it is available at www. gwu.edu/`nsarchiv/NSAEBB/NSAEBB80?wmd10.pdf (accessed 2 June 2003).

63. The Bush Administration continues to charge that Saddam Hussein's regime was helping al-Qaeda acquire CB weapons. American intelligence analysts are apparently not convinced. See 'Al Qaeda henchman says Iraq furnished chemical, biological arms aid: White House', 9 August 2003, available at www.spacewar. com/2003/030808224732.ifeiqrn2.html (accessed 13 August 2003); see also J. Risen, 'Prague discounts an Iraqi meeting', *New York Times*, 21 October 2002, available at www.nytimes.com (accessed 21 October 2002); B. Morton, 'Selling an Iraq–al Qaeda Connection', CNN.com, 11 March 2003 (accessed through CNN. com, 21 August 2003); W. Pincus, 'Report cast doubt on Iraq–Al Qaeda connection', *Washington Post*, 22 June 2003 available at www.washingtonpost.com/ac2/wp-dyn/ A19822-2003Jun21?language=printer (accessed 21 August 2003). For an analysis of reports of al-Qaeda's interest in, and pursuit of, CBN weapons, see G.A. Ackerman and J.M. Bale, 'Al-Qa'ida and Weapons of Mass Destruction' from the Center for Nonproliferation Studies, available at http://cns.miis.edu/pubs/other/alqwmd. htm (accessed 7 February 2004).

64. See, for example, United States, *National Security Strategy of the United States*, pp. 13–16.
65. Ibid., p. 15.
66. Pollack, *The Threatening Storm*, especially pp. 243–80; see also Avigdor Haselkorn, *The Continuing Storm*, New Haven, CT, Yale University Press, 1999.
67. Pollack, *The Threatening Storm*, p. 248; on oil wells see p. 265.
68. See Pollack, *The Threatening Storm*, p. 265 and Kenneth M. Pollack, 'Why Iraq can't be deterred', *New York Times*, 16 October 2002, available at http://usinfo.state.gov/topical/pol/02101611.htm, accessed 16 July 2003.
69. Pollack, *The Threatening Storm*, p. 254.
70. Ibid., p. 256.
71. K.N. Waltz, 'More May be Better', in S.D. Sagan and K.N. Waltz, *The Spread of Nuclear Weapons: A Debate*, New York, W.W. Norton and Company, 1995, pp. 8 and 7.
72. Pollack, *The Threatening Storm*, p. 256.
73. Ibid., p. 178.
74. See ibid., pp. 250–1, see also pp. 272–5. Possible scenarios described by Pollack include a second invasion of Kuwait and a takeover of Saudi oilfields, as well as intervention to promote regime change in Jordan and Syria.
75. For a deterrent threat to be successful, the negative expected utility of the threatened retaliation must outweigh the positive expected utility of a successful attack. The damage that can be done by a nuclear attack means that the likelihood of attack does not need to be very great in order to outweigh the successful utility of attack in most situations.
76. Pollack argues that a pure deterrent strategy would have entailed removing many US troops from the Middle East, hampering the ability to make a conventional counter to Iraqi aggression. But in the face of Iraqi aggression one would expect the threatened state(s) to welcome US troops, as they did in 1991; in addition, as mentioned above, the emphasis in current US military doctrine on long-range strikes and special operations lessens the need for a large military build-up before an attack. See Pollack, *The Threatening Storm*, pp. 273–4.
77. US Deputy Secretary of Defense Paul Wolfowitz links Saddam Hussein's overthrow with the removal of troops from Saudi Arabia in a May 2003 interview with Sam Tannenhaus of *Vanity Fair*. The transcript of the interview is available at www.defenselink.mil/transcripts/2003/tr20030509-depsecdef0223.html (accessed 7 February 2004).
78. The text of this and other UN Security Council resolutions is available at www.un.org/Docs/sc/unsc_resolutions.html (accessed 9 February 2004).
79. The sanctions were imposed under Security Council Resolution 661, passed on 6 August 1990.
80. As part of the ongoing monitoring and verification programme, Security Council Resolution 1051 (1996) set up an export/import control mechanism to govern materials related to CBN weapons.
81. The no-fly zones, first imposed by the United States, the United Kingdom and France, and later by only the first two states, were not authorised by the United Nations, although Security Council Resolution 688 (1991) did condemn the repression of civilian populations in Iraq.
82. See Schelling, *Arms and Influence*, p. 2.

83. Alternatively, some seem to have viewed Saddam Hussein as the fundamental cause of Iraq's pursuit of CBN weapons. This too may be a dangerously simplistic understanding of the role of these weapons.

84. UNSCR 687 (1991), para. 14.

85. For a related discussion, see Ritter, 'The Case for Iraq's Qualitative Disarmament'.

86. See, for example, S/1997/779, 8 October 1997, para. 79.

87. US Department of State, 'What Does Disarmament Look Like?', 23 January 2003. Available at www.state.gov/t/np/rls/other/16820pf.htm (accessed 21 August 2003).

88. G. Shelton, 'South Africa's Nuclear Weapons Experience and the Global Arms Control Agenda', Paper presented at the Conference on Unlocking South Africa's Nuclear Past at the University of the Witwatersrand on 31 July 2002. Available at www.wits/ac/za/saha/nuclearhistory/conf/contrib._Shelton.doc (accessed 21 August 2003). For further analysis of South Africa's nuclear programme, see also D. Albright, 'Nuclear Rollback: Understanding South Africa's Denuclearization Decision', in B.R. Schneider and W. L. Dowdy, eds, *Pulling Back from the Nuclear Brink*, London, Frank Cass, 1998, pp. 80–7; P. Liberman, 'The Rise and Fall of the South African Bomb', *International Security*, Vol. 26, No. 2 Fall 2001, pp. 45–86.

89. On South Africa's CB weapons programme, see H.E. Purkitt and S. Burgess, 'South Africa's Chemical and Biological Warfare Programme: A Historical and International Perspective', *Journal of Southern African Studies*, Vol. 28, No. 2, June 2002, pp. 229–53; S. Burgess and H. Purkitt, 'The Rollback of South Africa's Biological Weapons Program', INSS Occasional Paper 37, USAF Institute for National Security Studies, February 2001 available at www.usafa.af.mil/inss/ocp37.htm (accessed 13 February 2003).

90. Iraq's unilateral destruction of its CB programmes, which was a violation of its obligations under Security Council Resolution 687, complicated the attempt to verify its disarmament. While the UN inspectors continued to demand that Iraq turn over records of this destruction, it is possible that such records really do not exist: the example of both the United States and Canada suggests that states do not always keep careful records of such destruction, and to the extent that Iraq was attempting to hide the details of its programmes, it would have had an incentive not to keep detailed records. For news stories that reveal the incompleteness of US and Canadian records, see 'US finds evidence of WMD at last – buried in a field near Maryland', *Guardian*, 28 May 2003, accessed through ProQuest Direct; see also 'Canada searches for chemical, biological weapons', 5 July 2003, posted on the CBC website at http://cbc.ca/cgi-bin/templates/print.cgi?/2003/07/05/weapons_search030705 (accessed 8 July 2003).

91. See, for example, C. Hoyos and R. Khalaf, 'Trade becomes Iraq's strongest weapon', *Financial Times*, 10 September 2001 (accessed through Lexis-Nexis).

92. Others argue that Libya was ready to negotiate long before the Iraq war, and that overcoming its economic isolation was the main motivation for Libya's actions. See T. Lantos, 'A New Libya?', *Washington Post*, 31 January 2004, available at www.washingtonpost.com (accessed 7 February 2004); G. Hart, 'My secret talks with Libya and why they went nowhere', *Washington Post*, 18 January 2004, accessed through Lexis-Nexis; P.E. Tyler, 'Libyan stagnation a big factor in Qaddafi surprise', *New York Times*, 7 January 2004, available at www.nytimes.com (accessed 7 February 2004).

93. The United States has been working with China, Russia, South Korea and Japan in an effort to negotiate the end of North Korea's nuclear programme.

94. Avner Cohen and Benjamin Frankel argue that opaque proliferation is characterised by no nuclear tests, the denial of possession, a non-use of direct nuclear threats, a failure to incorporate nuclear weapons into military doctrine, no military deployment of nuclear weapons, organisational insulation of nuclear activities, and a lack of open debate about those activities. See A. Cohen and B. Frankel, 'Opaque Nuclear Proliferation' in B. Frankel, ed., *Opaque Nuclear Proliferation*, London, Frank Cass, 1991, pp. 21–2. An opaque capability is not one that is completely secret, and other states may know – or at least suspect – that the capability exists.

95. In January 2004, North Korea invited an unofficial delegation of American experts to view its 'nuclear deterrent'. The key evidence presented was evidently a sample of plutonium, along with a demonstration that the 8000 spent fuel rods that had been in cooling ponds under UN inspection had been removed and presumably reprocessed. But the group was not shown a nuclear device. See G. Kessler, 'North Korean evidence called uncertain', *Washington Post*, 22 January 2004, available at www.washingtonpost.com (accessed 22 January 2004); G. Kessler, 'North Korea displays "nuclear deterrent"', *Washington Post*, 11 January 2004, available at www.. washingtonpost.com (accessed 22 January 2004); D.E. Sanger, 'Visitors see North Korea nuclear capacity', *New York Times*, 11 January 2004, available at www.nytimes. com (accessed 12 January 2004); J. Yardley, 'Group of private U.S. experts visits North Korea nuclear plant', *New York Times*, 10 January 2004, available at www. nytimes.com (accessed 12 January 2004). For more information on North Korea's nuclear programme, see IISS, *North Korea's Weapons Programmes: A Net Assessment*, London, International Institute for Strategic Studies, January 2004.

96. The possible benefits of opaque proliferation included the possibility of stabilising an arms race short of the actual deployment of weapons, and the avoidance of direct violations of nonproliferation regimes. For various views on the virtues and liabilities of opaque proliferation, see Frankel, *Opaque Nuclear Proliferation*.

97. See, for example, 'Top secret Iraqi documents strewn across missile facility', CNN.com, 3 June 2003 (accessed 6 June 2003); 'Iraq: after the war: US dirty bomb fears after nuclear looting', *Guardian*, 21 May 2003 (accessed through ProQuest Direct).

12
Post-Conflict Reconstruction in Iraq: Lessons Unlearned

Karin von Hippel

Just after midnight, on 20 December 1989, and just one year into his presidency, President George Herbert Walker Bush ordered the invasion of Panama, a decision that would have far reaching implications not just for Panamanians, but also for the US government as it assumed its lone superpower role. Indeed, the mistakes made prior to this operation, during the invasion itself, and in the post-conflict period taught US and UN policy makers valuable lessons about nation-building[1] in the 1990s. Many of these were subsequently applied in Haiti, Bosnia, Kosovo and East Timor.

By the end of 2003, it appeared that most of the lessons learned in the 1990s had been ignored or overlooked by the next President Bush, who was sworn into office at the beginning of 2001 on an anti-nation-building platform. At that time, his soon-to-be National Security Adviser Condoleezza Rice outlined what would initially become President Bush's security strategy. She wrote,

> The president must remember that the military is a special instrument. It is lethal, and it is meant to be. It is not a civilian police force. It is not a political referee. And it is most certainly not designed to build a civilian society.[2]

On 26 February 2003, the *Washington Post* dug up a criticism of Al Gore by George Bush the day before the presidential elections. Bush declared, 'Let me tell you what else I'm worried about: I'm worried about an opponent who uses nation building and the military in the same sentence.'

The tragedy of 9/11 reversed President Bush's policy, and more closely aligned it to the activist foreign policy of his father and of President Clinton. Not only did President Bush subsequently endorse military assisted nation-building in Afghanistan and in Iraq, but he even sent troops into Liberia on a humanitarian mission in August 2003, a country not exactly of 'vital interest' to the United States, even given its special historical relationship. Yet despite his eventual embrace of President Clinton's policy, the Bush Administration has not incorporated the lessons-learning process of the 1990s with similar vigour, particularly in the case of Iraq, which, unlike Afghanistan, was intended from the start to be an all-out nation-building exercise. Indeed, if one considered the state of affairs in Iraq at the end of 2003, more than half a year after the official end of hostilities was declared on 1 May 2003, the situation looked dire, even taking into account Saddam Hussein's capture in mid December: coalition soldiers were cherry-picked on a daily basis, critical infrastructure regularly damaged, and large car bombs have killed hundreds of international aid workers, diplomats and Iraqi civilians. For the US government in particular, the costs have been enormous: an average of one US soldier per day has died in Iraq since the official end of hostilities: as of mid January 2004, 234 hostile US fatalities. In financial terms, the US treasury has been doling out $1 billion a week over the same period on the military costs alone.[3]

This chapter analyses post-conflict reconstruction in Iraq, focusing primarily on the first six months. It examines which of the major lessons learned since the end of the Cold War were ignored and which were applied. The initial six-month period is considered crucial by most analysts in determining the future course for a country emerging from violent conflict. Mistakes made during this time can have lasting effects, and the intervening power can often spend years undoing the damage done. Likewise, for the intervening power, it is imperative to get things right during this period as domestic support will still be high: Americans stand tall as they watch their troops land in overwhelming numbers, feed the starving, and stop the killing. After a few months, however, when the media has moved on to the next conflict, it is harder to keep the public engaged and willing to continue to pay the enormous costs necessary to establish a stable democracy, particularly when troops are being killed.

What lessons from the past 15 years of nation-building have been generally recognised as being core to enhancing post-conflict reconstruction during this critical initial period? The cases referred to are those in which the US government played a major role in the military intervention, as well as in the post-conflict reconstruction period – that is, in Panama, Somalia, Haiti, Bosnia, East Timor[4] and Kosovo – as they are instructive for understanding what has (and has not) happened in Iraq. From these experiences, numerous academic and policy studies have chronicled the lessons learned.[5] Just before the war in Iraq, a number of further studies by prominent policy makers and academics pointed to many of these lessons and how they should be applied to Iraq.[6]

Given that the focus of this chapter is on the first six months, the emphasis will be primarily security related, though other political and economic measures are also necessary to initiate reforms. A review of previous cases points to six lessons that have been unlearned, and only two that have been realised in this initial phase in Iraq. While it is likely that the intervention would still have encountered serious obstacles even if planning and initial responses had been perfectly executed from the beginning, the point of this article is that by ignoring basic lessons from recent experiences, the US-led coalition severely constrained progress, and lost critical support from the Iraqi population. The negative impact due to the lives lost – of international civil servants, coalition soldiers as well as Iraqis – and financial resources spent, could potentially have been minimised had planning and execution been more strategic and inclusive, though this is also impossible to prove.

Lessons unlearned

Power vacuums = looting and criminality

The establishment of security and the rule of law have generally been recognised as *the* priority in immediate post-conflict reconstruction. In the short-term, the establishment of security is central to prevent widespread looting and criminal elements from establishing a foothold. Lessons learned in Panama and Kosovo respectively should have been instructive.

Looting

In Panama, the massive looting and collapse of civilian agencies throughout the country, especially in Panama City, came as a complete surprise to US troops.[7] Moreover, its occurrence gave the impression that US troops were not managing the situation they had created by the intervention. Since Panama, contingency planning for similar pillaging has been incorporated into military strategy in the subsequent operations mentioned. Looting was hence not a problem to the same degree.

The massive looting in Iraq, therefore, should have been anticipated. Indeed, Iraqi advisers had also proposed the imposition of martial law for this exact reason, and there were Iraqi army units available, but they were not used. Yet there were too few troops in theatre to stop the looting because Secretary of Defense Donald Rumsfeld insisted on keeping troop numbers low, and Turkey refused passage for US troops.[8] It appears as well that the mistaken assumption on the part of the Pentagon planners was that the Iraqi police would remain in their posts and prevent such disorder from occurring. As one senior US soldier told this author, 'in Iraq, we didn't follow our own doctrine'.

Given the serious attention the US military placed on this part of the lessons learning process after Panama, it is unclear why this was not a critical component in the planning for Iraq. It is likely that if plans had been drawn up to deal with this contingency, they were not considered as critical by some in the Pentagon, and therefore not utilised. General Wesley Clark added: 'The ensuing disorder vitiated some of the boost in US credibility that was won on the battlefield, and it opened the way for deeper and more organized resistance during the following weeks.'[9]

Criminality

In Kosovo, the initial deployment of international police was too slow (as it was for other international representatives of the security sector). A dangerous power vacuum was thus created, and as with all power vacuums, was filled by the worst elements. The UN mission (UNMIK) henceforth spent far too much time in the first year trying to remove criminal gangs from political power in most of the municipalities as well as from businesses that were usurped when Serbs left the province in large numbers. The Kosovo Forces (KFOR) units were reluctant to assume policing duties, though on many occasions they did. Kosovo today still suffers from criminality: the few lucrative businesses, such as large hotels, remain in the hands of gangs, illegal construction mars most cities, and smuggling and trafficking of goods and people continue to blight most parts of the Balkans.[10] After Kosovo, many senior military and police figures recommended that planners for future operations consider the deployment of international police along with the military in the immediate post-combat phase to have a working police presence on the streets.[11]

In Iraq, the speed with which some of the national treasures were looted and most likely transported out of the country indicated well-organised criminal gangs far more attuned to the political vacuum that would be caused by the entry of US troops than the intervening power. And it was not just concerns over rare artefacts; there were legitimate fears that if Iraq had any weapons of mass destruction, some of these materials could have been looted.

Security sector reform

While police, military, judicial, penal reforms as well as civilian oversight of the military are all proceeding apace, and will in any case be long-term projects, problems have been encountered that could have been mitigated based on past experience. In previous operations, some states have chosen to abolish the armed forces entirely and maintain only the police, as in Costa Rica, Haiti or Panama. An alternative has also been the retraining of the military for civil emergencies and related domestic concerns.

In a similar vein, the creation of an entirely new police force has normally been necessary, one that could ensure public safety and gain the confidence of the local population. The goal of such initiatives is to achieve a comprehensive change in mindset of the local police and of the public, as previously the police in these countries had only served to terrify civilians through extortion and torture, instead of providing protection. In Panama, moreover, the US military considered it of utmost importance to have a working Panamanian presence on the streets so that the US troops would not be seen as an occupying force.

In most of the cases mentioned, newly trained forces have inevitably included some members of the old force due to the lack of experienced personnel, and the belief that it would take longer to train an entire corps of new officers than to retrain some of the old. Such a policy has not been without controversy, although the method applied in Haiti appeared to have garnered more domestic support. In Haiti, the approach was to phase out the old force in increments, while simultaneously recruiting and training new troops. The experience in Bosnia also shows the advantage of promoting accountability by international police trainers,[12] while in Kosovo, UNMIK initiated a similarly transparent multiethnic programme that included comprehensive background checks.

Many have argued that it did not make sense to disband the entire army, as Bremer did in late May 2003, if only to keep thousands of trained, armed and potentially disgruntled men busy.

In Kosovo, one of the motivations for maintaining the Kosovo Protection Corps, created from the former guerrilla group, the Kosovo Liberation Army, had been to keep these trained and armed men under watch and notionally disarmed so as to prevent them from causing trouble in the province and in neighbouring states. In Iraq as well, a large number of men had been employed in some form of security service, and while perhaps the top layers of the military and police, along with some of the paramilitary units, may have been tainted, the vast majority were not considered hard-line Ba'athists by most Iraqis.[13]

The role of the military

One of the most important shifts in the operations that has taken place in the past half-century concerns the role of the US military in political reconstruction. A conspicuous change had been the gradual reduction of US military control over nation-building activities, with the allied occupation of Germany and Japan representing the peak. Indeed, both of these operations were directed entirely by the military, with civilian agencies playing a subordinate role.

Panama was the last operation in which the military overtly directed political reconstruction, although there, at least, the US military had extensive experience and relations with Panamanians. Somalia was the last in which the military made important behind-the-scenes decisions (such as preparation of the nation-building resolutions for the Security Council). By Haiti, Bosnia, Kosovo and East Timor, the military's role was primarily confined to maintaining security and back-stopping democratisation activities.

A cardinal rule of democracy is to ensure that the military is subservient to civilian rule. It is extremely important for both symbolic and structural reasons not to allow these roles to be reversed, particularly by the occupying power and particularly when the aim of the entire exercise is to build a democratic and accountable state.

In Iraq, the US Department of Defense (DOD) did not transfer power to the State Department after the transition to the post-combat phase, and far too many soldiers were involved in political reconstruction activities throughout the country. While Bremer was a civilian, he still reported to the DOD, which remained the lead department for political reconstruction in Iraq.

Joint civil-military planning

Improvements in civil-military relations have been another striking development since Panama, when there was no initial cooperation with civilian agencies that would be involved in reconstruction due to the need to maintain secrecy about the timing – and indeed occurrence – of the invasion. This exclusion delayed the democratisation process. In Somalia, there was a conspicuous lack of cooperation on all sides and turf wars: between UN headquarters in New York and UN operations in Mogadishu, between civilian and military operators in Mogadishu, and even between US and foreign militaries. Additionally, while preparing for Somalia, there was no joint planning between the military and the heads of relief organisations, even though the military was originally deployed to provide protection for these organisations. In such a climate, it was hardly surprising that it became extremely difficult to carry out the mandate. By Haiti, Bosnia, Kosovo and East Timor, both were closely involved in the planning and implementation of political reconstruction.

Indeed, the Haiti operation experienced the fewest difficulties in implementation because military, humanitarian and development agencies were melded in a tight partnership due to the insistence of the Special Representative of the Secretary-General (SRSG), Lakhdar Brahimi. The development agenda was integral from the beginning, civilian and military actors trained together before deployment, and a civilian directed the entire operation. Within the US government, all civilian and military agencies that would be involved met regularly to plan out the mission. This did not guarantee that Haiti would develop a stable democracy, and indeed, the country is facing numerous problems today partly because the major intervening power lost interest after a short period of time. The point is that a well-coordinated initial phase provided the best possible environment for democratic reforms to take root.

In Iraq, in sharp contrast, although a number of US and UK agencies and think tanks participated in planning exercises, the Pentagon did not participate to a significant degree, nor did Pentagon officials take any of the major recommendations on board. The State Department had even prepared a lengthy document based on discussions initiated during the year prior to the war, which anticipated many of the problems, but this too was ignored.[14] While in general military staffs tend to develop and fine tune military plans for operations of this kind over years, it was striking that in this case planning for the post-combat phase only occurred in the final few months before the war. Moreover, General Garner's Office of Humanitarian and Reconstruction Assistance in the Pentagon was underfunded and understaffed from the outset. As General Wesley Clark noted, 'When planning finally began that autumn, it was based on the assumption that a US invasion would be welcomed as a liberation by most Iraqis.'[15] This was clearly not the case, and even if they had, as Louis Henkin wryly remarked after Panama, 'People have welcomed conquering armies since the beginning of time, especially when the conquering army is still there.'[16]

Civil-military relations

Beyond issues related to planning, the working relationship between civilian agencies and the military has also deteriorated since Somalia and Bosnia in the early 1990s, when UN peacekeeping troops provided security for delivery of assistance. UN agencies in general were happy with the role the military played in the latter instance as UN Protection Force (UNPROFOR) troops worked under the direction of the UN and did not act independently. In Kosovo, the picture grew more complicated as the military were tasked to establish refugee camps because the civilian actors did not have the capacity to do so. Here is where the UN considered that the military no longer worked under the guidance of the UN, and often operated at their own discretion without consulting the UN. Civilian agencies also worried about appearing too closely linked to belligerents.

Afghanistan and Iraq were further points of departure from this supportive role, where the US military (and also the UK and other militaries) assumed a direct humanitarian role, delivering aid and supporting civic restoration projects, while also having belligerent status. Some humanitarian organisations were involved in planning prior to the war in Iraq, and others prepared contingency plans for an eventual deployment, yet involvement for all too many NGOs and UN agencies remained controversial because many of these organisations had been against the war in the first place and did not want to become linked, at least in Iraqi eyes, with the aggressors.[17] In Iraq as well, because two of the major humanitarian donors were also the belligerents, the issue had become even more complicated for some agencies in terms of fundraising for their operations.

Issues of neutrality and impartiality are of great concern to humanitarian and development agencies, and many published guidelines for how they would coexist with the military in Iraq as well as in future operations.[18] A further difficulty arose in Iraq: the occupying powers were obliged by the Geneva Conventions to ensure the security and well-being of civilians, yet humanitarian agencies were reluctant to accept military protection and preferred to carry out the work on the ground themselves. Earlier in the decade, they had gone through a difficult but necessary adjustment period in order to adapt to each other's very different cultures, and had developed a *modus operandi*. Today, arguably, the gap between civilian and military agencies has re-emerged.

Multilateralism

The response to the unilateral US intervention in Panama was strikingly similar to Iraq. Subsequent interventions were multinational, and all but Kosovo were approved by the Security Council, despite the obvious problems inherent in making decisions by committee. The legitimacy conferred by international support and participation, and cost-sharing, were considered paramount by US policy makers.

The damage done to the US government by essentially going it alone in Iraq (albeit with the support of a handful of countries) will likely have reverberations far beyond the inability of the US government to obtain significant support from a larger coalition. Potential contributors – of soldiers, civilian personnel and financing – had been wary of entering a situation that would not give them commensurate decision making authority, nor grant the UN significantly more power, particularly as many of these potential contributors were against the war in the first place. Leaving humanitarian concerns aside, they wondered why they should be responsible for cleaning up a mess caused by the US government. They also wondered why they should entrust their soldiers to a coalition that was not exactly winning hearts and minds, in an environment that was terribly insecure. Even the unanimous agreement on Security Council Resolution 1511 (October 2003) could not secure the troop and financial contributions hoped for by the United States. Pre-emptive unilateral interventions lack legitimacy if not perceived to be in response to a manifest, imminent threat. Otherwise, pre-emptive use of military force sets a dangerous precedent in an already unstable international order, can be extremely costly, and in this case, can undermine the war against terror.

Indeed, the manifest US occupation of Iraq has only served to humiliate even moderate Muslims, enrage Islamic extremists, open the floodgates for Mujahadin fighters, and contribute to anti-Americanism in too many parts of the world.[19] While there was no established connection between Saddam Hussein and al-Qaeda prior to the war, as all too many analysts predicted, today one has been created.[20] It is extremely difficult to distinguish between hard-line Ba'athists fighting the occupation, Iraqis taking revenge for family members killed by the coalition, members of al-Qaeda who see this as an opportunity to attack America, and Mujahadin gunmen who may not be technically associated with al-Qaeda, but nevertheless have heeded bin Laden's call to fight the 'infidel' in Iraq. No matter how rich and technically proficient the US government may be, a unilateralist foreign policy in a globalised world can only be unpopular, impractical, and counter-productive.

Support from the population

Poor planning and bad coordination between civilian and military actors only serve to impair the operation once it is under way. And a poor initial phase undermines the local support required to tolerate a foreign occupation, which by definition would be considered humiliating even in the best of circumstances. Sergio de Mello rightly pointed out before he was tragically assassinated, 'This must be one of the most humiliating periods in history [for Iraqis]. Who would like to see their country occupied? I would not like to see foreign tanks in Copacabana.'[21] If the UN instead had been put in charge of political reconstruction, and the military under the direction of a multinational force, preferably under the stewardship of NATO,[22] the occupation would have been viewed as more legitimate. 'Provisional Authority' would have come to mean just that for Iraqis and others around the world who may mistrust the motivation of the US government.

The lesson from far too many other peace support operations is that once the occupying power is no longer seen to be in control and providing security, the population will start to attack that power and set up independent militias. The more anarchic the situation becomes, the more the population will tolerate another authoritarian ruler, if only to have security. In Iraq, as elsewhere, that leader could also be a religious extremist. Alternatively, the situation could lead to civil war. Neither are desired outcomes.

On numerous occasions since the post-combat phase began, US Administration officials have remarked that they 'underestimated' the challenges that were to face them, and did not 'anticipate' the sustained attacks against them. As is evident from the experiences in the 1990s, that should not have been the case. Two critical lessons have been realised, however, as discussed below.

Lessons learned

Staying power

The hasty exits from Afghanistan and Somalia in the late 1980s and early 1990s taught US policy makers the dangers of short-termism, although this lesson was not realised until the late 1990s. Indeed, in the early and mid 1990s, US policy makers frequently referred to the Vietnam-induced fear of 'Mission Creep', which adversely affected planning for all the operations. Once the Dayton peace process began to be realised on the ground in Bosnia, however, the vernacular evolved from 'Exit Strategies' to 'End States'. In 1999, Dave Scanlon, SFOR (Stabilisation Force) Spokesperson, told this author that

> SFOR is now working toward an 'end state', not an 'end date'. Deadlines no longer apply to the mission here ... What is left is to ensure a stable and secure environment so that ... a lasting peace [can be] established.[23]

A public, lengthy commitment to the operation was henceforth considered critical for allowing confidence-building measures sufficient time to be adopted.

Coupled with this was the improved understanding by policy makers in the US government and the UN that support for transitional elections in any country, such as in Haiti during the 1990 election, needs to be supplemented by meaningful, post-election programmes that can cope with 'inexperienced, weak, democratically elected governments coexisting with powerful anti-democratic structures of power'.[24] The common assumption among many policy makers in the United States had been that the bulk of the foreign presence could leave once elections were held.

In Iraq, the oft-repeated public commitment by the US Administration to a democratic future for Iraq, which by definition would require a prolongation of the international presence, depicts a continuation of this trend. On 27 August 2003, President Bush cited the allied occupations of Germany and Japan, noting the length of time that had been necessary to turn those countries into stable democracies. Indeed, after the Allies left, the US government continued to support German political and economic reforms for years until Germany became a stable, democratic state. Richard Merritt described the US success in democratising Germany in the following way: 'Its accomplishment require[d] clarity of goals, complete co-operation among the occupying powers, and withal persistence in the face of inner doubts, resistance to external criticism, and acceptance of the glacial pace inherent to the process.'[25]

In mid November, however, there was a setback on this commitment, with the promise to speed up the handover of power to Iraqi authorities by spring 2004. Whether political pressures and mounting American casualties will cause Bush to accelerate this process further remains to be seen. Similarly, in December 2003 the US government was pressuring the Afghani government to hold elections in June 2004, against the advice of the UN head of mission as well as many other experts. In both situations, it appears that the Bush Administration wants to be able to point to successes in democratic transitions due to the US presidential election in 2004, even if the policies may be myopic and likely to be harmful in the long-term.

Body bags

As noted previously, the interventions in the 1990s taught extremists that the US military (and government) was overly preoccupied with force protection, and had adopted what Thomas Weiss coined 'a zero-casualty foreign policy'.[26] Bin Laden also learned from Somalia of the US aversion to body-bags. Not only did this send the wrong message to terrorists, but it also prevented American troops from providing the necessary leadership in peace support missions, and interfered with relations with allies.

Force protection policies have interfered with the realisation of the mandates in all the operations except Panama. Even there, ironically, one of the justifications for the invasion was the 'threat to American lives', yet only one US citizen had been killed prior to the invasion, while 23 US troops were killed during Operation Just Cause. By Somalia, US soldiers were no longer allowed to die, at least not on a humanitarian mission. The fear of body-bags thus far has been mainly an American preoccupation, although in Bosnia, anxiety about Serb reprisals on British, Dutch and French peacekeepers put a stop to NATO bombing sorties for some time. Later during the Implementation Force (IFOR) and NATO's subsequent operation, SFOR, this fear impeded the active apprehension of indicted war criminals, particularly Karadzic and Mladic, by NATO troops.[27]

Many find it absurd that an American soldier's life abroad has been valued more highly than at home. This point does not mean that the lives of US soldiers are dispensable, but rather that their security will be enhanced by clearer and more robust rules of engagement. If strong signals are consistently sent out to errant leaders that mistreatment of foreign soldiers (and also humanitarian workers) will be met with serious reprisals, both will operate in a more secure environment. This policy was reversed after September 11, 2001, and although all US (and coalition) troops killed in Afghanistan and Iraq have been regrettable, the military now operates in a manner more appropriate to their training and mission. How patient the US public will be if the number of deaths and injuries continues to rise is another question, and certainly the lengthy deployment and insecure environment in Iraq has been the cause of numerous complaints by US soldiers.

Conclusion

While these two previous lessons are important and demonstrate some attention paid to prior experiences, even a full adoption of the first – the lengthy time commitment – appeared uncertain at the end of 2003. The balance during the first six months is therefore still weighed against a full acknowledgement and adoption of the most important lessons learned in the past 15 years by a ratio of 3 to 1. Numerous pundits have argued that they had warned the US government early on what would happen if it was not prepared. One often needs to display humility when claiming 'I told you so', as it could be argued that this only proves one's own irrelevancy. The evolution of best practice and incorporation of lessons learned during the operations in the 1990s, reflected in the many studies by prominent policy makers and researchers – from both sides of the political divide and both sides of the Atlantic – demonstrate that this administration was not interested in consultation.

After Panama, Richard Shultz explained:

At the most general level, the first [lesson] is the need to recognize post conflict situations as important and complex missions for the Department of Defense. This was clearly not discerned in Panama. The US did not have, at the time of Operation Just Cause, a policy for the period following the use of force.[28] It appears, in too many ways, that little has changed.

Notes

1. The term 'nation' in fact signifies what is known as a 'state', but in the United States, the term 'state' gets confused with the 50 states that comprise the United States. Although the term 'nation-building' incorrectly depicts what the US government is attempting to do, as it rarely strives to create a nation, inhabited by peoples of the same collective identity, this term has become synonymous with state-building. For example, when the US government and the UN attempted to rebuild Somalia, they did not try to reunite all Somalis living in Djibouti, Kenya and Ethiopia with Somalis in the former Somali Republic, which would have indeed created a Somali nation, but rather they focused on rebuilding the former Somali Republic.

2. 'Campaign 2000: Promoting the National Interest', *Foreign Affairs*, January–February 2000.

3. In September 2003, President Bush requested an additional $87 billion for Iraq and Afghanistan, all this from an already overstretched US economy.

4. The United States did not play such an overt role in East Timor, though it did play a role behind the scenes. East Timor is included as it was another example of an interim administration, and a serious nation-building effort led by the United Nations.

5. See, for example, Richard Caplan, *A New Trusteeship? The International Administration of War-torn Territories*, Adelphi Paper No. 341, Oxford, Oxford University Press/IISS, 2002; Nici Dahrendorf, ed., *A Review of Peace Operations: A Case for Change. Sierra Leone, Kosovo, East Timor, Afghanistan*, London, King's College, March 2003; *Play to Win: The Commission on Post-Conflict Reconstruction*, Washington DC, Center for Strategic and International Studies and the Association of the US Army, January 2003; Karin von Hippel, *Democracy by Force: US Military Intervention in the Post-Cold War World*, Cambridge, Cambridge University Press, 2000; *Report of the Panel on United Nations Peace Operations*, New York, United Nations, 21 August 2000 (also known as the 'Brahimi Report').

6. See, for example, *From Victory to Success: Afterwar Policy in Iraq*, Washington DC, Carnegie Endowment for International Peace and Foreign Policy, 24 July 2003; James Dobbins et al., *America's Role in Nation-Building: From Germany to Iraq*, Washington DC, Rand, 2003; Thomas R. Pickering and James R. Schlesinger, Co-Chairs, Eric P. Schwartz, Project Director, *Iraq: The Day After*, Report of an Independent Task Force Sponsored by the Council on Foreign Relations, 2003; Frederick D. Barton and Bathsheba N. Crocker (Project Directors), *Post-War Iraq: Are We Ready?*, Washington DC, Center for Strategic and International Studies, 25 March 2003; and William J. Durch, 'The UN System and Post-conflict Iraq', Washington DC, Henry L. Stimson Center, 18 April 2003.

7. See, for example, John T. Fishel, *The Fog of Peace: Planning and Executing the Restoration of Panama*, Strategic Studies Institute, Carlisle, PA, US Army War College, 15 April 1992, pp. 13, 26.

8. For quotes from US soldiers about the looting, see Tim Judah, 'The Fall of Baghdad', *New York Review of Books*, 50(8), 15 May 2003, p. 42.

9. General Wesley K. Clark, 'Iraq: What Went Wrong', *New York Review of Books*, 50(16), 23 October 2003.
10. For more information on this aspect, see Alexandros Yannis, 'Kosovo Under International Administration', *Survival*, 43(2), London, IISS, Summer 2001, pp. 37–8.
11. For example, at a conference held in London organised by the Centre for Defence Studies, King's College London, and sponsored by DFID, entitled 'Public Security and the Rule of Law from a European Perspective', 6 March 2001, several participants proposed this strategy. This conference was part of a series of seminars in support of the Brahimi Report.
12. See 'Bosnia and Hercegovina: Beyond Restraint', *Human Rights Watch Report*; and Report of the Secretary-General on the UN Interim Administration Mission in Kosovo, S/1999/987, 16 September 1999, para. 30.
13. From discussions held at the Centre for Defence Studies with a number of Iraqi exiles prior to the war.
14. See David Rieff, 'Blueprint for a Mess', *New York Times Magazine*, 2 November 2003.
15. Clark, 'Iraq: What Went Wrong'. See also Rieff, 'Blueprint for a Mess'.
16. From the American Society of International Law, Proceedings of the 84th Annual Meeting, Washington DC, 28–31 March 1990, pp. 251–2.
17. From interviews with numerous representatives of humanitarian agencies conducted by this author in Geneva, Brussels, Washington DC and New York in early 2003.
18. See, for example, OCHA, 'Guidelines on the Use of Military and Civil Defence Assets to Support United Nations Humanitarian Activities in Complex Emergencies', March 2003, or those published by Interaction and icva, two NGO consortia.
19. See Karin von Hippel, 'American Occupational Hazards', www.opendemocracy. net, 10 April 2003.
20. For example, see 'Combating Terrorism', Testimony of Daniel Benjamin, Senior Fellow, Center for Strategic and International Studies, Subcommittee on National Security, Veterans Affairs and International Relations, House Committee on Government Reform, 16 April 2002.
21. As cited in *The Economist*, 23–29 August 2003, p. 73.
22. NATO is the preferred option, over the current coalition force or even the UN (which still needs to improve its military capability in peacekeeping operations). NATO has demonstrated its competence in the Balkans, and would provide greater legitimacy.
23. From correspondence with Lt-Cmdr. Dave Scanlon, SFOR Spokesperson, April 1999.
24. Thomas Carothers, 'Lessons for Policymakers', in Georges A. Fauriol, ed., *Haitian Frustrations: Dilemmas for US Policy, A Report of the CSIS Americas Program*, Washington DC, CSIS, 1995, p. 18.
25. Richard L. Merritt, *Democracy Imposed: US Occupation Policy and the German Public, 1945–1949*, New Haven, Yale University Press, 1995, p. xiii.
26. Thomas G. Weiss, 'Collective Spinelessness: UN Actions in the Former Yugoslavia', in Richard H. Ullman, ed., *The World and Yugoslavia's Wars*, New York, Council on Foreign Relations, 1996, p. 91.
27. The British military conducted a poll in 1997 to see how many deaths of British soldiers the public would tolerate, and found the numbers quite high, about 15 per month. Respondents remarked that soldiers joined on a voluntary basis and

should therefore be well aware of the risks they might encounter. Indeed, the British, French and Dutch all lost more soldiers than the Americans did in the cases discussed here, while the Pakistanis suffered grave losses in Somalia without withdrawing.

28. Richard H. Shultz, Jr, *In the Aftermath of War: US Support for Reconstruction and Nation-Building in Panama Following Just Cause*, Maxwell Air Force Base, AL, Air University Press, 1993, p. 67.

13
Symbols and Slogans: Arab Responses to the War against Iraq

Alison Pargeter

I listened in growing dismay as the experts forecast, often in graphic terms, the coming disaster in the Gulf. Predictions of massive upheavals in every Islamic country, Americans slaughtered in the streets of Arab cities, airliners blown from the skies ... In actuality very little of this happened.[1]

These observations, by American commentator Norvell B. DeAtkine, were made in 1993 in the context of the 1990 Gulf War when allied forces ousted Saddam Hussein from Kuwait. A similar comment could be made with regard to the recent conflict in Iraq. As in previous crises in the Middle East that have involved western intervention, experts, pundits and the media alike warned that a US and British assault on Iraq would provoke major upheaval throughout the region from the Levant across to North Africa. It was predicted that the Arab masses would rise up against their governments, that the West's relations with the Arab world would never be the same again and that radicalism and religious extremism would reach new levels. But despite the strong Arab reaction against the war, very little of this has materialised. In many respects, this is no surprise; the predicted fallout from any crisis in the Middle East tends to be exaggerated and more often than not used by various factions, from the liberal left in the West to nationalist and Islamist groups in the Arab world, to score political and ideological points that have little bearing on the causes and consequences of the crisis itself. The recent conflict is no exception.

This is not to suggest, of course, that significant changes have not taken place as a result of the war. There has been a shift in the Gulf, for example, with the delicate balance of power between Iran, Iraq and Saudi Arabia being redefined once again. However, the outcome of this shift will be determined largely on what transpires in Iraq. Another major change has been in US relations with Saudi Arabia, albeit a result more of the fallout from 9/11 than a direct consequence of the conflict in 2003. To read DeAtkine's comments ten years later, therefore, is a salutary reminder both of the propensity among western and Arab analysts to misunderstand the Arab world, as well as a valuable indication of the stagnation that has characterised much of the Middle East over the past decade.

This chapter will trace Arab responses to the 2003 conflict at both the government and popular level, as well as assessing the reaction of Arab intellectuals and the Arab media to the crisis. It will also examine what has actually changed in the region and will explain why the predictions of uprising and revolution proved groundless.

Competing ideologies

In the post-colonial era, Arab politics have been dominated largely by the ideologies of Arab nationalism and conservative or traditional Islam. From the 1950s until the late 1970s, as in many parts of the developing world, Arab politics were driven predominantly by the nationalist agenda. Arab nationalism was first championed by Egyptian President Gamal Abdel Nasser after he came to power in 1954, and by the Ba'ath parties in Syria and later in Iraq. Arab nationalism advocated Arab unity as the means by which to gain freedom from colonialism and to achieve economic growth. Socialism was added subsequently, in large a reflection of the tendency among these nationalist states to ally with the Soviet bloc during the Cold War. The Algerian revolution (1962) and the coups that took place in Iraq (1958) and Libya (1969), for example, were viewed as great Arab nationalist successes. As a predominantly secular concept, Arab nationalism crossed all religious denominations and was seen by many Arabs as a means of regaining dignity after the humiliations of the colonial era. However, following the Arab defeat at the hands of Israel in 1967 and the death of President Nasser in 1970, Arab nationalism lost its power as a driving force in the region and was reduced to little more than a series of symbols and slogans. This entailed drawing on historical events and figures and harking back to the 'golden age' of the Arab Empire. Despite its demise, the rhetoric of nationalism continued to be used by Arab rulers across the region. As one academic has observed, 'Arab governments manipulated and deployed symbols that derived from their shared cultural foundations to persuade their audience that their definition of events and proposed response was appropriate, legitimate, and consistent with Arabism.'[2] As the post-Cold War world was changing, Arab leaders continued to cling to these outdated concepts as a means of legitimising their continuing hold on power and their unwillingness to adapt to the modern era.

Despite its popularity, Arab nationalism was not able to dislodge the conservative Islamic tradition that prevailed in the Gulf states, such as

Bahrain, Saudi Arabia, Qatar and Kuwait. The rulers of these Gulf states have traditionally maintained their hold on power by combining tribal politics with a conservative interpretation of religion. However, they were regarded by the nationalists as backward and stooges of the West, partly because many of them had been installed and maintained by colonial powers (in most cases Britain), and partly because they continued to ally themselves with western powers during the Cold War. As a means of countering the Arab nationalist movement, the ruling families of these Gulf states encouraged and supported Islamic movements, such as the Muslim Brotherhood, across the Middle East and North Africa that would serve to weaken and challenge the secular nationalist regimes. However, an unintended result of this policy was the emergence of radical rather than conservative Islamist movements that began to spring up throughout the region, threatening not only the power of the secular nationalists, but also the control of the conservative Islamist regimes. This, along with the end of the Cold War, that saw the collapse of the nationalists' Soviet backers, meant that the gap between these two camps began to narrow. As a result, leaders in both camps came to use the symbols of both Islam and Arabism as a means of explaining the 'Arab condition' and of maintaining the status quo.

Previous crises

Particularly at times of crisis in the region, symbols of Islam and Arabism have been conjured up by leaders throughout the Arab world both to play to their own populations and to justify any stance they have chosen to take. One heavily used symbol is that of the concept of Arab brotherhood or Arab unity which is often used in parallel with the idea that outside powers are to be blamed for the Arab world's internal divisions and weaknesses. Another much used metaphor is the conspiracy theory that is used to explain events that have an impact on the region. This links closely with the belief that the Zionists are behind many events, from the killing of John F. Kennedy to the attacks on the twin towers on 9/11. Arab nationalism also entails drawing heavily on historical events, and the likening of any intervention by the West to the medieval crusades is a central theme in any argument about dangers they face. Arab political culture is to a large extent plagued by these symbols and cliches, and despite the rhetoric of brotherhood, the Arab world remains deeply divided. This demonstrated itself at the time of the Israeli invasion of Lebanon in 1982. Arabs exploded with fury, denouncing Israel, expressing sympathy for their fellow Arabs and warning of the dangers that would engulf the region if Israel were not stopped. Yet aside from Syria that took up arms, the Arab states were unable to do anything other than verbally condemn the Israelis. Even the call for oil supplies to be cut, which had proved a successful tactic in 1973, fell on deaf ears and the region continued much as before.

Warnings of upheaval and impending disaster were repeated during the Gulf War of 1990. Arab governments and populations responded angrily to the US and allied forces attacks despite the fact that Iraq had invaded another Arab country. But as an Arab nationalist leader, Saddam was to receive more sympathy than the Kuwaiti royal family who were viewed as corrupt puppets of the West. There were many predictions of unrest. For example, in August 1990, prominent Palestinian scholar the late Edward Said warned:

Governments in Egypt, Saudi Arabia, and perhaps Jordan are likely to recover badly, if at all, from the US rush to military reaction. Immense economic and ecological changes unforeseen in their scope will, I think, radically change the face of the whole Middle East.[3]

These warnings also emanated from Arab leaders from both camps who were playing on nationalist and religious sentiment in order to convince their populations that they could be tough with the West and that they had sufficient feeling for their 'Iraqi brothers'. These predictions turned out to be exaggerated and the anticipated revolutions did not materialise. There were a number of demonstrations in some Arab capitals, but these were limited and short-lived. As another academic has commented,

At the time the Kuwait crisis was thought to have changed the face of the Near East but in retrospect it can be seen that the consequences were chiefly negative; Iraq's bid for dominance had been defeated. In other words the crisis largely confirmed what was already apparent: the Arab world was divided; the smaller Gulf states ultimately depended for their external security on outside powers; Egypt was the leading Arab state; the USA was the most powerful state in the world; and there was plenty of oil to go round.[4]

Perhaps no issue has been hostage to the trappings of Arab nationalist and Islamist ideology as much as the Palestinian one. This cause has been used by successive Arab leaders, intellectuals and factions alike to serve their own interests. For example, it is used by regimes as a means of justifying increased spending on arms and weaponry that more often than not are used against domestic populations. Furthermore, despite this continuing rhetoric, there has been very little unified Arab action to actually assist the Palestinians in the past three decades. Indeed, the Palestinians have generally been treated poorly by other Arab governments.[5] Therefore, despite the continued rhetoric about the 'central cause', as the Palestinian issue is known, aside from some financial assistance, the Arab world, including the so-called hard-line states, has done little to genuinely assist the Palestinians in their struggle against Israel.

Arab governments and Operation Iraqi Freedom

The rhetoric

As in previous crises in the region, the war against Iraq placed governments in the Arab world in a difficult position. They were caught between needing to safeguard their relations with the US whilst having to mollify their own populations, the majority of whom were stridently opposed to the war. This was clearly a more challenging task for the more pro-western or so called 'moderate' regimes, like Jordan, Egypt and Algeria, than for those countries that have traditionally had a more antagonistic relationship with the West, namely Syria and Libya, that were expected to launch anti-imperialist tirades against the bombing.

At the level of rhetoric, the first group, or 'moderates' were predictable in their official responses to Operation Iraqi Freedom. Almost all of them condemned the war and warned of dire consequences for the region as a whole if the US and Britain went ahead with the invasion. Egyptian President Hosni Mubarak stated: 'We did all we could to avoid a war and we were opposed to it being launched, but the great powers have their own calculations ... all of this has repercussions against the region.'[6] He also warned that the war against Iraq would unleash a hundred Osama bin Ladens. Algeria's ruling FLN party called the war a breach of international law that set a dangerous precedent.[7] King Abdullah of Jordan, in a play to the masses, likened the US troops in Iraq to Israeli tanks in the West Bank or Gaza.[8] The Saudi regime also opposed the conflict and tried to stop the fighting by presenting Baghdad and Washington with a proposal to end the fighting. The Gulf states, including Qatar, opposed the war and like most Arab countries hid their objections behind the lack of international support for the war, stating that there needed to be a UN mandate in order for military action to be justified. The one exception of course was Kuwait, which after having been invaded by Iraq in 1990, came out in full support of the US and British forces. The hard-line states also came out with the expected condemnations, accusing the US and Britain of illegal and imperialist invasion of a sovereign Arab state.

The Arab League, an institution that has long been viewed in the region and elsewhere as little more than a talking shop, strongly denounced US and British action against Iraq. On 21 March 2003, the League's Secretary-General and former Egyptian Foreign Minister, Amr Moussa, called for absolute Arab rejection of any military operation against Iraq or any other Arab country. This was backed up by a resolution on 22–25 March in which League members condemned the invasion and, amongst other things, called for 'the immediate and unconditional withdrawal of occupying US-British forces from Iraqi lands, and for making them accountable for the financial, moral and legal liabilities of this military aggression'.[9]

The reality

However, many Arab governments that had condemned the war continued to cooperate with the US and Britain, even to the extent of providing logistical support to their military operations in Iraq. Egypt permitted coalition warships to use the Suez Canal as a means of accessing the Red Sea, for example. Jordan authorised the deployment of US troops on its soil and the Bahraini government provided the coalition forces with use of a 50-year-old naval base that acted as an administrative support centre. Qatar, despite officially opposing the war, permitted coalition forces to set up their headquarters in the country. The reasons for this compliance, in spite of Arab states' opposition to the invasion and the deep resentment among Arab populations, are varied and complex. Broadly speaking, these countries are ruled by autocratic regimes or cliques and due to their lack of popular legitimacy rely heavily on the western world for support. Despite a strengthening of relations with the European Union, mainly through the Euro-Mediterranean Partnership Initiative,[10] it appears that despite the anti-war stance taken by some of the main players in Europe, the Arab states still look to the US as the key international player.

The Arab world can be divided into three main groups in this respect. The first group that includes Jordan, Egypt and Morocco rely heavily on western aid and assistance to survive due to their lack of natural resources and poor economic situation. USAID, for example, supplied Egypt with $615 million of development assistance in the 2003 financial year[11] and pledged over $1 billion worth of economic and financial assistance to Jordan in return for its 'support' in the war in Iraq. The second group consists of the rich Gulf states whose ruling families and elites look to the outside world to protect their internal and external security and also to provide them with a ready supply of arms. This reliance was strengthened after the Kuwait crisis in 1990, and since then weapons supplies have increased to countries such as the United Arab Emirates. As such, these regimes have been less staunchly opposed to the new administration in Iraq; a number of Gulf countries, including Saudi Arabia, welcomed a delegation from the Iraqi governing council in August 2003.

The last group, comprising Syria, Libya and Algeria, consists of those countries that allied themselves with the Soviet Union during the Cold War. Following the collapse of the Soviet bloc, these states came to realise that they have no real alternative other than to deal with the only remaining superpower. Whilst Syria and Libya both denounced the invasion, their leaders were concerned about the possibility that they might be next to suffer the fate of Saddam Hussein. Syria therefore initially condemned the war, but later appeared to be more compliant, reportedly handing over a number of Iraqi Ba'athists at the request of the US. Although he criticised the attacks on Iraq, Libya's Colonel Qadhafi also took steps to ensure his attempts at mending relations with Washington were not hampered. Algeria had already succeeded in developing closer relations with the US and following 9/11, like a number of Arab states, has also come to rely even more heavily on the

US citing its 'terrorist' problem as a reason for increased weaponry as well as financial and political support.

Selective solidarity

During the war, Arab governments were quick to express solidarity with the Iraqi people, stressing their empathy with those Iraqis who were suffering under the invasion. Yet this empathy looks rather thin when one considers that these same governments remained silent whilst Saddam Hussein was killing Iraqis in their thousands. There was no sympathy expressed for the Iraqi Kurds, Shia and Sunnis who were slaughtered at the hands of the Ba'ath party during its long and bloody rule. This perhaps is not surprising in view of the questionable human rights records of all the Arab states. However, more shocking has been the unwillingness of these leaders after the war to condemn or even acknowledge the human rights abuses that took place under the Saddam regime. Arab parliamentarians at a meeting in Beirut in June 2003 reportedly refused to make any condemnation of the mass graves that were discovered after the toppling of the Ba'athist regime. The editor of the Saudi-owned newspaper *Al-Sharq al-Awsat* wrote:

> At every conference these parliamentarians fail to express a single word of regret for what happened to the Iraqi people – many of whom were lost in graves dug around mosques, schools, and prisons. A word of sympathy is not a lot to ask for Iraqis agonized by the sight of the mountains of bones that were the thousands of citizens killed and buried in their clothes. Arab parliamentarians limit their condemnation to the Zionists and the foreign invasion and have purposefully forgotten the crimes committed under our noses.[12]

Arab governments have maintained an ambiguous stance and clothed all discussion about Iraq in expressions of concern for the Iraqis, rather than choosing to address real issues.

The support that these regimes gave to Saddam Hussein was not for any particular affection for the Ba'athist regime in Iraq. None of these governments, aside perhaps from the Palestinian Authority and Syrian regime, was particularly sorry to see the collapse of the Iraqi regime, but for many Saddam was preferable to any potentially democratic solution for Iraq. Not that these Arab states were convinced that the US would be able to or indeed was even interested in installing a genuinely pluralistic government in Iraq, but anything that placed a spotlight on their own lack of democratic credentials would make them feel distinctly uncomfortable. As a result, playing to the old Arab nationalist and Islamist tunes relieved them from discussing issues such as democratisation and human rights at any level other than the superficial. Backing Saddam Hussein was also a means of trying to prevent a Shia leadership in Iraq. Indeed Egypt and Saudi Arabia encouraged the US not to finish off Saddam at the end of the Gulf War of 1991 in order to conserve Sunni rule there.

Following the war, the Arab states largely rejected the new administration in Iraq, insisting on viewing the Americans and British as colonial occupiers. The Arab League initially rejected the newly formed Iraq Council, and shortly after it was appointed, Arab League Head Amr Moussa stated that the Council would have had more power and credibility if it had been elected. In response to Moussa's comments, Thomas Friedman, writing in the *New York Times*, observed:

> Mr Moussa presides over an Arab League in which not one of the 22 member states has a leader elected in a free and fair election. On top of it, before the war, Mr Moussa did all he could to shield Saddam Hussein from attack, although Saddam had never held a real election in his life. Yet, there was Mr Moussa questioning the new US-appointed Iraqi Council, which, even in its infant form, is already the most representative government Iraq has ever had.[13]

Thomas Friedman could also have added that Amr Moussa himself was not elected to be Head of the Arab League, but rather was appointed by unelected Arab governments, not to mention Moussa's former post as Foreign Minister of Egypt – a position that he did not gain through a free and fair election.

It appears therefore that in this crisis, as in previous crises in the region, Arab governments have been prepared to use whatever rhetoric they deem necessary to appease their populations, regardless of whether that rhetoric corresponds with any sort of political reality. They have played on Arab nationalist and conservative Islamist sentiment, ensuring that they cannot be accused of not supporting their 'Arab brothers', but in reality have done very little up until now to try to alleviate the suffering of the population of Iraq or to assist in the reconstruction process.

Arab popular responses

An attack on Arab pride

As predicted, at the popular level the vast majority of Arabs across the Middle East as well as those residing abroad were strongly opposed to military intervention in Iraq. American and British motives were questioned and the fact that the action was taken without the backing of the United Nations only added to suspicions. In addition, American and British determination to link the Saddam Hussein regime with terrorism and al-Qaeda – an accusation widely understood to be lacking in substance – fuelled further mistrust over the coalition's true intent in the region.

The predominant beliefs held by the majority of Arabs about the conflict are:

1. The US invaded Iraq because they wanted to exploit Iraq's natural resources and control its oil
2. Military action was taken against Iraq to protect Israel[14]
3. The US wanted to humiliate the Arabs and to destroy the Islamic/Arab culture primarily because it felt threatened by it.

These beliefs are clearly shaped by the discourse of Arab nationalism and conservative Islam. Also reminiscent of the Arab nationalist stance was that the action against Iraq was viewed by most not only as an attack on the Iraqi people, but as an attack on all Arabs. In parallel, for the Islamists, an attack against Iraq, despite the fact that Saddam Hussein's regime was largely secular, was considered as an attack against all Muslims. Whilst there was widespread acknowledgement among many Arabs that Saddam Hussein was a tyrant, once he had become a target of the US and Britain, he had to be supported in the name of the Arab brotherhood. As a result, there was widespread reluctance to acknowledge that certain sections of the Iraqi population were happy to be rid of the Ba'athist regime – something that prompted great resentment among the Iraqi population, especially those in exile. To many Arabs who had not lived under the brutality of the Iraqi regime, Saddam became a sort of hero, who, despite having killed thousands of his own citizens, was worthy of praise because he was standing up to the US. As one Egyptian commented at the start of the war, 'Saddam is so brave and is making us proud. When I meet Saddam, I will shake his hand and say "You are my Arab warrior".'[15] Another voiced the opinion, 'I used to find Saddam disgusting, but now I admit, he makes us proud. He is fighting back when no one thought he could. If someone told me "Get in this bus, fight for Saddam", I would clap and cheer and go.'[16]

Due to the high expectations that had come to surround Saddam, the ease with which the coalition forces were able to destroy the Ba'athist military machine – supposed to be one of the greatest military powers of the region – brought crushing disappointment. Saddam was revered because he had fought the Iranians, becoming known as the defender of the eastern gate of the Arab world against the Persians and for many Gulf states also a defender against the spread of Shiism. He was also applauded after he launched Scud missiles at Israel during the Gulf War of 1990. As such, Saddam Hussein had come to represent Arab pride and was viewed as a new modern leader who could combine technological advancement with traditional Arab values. However, out of desperation, the Arabs inflated Saddam's ability to confront the coalition forces during this conflict, and his defeat was compared to 1967 when Israeli forces routed the Arabs in a matter of days – a moment still regarded in the Arab world as one of the utmost humiliation. As one Egyptian human rights activist commented after the Iraqi regime had been toppled: 'I feel defeated. In my adult life, this is the first Arab capital to completely fall into the hands of a foreign power.'[17] Another Egyptian commented:

'We had all hoped that Iraq would resist longer than this'[18] and a researcher in Jordan stated: 'He fled in a disgraceful manner. He didn't fight.'[19] This disappointment was compounded when coalition forces captured Saddam Hussein in December 2003, and this prompted many in the Arab world to complain that the former Iraqi leader did not put up more of a struggle. Yet there appeared to have been no real questioning by the Arab masses as to why the Iraqi army did not stay to fight with Saddam in the first place.

Grievances

It is indisputable that the Arab masses were greatly angered by the conflict, but to assert that the war in Iraq created a swathe of hatred for the US is somewhat misjudged. Hatred for the US was already running extremely high prior to the war, and it is for this reason that bin Laden attained and continues to have heroic status in many parts of the Middle East. Anger has been rising steadily among Arab populations, especially in recent years. It is centred around the continued lack of a solution to the Palestinian problem, unwavering US support for Israel, the perceived heavy-handed US response to 9/11 (which many Arabs still do not believe to have been carried out by al-Qaeda) and the subsequent bombing of Afghanistan. The war in Iraq served as yet another grievance to add to this list. There is also significant resentment of the west's hypocrisy in its dealings with the regimes of the region, and its selectivity in condemning certain governments for being corrupt, brutal and undemocratic, whilst supporting others of a similar nature. Indeed, the war in Iraq caused many Arabs to reflect painfully on their inability to oust a ruler like Saddam Hussein themselves, and the conflict only served to heighten a sense of impotence against their own tyrannical rulers, many of whom have been backed by the US and Europe. Therefore, to claim that the war in Iraq has resulted in an increase in hatred for the US is perhaps to have underestimated and misunderstood how much the US was detested prior to the war.

Despite the strength of anti-American and anti-British feeling during the war, demonstrations against it were relatively modest and short-lived. The most notable protests were in Morocco where tens of thousands of students took to the streets in various cities, in Syria where 500,000 demonstrators turned out, in Yemen where tens of thousands protested in Sanaa, and in Egypt where more than 10,000 students demonstrated. However, in all cases, protests were broken up or limited by the police – the Egyptian authorities arrested and imprisoned a number of demonstrators and two protesters were shot dead in Yemen. Protests were also held in Libya, but as usual these were orchestrated by the Libyan authorities. The limited nature of protest partly reflects the reasons why there were none of the predicted revolutions or major uprisings as a result of the war in Iraq. All of the regimes in the Arab world forbade unauthorised public demonstrations, and all countries to varying degrees maintain authoritarian systems that rely heavily on the security services to maintain order. The Saudi regime, for example, prohibits demonstrations on the justification that they are unnecessary because the government represents the view of the people. The suggestion therefore that US action would lead to widespread and uncontrolled spontaneous protest or the toppling of regimes in countries such as Jordan or Morocco was grossly exaggerated. In fact, traditionally these regimes have authorised demonstrations about Palestine or issues such as Iraq as a means of trying to dispel some of the tension and frustration among their own populations. If Arabs cannot override their rulers to protest when their own families are being tortured, imprisoned and killed, or when they are denied participation in the political and material life of their own countries, it is unlikely they will be able to do so because another country, in some cases many miles away, is being attacked.

Nevertheless, the toppling of Saddam and evident fallibility of one of the longest serving dictators in the region gave Arab populations much food for thought. In Libya, for example, football crowds reportedly chanted slogans about Qadhafi's son, Saadi, along the lines of 'Saadi, Saadi, look what happened to Uday [Saddam's son]'. Indeed, in private, many Arabs acknowledged that they wished the Americans had removed the regime in their own country, but felt unable to voice this in public, because of the need to conform to the Arab nationalist agenda that required supporting Saddam in the face of US aggression.

Arab intellectuals and the Arab media

During the conflict in 2003, Arab intellectuals as well as the Arab media proved themselves to be far from immune to the rhetoric of nationalism. Indeed, Arab intellectuals appear to have done little more than echo the general sentiments of many Arab governments and the masses. They have played on Arabist and Islamist ideology, venting their anger against the West and giving substance to the view that the war should have been seen as an attack on the whole Arab world. Whilst most claimed to be on the side of the Iraqi people, they also appeared to be willing the prolongation of the war for the sake of Arab pride. Sadik Jalal al-Azam, a celebrated Syrian author and academic, stated: 'If Saddam's regime is going to fall, it's better for our future, for our self-confidence and for our image that it falls fighting.'[20] A sentiment perhaps unlikely to be shared by those experiencing the regular bombing raids in Baghdad. The motives of these same intellectuals who stress their concern for the Iraqis now, but remained largely silent when Saddam Hussein dumped thousands of Faili Kurds (Shia Kurds) on the Iranian border in the late 1970s with the excuse that they were not Arabs, and when he was gassing the Kurds in the 1980s, should also be questioned. As Iraqi scholar Kanan Makiya wrote after the First Gulf War, 'I will note how uninteresting were the deaths of between 500,000 and one million Iraqis and Iranians in that war to the very same people who talked only about the hypocrisy of the west during the Gulf War.'[21] Those Arab intellectuals who had railed so hard against the West during 1990/1 kept largely silent when Iraqis rose up against Saddam after the war and were brutally put down and killed by Iraqi forces. As Makiya has also described, 'Leaders like Saddam Hussein thrive on the silence of the Arab intelligentsia toward cruelty.'[22] In much the same way as the masses and governments in the region reacted, despite their dislike for Saddam Hussein, most Arab intellectuals chose to back him in the face of the US and British attacks. There have of course been notable exceptions to this rule. Wahid Magid, Deputy Director of the Egyptian think tank al-Ahram Centre for Political and Strategic Studies, commented: 'The Arabs would like to see the American project fail in Iraq and if they had the means to contribute to its failure, they would do it. For the moment, they're doing that by not getting involved.'[23] However, such voices have been few and far between.

Many Arab intellectuals have also been unable to decouple the issue of Iraq from that of Palestine. Much of the late Edward Said's commentary on Iraq, for example, focuses more on the Palestinian issue, reflecting his own particular interest in the region. One wonders whether Said and others had hoped Saddam would be the one Arab leader with the power to confront Israel. Said wistfully wrote in April 2003: 'Iraq might once have been a potential challenge to Israel. It was the one Arab country with the human and natural resources, as well as the infrastructure, to take on Israel's arrogant brutality.'[24] This view, shared by many Arab intellectuals, appears to be born out of desperation rather than reality. Even when Iraq was at its military peak, Saddam Hussein chose to fight Iran in a war that lasted for eight years, rather than to challenge Israel. This linkage of the crisis in Iraq with Israel drove Palestinian novelist, Ziyad Khaddash, to publish a short story in response to the war, entitled 'As if I am in Basra, as if You are in Ramallah', in which he likens US attacks on Iraq to those of the Israelis against the Palestinians.[25] While not seeking to detract from the suffering the Palestinians have endured under Israeli occupation, it is noteworthy that several Iraqis who fled their country at the hands of Saddam indicated that they found such sentiments insulting and suggestive of a complete misunderstanding of the horrors to which Saddam Hussein had subjected his population.[26]

Arab satellite channels such as al-Jazeera, the Arab News Network (ANN), al-Arabia and Abu Dhabi TV also borrowed heavily from the nationalist rhetoric in their coverage of the war in a bid to appeal to the masses. Despite their claim to objectivity, their language was highly emotive and terms such as 'occupation', 'aggressor' and 'Zionist', which filled their commentary reflected their very obvious stance on the war. Like their western counterparts, they were also highly selective in the scenes they chose to broadcast. When the statue of Saddam Hussein was pulled down, for example, some channels tried to lessen the impact of the symbolism by broadcasting reports from their correspondents in Baghdad about the Iraqi resistance rather than focusing on those Iraqis who were jubilant. Some of these channels also chose to belittle the scenes of Iraqis celebrating at the fall of the regime, even going as far as to imply that their joy was less valid because they were either Shia or looters and therefore could not be considered 'real Arabs'.[27] As one Palestinian scholar observed: 'In Arab eyes, this was an event staged by the international media, who challenged a handful of Iraqi youngsters to attack the statue, and so start to win the battle for "Iraqi hearts and minds".'[28]

Radicalisation

Whilst the war has undoubtedly inflamed Arab passions, pushing some to go to Iraq to fight, arguably there was enough anger and resentment prior to the war to encourage radical behaviour. As Robin Banerji has argued, the war will not necessarily create more recruits to terrorist organisations. He writes:

> It is not clear, that following this war, Arabs will turn in any greater numbers to physically attacking the west, or their own governments, than they have in the past…Previous experience of wars in the area suggests that the upsurge of violence may be short…before it falls back to pre-war levels.[29]

However, what the war in Iraq has done is to create a space in which Islamic radicals who subscribe to the idea of going to fight jihad (Holy War) can operate. With the bombing of Afghanistan that destroyed their base as well as the continued repression in their own countries, post-Saddam Iraq represents a key opportunity for these radical elements. Iraq also represents a more attractive opportunity than other countries where recruits have gone to fight jihad – such as Chechnya – because it is in the heart of the Arab world and can therefore be depicted as a more 'noble' and important struggle. Iraq's porous borders, weak local security forces, general insecurity and increasingly frustrated citizens also make it a key target for radicals who are able to attack US and international personnel and interests within Iraq. Indeed there have been reports that money is being offered to Iraqis to attack or kill coalition forces. Furthermore, there appears to be a realisation among radicals in the region that Iraq's Sunni population is in danger. In the last few years of his rule, Saddam Hussein began to encourage Sunni Islamism as a means of further containing the Shia. Following the war, these Sunnis are increasingly feeling threatened, as the Shia increase their power and the Kurds insist upon a federal solution for Iraq. Some of these radical elements going to Iraq may therefore be assuming that as well as fighting the Americans, they are also protecting their Sunni brothers.

There has been a steady flow of Arabs who have gone to Iraq to fight alongside Ba'athist loyalists and the new Sunni Islamist movements that have sprung up in Iraq, such as Salafiya Jihadiya. This process began prior to the start of Operation Iraqi Freedom and Saddam welcomed them into the country.

Indeed, the Iraqi interests section in Damascus was reportedly providing a free bus service for those volunteers who wanted to cross the border into Iraq to fight.[30] Although officially the Syrian authorities discouraged anyone from going into Iraq, it appears that in practice they turned a blind eye to the scores moving across the border. Jordan also officially prohibited fighters from going, but not very effectively. Many of those who are going to fight appear to be Palestinians, although they seem to be resident in Syria, Lebanon and Jordan rather than from the West Bank or Gaza. There are also reports of large numbers of Wahabis from Saudi Arabia moving into Iraq following the crackdowns on Islamic radicals imposed by the Saudi regime. In view of Saudi concerns about a Shia-dominated Iraq, it is not inconceivable that elements within the Saudi government are offering tacit support to these radicals. Nevertheless, the creation of a space for such radical Islamist elements is likely to be of concern to many regimes in the Arab world that have been trying to eliminate such militants in their own countries since the mid 1990s.

These fighters have been helped by the tacit acceptance and encouragement offered them by some of the leading religious authorities in the Arab world. At the start of the war, the Sunni Islamic authority al-Azhar in Cairo issued an edict calling for jihad, although later watered down its call, claiming that it meant jihad in the sense of the non-violent struggle. Syrian Islamic authority Sheikh Ahmad Kafaro stated in March: 'I call on Muslims everywhere to use all means possible to thwart the aggression, including martyr operations against the belligerent American, British and Zionist invaders.'[31] There are of course exceptions to this stance, such as Egyptian Islamic scholar Gamal El-Banna who opposed the idea of Arabs going to fight for Saddam Hussein. He commented: 'This is total foolish nonsense. This man was slaughtering brother Muslims. He is worse than a tyrant and dictator and the truth is we Arabs didn't do enough to stop him.'[32]

Despite the fact that many Arabs going to Iraq have claimed they would undertake martyr operations there, to date the number of attacks actually involving suicide have been relatively few in comparison to other attacks. That is not to discount the horrendous attacks on the Jordanian embassy and on the United Nations headquarters in August 2003, as well as the suicide bombing in November the same year on the Italian police headquarters in Nasiriyah and the suicide attack outside US headquarters in Baghdad in January 2004. It appears therefore that either the numbers of volunteers entering Iraq has been exaggerated, that those who have entered are largely ineffective, or that they have been thwarted by coalition forces. But even if more attacks do occur, this should not be overplayed, and it should also be borne in mind that much of the guerrilla fighting is being undertaken by Ba'athist loyalists and some Sunni tribes linked to the regime who lost much in the war. Furthermore, reports from Iraq suggest that these Arab fighters are regarded with contempt by the majority of Iraqis, especially Shia, who see them as supporters of Saddam and who have no interest in prolonging the conflict. Ordinary Iraqis also resent the fact that their fellow nationals are being killed in these attacks. There have even been reports of attacks on foreign fighters by Iraqis.[33]

The Shia/Sunni divide

Although in general terms the war in Iraq has not dramatically altered the face of the region or the West's relations with the Arab world, the conflict has inevitably brought about a number of changes. It is of course too early to assess the full extent of the impact on the region, as much will depend on what transpires in Iraq during 2004. However, crucially the Arab world will have to come to terms with the fact that Iraq is no longer a brethren Sunni Arab country as it had been able to project itself in the past. The Shia, the Kurds and to a certain extent the Turkmen, will all be represented in any future power sharing agreement and this will dramatically alter the ethnic complexion of the Iraqi government. As such, many Arabs will feel they have lost one of the major Sunni Arab powers and defender of the eastern border. It seems likely, therefore, that an ethnically mixed government in Iraq will sit uncomfortably in the structure of the region. This change will also affect the balance of power in the Gulf. The three main states in the area – Iraq, Saudi Arabia and Iran – have traditionally competed to be the regional hegemon. As three states of a similar size and strength, any alliance between two of them inevitably threatens the third. In this vein, the emergence of the Shia in Iraq might bring the new Iraqi leadership closer to that of Iran, although this will depend on the components of the new Iraqi government, and perhaps more crucially on the wishes of the Americans.

The materialisation of another Shia power base in the Gulf has also encouraged a new boldness among other Shia minorities in the region. For example, following the war, 450 notables from Saudi Arabia's long-oppressed Shia minority submitted a petition to Crown Prince Abdullah to protest at their continuing discrimination. The fact that the Crown Price accepted the petition at all is in itself surprising, as the Saudi regime had previously refused to even acknowledge the existence of its Shia minority. The southern Gulf states, including Bahrain and Kuwait, are also concerned about a Shia-dominated leadership in Iraq that might prove more sympathetic to Iran than to the Sunni Arab states. As a result of the war, these Gulf leaderships will therefore have to find a way to deal with the growing empowerment of their Shia minorities. The choice seems stark; Shia minorities will either be given more rights and a greater role, or they will find themselves the victim of yet more repression.

In the new atmosphere in the Gulf, Saudi Arabia is also having to come to terms with the fact that it is no longer the favoured partner of the US in the region. However, much of this is to do with 9/11, and the recognition on the part of the US that the Saudi regime has been exporting Wahabist ideology along with significant financial backing. The July 2003 report by the US joint congressional committee on intelligence into security failures before 9/11, contained 28 blanked out pages which, it was widely alleged, detailed links between the Saudi ruling family and al-Qaeda members.[34] Significantly, the paper marked a new willingness on the part of the United States to criticise and publicly embarrass the Saudi regime. As American reliance on Saudi Arabia is being recalculated, the US is refocusing more of its attentions on Qatar as a key ally in the region, as well as consolidating its longstanding ties with Kuwait. This appears therefore to be more of a reshuffling and a realignment with a different selection of unelected elites rather than any deep change in the way the US deals with the region. The extent to which the US will be able to rely on Baghdad as a partner will depend on what develops in Iraq itself. As David Gardner writes:

> The US is now a power in the Gulf and the Levant in the most blunt and front-line way. Neither the Americans nor the Arabs seem to have a clear idea what that means, but they all know it spells the end of the status quo.[35]

Conclusion

Now that the Saddam Hussein regime has gone and the Arab world is begrudgingly accepting the new Iraqi governing body, it should be asked why upheavals and uprisings across the Arab world did not occur as predicted. Why did certain people have such faith in the so-called 'Arab street' when, as journalist David Pollock noted of the region in 1992, 'There has not been a successful popular uprising ... for at least the past thirty-five years, if ever.'[36] More importantly, why did so many people buy into the outdated slogans of the Arab nationalists? Perhaps assessment of the Arab world has become as stagnant as those very regimes that have remained in power for generations. Arab nationalism has proved itself to be little more than a simplistic set of ideas encompassing a belief in Arab unity, the primacy of the Palestinian issue and a harking back to the historical golden age of the Arabs. Arguably, Arab nationalism has evolved largely into empty rhetoric exploited by authoritarian regimes to obtain popular acquiescence in the maintenance of the status quo. The war in Iraq was yet another example of this trend, and seems unlikely to be the last.

The war also served the interests of local Islamist movements across the region that were able to use their opposition to the conflict to bolster their support base. With the left-wing movement that used to represent the only credible source of opposition to Arab governments having been destroyed or co-opted into the ruling elite, as in Morocco for example, the Islamists are the only relevant source of opposition throughout the region. Although militant Islam is largely on the wane due to the fact that its followers were brutally repressed by governments throughout the Middle East and North Africa in the mid 1990s, the so-called moderate Islamists are gaining ground in many countries, including Syria, Morocco and Egypt. These movements have altered the Arab nationalist discourse of the past to fit their own agendas and as such they are currently stepping into the role played by the nationalist movement in the 1950s and 1960s, polarising Arab politics between themselves and the regimes. The conflict in Iraq has provided them with a good source of propaganda and as such has contributed to the already widening gap between Arab populations and regimes.

It appears therefore that yet again the true nature of the regimes in the region, as well as the reactions of the Arab masses, have been misunderstood. What has also been underestimated is the strength of hatred that existed for the West prior to the war. The conflict in Iraq is unlikely to alter the West's continuing support for authoritarian regimes in the region, will not lead to a sustainable solution to the Arab-Israeli conflict, and will not result in a reduction in the development gap. Therefore, this bitterness and resentment towards the West will grow and the stagnation in the region will continue regardless of what transpires in Iraq. It seems reasonable to suppose, therefore, that this stagnation suits not only those in power in the region, but also those in power in the West.

Notes

1. N. DeAtkine, 'The Middle East Scholars and the Gulf War', *Parameters*, Vol. XXIII, Summer 1993, pp. 53–63.
2. M. Barnett, *Dialogues in Arab Politics*, New York, Columbia University Press, 1998, p. 10.
3. E. Said, 'Behind Saddam Hussein's Moves', *Christian Science Monitor*, 13 August 1990.
4. M.E. Yapp, *The Near East Since the First World War*, 2nd edn, London, Longman, 1996, pp. 504–5.
5. Libya expelled large numbers of Palestinian workers in the mid 1990s, for example, leaving them stranded on the Egyptian border. The Arab League also ruled that Palestinians should not be granted the nationality of their country of residence in the belief that if they are given a new nationality they might forget about their homeland and the struggle.
6. Council for Advanced Arab British Understanding (CAABU) Briefing, *Arab and International Reaction of Governments and Peoples to the Attack against Iraq*, 24 March 2003. Available on www.caabu.org.
7. Ibid.
8. Ibid.
9. League of Arab States, Resolution, *The US-British Military Aggression on Iraq and its Import for the Security and Peace of Neighbouring Arab Countries and for Arab National Security*, 22–25 March 2003. Available on www.caabu.org.
10. This partnership between the European Union and the states on the southern shores of the Mediterranean, except Libya, was launched in November 1995 and

aims to create an area of peace, stability and prosperity in the Mediterranean and a Mediterranean Free Trade Zone by the year 2010.

11. USAID, *Egypt, Program Briefing*, undated. Available on www.usaid.gov/locations/asia_near_east/countries/egypt/egypt_brief.html.

12. Abd Al-Rahman Al Rashed: 'The Silence of Arab Parliaments', *Al-Sharq al-Awsat*, 25 June 2003.

13. T. Friedman, 'Shaking up the neighbours', *New York Times*, 6 August 2003.

14. Indeed, there have been suggestions linking the war to a report published by an Israeli think tank in 1996 that claimed Benjamin Netanyahu had stated that removing Saddam from power was an important Israeli strategic objective. Quoted in 'Beyond Regime Change', *Los Angeles Times*, 1 December 2002.

15. 'Iraqi leader finds growing support among Arabs', *Washington Post*, 26 March 2003.

16. Ibid.

17. 'Arab reaction', *Detroit Free Press*, 10 April 2003.

18. Ibid.

19. Ibid.

20. N. MacFarquhar, 'Why Arab intellectuals are now praying for Saddam', *New York Times*, 27 March 2003.

21. K. Makiya, *Cruelty and Silence*, London, Random House, 1993, p. 308.

22. Ibid., p. 325.

23. K. Ghattas, 'Arabs watch Iraq with mixed feelings', *Financial Times*, 20 August 2003.

24. E. Said, 'Diary', *London Review of Books*, 3 April 2003.

25. M. Khoury-Machool, *Losing the Battle for Arab Hearts and Minds*, 2 May 2003, available on www.opendemocracy.org.

26. Conversations with Iraqi exiles in the UK.

27. Conversation with Iraqi writer.

28. Khoury-Machool, *Losing the Battle for Arab Hearts and Minds*.

29. R. Banerji, 'Radicalisation?', *Prospect Magazine*, May 2003.

30. N. MacFarquhar, 'Arabs rally to Baghdad's cause: shared ties fuel zeal, though States discourage action', *New York Times*, 1 April 2003. Available on www.jsonline.com/news/gen/apr03/130341.asp.

31. *New York Times*, 'Some Arabs "Going to the Jihad in Iraq"', 2 April 2003.

32. 'Iraqi leader finds growing support among Arabs'.

33. Conversation with Iraqi journalist in Baghdad.

34. BBC News Online, *Saudi Arabia Denies Terror Links*, 25 July 2003. Available on www.bbc.co.uk.

35. 'Time of the Shia', *Financial Times*, 30/31 August 2003.

36. J. Schanzer, 'The Arab Street and the War', *Policywatch*, No. 729, 21 March 2003.

14
The Economic Consequences of the War

Domitilla Sagramoso

With all the controversy surrounding the decision to go to war against Iraq, only passing attention was paid to the potential implications for the world economy of a prolonged and protracted conflict, as well as to the effects of raising energy costs. The US and most European economies experienced a major slowdown during 2000 and 2001, and although signs of stronger growth appeared in 2002, doubts remained as to the sustainability of the recovery. The risk existed that a prolonged war in Iraq would slow productivity growth, boost oil prices and trigger a world recession. However, the war in its most active phase turned out to be quick and decisive, and therefore its impact on the world economy remained quite limited. On the other hand, the costs of what might become a long and costly occupation could end up being much higher than those incurred before and during the actual military campaign.

This chapter will provide a broad overview of the implications of the war – understood as the more active phase of the military campaign undertaken in the spring of 2003 – on the world economy and on the oil markets. It is probably too early to make a proper assessment of the impact and costs of the Second Gulf War, primarily because most official data have not been released yet. At the time of writing, the US and the UK, the two main actors in the war, had not yet published all the details of the costs incurred, and the existing estimates tended to exclude costs such as veterans' benefits and health costs, the costs of replacing used or damaged equipment, as well as the costs of continued military occupation and reconstruction. Nevertheless, it has still been possible to assess broadly the impact of the war on the world economy, in particular on the US and Europe, and on countries in the Middle East, as well as on the oil market.

The world economy

Although the world economy was showing signs of recovery during most of 2002 – trade and industrial production picked up across the globe – by the end of that year, the pace of recovery slowed down, particularly in industrialised countries. Industrial production stagnated, while the growth in global trade faltered, amid rising uncertainties concerning the war in Iraq and the continued negative effects of the 2000 equity bubble. In early 2003, financial markets fell back, with equity markets declining between 40 and 60 per cent below their early 2000 peaks.[1] The anxieties caused by the war in Iraq partly accounted for the slowdown in the global economy during late 2002 and early 2003. However, the negative effects of the bursting of the equity bubble, excess capacity in the corporate sector, high levels of debt and the SARS outbreak also played an important part. All these factors led to a drop in consumer and business confidence as companies remained cautious as far as new investments were concerned. Oil prices were also affected by the uncertainties surrounding the Second Gulf War and its potential consequences. After exhibiting significant volatility throughout much of 2002, oil prices rose sharply in late 2002 and early 2003. Besides the war in Iraq, prices were also affected by supply disruptions associated with the political crisis in Venezuela, a major oil producer. Despite OPEC's decision in early January 2003 to raise its output target by 1.5 million barrels a day, prices continued to climb, peaking in mid March at $34 a barrel. As a result, households worldwide faced higher bills for fuel and heating oil, and many firms were burdened with rising energy costs.

The swift prosecution of the war in Iraq resolved some of the exceptional uncertainties that were undermining the US and other major economies. Worst-case scenarios, such as the development of a prolonged conflict involving a high number of casualties, an Iraqi urban defence strategy around Baghdad and Basra, and the outbreak of a wave of fatal terrorist attacks against the US and its allies, failed to materialise. Similarly, an Iraqi attack on Israel, the systematic destruction of Iraqi oilfields, and the use by the Iraqi regime of weapons of mass destruction, did not occur either. Neither did the Iraqi army use chemical or biological weapons against coalition troops, nor did the allies completely destroy Iraq's basic social and economic infrastructure. The damage was very limited, and this in turn helped to lower the costs of the war. As a result, just as the war ended, oil prices began to fall and the global economic climate began to improve. Share prices rallied and consumer and business confidence rebounded in the more developed economies.

The United States' economy

Once it became clear that military action in Iraq was imminent, US equity and bond markets rallied, as some of the uncertainties dissipated and investors began to show a greater appetite for riskier assets. Equity indexes jumped about 8 per cent right after Bush issued an ultimatum to Saddam Hussein on 17 March 2003.[2] Moreover, during the second and third quarters of 2003, the US economy showed unexpectedly high rates of growth. The figures released on 31 July by the US Department of Commerce indicated a 2.4 per cent annual GDP growth for the second quarter of 2003, the fastest rate since the third quarter in 2002.[3] In the third quarter of 2003, real GDP increased at an annual rate of 8.2 per cent, the fastest rate since 1984.[4] Although data from labour markets and the manufacturing sector showed continued sluggishness – jobs failed to grow and wage and salary incomes increased particularly slowly – other signs pointed to an improving economic outlook in the second half of 2003. Such positive indicators included a rebound in the stock market, nascent signs of improvement in the manufacturing sector, higher non-manufacturing business activity, improved consumer and business confidence, and a decline in businesses inventories.[5]

Despite such positive signs, many experts expressed doubts regarding the durability and sustainability of the recovery. They warned that growth could slow down once the effects of tax rebates and a surge in mortgage refinancing wore off.[6] The high growth rates experienced by the US economy were caused, on the one hand, by continued spending among US consumers. Positive consumer spending was boosted by the significant tax cuts introduced by the Bush Administration in 2003 and by the end of the uncertainties surrounding the war in Iraq. Growth was also boosted by substantial increases in US government spending in general, and defence spending in particular, which was up nearly 45 per cent in the second quarter of 2003 – the fastest pace at which it had grown since the early 1950s.[7] The substantial increases in spending and the lower-than-expected tax revenues resulted, however, in the emergence of a record budget deficit, which reached $374 billion in FY2003, and was expected to reach $475 billion in FY2004.[8] Joshua B. Bolten, Director of the White House's Office of Management and Budget (OMB), argued in July 2003 that a deficit of such magnitude was actually manageable, as long as pro-growth economic policies were pursued and serious spending discipline was exercised. In his view, a deficit of 4.2 per cent of GDP could well be sustained by the US economy.[9] However, defence spending, and specifically the costs of the Iraqi war and the subsequent occupation, turned out to be much higher than initially expected, and therefore had and will probably continue to have a much bigger impact on the budget, especially in 2004 and 2005. The government calculations in 2003 did not take full account of the costs of maintaining troops in Iraq and Afghanistan beyond 2003, and of rebuilding the collapsed infrastructures of those countries.[10]

Preliminary costs of the war and their impact on the US budget

The cost of the Second Gulf War to the US was estimated by Secretary of Defense Donald Rumsfeld in July 2003 to reach roughly $3.9 billion per month, or $35.1 billion for the financial year 2003 – from January to September 2003.[11] The US General Accounting Office produced a rather similar figure, by reporting in May 2004 that the costs of Operation Iraqi Freedom for the financial year 2003 amounted to $38,838,856.[12] However, the costs of the war thereafter increased substantially. In April 2003, the US Congress approved a government proposal for $74.7 billion in supplemental appropriations to cover primarily the costs involved in the war in Iraq, as well as the global war on terrorism during 2003. The supplemental was expected to cover the costs of the Iraqi war from January 2003 until end of the financial year on 30 September 2003, and included $62.6 billion granted to the Department of Defense to cover the costs of military operations in Iraq and the war on terrorism. Of that figure, $59.9 billion was allocated to the war in Iraq. An additional $5 billion was available to the Department of Defense, the State Department and other agencies for relief and reconstruction operations in Iraq.[13] The supplemental, however, was not all spent and $17 billion was passed on to the following financial year. These delays in expenditure partly accounted for a lower-than-expected budget deficit of $374 billion, instead of the estimated $455 billion in the Mid-Session Review.[14]

In November 2003, an additional war supplemental for Iraq and Afghanistan for a total of $87.5 billion was approved. Some $64.7 billion was assigned to military operations in Iraq and Afghanistan, with a further $18.7 billion allocated to the Iraqi Relief and Reconstruction Fund, to be spent by the Coalition Provisional Authority in Iraq during the financial year 2004. On the basis of these figures and the supplemental initially proposed by President Bush, which allocated $51 billion to military operations in Iraq, expenditures for Iraq can be expected to total roughly $69.7 billion in FY2004. This figure sharply contrasts with earlier government projections of expenditures in Iraq for 2004 of $26.8 billion. If these funds are all spent, which seems likely given the current US commitment in Iraq, they could add $42.9 billion to the estimated US budget deficit for 2004 of $475 billion. The budget could increase even further if account is taken of expenses incurred in the war in Afghanistan. A similar situation can be expected to take place in FY2005, given that the costs of military operations in Iraq and Afghanistan have been estimated at $40–$55 billion per year, and the Bush Administration has only requested $25 billion from Congress.[15]

The budget deficit can be expected to be even larger if the US economy does not grow as rapidly as expected in 2004–5. In its Mid-Session Review of the 2003 budget, the OMB used optimistic economic assumptions which presupposed strong and constant economic growth. Although the economy grew quite substantially in the first quarter of 2004 – 4.4 per cent of GDP – there is still a risk that if the budget deficit continues to grow, it will become unsustainable and impossible to eradicate. OMB figures show public debt growing faster than the economy, a situation which is not really sustainable in the long-run.[16] If deficit levels fail to decline relative to GDP once economic recovery is under way, global investors might begin to shy away from dollar-denominated assets. There is also the risk that long-term deficits might result in increases in interest rates, which in turn might significantly impair economic growth. Moreover, the financing of the war risks absorbing productive resources which would have been more efficiently used elsewhere (in the private sector, for example).

During the 1990–91 Gulf War, America's costs were almost entirely covered by others – mainly Arab countries, together with Germany and Japan. This time instead, the US has been forced to furnish the vast majority of the military forces required to keep the peace in Iraq and to pay for the costs. Although the US has received substantial military support from the UK, as well as some support from Australia, Spain, Italy, Poland and others, it has failed to obtain contributions from major countries such as Germany, France, Russia, India, Pakistan and Turkey, and some countries like Spain are withdrawing their support. Also, the US will most likely cover the majority of the reconstruction costs, given that Iraqi oil revenues remain rather limited – $10 billion a year – and that the contributions pledged by all other countries at the Iraq donors' conference held in Madrid on 23 October 2003 have not exceeded $13 billion.[17] The US thus finds itself in the historically familiar position of financing a war through government debt, the burden of which will pass to future generations unless it is eroded by inflation.[18]

Lawrence Lindsay, head of the White House's National Economic Council dismissed the potential negative economic consequences of governmental spending on the war, arguing that such expenses would not have an appreciable effect on interest rates or add much to federal debt. However, he also remained doubtful that the additional spending would actually give a strong lift to the economy, noting that 'building weapons and expending them [was] not the basis for sustained economic growth'.[19] Similarly, Charles Shultze, former US budget director in the 1960s, claimed that existing spending levels in Iraq were in themselves not substantial. According to the OMB, the war would add $47 billion to the deficit in 2003, which actually represented only 10.3 per cent of the projected 2003 deficit. However, taken together with broader spending and taxation trends, these figures do raise concerns.[20] The main concern is not the direct costs of the war in Iraq, but the lack of appropriate plans to deal with the substantial additional and indirect costs, in view of the existing record deficits.[21] On the other hand, one could also argue that the war had a positive effect on the economy, because it removed some of the uncertainties and dangers related to global terrorism, and therefore it represented an investment in the removal of a threat to the economy which far outweighed the costs.[22] That said, whether Iraq without Saddam Hussein represents less of a threat to world peace than Iraq with Saddam, remains to be seen.

The European economies in the euro zone

The European economies were less directly affected by the war in Iraq than the American economy, although they also suffered from the geopolitical uncertainties surrounding the war and its immediate aftermath – prolonged violence in Iraq, instability in the Middle East, growing violence in the Arab-Israeli conflict, strains in the transatlantic relationship and risks of further terrorists attacks.[23] Consumer and business confidence plummeted during the first half of 2003, equity markets continued to decline and economic growth failed to pick up. Moreover, the European economies also suffered from high and volatile oil prices that led to temporary boosts in inflation during the first quarter of 2003. The difficulties faced by most European economies were not primarily related to the war in Iraq. The weak performances of the European economies during the first half of 2003 were also determined by the slowness of the recovery in the world economy, the absence of a substantial increase in global trade, the SARS outbreak, and the lack of effective structural reforms in most of the euro-zone economies.[24] As opposed to the US and Japan, which experienced economic growth once the war ended, the European economies – primarily in the euro zone – failed to grow once the main phase of the military operations of the war in Iraq was over. Although consumer and business confidence grew substantially after the war ended, during most of 2003, the euro-zone economies stagnated. Recession gripped Germany, Italy and the Netherlands in the second quarter of 2003, and the French economy grew by a meagre 0.2 per cent.[25] Growth for the entire euro zone for 2003 has reached only 0.5 per cent.[26]

The underlying reasons for the subdued economic growth of most euro-zone economies in 2003 are to be found largely in unfavourable domestic conditions in most European economies – primarily the existing structural rigidities – rather than in the overall world recession. Inflexible labour markets, with high wage costs and protection against redundancy have made it difficult for European companies to adjust to downturns, and have inhibited natural job creation during upturns. European companies have tended to adjust to the erosion of revenues by cutting down capital costs and overlooking labour costs. Such actions resulted in only limited increases in labour productivity, which then translated into depressed profit margins.[27] Moreover, the 3 per cent of GDP budget deficit limit under the euro zone's Growth and Stability Pact significantly limited the scope for economic stimulus from lower taxes and higher public spending. Some relief was received from the decision taken right after the war broke out to relax the pact rules as a result of the 'exceptional circumstances' surrounding the war.[28] The tentative signs of rebound in the United States and the European stimulus programmes lifted business and consumer confidence; however, that optimism did not translate into real economic gains. Moreover, the rise in the exchange rate value of the euro during 2003 hurt euro-zone manufacturers quite significantly, with a reduction in overseas demand for European goods. Although growth is expected to pick up in 2004 and reach 2.5 per cent in 2005, according to OECD estimates, structural reforms, especially in the labour market, remain essential if growth is to remain substantial.[29] The boost in manufacturing experienced by some euro-zone economies in late 2003, was driven primarily by increases in global exports rather than by increases in domestic demand – a clear indication that the euro-zone economies remain dependent on the US for growth and are unable themselves to become the engines of growth.

The UK economy and the cost of war

Growth in the United Kingdom weakened in the first half of 2003, reflecting a slowing of investment and private consumption, as well as a deterioration of external demand due to the slow growth of the world economy. Concern over the Iraqi conflict also played an important part in pulling global equity markets down to a seven-year low in March 2003. However, once the conflict ended, equity markets made significant gains, with the FTSE World index increasing by 40 per cent as recovery in the world economy gained momentum.[30] Moreover, January 2004 indicators, including business surveys and retail sales, pointed to an improving outlook. According to data published in January 2004, manufacturing in the UK was growing at about 3.5 per cent on an annualised basis, clearly indicating an improvement in companies' sales, orders and investment intentions in the last quarter of 2003.[31] The labour market also remained resilient during 2003, with continuing low unemployment and relative stable earning growth. In July 2003, the Bank of England cut the benchmark interest rate by 0.5 per cent to 3.5 per cent, in response to weakening economic prospects.

A more lax fiscal policy during 2003 provided an important support for activity during the year's slowdown, drawing on the room for manoeuvre built up over preceding years. However, increases in public spending resulted in a widening of the public deficit. Although debt in Britain remained low during 2003 – 32.8 per cent of national income – when compared to other industrialised economies (42 per cent in France, 50 per cent in Germany, just under 50 per cent in the US, 80 per cent in Japan), it started to grow. Britain's public deficit was expected to reach 3.4 per cent of GDP in 2003, breaching the 3 per cent limit imposed by the EU Growth and Stability Pact.[32] The UK deficit grew in 2003 primarily as a result of increases in spending for public services and because of lower-than-expected tax receipts. However, the costs of the war in Iraq also played an important part. In December 2003, the UK Treasury allocated an additional £800 million to finance military operations in Iraq in 2003 and 2004, taking the total earmarked for the conflict and its aftermath to £3.8 billion.

In the financial year leading up to April 2003, the government allocated £3 billion for Iraq, of which £1 billion was spent in 2002–3, with the remaining £2 billion carried forward to 2003–4. At the time of writing, the UK was spending between £100 million and £200 million a month in operations in Iraq, which meant that the yearly costs approached £2.4 billion. The Treasury agreed in December 2003 to allocate a total of £500 million to the war expenses in 2003–4, in order to meet the expected costs of £2.5 billion, while the remaining £300 million were passed on to the following financial year. Together with the war in Afghanistan, the costs were expected to reach a total of £6.3 billion for the two financial years 2003 and 2004.[33] However, the UK military involvement in Iraq is expected to continue for some time, and as a result, costs are expected to grow. In addition, at the time of writing, the UK Ministry of Defence had not yet fully accounted for the cost of the replacement of lost or damaged equipment, which could substantially increase the overall bill. Nevertheless, despite the risks involved in a broadening deficit resulting from the Second Gulf War and increased public spending, the supportive macroeconomic policies, together with relatively favourable domestic conditions and a gradual improvement in external trade, were expected to lead to stronger growth in 2004. The UK economy grew by 2.1 per cent in 2003, and was expected to grow between 3 per cent and 3.5 per cent in 2004.[34]

The Asian and East European economies undeterred and unaffected

The major Japanese and Chinese economies and the smaller economies of South East Asia were not significantly affected by the war in Iraq. The Japanese economy experienced unexpectedly high rates of growth in 2003 – it grew by 3.9 per cent between April and June 2003 – and was expected to grow by 2.5 per cent in 2004.[35] However, a note of caution is required. Although exports grew strongly and industrial production picked up significantly in July 2003, retail sales continued to fall, and the apparent strength of business fixed investment in national data accounts appeared at odds with weaker trends in shipments of capital goods and construction materials.[36] Moreover, forecasts remained clouded by entrenched deflation and by the persistent weakness in Japan's corporate, financial and public sector balance sheets. Other Asia-Pacific countries, by comparison, continued to experience relentless growth. Despite a slowdown during the first quarter of 2003, partly as a result of the SARS outbreak, the uncertainties surrounding the war and the increase in oil prices, Asia-Pacific countries – excluding Japan – became the world's fastest-growing economies in 2003. The Chinese economy, undeterred by the global slowdown, continued to grow at high rates in 2003, following previous growth records – 7.5 per cent in 2001, 8 per cent in 2002, and 8.5 per cent in 2003.[37] Such astounding rates of economic growth created concerns over a potential overheating of the economy that could result in a major bust once the positive cycle ends.[38] High rates of growth were also envisioned elsewhere in Asia. India, Pakistan and Bangladesh were expected to grow by 5.5 per cent in 2003 and 5.8 in 2004, whereas Indonesia, Malaysia, the Philippines and Thailand were expected to grow by 4.1 per cent in 2003 and 4.4 per cent in

2004. The Asian Tigers – Hong Kong, South Korea, Singapore and Taiwan – were expected to grow by 2.3 per cent in 2003 and 4.2 in 2004.

Significant growth was also experienced by the Russian economy, which strongly benefited from sharp increases in energy prices. Russia's GDP grew at an average of 6.2 per cent between 1999 and 2003. The recovery resulted primarily from a combination of prudent fiscal and monetary policies, political stability, the devaluation of the rouble, and quite high energy prices. Despite the conduct of structural reforms during 2001–3, energy exports still represented a high percentage of the Russian economy in 2003. As a result of an increase in oil prices and an expansion in output, crude oil, oil products and natural gas accounted for 63 per cent of Russia's exports in the first quarter of 2003. In 2002, oil production reached 7.4 million barrels per day (b/d) and, as production increased towards the end of the year, Russia actually exceeded Saudi Arabia in daily output, with crude oil output hitting a record of 8.82 million b/d.[39] Despite the existing constraints of insufficient export pipeline capacity, Russia became a major oil exporter. In 2002, the country exported over 5 million b/d of oil, second only to Saudi Arabia, and between January and September 2003 Russia's oil exports increased by 18 per cent year-on-year.[40] As a result, Russia's export earnings on crude rose over 35 per cent during 2003, reaching $40 billion.

In central and eastern Europe, growth remained solid during 2002 and 2003, despite a difficult international environment. Undeterred by higher oil prices and global economic sluggishness, EU accession countries grew by an average of 3 per cent in 2003 outstripping the euro-zone countries. Growth was driven primarily by exports and by a resumption of industrial production. Private consumption remained robust, while additional support was provided by low interest rates.[41]

The weakest economies: the Middle East, Africa and Latin America

Security concerns and high oil prices negatively affected the economic development of the weakest economies worldwide. The Middle East, and in particular the region's non-oil producing countries, was the area most negatively affected by war. GDP growth in the Middle East continued to weaken in 2002, reflecting lower oil production as a result of reduced OPEC quotas, the after-effects on tourism of 9/11, and the tense political and security situation in the region. The picture, of course, varies considerably across countries. While higher oil prices in late 2002 and early 2003 benefited oil-producing countries – Saudi Arabia, the United Arab Emirates, Kuwait and Iran – oil importers in the region suffered as a result of it. Countries dependent on tourism, such as Egypt, or with close economic links to Iraq, notably Jordan and Syria, were most seriously affected in terms of disruptions to trade and investment flows, and reduced numbers of foreign visitors. However, the impact turned out to be only temporary and most economies in the region, except for Iraq, eventually recovered.

The Egyptian economy was severely affected by 9/11, as tourism collapsed and GDP growth slowed down from 3.5 per cent in 2001 to 2 per cent in 2002. Although GDP growth began to recover in late 2002 aided by higher tourist arrivals, the war in Iraq again led to a decline in tourism. In the spring of 2003, local economists estimated that the war could cost Egypt up to $8 billion in lost revenue from a fall in tourism, reduced traffic along the Suez Canal and a fall in exports to Iraq, one of Egypt's largest trading partners.[42] However, the impact of the war turned out to be less severe than expected. Economic growth picked up quite quickly in the spring of 2003 while tourism activities soared during the summer. As a result, the Egyptian Central Bank estimated that Egypt's GDP grew by 3.1 per cent during the fiscal year 2002–3.[43] Lebanon also saw a boom in tourism during the summer of 2003, despite a slowdown in March, April and May 2003 because of the war in Iraq, with an increase of 4 per cent in foreign visitors during the first eight months of 2003 compared to the previous years.

Syria, a major trading partner of Iraq, was also adversely affected by the war during its initial phases. Syria imported Iraqi oil at discounted prices, and sold many of its goods in the Iraqi market. Rateb Challah, head of the Federation of Syrian Chambers of Commerce, estimated in August 2003 that trade with Iraq was running at an annual equivalent of between $100 million and $200 million, a far cry from the $3 billion estimated by western diplomats before the outbreak of the war.[44] However, trade was picking up and the prospects for commerce were improving. Moreover, although the total trade between Syria and Iraq amounted to more than 10 per cent of Syrian GDP, analysts believed that the impact of the fall in trade on the Syrian economy would be quite limited. Iraqi payments to Syria apparently continued until the day before the war started, providing a comfortable cushion to the country's foreign exchange reserves. Moreover, according to some experts, very little of this money actually went into the economy, and instead ended in the pockets of politicians.[45] Furthermore, the war ended up being short and contained, and therefore it is believed that the losses resulting from the war were overstated. However, it will be impossible accurately to tally up the costs and assess the long-term economic effect of the war until Iraq's future is clearer and the implication of Saddam Hussein's overthrow on regional balances becomes more apparent. Other countries in the region, such as Jordan and Turkey, also suffered from the war. However, the negative impact was limited by the brevity of the war, and was alleviated by the financial aid provided by the US to both countries – $1 billion for each.[46]

Uncertainty over Iraq, as well as bad weather, declining world trade, and government agricultural subsidies in the industrialised economies, also negatively affected the African economies. Average GDP growth in Africa fell from 4.3 per cent in 2001 to 3.2 per cent in 2002, despite relatively sound monetary policies, falling inflation and improvements in governance throughout the continent.[47] However, the African economies recovered during the second and third quarters of 2003, and were expected to grow by 4.2 per cent in 2003. The figures of course could be revised downwards if the economic and political situations in Zimbabwe and Liberia deteriorated further. Latin American countries experienced a slight recovery during 2003, after having undergone a major downturn during 2001–2. However, growth remained highly differentiated across the region with political uncertainties weighing heavily in the most unstable regions. Although not directly affected by the war, Latin America benefited from an increase in the price of its exporting commodities – energy, metals and agricultural products – which allowed for an increase in most countries' revenues. However, the region also witnessed a fall of 11 per cent in United States' aid.[48]

The oil market

Following a decline which reached $20 a barrel in late 2001, oil prices climbed steadily in 2002, reaching about $37 a barrel in mid March 2003.[49] The increase in prices was related primarily to market perceptions of potential supply disruptions as a result of the war in Iraq, as well as to prospective increases in demand, rather than to an actual shortage of supply. Worsening tensions between the United States and Iraq during late 2002 and early 2003 sparked concern over the possibility of military action in the Middle East where two-thirds of the world's proven crude oil reserves are located. This led to a sharp rise in oil prices, despite a significant expansion in global production during the course of 2002. In early December 2002, a general strike that virtually halted oil production in Venezuela resulted in a sharp tightening of supply in global oil markets, and this in turn led to a further increase in prices. Prices were also boosted at the end of 2002 by OPEC's mid December call on its members to bring actual output down by 2 million b/d. In the event, the OPEC call did not materialise, as OPEC members increased output to cover for Venezuela's supply shortfall. Although Venezuelan production gradually recovered, further escalation in US–Iraq tensions and the prospect of war and supply disruptions continued to push prices up through early March 2003.

The price of oil in the aftermath of the war

In late March, as military action against Iraq became certain, prices fell from over $37 a barrel to $25.5 a barrel in just two weeks. Economists and governments had feared that war in Iraq would lead to a sustained spike in oil prices. Worst-case scenarios had envisaged the oil price reaching $50 a barrel or more for months, tipping the global economy into recession.[50] Besides the removal of Iraqi oil from the market during the war, western governments worried that another major oil supplier in the Middle East – Saudi Arabia, for example – would stop selling oil to the US, either because of an Iraqi attack against it or out of solidarity with Saddam Hussein. However, such predicaments failed to materialise. The war turned out to be swift and contained, most Iraqi oil infrastructure remained intact and the disruption to deliveries remained minimal. In order to offset the losses of Iraqi oil, OPEC members sent an additional 1.7 million barrels of oil per day to the market.[51] Moreover, oil markets anticipated the disappearance of Iraqi oil from the market due to war and the end of the UN Oil-for-Food programme and reacted accordingly. Therefore, when the active phase of the military campaign finished in mid-April, prices dropped to around $25 a barrel from almost $40 a barrel in the run-up to the war.

While oil prices declined sharply in mid April, they recovered soon thereafter, reaching $32 a barrel in early August 2003. The second and third quarters of 2003 were characterised both by high oil prices and high price volatility. Between April and November 2003, despite excess oil production by OPEC members of over 1 million barrels a day, prices oscillated between $28 and $32 a barrel – much higher than the $18–25 price range considered appropriate by the US and other energy consumers. Such high prices were caused primarily by global geopolitical instabilities, rather than by a drop in supplies or a sharp increase in demand, although the increase in demand driven by the rapid expansion in global economic activity also affected prices.[52] Ever since the end of the Second Gulf War, world oil markets have remained sensitive to the difficulties faced by the US-led coalition in Iraq, the civil unrest experienced by Nigeria, the political upheavals taking place in Venezuela and the terrorist activities besetting Saudi Arabia.[53] Moreover, contrary to expectations, Iraqi oil has failed to flow back in big quantities to the market. Lack of adequate and properly functioning infrastructure, continued unrest, persistent looting and sabotage have significantly reduced and delayed the flow of Iraqi oil to world markets. Such developments have contributed significantly to a high level of oil prices. However, during late 2003 and early 2004, prices were also affected by the seasonal fall in US crude inventories, which in November 2003 remained 11.2 million barrels below their five-year average, according to the US Energy Information Administration.[54]

High oil prices have benefited OPEC members, which, despite failed efforts to cut production, have managed to keep the oil target price at $28 a barrel, and have enjoyed a real oil price of $37 a barrel. However, high prices are forcing consuming countries to look outside OPEC for supplies, thus encouraging marginal producers to increase output. Moreover, if maintained for long, high prices might lead to increased energy conservation and a shift away from oil to other sources of energy. More worryingly, however, high oil prices might impair economic growth and curb future energy demand. Studies on the impact of higher oil prices on the world economy have shown that in the recent past, higher oil prices have a negative impact on economic growth in a variety of ways.[55] First, a transfer of income from oil consumers to oil producers occurs, which often results in a fall in demand, primarily because oil consumers tend to spend more than oil producers. Also, a reduction in demand also tends to occur within producing countries, given that they often allow higher oil prices to feed through to consumers. Second, there is usually a rise in the cost of the production of goods and services in the economy, given the increase in the relative price of energy inputs that puts pressure on profit margins. Third, there tends to be an impact on price levels and on inflation. Its magnitude depends on the degree of monetary tightening and the extent to which consumers seek to offset the decline in their real incomes through higher wage increases. Fourth, there tends to be a direct and indirect impact on financial markets. As a result, it has been estimated that a $5 per barrel increase in the price of oil would reduce the level of global output by around a quarter of a percentage point over the first four years, after which the output losses slowly fade away. Actual as well as anticipated changes in economic activity, corporate earnings, inflation and monetary policy following the oil price increases tend to affect equity and bond valuations, and currency exchange rates.[56]

Despite the current trends, however, experts estimate that in the absence of any major shocks in the future, prices will probably fall because of higher global oil supplies. Non-OPEC supply, primarily coming from Russia, Norway, Brazil and Angola, is expected to increase by 1.4 million b/d in 2004. Nigeria, an OPEC member, is also expected to increase supply by 2.1 million b/d. At the end of 2003, there were expectations that Iraq might, in the short to medium term, become an important player in the market. Its output at the time was growing and the Iraqi authorities were hoping to raise exports by another 1 million b/d by April 2004. However, growing instability and constant acts of sabotage reduced Iraqi production to 1.5 million b/d in mid June 2004. Even without Iraq, however, OPEC apparently faces a potential 2 million b/d shortfall in demand for its crude by the second half of 2004.[57]

Iraqi oil prospects

Iraq's northern oilfields resumed production almost immediately after the US-British occupation. However, sabotaging and looting dogged efforts to rehabilitate, and eventually properly run, the northern pipeline to Turkey. Exports from Iraq's southern fields through the Gulf export terminal at Mina al-Bakr near Basra also witnessed regular interruptions primarily because of power shortages at the terminal. Such developments substantially reduced the production and export of Iraqi oil during the summer of 2003, although production slightly recovered during the autumn. In November 2003, Iraq was producing some 1.9 million b/d, of which 1.55 million were exported to the outside world, almost entirely through the Basra terminal in Southern Iraq.[58] Such production and export levels, although significant compared to oil outputs at the end of the war, remained small compared to the levels achieved by Iraq before the fall of Saddam Hussein in April 2003. In February 2003, Iraq was producing 2.48 million b/d and was exporting 2 million b/d. In order for Iraqi oil exports to flow on a substantial basis, Iraqi production still has to overcome some major obstacles, namely lack of secure pipelines and exit routes, the absence of a stable central government, as well as the need for substantial investment. Over the past months, the inability of the US-led coalition to bring security to Iraq has forced oil companies to shy away from investing and setting up an important presence in the country.[59]

Iraq is home to the second largest oil reserves in the world, with proven reserves equalling 113 billion barrels, according to some estimates.[60] However, experts believe it will take years before a significant volume of this oil reaches the market. Experts have estimated that it could take Iraq as much as three years and $5 billion of investment to achieve the production of 3.5 million b/d, the volume Iraq pumped before its 1990 invasion of Kuwait.[61] In order to increase oil production from the current levels to the expected 6–7 million b/d by 2010, it has been estimated that an investment of $35–40 billion over ten years is required.[62] Given the current difficulties in attracting investment, there is little doubt therefore that in the shorter and medium term, Iraq will not become a major oil producer. However, as Iraq slowly returns to its pre-2003 war production and export levels, several key questions arise. Will Iraq be forced to join the OPEC production quota system? How will other OPEC members react to the Iraqi production quota? And more crucially, might Iraq decide, under US influence, to withdraw from the organisation altogether? The answer to this last question will depend very much on the future political configuration of Iraq and its relationship with the United States. Iraq has been a member of OPEC since its foundation. However, since the First Gulf War in 1991, Iraq's oil production has been controlled by the United Nations, through the Oil-for-Food programme. This might argue in favour of playing an independent game. Yet some experts believe that it is highly unlikely that Iraq will distance itself completely from OPEC. The country is in such dire need of funding to finance its reconstruction and development that it will probably avoid a collapse in prices that might result from a confrontation with its neighbours in the cartel.[63]

Conclusion

Most economic indicators for 2003 and 2004 point to a worldwide economic recovery, excluding western Europe, as well as some Middle Eastern and African countries. Contrary to expectations, the Second Gulf War did not drag the world economy into recession, to a great extent because it was swift and contained, and because the damage to Iraqi infrastructure and oilfields was limited. It seems likely, as noted by William D. Nordhaus, that the most adverse psychological reaction to a short war took place even before the war started.[64] Nordhaus' predictions seem reasonable enough; if oil prices remain stable (as they more or less have) and victory is swift (as it seems to have been) then there will not be a repetition of the 1990–91 recession and the macroeconomic impact of the 2003 war will be negligible.

Yet the situation in Iraq remains volatile, the prospects of democratisation and stability remain uncertain and the price of oil remains too high. Moreover, the US economy faces growing budget deficits, which could worsen if the US is compelled to stay in Iraq longer than planned and the security situation deteriorates further. In addition, a host of structural challenges – particularly the continued hangover of the 1990s equity bubble – have left the world economy, primarily in the US and Europe, extraordinarily vulnerable. Although the war did not lead to a major rift between the US and its European allies as far as economic relations are concerned, there is little doubt that the spirit of cooperation that characterised relations among industrialised nations during the 1990s has been eroded significantly. There is a growing tendency in the US to give preference to bilateral trade agreements as opposed to multilateral accords, thus undermining the relevance of multilateral institutions like the World Trade Organisation. There is a marked lack of concern in the US over global financial developments and the impact on the world economy, primarily the European economy, of a falling dollar and an overvalued euro. Such worrying developments, although not caused by the war in Iraq, have certainly been exacerbated by the tensions that emerged among transatlantic allies, and need to be monitored carefully.

The Asian economies, on the other hand, seem less affected by the war as they continue to experience significant growth. The oil-producing countries, both in the Middle East and the former Soviet Union, seem to be benefiting enormously from the current high prices. However, such a positive conjuncture might end up being counter-productive as it prevents oil exporting countries from conducting the necessary reforms to become less dependent on energy exports. The future of Iraq and of its oil industry will have an important impact on the oil market, although its full integration into the system will take quite some time to complete.

Notes

1. IMF, *World Economic Outlook: Growth and Institutions*, Washington DC, IMF, April 2003, p. 1.
2. Board of Governors of the Federal Reserve System, *Monetary Policy Report to Congress*, 15 July 2003, p. 20.
3. Peronet Despeignes, 'Growth figures fuel hopes of US recovery', *Financial Times*, 31 July 2003.
4. David Leonhardt, 'Economy records speediest growth since the mid-80s', *New York Times*, 31 October 2003, p. 1.
5. US House of Representatives, Committee on the Budget, Majority Caucus, Economic Update, 'Emerging Evidence Anticipates Stronger Growth but Employment Lags', 14 July 2003.
6. Leonhardt, 'Economy records speediest growth since the mid-80s'.
7. 'An Ocean Apart', *The Economist*, 1 August 2003.
8. OMB, the Executive Office of the President, *Mid-Session Review*, Summary, p. 3, available at www.whitehouse.gov/omb/budget/fy2004/summary.html.

9. 'White House sees a $455 billion gap in the '03 budget', *New York Times*, 16 July 2003.
10. OMB, *Mid-Session Review*, Summary, p. 3.
11. 'The Cost of the War', *New York Times*, 20 July 2003.
12. United States General Accounting Office, *Military Operations: DoD's Fiscal Year 2003 Funding and Reported Obligations in Support of the Global War on Terrorism*, GAO-04–668, May 2004, Highlights.
13. 'President Submits $74.7 Billion Supplemental Appropriations Request for Funding War on Terrorism', Executive Office of the President, Office of Management and Budget, Washington DC, 25 March 2003.
14. OMB, 'Joint Statement of John W. Snow, Secretary of the Treasury, and Joshua B. Bolten, Director of the Office of Management and Budget, on Budget Results for Fiscal Year 2003', 20 October 2003, p. 4.
15. House Budget Committee, Democratic Caucus, *House Budget Committee Democratic Staff Analysis: Administration's $25 Billion Request for Iraq and Afghanistan Operations will Cover Only a Fraction of Fiscal Year 2005 Costs*, 11 May 2005, p. 1.
16. House Budget Committee, Democratic Caucus, *Deficits Hit Record Levels: Administration Shows No Shame, Shock or Solution*, 16 July 2003, p. 8.
17. Steven R. Weisman, '$13 billion raised at Iraq aid talks', *International Herald Tribune*, 25–26 October 2003, p. 1.
18. Brigitte Granville, 'Economic consequences of the war: downslides all around', *World Today*, May 2003, p. 21.
19. Bob Davis, 'Cost of Iraq war may top $100 billion', *Wall Street Journal*, 16 September 2002.
20. Brian Knowlton, 'US budget deficit put at $455 billion', *International Herald Tribune*, 16 July 2003.
21. House Budget Committee, *Deficits Hit Record Levels*.
22. Davis, 'Cost of Iraq war may top $100 billion'.
23. EU, *European Economy: Economic Forecasts Spring 2003*, Commission of the European Communities, DG Economic and Financial Affairs, p. 7.
24. EU, *The EU Economy: 2003 Review*, Commission of the European Communities, DG European and Financial Affairs, Brussels, 26 November 2003, p. 7.
25. Robert Graham and Tony Major, 'Gloomy French data add to Eurozone woes', *Financial Times*, 21 August 2003.
26. OECD, *OECD Economic Outlook, no. 74*, Paris, December 2003, 'The Euro Area', available at www.oecd.org/dataoecd/2/29/22545260.pdf.
27. EU, *The EU Economy: 2003 Review*, p. 9.
28. Granville, 'Economic Consequences of the War', p. 21.
29. OECD, *OECD Economic Outlook, no. 75*, Paris, May 2004, 'The Euro Area'.
30. Chris Flood, 'Economic fundamentals still in the ascendant', *Financial Times*, 14 December 2003, p. 2.
31. Anna Fifield, 'Sharp pick-up in activity signals business upturn', *Financial Times*, 23 January 2004, p. 4.
32. 'British deficit widens', *International Herald Tribune*, 11 December 2003, p. 11.
33. Ibid.; James Blitz, 'Brown to boost Iraq operations by £800m', *Financial Times*, 10 December 2003, p. 2.
34. 'Pre-budget report', edited version of Chancellor Gordon Brown's speech to the Commons, *Financial Times*, 11 December 2003, p. 4.
35. Ken Belson, 'Japan sees expansion persisting next year', *International Herald Tribune*, 1 November 2003, p. 11.

36. IMF, *World Economic Outlook: Public Debt in Emerging Markets*, September 2003, p. 29.
37. Ibid., p. 35.
38. Keith Bradsher, 'As China's economy races ahead, bubble worries are afloat', *International Herald Tribune*, 19 January 2004, p. 6.
39. 'Oil: Russian gambit threatens to change game', *Middle East Economic Digest*, 7 November 2003, p. 4.
40. Bank of Finland, Institute for Economies in Transition, *BOFIT Russian Review*, Issue no. 1, 13 January 2004, p. 1.
41. EU, *Autumn 2003 Economic Forecast*, European Commission, DG for Economic and Financial Affairs, 29 October 2003, p. 5.
42. David Lamb, 'Economies of Arab Countries Shaken by Invasion', *Guardian* News Service, *Los Angeles Times*, 20 April 2003.
43. Agence France-Presse, 10 October 2003.
44. Roula Khalaf, 'Syria resumes trade with Iraq unhindered by US', *Financial Times*, 6 August 2003, p. 5.
45. Ibid.
46. Christian Miller, 'Jordan tastes the fruits of US friendship', *Los Angeles Times*, 14 July 2003, p. 1.
47. Mark Turner, 'Rich world's subsidies hitting African growth: UN economic report', *Financial Times*, 31 July 2003, p. 1
48. 'Powell to Latin America: you are not a priority', Democratic Caucus, US House of Representatives, 12 February 2004.
49. 'Oil Prices on the Rise', BBC News, 12 March 2003, available at http://news.bbc.co.uk/1/hi/business/2844205.stm.
50. The past four world/US recessions have been preceded by the price of oil jumping to higher than $30 a barrel.
51. Piero Fornara, 'Il Ministro Saudita Ali al Naimi: "Riduciamo la produzione"', *Il Sole 24 Ore*, 24 April 2003.
52. International Energy Agency, *Oil Market Report*, 10 December 2003, p. 15, available at www.oilmarketreport.org.
53. IMF, *World Economic Outlook: Growth and Institutions*, April 2003, p. 50.
54. Daniel Hanna, 'High oil prices set to continue well into 2004', *SCB Economic Update*, 10 November 2003, available at www.amefino.com/news/Detailed/31018.html.
55. IMF, *The Impact of Higher Oil Prices on the Global Economy*, Washington DC, 8 December 2000, pp. 10–15.
56. Ibid.
57. Hanna, 'High oil prices set to continue well into 2004'.
58. International Energy Agency, *Oil Market Report*, 10 December 2003, p. 16, available at www.oilmarketreport.org.
59. Carola Hoyos, 'Oil groups snub US on Iraq deals', *Financial Times*, 24 July 2003.
60. Nicola Pedde, 'The making of a New World Energy Order', *International Spectator*, April 2002, p. 27.
61. Carola Hoyos and Kevin Morrison, 'Iraq returns to the international Oil Market', *Financial Times*, 5 June 2003.
62. Global Investment House, McKinsey, cited by BBC News, 'Oil slides on Saddam's sons' death', 23 July 2003.
63. Panos Cavoulacos, Vice-President of Booz Allen Hamilton, interviewed by *Le Figaro*, 'Les Etats-Unis ne prendront pas le risque d'ecarter la concurrence', 4 June 2003.

64. William D. Nordhaus, 'The Economic Consequences of a War in Iraq', in Carl Kaysen, Steven E. Miller, Martin B. Malin, William D. Nordhaus and John D. Steinbrunner, eds, *War with Iraq: Costs Consequences and Alternatives*, American Academy of Arts and Sciences, Committee on International Security, Cambridge, MA, 2002, p. 76.

15
Unfinished Business

John C. Garnett

Given the capability of Coalition forces, the outcome of the Second Gulf War was inevitable, despite fears that the Republican Guard, particularly its elite units surrounding Baghdad, would put up fierce resistance. In the event, resistance was minimal and the whole campaign was over inside seven weeks. But even though the war was quickly won, the 'peace' has proved more difficult to achieve, and those who risk commenting on it find themselves in the unenviable position of a theatre critic trying to review a play without knowing how it ends.

Winning the peace has turned out to be not only much more problematic, but also far more costly in terms of Coalition lives than the war itself. A year after President Bush declared the war to be over, meaningful peace and stability in Iraq has still not been restored, and the evidence suggests that it is not likely to be restored in the foreseeable future. Indeed, there is plenty of evidence that the level of violence is escalating and that Coalition forces are incapable of containing it. From the outset Coalition forces have never been able to provide the kind of security environment which is a prerequisite for economic recovery and political stability. Iraq has been plagued on a daily basis by car bombs, suicide bombers, assassinations, kidnappings, looting incidents and infrastructure damage. As the months rolled by, the level of lawlessness encouraged key foreign workers to leave the country and from time to time virtually halted the rebuilding mission. Arguably, the only growth industry in Iraq has been the security business – providing protection for essential facilities and for foreign contractors. Safeguarding the lives of up to 20,000 civilian contractors is now a big and lucrative business. The crude idea that, once war was over, democratic government could be swiftly implemented, the economy revived and order restored, enabling the Coalition forces to withdraw, leaving behind a stable and democratic country which would provide an example for the whole of the Middle East, has proved to be unfounded.

Nevertheless, despite the gloomy headlines of the western press, some progress has been made. A 24-member interim Iraqi Governing Council was quickly created, with the hope that this might form the nucleus of a new government. And it has enjoyed some success, particularly in the area of devising an interim constitution. Work on the reconstruction of Iraq's infrastructure and oil industry has progressed, albeit not as quickly as many had hoped. Iraq is now producing 2.4 million barrels of oil per day, an equivalent rate to that which prevailed before the war began. Electricity generation is also back to pre-war levels. Irrigation systems are being repaired, water purification and sewage treatment plants restored, transport developed, and the banking system has been overhauled. In November 2003 the United States government earmarked $13 billion for infrastructure improvement, and though it is taking some time, the benefits of this expenditure are defusing some of the anti-coalition feeling among the Iraqi people. Significant progress has been made in restoring a semblance of normality to the lives of many ordinary Iraqis. In a poll conducted by the BBC in Iraq during March 2004, more than 50 per cent of those questioned thought that conditions were better than those which prevailed before the war and were optimistic about the future. Even so, Iraq is still unstable, and continuing violence overshadows economic recovery.

So what has gone wrong? Basically, many of the assumptions which underpinned the policy of intervention have proved to be mistaken. First, the idea that Saddam's government was *universally* unpopular has been shown to be false. It is true that basic freedoms were curtailed in a tightly controlled police state. It is true that enemies of the regime were ruthlessly rooted out, tortured and killed in their thousands. It is also true that the economy was severely damaged by international sanctions and neglect. Nevertheless, for many Iraqis who were not 'political' it was still possible to lead a more or less normal, though impoverished, life, and Saddam was astute enough to allow a significant number of citizens to acquire a stake in the continuation of his regime. What has emerged since the end of the war is the fact that Saddam's ruthless autocracy was much less centralised than western observers believed. Saddam delegated power at local levels to different elites – tribal and religious leaders and businessmen – whose loyalty was guaranteed by a mixture of bribery and fear. These groups cannot be compared to the warlords who filled the power vacuum in Afghanistan when the Taliban were defeated, but when the Coalition dismantled the Ba'athist apparatus of power – including the armed forces – on which government and order depended, it was inevitable that these groups, including Ba'athist loyalists, would emerge as competing sources of authority able to disrupt the process of transition to democratic government.

Saddam's supporters and the quarrelling religious and political factions in post-war Iraq have proved to be more numerous and more disruptive than the Coalition believed possible. At first, the Americans found it convenient to explain armed resistance to the Coalition occupation in terms of a hard core of Saddam loyalists trying to turn the clock back. But it was clear even before his capture that Saddam could not possibly have controlled the numerous groups of insurgents who were attacking Coalition forces on a daily basis. Those who were involved in armed resistance were not just disaffected Ba'athists, and their main aim was not to restore the Ba'athist regime but to get the Americans out as quickly as possible. The scale of the attacks on Coalition forces suggests that the downfall of the previous regime was by no mean *universally* welcomed, despite its overall unpopularity. Donald Rumsfeld's contention that the Coalition forces faced only 'a limited number of adversaries' always had a hollow ring to it.

In retrospect, and, of course, with the benefit of hindsight, it is easy to be critical, we can now see that serious mistakes have been made. The failure to control widespread looting in the early weeks of Coalition occupation encouraged habits of lawlessness which have never entirely disappeared. And the disbanding of the Iraqi army and police – which were the only forces capable of maintaining a semblance of order – was a serious error. It created a power vacuum which has been filled by fundamentalist warlords and criminal groups.

It has also become clear that from the beginning the Americans seriously underestimated the security problem and the implications of a total collapse of authority in Iraq. They never considered the security problem seriously, and they were never willing to provide the massive resources needed to deal with this problem. Even as sovereignty is handed over to the new government, adequate security forces and arrangements are not in place.

The escalating security problem has demonstrated another weakness in American strategy, namely the failure of American soldiers to operate with any degree of subtlety or sensitivity in the post-conflict but highly dangerous conditions of civil strife which prevail in Iraq. However good their war-fighting qualities, peacekeeping and peacemaking are not their forte, and their heavy handed approach has almost certainly exacerbated the tense relationship between the civilian population and the Coalition authorities. The British, no doubt benefiting from their colonial history and their experience in Northern Ireland and the Balkans, have shown themselves to be much better at the 'hearts and minds' strategy needed in dealing with fractured societies.

Why did we get it so wrong? Perhaps one of the reasons is that Coalition intelligence before the war relied far too heavily on disaffected refugees who had a vested interest in seeing the regime toppled, and who insisted that Coalition troops would be welcomed with open arms. The authentic voice of the street Arab in Baghdad was never properly ascertained. Heavy reliance on westernised Iraqis who had been out of Iraq for years and who had an axe to grind anyway may have fuelled unreasonable optimism in both London and Washington.

A second mistake made by the American and British governments was to seriously underestimate the strength of Iraqi nationalism. Saddam may have been a tyrant but he was an *Iraqi* tyrant. To be sure, the Americans and the British were seen by most Iraqis as liberators freeing their country from a despot, but they were also seen as occupying forces which had invaded their territory, bombed their buildings and killed many innocent people. This ambivalence towards the Coalition forces has existed from the beginning of the war. It has been fuelled by speculation that the Americans are really only interested in Iraqi oil and the removal of the threat to them posed by the weapons of mass destruction which they believed Saddam possessed.

And anti-American sentiments have been exacerbated by the heavy handed ineptness of US forces on the ground and the devastating media coverage of the human rights abuse which took place in the Abu Ghraib prison. No one seriously argues that the inhumane and brutal treatment meted out to prisoners under interrogation can be compared to the institutional and systematic torture which was a matter of routine under Saddam's regime, but the impact of those grotesque photographic images which flashed around the world in May 2004 cannot be overestimated. After all, the invasion of Iraq was supposed to stop this kind of behaviour. Small wonder that Iraqi and world opinion was enraged. And the longer the Coalition forces remain, the more uneasy the Iraqis are likely to become about the reasons for their presence. Outside Iraq hardly anyone believes that the United States or Britain is bent on old-fashioned imperialism. Neither wishes to create a physical empire, but an empire of influence is less far-fetched, and, anyway, what matters is not Coalition intentions but Iraqi perceptions.

The Bush Administration responded to the pressure it was under by dramatically shortening their original timetable for an orderly handover of power to a democratically elected Iraqi government. In November 2003 the Americans announced their clear intention to withdraw substantial Coalition forces by the middle of 2004 and to introduce civilian rule at the same time. Over 100,000 US troops will remain in Iraq after that date, but since their presence will be at the invitation of the Iraqi government, the 'occupying power' accusation should lose its potency. The precise nature of the degree of control which the new government will exercise over the Coalition forces which remain in Iraq is not clear. The Americans (and the British) understandably reserve the right to manage their own forces, but if the stigma attached to 'forces of occupation' is to be dispelled, the government of Iraq must be seen to be in overall control. The Iraqi government's right of veto over Coalition activities has now been accepted, but not their right to order Coalition forces into action. Arguably, if the political/security situation deteriorates it is this positive power which is more important than the power to veto.

A third questionable assumption made by the Coalition countries before the war began was that the physical and political reconstruction of Iraq would be a relatively painless process compared with the military task of toppling Saddam's government. This assumption led the Coalition to put enormous effort into planning the war while giving less thought to planning the peace and reconstructing the Iraqi economy. Nevertheless, the problem was not ignored on either side of the Atlantic. In the US, an interagency planning group was created comprising representatives of the National Security Council, the Office of Management and Budget, the Department of Defense and the US Agency for International Development. A Disaster Assistance Response Team was created, and humanitarian material including food was stockpiled in the region. As early as February 2003, President Bush explained that 3 million emergency rations were being moved to the region.[1]

The provision of humanitarian relief for the immediate post-conflict environment was relatively successful, though conditions of chaos and lawlessness slowed down the provision of help in many areas. Longer-term reconstruction has been more difficult. The pre-war hope that the oil industry could be quickly put back on its feet and that the revenue which it generated could be used to finance a good deal of infrastructure reconstruction proved to be wildly overoptimistic. Neither the British nor the US government seem to have realised the scale of the problem facing them. War, sanctions and neglect had reduced the Iraqi economy to a shadow of its former strength. Putting it back on its feet will be a long and expensive process. Current estimates of the costs of continuing occupation and reconstruction vary, but a realistic figure for the American contribution during the calendar year 2003–4 is $97 billion. Admittedly that includes the cost of the war itself – say $15 billion – which it is reasonable to regard as a one-off cost which ought not to be included in future estimates. Assuming that up to 150,000 troops remain in Iraq for the foreseeable future, the operational costs for the military look like $45 billion per year, and, of course, on top of that should be added the costs for reconstruction, at present estimated at $18 billion. These are not insignificant sums to be spending on a country which to date has not shown much gratitude to its liberators. It remains to be seen how much longer the United States will be willing to shoulder this burden, and it is not altogether surprising that it is anxious to unload some of it on to NATO allies who, equally unsurprisingly, are reluctant to pick it up.

If the physical problems of rebuilding the Iraqi economy are huge, the political task of turning it into a democracy is at least as daunting. Again, the Coalition may have underestimated the difficulties which lay ahead of them. Modern Iraq has no tradition of democracy and none of the values which underpin it and are a precondition for its success. Iraq is an artificial creation of British colonialism. When the British drew the map of Iraq they threw hostile tribes into a state which had no meaning for those who lived within its borders. Iraq was an impoverished country, seriously divided on ethnic, tribal and religious lines. Its population had no strong sense of national identity or national loyalty, and throughout its history it has been troubled by internal quarrels between constituent communities whose relations with each other are characterised by fear and suspicion.

Arguably, Saddam's policy of 'divide and rule' actually exacerbated the ethnic, tribal and religious tensions which divided the Iraqi people. Memories of recent intercommunal violence and the fault lines which continue to exist between the Kurdish, Sunni and Shia communities suggest that Iraq is no more cohesive today than it was when it became independent in 1932. In short, Iraq is a fractured society and does not offer promising ground for the seeds of democracy to germinate and take root. It is almost certainly a mistake to believe that imposing a democratic constitution – however carefully thought out – will somehow solve the problem. Without an underpinning foundation of shared values, any constitutional superstructure is likely to be a fragile edifice. One of the worries about the current accelerated exit policy of the Coalition is that as a result of political pressure, both from within Iraq and from the international community, it may be forcing the pace of democratic change before the underlying building blocks are in place.

From the outset of the military campaign against Iraq, the Coalition made it clear that once Saddam was deposed their intention was to hand over the reins of power to a democratic government as soon as one was elected. Unfortunately, one of the consequences of prolonged oppression by the Ba'athist regime was that within the body politic no potential opposition party existed which could assume power and lead Iraq towards democracy. When a significant opposition exists it can usually be supported and assisted by outside forces and it has a kind of legitimacy at least in the sense of being home-grown. Success rates in building stable democratic regimes where there is a popular in-country opposition party waiting in the wings are much higher than in those countries where a surrogate regime hand-picked by the occupying power is given the responsibility of government. Case studies of Vietnam, Haiti, Cambodia and others make the point that countries ruled by surrogate US-appointed governments rarely make the transition to democracy and, after ten years, are almost invariably autocratic. In Iraq the Coalition were forced to create an Interim Governing Council which contained no charismatic figure capable of driving the democratic process forward and which had no real credibility with the Iraqi people who have become increasingly disillusioned with their liberators.[2]

The original exit timetable contained no precise date for US withdrawal, but it had a certain logic. An Interim Governing Council would be appointed; it would devise a new constitution; there would be a census and a constitutional convention, and, finally, elections would be held after which government and sovereignty would be handed to the Iraqi people. Coalition security forces would, however, remain until it was deemed safe for them to depart. Unfortunately, this fairly leisurely timetable left the Coalition looking like a semi-permanent army of occupation with all the opprobrium that that generated, and it also meant that during the interim period before the election took place, the police and security forces, whose high profile role was crucially important in getting to grips with the post-war conditions of chaos, were not anchored in a democratic framework and therefore lacked the legitimacy for effective action. It is interesting to note how the rhetoric surrounding the handover of sovereignty and the withdrawal of Coalition forces has changed since the war ended. There had always been a plan for 'eventual withdrawal' and that is still the clear intention of both the US and British governments; but in the immediate aftermath of the military campaign the intention was to remain in Iraq 'for as long as it takes', and the feeling was that Coalition forces would probably be required for many months, perhaps even years. A year later there is evidence that both the Americans and the British want out as quickly as possible. Overall, the Iraqi experience has not been a pleasant one for either President Bush or Prime Minister Blair, and both would like to draw a line under the experience. The handover of sovereignty, which was once regarded as the beginning of a process, is now being seen as the end of a process and an excuse for pulling out. Whether the security situation in Iraq justifies any optimism about an accelerated pace of withdrawal is very debatable, and in these circumstances a premature withdrawal of forces could plunge Iraq into chaos.

Clearly, a good case can be made for shortening the period of transition to democracy, but an accelerated exit timetable has clear dangers, particularly if it is seen as a 'cop-out' by an American president worried about the next election, growing public unease about escalating costs, continuing attacks on American personnel and no end in sight. It would also be disastrous if, as a result of undue haste, the permanent constitutional arrangements for the government are flawed. In March 2004, after much wrangling and disagreement and a good deal of American pressure, Iraq's Governing Council finally agreed the terms of a temporary constitution which would guide the country's government after sovereignty was handed over to it on 30 June. The Interim Constitution enshrines the principles of a democratic, federal and pluralistic system of government. It allows the Kurds much of the self-government they have enjoyed since 1991; it gives women up to 20 per cent of the seats in the transitional parliament; it insists on an independent judiciary; it makes Islam the official religion and 'a main source' but not '*the* main source' of legislation; it contains a Bill of Rights to ensure personal, political and religious freedom.

For the optimists the Interim Constitution augurs well for the future of Iraq because they believe it sets the parameters within which the Permanent Constitution will be conceived. But the Interim Constitution is a fragile edifice, a compromise which satisfies none of the parties to it. For example, feminists groups in Iraq demanded 40 per cent women members in a future parliament, not the 20 per cent they were given. Radical Islamic groups wanted a fully

Islamic state under Sharia law, not a state where Islam is only *one* source of legislation. The Kurds wanted to extend their area of control (particularly in Kirkuk) and are not content with simply retaining the independence they currently enjoy.

Arguably, the Governing Council went along with the Interim Constitution not out of genuine enthusiasm but for two less respectable reasons. First, because it was seen as the only way of getting sovereignty transferred to an Iraqi government, and second, because it did not preclude significant amendments being implemented when the real struggle for power takes place in 2005 when the Permanent Constitution is negotiated. This second reason is a serious cause of concern – that once the Americans are out, the cracks which the Interim Constitution papered over will reappear and deepen as the various factions struggle to mould Iraq in their own images. If this happens – and given the tensions in Iraqi society it is quite likely to happen – the optimism generated by the Interim Constitution will be seen as a false dawn, a facade of unity unable to survive the internecine warfare which simmers away in the body politic of Iraq.

Instead of propping up autocratic regimes, President Bush has now firmly committed the US to the spread of democracy which he believes is a prerequisite for American security in the long run.[3] In a recent speech to the National Endowment for Democracy he made his position clear: 'We believe that liberty is the design of nature; we believe that liberty is the direction of history.'[4] Unfortunately, within the region this 'forward strategy of freedom' may be interpreted by some as yet another example of the cultural imperialism which causes so much anti-American feeling around the world. Though it may be driven by idealism (as well as self-interest), the tendency to universalise American values, to engage in what Hans Morgenthau used to call 'nationalistic universalism', raises hackles wherever it is encountered and has always suggested overconfidence in the superiority of American ways of thinking.[5]

Equally serious, there remains the fundamental question of whether democracy is compatible with Islam. Apart from the fact that Islam, like most religious doctrines, can be interpreted in very different ways, there is nothing unambiguously anti-democratic about it, apart, perhaps, from the fact that fundamentalist interpretations encourage an authoritarian, deferential mind-set which sits uneasily with democratic values like pluralism and tolerance. But President Bush has no doubts on this issue: 'It should be clear to all that Islam – the faith of one fifth of humanity – is consistent with democratic rule.'[6] Let us hope he is right. The trouble with President Bush and Prime Minister Blair is that they are both 'conviction' politicians. In some situations a strong belief in the rightness of their cause is an asset which makes for decisiveness and clarity on the part of policy makers. But in dealing with complex problems, a degree of 'dithering' may be excusable; a sign of wisdom, not weakness. Many of us feel more comfortable with politicians who, if not wracked with self-doubt, are at least troubled by the possibility that they might be wrong. Neither Bush nor Blair fall into that category and, as a consequence, for many people their foreign policy style is a source of considerable unease.

In the West no one has seriously challenged the view that Iraq must be turned into a democracy, but it is worth considering how prominently this objective has featured in the Coalition's list of reasons for going to war. In the months preceding the invasion all sorts of reasons for regime change were advanced; amongst them the supposed possession by Iraq of weapons of mass destruction, the tyrannical nature of Saddam's government, the failure of Iraq to comply with UN resolutions, the need to deal with a 'rogue state', and so on. The relative weight given to these various justifications for military action has varied over time. Before the war began, Saddam's failure to comply with UN resolutions and his supposed possession of WMD were emphasised; since the invasion and the failure to find any WMD, the emphasis has shifted towards the argument that regime change was necessary because Saddam was a tyrant.

Much of this political rhetoric has a hollow ring to it. After all, lots of states have weapons of mass destruction and we are not contemplating invading them. Even more states are ruled by tyrants and we do not seek to usurp them. Numerous states, including Israel, are in breach of UN resolutions, and we tolerate them. And, arguably, there are more than a handful of 'rogue states' against which no action is contemplated. So we need to be clear that the real reason for invading Iraq was that it was seen as being hostile to the United States and a threat to its security. In other words, whatever the rhetoric, the main point of the war was to replace an unfriendly regime with a friendly one, not to replace a despotism with a democracy. Whether the new government of Iraq was democratic or not was always less important than whether it was well disposed towards the United States. Of course, there are many who argued that the best way of making sure that it would be friendly was to make sure that is was democratic.

It has become conventional wisdom in academic circles that democratic states do not fight each other and that the spread of democracy worldwide would eliminate the phenomenon of war.[7] Though there is some empirical evidence to support this proposition, it is difficult to identify a persuasive reason why democratic states should *not* fight each other. After all, despite being democratic they may still have clashing vital interests worth fighting over. It is probably fair to say that in this important academic debate the evidence is inconclusive and the jury is still out. The point that needs to be made in the context of post-war Iraq and the Middle East in general is that it may be naive of the West to believe that the spread of democracy will automatically promote friendlier relations.

Indeed, there are some grounds for thinking that the reverse may be the case. In Saudi Arabia, for example, it is the *autocratic* government which is friendly and well disposed towards western interests, and the population which would be empowered by a democratic constitution which is hostile. Now it may be argued that ordinary people throughout the Middle East are hostile precisely because the US has traditionally supported the authoritarian governments which oppress them, and that if it stopped doing this, anti-Americanism at the grassroots level would evaporate. Clearly, the validity of this argument depends on the proposition that the United States is loathed *solely* because it has supported autocratic regimes. In practice, of course, the US is hated for a plethora of other reasons as well – its support for Israel, its neglect of the Palestinians, its cultural imperialism, its heavy-handed muscular foreign policy in the region, and so on. These explanations for anti-Americanism would remain even if democracy caught on in the Middle East. If this analysis has some merit then it suggests that it may be perverse for western countries to try to remove despots who are friendly with democrats who are not. President Bush's vision of how democracy might unfold in the Middle East may produce quite unintended consequences. There is, for example, a real possibility that democratic elections could produce Islamist governments (as happened in Algeria in 1992) which are more, not less, hostile to the United States. And this is not an implausible scenario for Iraq.

However, until very recently, the democratic deficit in the Arab world as a whole did not figure at all prominently on the agenda of US policy makers who were more interested in supporting regimes which were friendly to the West and would keep the oil flowing than in worrying about their political complexion. It is true that in the 1990s the United States did fund modest democracy assistance programmes in a number of Middle Eastern countries, but the point of this policy was not to bring about genuine democratic change but to prolong the life of autocratic regimes by defusing opposition to them. It was 9/11 which forced a rethink, as many Americans concluded that one of the most important underlying causes of terrorism and anti-American feeling in the Arab world was US support for non-democratic regimes. The most recent manifestation of this change of heart is President Bush's 'road map' for the Middle East.

This is an ambitious vision of how the United States can use its power to promote democracy, peace and freedom across the region, but, given the political realities of the Middle East, turning the vision into reality is fraught with difficulty. Indeed, it is difficult to quarrel with Philip Gordon's sober judgement 'that much of the Bush vision ... is problematic and ... will take generations to realise'. As he says, 'While it is fine for the United States to talk about democracy and freedom in the Arab World Bush is unlikely to achieve it during his presidency or even in his lifetime.'[8]

Imposing democracy on states is not an impossible task, but it is not an easy one. When autocratic regimes crumble, two of the most likely outcomes are chaos – as happened in Yugoslavia when President Tito died, and the rise of equally repressive regimes, which is what has happened on a number of occasions in Haiti. When outside powers intervene to topple regimes they dislike, they have an obligation to see that neither of the above outcomes occur. Unfortunately, this task involves the expenditure of enormous amounts of money and effort over many years. In the case of Germany and Japan after the Second World War, both were forthcoming and a successful transition to democracy was achieved. Since then the appetite for expensive reconstruction has diminished – particularly in the United States where there is growing unease about a long-term presence in countries like Iraq and Afghanistan.

Iraq is not a 'basket-case' and the prospects for democracy are certainly better than those prevailing in that other Muslim country liberated by US intervention and where 'warlordism' and insecurity continue to exist almost two years after the defeat of the Taliban. Iraq has fertile land, an industrial infrastructure, an educated workforce, a bureaucracy, a capitalist ethos, a middle class and, most important, the second-largest reserves of oil in the world. Although it has been damaged by war and neglect, its potential for recovery is unquestioned if sufficient outside resources are pumped into its economy. Whether it can be turned into a democracy which bears comparison with anything that exists in Europe or America is more problematic.

There are particular difficulties in creating democracies in states which are ethnically, culturally, tribally and religiously divided. Where these conditions prevail, 'one man, one vote' can easily result in tyranny of the majority. For that reason alone it is important to devise a constitution for Iraq which balances conflicting interests in such a way that neither the Kurds, the Sunnis nor the Shias are able to exploit each other. The Shia community, comprising about 60 per cent of the population, might be expected to favour majority voting, but the Kurds and Sunnis are certain to be much less enthusiastic about any system which condemns them to permanent vulnerability.

A unitary, democratic, secular and stable Iraq in which internecine and anti-government violence has been marginalised is the best that can be hoped for. No one expects progress towards this goal to be smooth or untroubled, and the period between the end of June 2004 and the elections which are planned for 2005 may be particularly difficult. But there is more cohesion in Iraq than the lurid headlines suggest, and if a strong central government can control the security situation and win the confidence of the Iraqi people by pursuing consensus politics calculated to unify rather than divide the country, then Iraq can look forward to a bright future.

At the moment there is general agreement that Iraq should remain a unitary state with a federal, decentralised structure, and that the 'Balkanisation' of the country would be a disaster. The trouble with federal, decentralised structures in which significant powers are vested in local communities is that they sometimes exacerbate differences rather than soften them. To the extent that Kurds, Sunnis and Shia are encouraged to pursue their own religious beliefs, organise their own educational systems and promote their distinctive cultures, the differences between them and the tensions which divide them are likely to be heightened. Since Iraq is already a seriously divided society where there is a good deal of intercommunal suspicion, violence and revenge killings, there is a sense in which it needs *more*, not less, centralisation if it is to remain a viable unitary state.[9]

For those interested in creating a federal, democratic Iraq where the principle of 'subsidiarity' delegates power, wherever possible, to the lowest local level, it is almost a contradiction in terms to hope for the emergence of a strong leader capable of uniting the country and holding it together. Strong leaders have a nasty habit of forgetting their democratic origins and responsibilities, and if that should happen in Iraq once the restraining hand of the Coalition is removed, we might end up with a new despot, perhaps a Tito-like figure, more benevolent than his predecessor but a despot nevertheless. There is not much to be said for this scenario, but if the alternative is continuing intercommunal violence and weak government, it may have something to recommend it. If the new government shows signs of weakness it may not be able to control the irreconcilable ethnic forces that simmer away just below the surface of the Iraqi politics. It is easy to envisage serious friction between Kurds, Sunni Arabs, Shia Arabs, Sunni Turkmen and Shia Turkmen over the oil riches of Kirkuk. And one can plausibly imagine a situation in which there is a clash between an elected Shia-dominated government trying to improve its will across the entire country, and the Kurdish 'government' determined to hang on to the *de facto* independent status it currently enjoys. To further complicate the picture, a surge of religious fundamentalism may yet destroy any chance of a unitary secular state.

The possibility that a weak Coalition government may be unable to control divisions which are tearing the country apart has raised the spectre of the fragmentation or partition of Iraq into mini states built around the three major groupings, Kurds, Sunnis and Shia. This is a last-resort solution built on the proposition that those who cannot be persuaded to live together should be permitted to live apart. A divided Iraq would be a *weak* Iraq, a power vacuum, vulnerable to outside pressure if not intervention from Iran and Turkey and permanently troubled by internal border disputes between the various ethnic groupings. Again, this is a solution with little to recommend it, but it cannot be ruled out and it is better than the 'ethnic cleansing' solution which has prevailed in some other parts of the world where communities have found it impossible to coexist.

From the perspective of the Coalition and the international community as a whole, the stakes in Iraq are now very high. The United States and Britain have both gambled heavily on success and the credibility of their pre-emptive interventionist foreign policy hangs in the balance. Failure of such a high-profile policy would seriously damage the reputations of both President Bush and Prime Minister Blair, both of whom are close enough to elections for their respective publics not to have forgotten any spectacular failure of foreign policy.

More seriously, American policy in the Middle East – particularly President Bush's vision of spreading democracy throughout a region in which it is in very short supply – would be in shreds. Indeed, the whole idea of taking military action against 'rogue states' or 'states of concern' as they are now called, would be discredited, and with it a major plank in the war against terrorism would collapse. If it does not work in Iraq, what chance does it have elsewhere? Worst of all, anti-western feeling throughout the Islamic world is likely to be inflamed by the spectacle of an Iraq devastated by war, and now either reduced to chaos by internecine strife or ruled by a dictator no better than Saddam.

The future of Iraq is in the balance. Arguably, neither the optimistic vision of a stable democratic state nor the gloomy predictions of civil war, theocracy, dictatorship and fragmentation will come about. Instead, we may be confronted with a messy Afghanistan-type scenario where a weak central government survives but is unable to control the country or to provide the stability necessary to encourage investment and facilitate long-term prosperity. It will not be a disaster – though it will have the potential to turn into one – but no one will be able to regard it as a success. Those who opposed the war from the beginning may glean some comfort from this mixed outcome, but apart from the hollow satisfaction of being able to say 'we told you so', the critics would have little to celebrate. Of course, those who lined up against the war will almost certainly be equally disturbed if Iraq turns out to be a runaway success. An unambiguous success story might encourage a triumphant President Bush to turn his attention to Iran and other states of concern, with all the imponderables and dangerous consequences that a more ambitious interventionist policy might engender.

Notes

1. The USA began detailed post-war reconstruction planning as early as September 2002, seven months before hostilities began. A comprehensive account of the measures taken can be found in Roger Macginty, 'The Pre-war Reconstruction of Post-war Iraq', *Third World Quarterly*, Vol. 24, No. 4, 2003, pp. 601–17. At the end of his article Macginty speculates about whether planning was 'merely a moral balm for a pre-emptive war with a questionable status under international law' (p. 615).

2. Not everyone is pessimistic about the future prospects of democracy in Iraq. Rosemary Hollis had made the point that a number of commentators regard Iraq as a promising starting point for democratisation 'because it has or had had a secularist tradition, a well-educated professional class and a reputation for industriousness'. See R. Hollis, 'Getting Out of the Iraq Trap', *International Affairs*, Vol. 79, No. 1, 2003, p. 31.

3. An interesting analysis of President Bush's Middle East Vision is to be found in Philip H. Gordon, 'Bush's Middle East Vision', *Survival*, Vol. 45, No. 1, Spring 2003, pp. 155–65. See also Amy Hawthorne, 'Can the United States Promote Democracy in the Middle East?', *Current History*, January 2003, pp. 21–6.

4. See his speech at the 20th Anniversary of the National Endowment for Democracy, 'Freedom in Iraq and Middle East', United States Chamber of Commerce, Washington DC, 6 November 2003.
5. H. Morgenthau, *Politics Among Nations: The Struggle for Power and Peace*, 4th edn, New York, Alfred Knopf, 1966, pp. 321–31.
6. Speech at the 20th Anniversary of the National Endowment for Democracy.
7. See M.W. Doyle, 'Kant Liberal Legacies and Foreign Affairs', *Philosophy and Public Affairs*, Vol. 12, 1983. Also 'Liberalism and World Politics', *American Political Science Review*, Vol. 80, 1986.
8. Gordon, 'Bush's Middle East Vision', p. 163.
9. The point is well-made by Daniel Byman in 'Constructing a Democratic Iraq', *International Security*, Vol. 28, No. 1, Summer 2003, pp. 57–8. This article provides an excellent overview of the problems confronting post-war Iraq.

16
Conclusion: Iraq 2003 – Parallel Warfare and Parallel Politics

Paul Cornish

The uses and abuses of instant history

If war is an activity shaped, defined and evaluated in terms of causes, conduct and consequences, then the war fought against the regime of Saddam Hussein by the United States and its allies between March and May 2003 could scarcely be said to have been concluded one year later, as the chapters in this volume were being compiled. Until the consequences of the campaign can be known with some more confidence, it would be premature to attempt a synoptic assessment of the war. In that vein, some protagonists such as the UK's Prime Minister Tony Blair have argued for a general suspension of judgement until the outcomes of the war can be more clearly discerned. Yet while there is much to be said for allowing history to take its course – what took place in Iraq in 2003 and 2004 could well have political potency for several generations to come – this is a difficult argument to accept in principle. Should judgement be suspended indefinitely until the 'correct' consequences have emerged, whatever they might be, and should all contrary evidence be ignored in the meantime? And will a complete assessment of the war ever be possible? After all, there is not much in human history about which perfect knowledge is claimed and under which a line can be drawn for once and for all.

Whatever its flaws, 'instant history' is appropriate here simply because the war is too important, politically and morally, to be left to historians. For some, the very inconclusiveness of the war merely sharpens focus on its more tangible aspects – its causes and its conduct. We might not yet know very much about the consequences of the war, but we do know that war*fare* took place in Iraq, and we do therefore have a sufficient and necessary case for asking questions about why and how it began, and what took place.

Various contending explanations have been offered for the resort to armed force against Iraq. For some, this was a war of ideas: the West versus the rest; unilateralism versus multilateralism; Christianity versus Islam; the European Enlightenment versus medievalism; democracy versus despotism; humanitarianism versus repression and mass murder; a just war in the western tradition. For others this was a war to reclaim the honour of the Bush family in their historic struggle against Saddam Hussein, a war of revenge for 9/11, or a war of self-defence against further terrorism and the threat of weapons of mass destruction. Then there are those who describe the war in straightforwardly Machiavellian terms; a war for oil, territory and military bases, and for the aggrandisement of the American imperium. The diplomatic and politico-military background to the conflict – *how* the conflict began – raises another set of questions. Was this a war of last resort, with all other legal and diplomatic approaches having been exhausted? Was this a war in direct breach of the UN Charter and international law? Or was it a war of necessity that, incidentally, demonstrated the inadequacy of international law and the urgent need for more robust legal thinking and diplomatic practice? What forces were at play within the Bush Administration, and to what extent can the war in Iraq be explained in terms of rivalry between the US State Department and the US Department of Defense? And finally, the way in which the campaign was fought fuels discussion about, *inter alia*, the speed and efficiency of the recently 'transformed' US military forces, about the apparent reluctance of US troops to engage in post-conflict stabilisation and peace-building, and about the differences in capability and operational style between US armed forces and those of their close allies.

Other commentators argue that history has already moved on sufficiently for a more rounded debate to take place; even though the complete picture is not yet clear, and may not be for decades, there are more than enough interim consequences to be going on with. Some such outcomes were apparently unforeseen (for example, the resilience of the Ba'athist opposition), begging questions about the quality of analysis and policy making in the approach to the war. Other consequences were foreseen (for example, the aggregation of anti-western terrorist groups in Iraq), but it seems not by the governments of the United States and its allies, or at least not to the extent of influencing policy. Some outcomes, such as Libya's public abandonment of weapons of mass destruction, were predicted in such general terms by the Bush Administration that to claim them as a favourable consequence of the campaign against Iraq would be to stretch cause and effect to breaking point. Searching questions can, therefore, already be asked about the decision making processes, about the declared motives for going to war, and about the means employed. More usefully, it is becoming possible to set the claimed rationales and benefits of going to war against known costs. In other words, even at this early stage a balanced discussion of the Iraq war can be had, one in which motives, means and consequences are subject to a net assessment.

For example, whatever the alleged shortcomings of international law and the UN system, have these central features of international politics been damaged, and if so to what (and whose) purpose, and at what cost? If there is a case to be made for pre-emptive (and perhaps even preventive) military action against terrorism- and proliferation-inclined organisations and governments, how much collateral damage could be (or has been) caused to an international system which, for the past 60 years or so, has sought to minimise the use of armed force and armed intervention? Is that damage acceptable in the face of terrorism and proliferation? Similarly, have the cohesion of the US-European relationship, manifested most obviously in NATO, and of the European Union been undermined irreparably, and if so does that matter? And finally, has the war in Iraq (like the so-called war against terrorism), been described and rationalised in such terms as to fulfil Huntington's prophecy of a 'clash of civilisations' between the Judaeo-Christian, democratic-capitalist West and the Arab-Islamic world?

Rather than await the verdict of history, *Conflict in Iraq* has sought to provide a balanced assessment of the war; its diplomatic and military context, its conduct and its consequences up to one year after George Bush's declaration of the end of military action on 1 May 2003. The aim of this concluding chapter is not to summarise or synthesise arguments presented elsewhere in the book, but to offer an analysis of the significance and implications of the conflict for strategic thinking and practice in the early twenty-first century.

A revolution in warfare?

For many observers, the war in Iraq in 2003 saw the manifestation and, indeed, validation of a decades-long transformation of US and other western armed forces. History has played its part in the impulse to improve armed forces: the US experience in Vietnam and, much later, Somalia; the end of the Cold War; peace support operations in former Yugoslavia; the start of the so-called war on terror after 9/11. But the transformation from vast, armour-heavy, largely static Cold War-style armed forces to the lighter and more responsive forces deployed to Afghanistan and Iraq has also been prompted by the availability of new technology in communications, intelligence gathering and target acquisition, and in the capabilities of weapons. In the 1990s, this 'Revolution in Military Affairs' (RMA) as it became widely known, spawned a sub-genre of strategic analysis.[1] What were the historical standards against which developments in military capability and practice could be judged 'revolutionary'? Was the RMA of the 1990s a real revolution, or merely an evolution (albeit rather dramatic) in western military capability? What was the balance in the supposed RMA between technological and conceptual development; did doctrine drive technology, or had the relationship finally been reversed? Had the principles of western warfare been overturned and replaced? Had the information age given rise to a whole new theory of war?

Latterly, the terms of debate have tended to shift away from RMA, perhaps in order to stifle the by now rather inconclusive 'revolution *versus* evolution' discussion. The preferred term in both the United States and the United Kingdom became 'defence transformation'; a term so bland that it was soon supplemented by far more arcane and therefore impressive expressions such as 'network centric warfare' (NCW) in the United States and, rather easier on the ear, 'network enabled capability' (NEC) in the United Kingdom. At its simplest, new technology is seen to offer military advantage in three areas: communications and computing; target sensing and identification; and target acquisition and attack. Thus, military command and control and intelligence gathering have become faster and more responsive, as well as better informed through real-time networking. Modern weapon platforms not only provide greater mobility and stealth, longer range, improved accuracy and ever more destructive impact on the target, they are also closely connected to the improved command and control system and to the network of sensors, thus ensuring decisive effect. Acknowledging these developments and possibilities, American, British and other armed forces have become preoccupied with a new set of military terms; 'tempo', 'agility', 'knowledge superiority', 'synchronicity', 'connectivity', 'operations in depth' and 'lethality'. And the key components in a military operation, ranging from the command and control organisation through to the intelligence gatherers, the logistics providers and the combat elements, have all become integrated in a very close, so-called 'sensor-shooter' link.

Of course, there have been many occasions in the history of warfare when technological developments or social changes have had a momentous effect on the conduct of war; the stirrup, the longbow, the mass-produced rifle, the *levée en masse*, the telegraph, the machine gun, universal emancipation, the tank, the atomic bomb, and so on. What is claimed to be distinctive about the military-technological developments of the late twentieth and early twenty-first centuries, however, is that they create the opportunity for armed force to have more effect, in more places, and more quickly than ever before. Two new jargon expressions – 'effects-based warfare' and 'parallel warfare' – describe the uses to which all this new technology is being put, and set out a number of intellectual and political challenges inherent in the new (revolutionary or evolutionary) style of warfare.

The term 'effects-based warfare' signifies a clean break from the 'threat based' strategic planning of the Cold War, where the focus of strategic planning was a prospective adversary's capabilities and intentions, and the aim of the strategist was to devise the best ways to anticipate or respond to that threat. Following the Cold War, when western governments became politically and financially uneasy about fixing defence planning around explicit threats, several western armed forces pursued 'capability based' planning, with force structures designed to produce a 'toolbox' of generic capabilities that would be available to government in defined circumstances (that is, peacekeeping and peace support operations, home defence, defence of overseas territories and allies, protection of supply routes, and so on), without having to be so confrontational as to name a specific enemy.

Effects-based warfare offers the triumph of quality over quantity. As in any military campaign, past or present, the first step is to identify the strategic goal; the purpose of military operations. The goal might, for example, be to remove an enemy government's ability to deploy and control its armed forces, and therefore remove the enemy's capacity to resist. In the past, that goal might typically have been pursued by concentrating ground forces against the enemy's army in order to destroy it, or by massing bomber forces against the enemy's capital in order to prevent decision making and communication. By exploiting modern communications, intelligence and weapon technologies, effects-based warfare means that armed forces can now be far more exact in their pursuit of the strategic goal, achieving that goal without the massive military outlay seen in the past. The desired strategic goal might be achieved by a series of limited and precise attacks against communications nodes, leaving both government and army intact but ineffective. The war can be won, in other words, without having to bring about the 'total destruction' of the enemy.[2] Sun Tzu, the ancient Chinese strategic thinker, would doubtless be impressed; 'For to win one hundred victories in one hundred battles is not the acme of skill. To subdue the enemy without fighting is the acme of skill.'[3]

By encouraging *economy* of effort – the most efficient use of military resources – effects-based warfare also offers *concurrency* of effort, or 'parallel war'. Rather than fight a sequential war – typically, with suppression of enemy air defence systems being the first requirement, enabling subsequent attacks against enemy air and ground forces – effects-based warfare makes it possible for all the different phases of a military campaign to be fought in great detail, at once. The enemy can thus be attacked as a whole system, across the spectrum, rather than as a series of distinct operations. Seen in this way, effects-based and parallel warfare could have profound implications for military practice and strategic thinking.

By one account, new technology makes it possible to exploit time – 'the temporal dimension' – more decisively on the battlefield than ever before.[4] The ability to observe, think, decide and act faster than an enemy has long been the goal of military commanders, and military innovations have often been assessed in terms of the contribution they can make to tightening the so-called 'OODA loop' ('Observation, Orientation, Decision, Action').[5] The argument of Dahl and others is that effects-based (offering economy of effort), and parallel warfare (offering concurrency of effort), combine to tighten the OODA loop so considerably that an enemy would immediately perceive himself to be overwhelmed, would capitulate at an early stage, or would even be deterred from fighting in the first place.[6] At the strategic level, these new technologies ought to make warfare not only more contained in terms of the damage and destruction caused (thereby making recovery and reconstruction easier), but also more containable politically. That is to say, rather than give weight to the old argument, still pursued by some, that politicians should leave warfare to the military,[7] effects-based and parallel warfare invite *closer* involvement and control by political leaders; although new in style, warfare is still explicitly purposive, rather than an end in itself, and the purpose of war is (or should be) political. Finally, just as new technology and thinking makes it possible for different battles and operations to be fought simultaneously, so it should be possible at the strategic level to pursue combat operations in parallel with other, non-combat activities such as immediate post-conflict reconstruction and humanitarian assistance.

If effects-based, parallel warfare offers new opportunities for the decisive use of armed force, it also presents important challenges for those concerned to ensure that warfare is both managed and moderated politically. Civilian control might in practice be difficult to maintain. As we have seen, a central feature of effects-based, parallel warfare is that the size and capability of armed forces is no longer the starting point in military analysis and planning; what matters is the precise, timely, appropriate and decisive achievement of effect, and the ability to exploit time in more complex, multifaceted and effective manner than the enemy. If the desired effect can be achieved with a small number of precision-guided munitions, or with just a handful of troops deployed and extracted with great rapidity, or by moving into one phase of war (to use the traditional paradigm) and then switching rapidly and unexpectedly to another, then so much the better. But if, as many commentators suggest, the implications of all this are that armed forces will adopt a flatter, less hierarchical structure, that the 'levels of war' (tactical, operational and strategic) will lose their distinctive characteristics and be folded into each other, and that war will no longer be a sequential activity, then the civilian management of military operations could actually become far more complex and perhaps less effective. In the traditional model, the application of armed force was understood and described organisationally in hierarchical terms. At the apex of the organisational hierarchy would be found grand strategy or political strategy, beneath it military strategy, then military operations, and finally, the basis of the entire effort, tactical and individual effort. In the traditional view, war was also considered in temporal terms to be a linear activity, in which time would serve the organisational hierarchy. Thus instructions and objectives would be passed from the top to the bottom of the hierarchy, with objectives at each level being allocated a certain amount of time. A tactical commander would use the time available to ensure that his objectives were met, enabling operational objectives to be achieved on time, and so on.

In effects-based and parallel warfare, however, it is assumed that tactical activity – one pilot with one bomb, and possibly even one soldier with one rifle – can have strategic effect without having to be orchestrated and multiplied through the various levels of war. Furthermore, this strategic effect might be achieved almost instantaneously or at least well within the news cycle. The desired effect could also, conceivably, be achieved even before its operational or strategic desirability has been realised, as a result of intelligent 'mission command' and opportunist use of armed force at the tactical level. This should sound alarms for western political leaders. Having traditionally assumed that the control of armed forces in war required a close relationship with only the highest levels of the military hierarchy, the new situation could be overwhelming and deeply confusing. Political leaders might be faced with two possible solutions. If strategy is to be the responsibility of small units and even individual soldiers, then the civilian leadership must either become massively involved in the minutiae of military activity (something which would not be welcome in military circles), or renounce altogether their claim to control armed forces and their application; a prospect which must surely be anathema for democratic societies.

In terms of planning, execution, force posture and equipment, US and allied operations in Iraq in 2003 were to be a demonstration of the scope of 'transformed' warfare. From the highest level, planning was nothing if not bold and assertive, with respect not only to the balance of forces and capabilities in Iraq, but also to the balance of influence and initiative in Washington. By one account, US Secretary of Defense Donald Rumsfeld made an early judgement which shaped the conduct both of US and allied military operations in Iraq, and the Bush Administration's domestic political operations in Washington. Rumsfeld's judgement was that in spite of numerical superiority in troops (about 400,000 against the Coalition's 300,000) and tanks, armoured fighting vehicles and artillery (about 8500 to the Coalition's 2200),[8] Iraq's armed forces were less well organised and militarily less capable than generally supposed. Rumsfeld's judgement was vindicated, goes the argument, by the conduct of the campaign, in which the organisation and capability of Iraqi troops – particularly the much-vaunted Republican Guard divisions – proved to be groundless.[9] But it was in the planning phase that Rumsfeld's assessment was most significant. Rumsfeld provided an alternative organising vision of the way operations in Iraq might be conducted, a vision of 'an unprecedented combination of speed, precision, surprise, and flexibility'.[10] Without that alternative, the prevailing view would have been that Rumsfeld's approach represented a 'reckless gamble' that would result in catastrophe and humiliation for the United States and its allies.[11] Some would argue, of course, that warnings of humiliation were indeed borne out, in the insurrection in various parts of Iraq in spring and summer 2004. Rumsfeld's assessment also provided the clear political direction called for by advocates of effects-based, parallel warfare; an unequivocal mission statement which could become the central driving force and rationale for effects-based, parallel warfare in all its aspects.

Planning did not come to an end when combat operations began in late March 2003. US-led operations required constant supervision of the battlespace by commanders and headquarters, and the flexibility to adapt or replace plans according to circumstances.[12] But the breadth and rapidity of the communications networks at the core of the new style of warfare do imply a step-change in command responsiveness, with changes in circumstances being identified and reported promptly (if not in 'real time'), and plans being changed rapidly, efficiently and with confidence. The new responsiveness of US command and decision making was also enabled by 'real time' operational analysis, allowing for faults to be remedied and unexpected opportunities to be exploited during operations, rather than wait for a complex and drawn-out post-conflict 'lessons learned' process. The execution of US and allied plans for operations in Iraq was characterised by economy of strategic effort. On the ground, US and British contingents amounted to one heavy and four light divisions; fewer than half the troops committed to the Gulf War in 1991. The much-debated and diplomatically contentious northern front was, in the end, not required, and the redeployed US 4th Infantry Division not committed until late in the campaign.[13] For domestic US and international consumption, the political message was clear and deliberate; with its transformed military capability, the United States could lead Operation Iraqi Freedom[14] and destroy Saddam Hussein's regime without requiring full mobilisation.[15] Militarily, particularly for sceptics of Rumsfeld's so-called 'invasion-lite', the message was just as clear; the success of this relatively lightweight operation could only be explained by the transformation of strategic and operational thinking and military capability.

US and allied plans were executed at a remarkably fast pace, by closely integrated forces, and with relatively few casualties to allied troops. With key bridges having been secured on their behalf, the US 3rd Infantry Division advanced some 300 miles in just four days to a position 50 miles south of Baghdad, incurring just two casualties along the way.[16] The allied use of time was far more than mere speed of manoeuvre, however. The predictable, linear style of warfare was abandoned, just as the advocates of effects-based, parallel warfare had been insisting. Rather than wait for the conclusion of a 38-day bombing campaign (as in the Gulf War of 1991), the ground attack on Iraq actually began *before* the air campaign, with US, British and Australian Special Forces being deployed to western Iraq and the Kurdish region to secure airfields and attack other objectives. And US and allied forces understood that by dictating the tempo of the conflict, they would maintain the initiative over the Iraqis. In the words of Lieutenant General Scott Wallace, commander of US 5th Corps: 'I would suggest to you that "tempo" can be fast or slow, either of which is OK as long as you are in control of the tempo and the enemy is not."[17] US and allied armed forces were more closely and genuinely integrated into one composite fighting force than ever before, with all contingents conforming to a Common Operating Picture.[18] As Cordesman notes: 'The United States and Britain [fought] a kind of joint warfare different from any previous conflict. ... air and missile power, rapid and focused armoured manoeuvre, the creative use of Special Forces and air mobile forces, and sea power were combined to inflict a massive and sudden defeat on a large traditional army.'[19] As for casualties, between 20 March and 1 May 2003, when Bush announced the end of combat activity, the United States had lost 138 troops, 114 from combat; while their British allies had lost 42 dead, 23 from combat. By comparison, the United States lost an average of 211 dead *per day* from combat during the Second World War, and 18 per day in Vietnam. During the Gulf War in 1991, the US lost 146 in combat.[20] The number of US casualties taken during and after the 2003 campaign is gratifyingly low, but possibly sufficient to dispel the image, so widespread in the 1990s, of 'casualty-averse' US political and military leaders, obsessed to the point of inactivity by the so-called 'body-bag syndrome'.[21] Indeed, the low level of casualties taken by the Coalition surprised many commentators, even as the campaign was in its stride,[22] and gave way to speculation that vast numbers of casualties would be taken by the US and allied troops once predicted intense urban warfare began. This prediction was not borne out, at least not until the insurgency of March–April 2004. Iraqi combat casualties do not appear to have been reliably assessed, by either side, but have been estimated at between 30,000 and 40,000.[23] Iraqi civilian or non-combatant casualty figures are even less certain.

Even without the conceptual framework of effects-based, parallel warfare, Coalition forces in Iraq had battle-winning equipment at their disposal; weapons and technology which Iraqi forces simply could not match. Vast computing power enabled close coordination of every aspect of the campaign. Ships, vehicles and aircraft were generally reliable and dependable; a return on huge investments made in the development and production of weapons and equipment, and in military training. At sea, Coalition forces achieved complete dominance, with the US, UK and Australia between them deploying 54 major surface warships, 13 submarines and a host of support ships. On the ground, although so-called 'friendly fire' incidents did occur, US troops benefited from new combat identification systems such as Blue Force Tracking, whereby positions of vehicles were automatically logged by GPS, reported and updated. Coalition forces very quickly established control of the air over Iraq. At the peak of operations, Coalition air forces mustered some 1800 combat aircraft of various types, plus helicopters. Over 40,000 fixed-wing sorties were launched, some 20,000 of which were strike sorties. There was no Iraqi air response. No Coalition aircraft were lost to Iraqi airpower, although there were losses (fewer than ten) to Iraqi ground-based air defences. Thirteen aircraft were lost to non-combat causes, and there were 25 accidents involving aircraft.[24] Coalition forces launched almost 20,000 precision-guided munitions (PGMs) against Iraqi targets, and dropped a further 9000 unguided weapons. Whereas during the Gulf War of 1991, some 7 per cent of munitions had been precision-guided, in Iraq in 2003 that percentage had increased almost by a factor of ten. Many of the PGMs were GPS-guided, a system which proved to be more reliable and accurate than laser-guidance. As well as providing accurate guidance, the unrivalled network of US military satellites was used for communications and intelligence gathering. Command and control of coalition forces was made more effective by aircraft such as the E-8C JSTARS and the RC-135 Rivet Joint, and by the ability to keep such key aircraft constantly on station by air-to-air refuelling. Unmanned aerial vehicles (UAVs), or remote-controlled reconnaissance aircraft, also provided vital intelligence. At the tactical level, the short-range Dragon Eye could be carried, assembled and launched in ten minutes by a team of two. At the opposite end of the spectrum, Global Hawk aircraft, flown from an airfield in the United Arab Emirates and controlled from Beale Air Force Base in California, provided real-time surveillance and reconnaissance over Iraq for every day of the campaign. Aerospace dominance made it possible to pursue 'effects-based bombing', whereby the United States and Britain could

> seek to paralyse and destroy a regime, not bomb a country. It allowed them to avoid attacking most urban and populated areas unless there were time-urgent targets or Iraqi forces that actively threatened coalition forces.[25]

The planning of the Iraq campaign was bold, and the plan was executed with speed, confidence and imagination. The coalition force posture was proved to be appropriate for the immediate task of collapsing Saddam Hussein's regime, and the weaponry and equipment deployed conferred decisive advantage to the Coalition. After all the debate of the 1990s, it might indeed be appropriate to describe the 2003 campaign as 'revolutionary'. But for all the conceptual, mechanical and digital sophistication of the campaign, the performance was not flawless. For example, detailed 'battle damage assessment' – the process of gauging the accuracy and effect of attacks and even individual munitions – was difficult to carry out reliably; an unexpected consequence of the speed and comprehensiveness of operations. Plenty of assessments were made, however, of the initial 'shock and awe' bombardment. Although this modern-day blitzkrieg appears not to have been a complete failure,[26] many commentators argue that expectations (and even promises) that it would bring about an immediate and complete conclusion to the campaign proved unrealistic. The slick sophistication of the campaign was, in some cases, more apparent than real. Cordesman warns against reading too much into the advantages and capabilities of network-centric warfare; some computing and communications networks were more advanced than others, and the system as a whole was held together rather haphazardly in some cases.[27] And when the various networks did function as intended, they gave weight to the long-established concern that network-centric, effects-based, parallel warfare invites micro-management of the planning and conduct of military operations by senior political and military leaders.[28] Arguably the greatest flaw, however, was that the 'revolutionary' use of military force in Iraq was neither accompanied by, nor did it cause, a revolution in the politics of the use of armed force. Indeed, the conduct of the campaign and subsequent events might have prompted a fracturing of politics, and perhaps even a *counter*-revolutionary climate, both domestically and internationally, where the resort to armed force is concerned.

A counter-revolution in politics?

Rumsfeld was evidently correct to argue that the Coalition invasion force was not too small. In important respects, the invasion worked; the regime of Saddam Hussein was destroyed rapidly and decisively. But, just as evidently, Rumsfeld and his associates were wrong if they supposed that the deployment of a small, light, mobile invasion force would be as constructive politically and ideationally as it had been destructive physically.

The so-called 'Rumsfeld Doctrine' can be debated on two levels; the practical and conceptual. In the first place, critics argue for example that allied forces deployed to Iraq were simply too small and light to be reconfigured rapidly into a full-scale occupation force. Others have claimed that allied troops (particularly US troops) were inadequately trained in urban warfare and in counter-insurgency or 'hearts and minds' operations. Or indeed, in basic military responsibilities and political awareness, as the abuse of Iraqi prisoners by Coalition military personnel would seem to indicate. Furthermore, while US forces had been transformed into an impressive combat machine, and while the Pentagon and commanders in the field certainly did give some consideration to matters of civil affairs and post-conflict operations,[29] insufficient thought had been given in US military doctrine and planning to the transition from combat operations to stability and reconstruction projects. Overall, the US approach was, in other words, monochromatic and lacking in subtlety. To this list of charges might be added the claim that technology had been allowed to precede doctrine, thought and politics. By this view, the war in Iraq was fought *because* new technology and weapons were available, and the opportunity was seized both to demonstrate the efficacy of American military might and to prove that the military transformation led by Rumsfeld had been well conceived.

These practical aspects of the allied deployment to, and operations in Iraq will rightly continue to provoke debate among specialists in military equipment, force posture, training and doctrine. For example, in response to the claim that the intervention was driven by the availability of new weaponry and technology, Cordesman observes that

> the Iraq war could [not] have been fought with the kind of force transformation that Secretary Rumsfeld sought. ... The transformational forces that Rumsfeld has sought will not be ready for at least five to seven years [from 2004].[30]

However, unless warfare is defined narrowly and exclusively in terms of its physical manifestations, then the net must be cast wider in order fully to understand what took place in Iraq. To gauge whether the use of armed force in Iraq was 'revolutionary', 'evolutionary' or something else altogether, it is necessary to look beyond the symptoms of effects-based, parallel warfare, to ask what was the relationship between politics and armed force in the intervention in Iraq. Carl von Clausewitz, the nineteenth-century Prussian strategist so esteemed in western military establishments, famously insisted that 'war is simply a continuation of political intercourse, with the addition of other means'.[31] As far as the intervention in Iraq is concerned, several interpretations of the political-military relationship have been offered. In four such interpretations, each hotly debated, a clear enough political rationale is suggested for the use of armed force: to replace a repellent regime and democratise Iraq; to achieve US-oriented geostrategic stability in Iraq and the broader region; to use armed force to prevent further proliferation of weapons of mass destruction; and to use armed force for purposes of retribution and pre-emption against America's actual and/or perceived enemies. Another interpretation might be that effects-based, parallel warfare was expected to generate a political rationale appropriate to the means being used, with the Clausewitzian political-military relationship therefore developing after the military event. Still another interpretation might be that there was no political-military relationship at all, because the new style of warfare proved to be so complex and fast-moving that politics could not keep pace. Whatever the merit of these different explanations, what is significant for strategic analysis is that each has generated its own backlash. The overall result is that the coherence of the political case for using armed force in Iraq has been weakened and that certain of the claims made on behalf of effects-based, parallel warfare have been brought into question.

The liberalisation/democratisation thesis suggests, from the outset, that certain assumptions had been made about the ripeness for change in Iraq, and about the innate perfectibility of the Iraqi state, society and people. In the early stages of the conflict, frequent reference was made to the elusive 'tipping point', whereby the application of just a little more military force here or there would initiate a domino effect and see the rapid collapse of the regime. This would have been effects-based operations on the grandest possible scale; careful and limited application of military force would not merely defeat the enemy but would bring about a revolutionary transformation of Iraqi society from the inside out, and relatively peacefully. The wisdom of the 'tipping point' strategy needs further debate, but for my purposes its significance lies in the sense of latency that it conveyed. The Iraqi people were, it would seem, regarded as desperate for change and to be liberated from Saddam Hussein, but needing to be convinced more thoroughly before turning finally against the regime. So the intervention in Iraq became in part an enlightened act to enable self-redemption, to unlock the natural capacity and tendency of Iraqi people to be something else, something better. But the question, of course, is what? If improvement is introduced and sought by outside agents, it seems reasonable to ask what is the goal these agents have in mind? According to the democratisation thesis, the US-led intervention was driven by the conviction that democracy should be encouraged around the world as a good in itself, and that Americans should assist in the process. But any authority this explanation might have had was soon undermined by the observation that a genuinely democratised Iraq could choose to be an Islamic republic, could make inconvenient alliances, could decide to breach international arms control and non-proliferation treaties, and could be generally indisposed to the west and the United States. Why would the United States and its allies intervene if this could or would be the outcome? In this case, the political backlash takes the form of the democratisation project being regarded at best as naïve, condescending and unconvincing, and at worst as hypocritical; a project to create a *US-style* and *US-friendly* democracy in Iraq. For some critics, the democratisation project was simply infantile, driven by the conviction that, once liberated, Iraqis would be able to realise their manifest destiny of becoming Middle Eastern Americans.[32]

The second interpretation springs from the first. The claim here is that the language of democracy and liberal values were deployed in order to mask the real, power political intent of the United States: 'A compliant not democratic Iraq is [the Bush Administration's] objective, the aim being to secure a compliant Middle East.'[33] Once again, the test of US motives is to imagine what could have been (and could still be) the outcome of genuine, disinterested democratisation and self-determination in Iraq. The result could be the fracturing of the country into Kurd, Sunni and Shia sectors, inviting intervention from neighbouring countries and creating a pocket of instability in the Middle East. Since this outcome would be as unattractive to the United States and its allies as an anti-western Islamic republic of Iraq, it follows that some other rationale must have been at work, namely, so the argument goes, the consolidation of the US imperium in the Middle East. While there are some scholars who argue that a new, benign American imperialism (preferably as close as possible to the British imperial ethic) would be good for large parts of the world,[34] the problem is that many other scholars and most of the targets of this enlightened imperialism see it as anything but benign. In the consequent backlash, geostrategic stability will be prevented if it is to be only on American terms, frustration will mount over western promises made but not fulfilled, and mistrust and hostility toward the United States and the West will deepen. The third possibility, that the intervention was designed to prevent proliferation of weapons of mass destruction, faces the difficulty that firm evidence of Iraqi WMD capability was not much in evidence one year after the end of the conflict, and that there had arguably been a functioning alternative to military intervention, in the form of UN inspection and monitoring visits. Here, the backlash could come in the form of deep scepticism over any future arguments for forceful counter-proliferation. With the fourth interpretation – that operations in Iraq were simply about capturing and destroying enemies of the United States, actual and potential – the backlash is clearest of all. Domestic electorates in the United States and Europe will regard talk of counter-proliferation and humanitarian relief as a deception perpetrated on them by their elected government, and the western alliance will become strained to breaking point as governments sense they have been duped into providing multilateral 'cover' and legitimacy to a policy driven by straightforward, self-interested US unilateralism.

With each of the four interpretations just discussed, the notion that armed force should be used in Clausewitzian style to pursue political ends becomes widely disputed and generally discredited. But perhaps of even greater concern for devotees of Clausewitz is a fifth possibility; that it was assumed by the political and military leaders of the Coalition that the use of force in Iraq would not merely serve one or another political agenda, but would clarify and perhaps even create an appropriate political framework *ex post facto*, in Iraq and the wider Middle East, and within the countries contributing to the US-led Coalition. In this way, the Clausewitzian model would be achieved only after the event; an approach which represents at best a misunderstanding of Clausewitz, and at worst complete contempt for the western ideal that warfare must serve politics. Cordesman gives warning of this when he writes of 'the inability of the U.S. military to properly conceptualise and understand grand strategy'.[35] Clausewitz was entirely clear on this point: 'The political object is the goal, war is the means of reaching it, and means can never be considered in isolation from their purpose.'[36] And later in *On War*:

> Subordinating the political point of view to the military would be absurd, for it is policy that creates war. Policy is the guiding intelligence and war only the instrument, not vice versa. No other possibility exists, then, than to subordinate the military point of view to the political.[37]

Although this interpretation of events could prompt a rush of papers describing the merits of Clausewitz and castigating the US armed forces for their lack of understanding, the political backlash here is likely to consist of more than intellectual pique.[38] The suspicion that western armed forces have become an authority to themselves could see diminishing trust in armed forces, reflected in declining recruitment and in reduced defence spending. More significantly, if an assault has occurred on the elaborate and delicate (and Clausewitzian) structure of civil-military relations in the West, the result might be a temporary separation of the civil and the military, a separation which eventually proves untenable and results either in the militarisation of politics, or the politicisation of the military.

The sixth and final suggestion is that effects-based, parallel warfare was so successful, and so overwhelming, that the domestic politics by which it should have been shaped and guided were simply unable to keep pace. At the heart of modern western military doctrine and practice lies the idea of 'manoeuvre warfare'. Recent writing on the subject often refers approvingly to the words of Winston Churchill:

> There are many kinds of manoeuvre in war ... some only of which take place on [or near] the battlefield. There are manoeuvres to the flank or rear. There are manoeuvres in time, in diplomacy, in mechanics, in psychology; all of which are removed from the battlefield, but react often decisively upon it, and the object of all is to find easier ways, other than sheer slaughter, of achieving the main purpose.[39]

In other words, manoeuvre in war is much more than movement; manoeuvr*ism* calls for breadth and speed of operations, and for imagination and intelligence on the part of commanders. Although written over 80 years ago, Churchill's prescription easily captures the sense of today's effects-based, parallel warfare. However, what Churchill and his modern disciples seem not to have anticipated is that the clever use of manoeuvre warfare to undermine and disable the relationship between an adversary's army and government could have a disturbingly similar effect in reverse. Put another way, the US-led Coalition in Iraq in 2003 manoeuvred inside its own political OODA loop as well as that of Saddam Hussein's regime. Effects-based, parallel warfare, as seen in Iraq, functions at a very rapid pace, in many areas and on many levels (strategic, operational, tactical and individual) simultaneously. But the domestic politics of a western democracy, however efficient, do not work in quite the same way, at quite the same speed; military transformation has not, in other words, been accompanied by a transformation of politics. The rapidity of the advance to Baghdad, the use of precision-guided weapons to achieve overlapping and overwhelming effect in order to impose a 'picture of defeat'[40] on the Iraqi opposition; all this is too fast and too complex for a modern democratic government to comprehend and control. In circumstances such as these, the understandable tendency is for democratic politicians to hold their breath and hope that the use of effects-based, parallel warfare will in time return things to a more manageable and predictable state.

But this threatens a suspension of Clausewitz's 'political intercourse', rather than its 'continuation by other means'. This possibility has not attracted much attention in the debate, perhaps because in the rush to abandon 'linearity' and embrace 'post-Newtonian' ideas about strategy,[41] it has not been realised that it is impossible to be non-linear in only one direction. In other words, 'non-linear warfare' which determinedly thinks only about how 'we' can impose our will on 'them' in battle, overlooks the likelihood that 'we' will also be changed in the process. This change is not only that the political-military link becomes more difficult to sustain in the midst of war – a worrying prospect, many would argue, since this is precisely where the link is most needed – but also that politics generally could become ever more fractured and incoherent where the use of force is concerned. The politics of the military intervention in Iraq were by no means the exclusive domain of the governments most closely involved. The politics of the intervention were fiercely and authoritatively debated by the public (domestic and foreign) and by parliaments, judiciaries, intelligence services, armed services, NGOs and advocacy organisations and foreign governments. This is as it should be; anything other than a free and vigorous debate on the use of armed force would be unpalatable for democratic polities. But there was a sense in which the breadth and vigour of the debate undermined any residual respect for the notion that the only legitimate user of armed force domestically and internationally is the government of a state. If this impression is accurate and proves to be durable, then the estrangement between politics and the military prompted by effects-based, parallel warfare and other innovations, will have created a conceptual vacuum to be filled by 'parallel politics', whereby no authority on the use of armed force is regarded as greater or more legitimate than any other. If it is becoming increasingly difficult for a unitary, coherent democratic government to manage the new style of warfare in all its rapidity and complexity, then 'parallel politics' can only make the aspiration for democratic control of the armed services and what they do in war even more hopeless. This combination of 'parallel warfare' and 'parallel politics' suggests three possible outcomes, none of them welcome. In the first, the norms and processes of democratic control of military activity will be pushed to the margins as the executive branch of government insists on an ever more exclusive role as both legitimator and user of armed force. The second possible outcome is that a general presumption against the use of armed force in most if not all circumstances will take hold, as governments become progressively overwhelmed by the sense of political risk. The final possibility is that the bond between state and organised armed force will be broken, and the responsibility or opportunity to use armed force will be displaced either to some international body such as the United Nations, or to private military companies (PMCs) competing in the marketplace, or to some combination of the two, exemplified by PMCs being contracted by the UN to undertake complex tasks involving the use of armed force in Afghanistan, Iraq and elsewhere.

Conclusion: anti-strategic warfare

If strategy is understood to mean the organised use of armed force to achieve political ends, then the significance of the conflict fought by the US-led Coalition in Iraq in 2003 could lie less in its 'revolutionary' military aspects than in its 'counter-revolutionary' political implications. As a consequence, this conflict could, perversely, prove to have been anti-strategic. However impressive its effect on Saddam Hussein's regime, the 'effects-based, parallel warfare' seen in Iraq has prompted the development of a diffused, incoherent and bitterly disputed 'parallel politics'. The paradox here is that while advocates of effects-based, parallel warfare call for close and coherent political direction and an unequivocal decision as to the 'effect' being sought, in practice the new ways of war were not sufficient to overcome deep divisions about the legitimacy and wisdom of the war in Iraq. Worse still, effects-based, parallel warfare could have been destructive of the politico-military relationship, either by assuming that a political framework in Iraq could be constructed after the military event, or by ensuring that politics was simply incapable of keeping pace with warfare. In the end, effects-based, parallel warfare has proved to be less, rather than more responsive to politics, and the relationship between politics and warfare, whereby the former provides legitimacy, purpose and boundaries to the latter, has come under very severe strain.

Quite apart from the intellectual challenge to assumptions long held in the United States, the UK, Australia and other Coalition members regarding the political control of armed forces, the broader implications of this politico-military estrangement could be profound. When it comes to the use of armed force for whatever purpose, these governments will in future face an uphill struggle to re-establish their bona fides, nationally and internationally. Widespread public reluctance to accept the use of armed force other than in unequivocal cases of national, territorial self-defence will mean that compelling arguments to use armed force to pre-empt either a humanitarian catastrophe, a terrorist attack or the proliferation and use of weapons of mass destruction, will go unheard. Western governments which profess the legitimacy and necessity of intervening against tyrannical regimes and gross humanitarian abuses will have little moral and diplomatic credibility if their strategic posture is capable only of reaction and outrage after the event, rather than prevention. Western governments concerned to defeat more direct threats to their security from terrorist groups and other adversaries, will be dependent upon a strategic posture which on the one hand is technologically and organisationally astounding, but on the other hesitant and reactive. The initiative will thus have been lost to adversaries for whom the use of asymmetric means to gain initiative is everything, and for whom the ideal western target is one that can only react – preferably immoderately, in panic and at great volume – rather than anticipate.

Notes

1. See, for example, D. Jablonsky, *The Owl of Minerva Flies at Twilight: Doctrinal Change and Continuity and the Revolution in Military Affairs*, US Army War College, Strategic Studies Institute, May 1994; M.J. Mazarr, *The Revolution in Military Affairs: A Framework for Defense Planning*, US Army War College, Strategic Studies Institute, June 1994; and for a broader view, C. Gray, *Modern Strategy*, Oxford University Press, 1999, pp. 200–5, 243–54.

2. G.L. Crowder, 'Effects-based Operations: The Impact of Precision Strike Weapons on Air Warfare Doctrines', *Military Technology*, June 2003, p. 20.
3. Sun Tzu, *The Art of War*, trans. S.B. Griffith, Oxford, Oxford University Press, 1971, p. 77.
4. E.J. Dahl, 'Network Centric Warfare and the Death of Operational Art', *Defence Studies*, Vol. 2, No. 1, Spring 2002, p. 10.
5. Coined by Colonel John Boyd, US strategic analyst and commentator. In combat (indeed, in any walk of life), the goal should be to complete the OODA cycle before the adversary, thereby retaining the initiative and ensuring success. For a full account and explanation of Boyd's insight see B. Berkowitz, *The New Face of War: How War Will be Fought in the 21st Century*, New York, Free Press, 2003, pp. 38–45.
6. Crowder, 'Effects-based Operations', p. 22.
7. Helmuth von Moltke, mid-nineteenth-century Chief of the Prussian General Staff, once voiced 'the universal wish of military commanders: "The politician should fall silent the moment that mobilization begins."' Quoted in J. Snyder, 'The Cult of the Offensive in 1914', in R.J. Art and K.N. Waltz, *The Use of Force: Military Power and International Politics*, New York, Rowman and Littlefield, 1999, p. 118.
8. A.H. Cordesman, *The Iraq War: Strategy, Tactics and Military Lessons*, Westport, CT, Praeger Publishers, 2003, pp. 40–1.
9. D.A. Macgregor, *Transformation Under Fire: Revolutionizing how America Fights*, Westport, CT, Praeger, 2003, p. 235.
10. D. Rumsfeld, testimony to US Congress, 9 July 2003, quoted in Cordesman, *The Iraq War*, p. 1.
11. 'How the Pentagon was told to change the rules', *Financial Times*, 1 April 2003.
12. Cordesman, *The Iraq War*, p. 178.
13. According to Rumsfeld, the necessary redeployment of the US 4th Infantry Division was turned to military advantage. By holding the division on its transport ships in the Mediterranean, US commander General Tommy Franks fuelled Saddam Hussein's miscalculation that the war would not begin until a northern front had been opened. As a result, the start of the campaign came as something of a surprise to the Iraqis, who continued to hold 13 divisions north of Baghdad. See Rumsfeld in Cordesman, *The Iraq War*, p. 2; see also *ibid.*, p. 115.
14. Operation Iraqi Freedom was the US planning term. National contingents chose their own operational title; British troops used 'Operation Telic', and Australians 'Operation Falconer'.
15. Although, as Cordesman notes, together with existing US deployments in Afghanistan, Germany and Korea, the deployment to Iraq meant that a 'significant amount' of the US Army's combat strength was now deployed: *The Iraq War*, p. 38.
16. Macgregor, *Transformation under Fire*, p. 237.
17. Lieutenant General Scott Wallace quoted in Cordesman, *The Iraq War*, p. 157.
18. At the national level, integration of navy, army and air forces is described as 'joint warfare', with the goal being to have all different elements functioning as one force (rather than as different forces, with different styles and objectives, cooperating more or less closely with one another). Integration of closely allied contingents (such as the US and UK, and other NATO members) is described as 'combined warfare', with other contributions to a coalition described as 'multinational'.
19. Cordesman, *The Iraq War*, p. 57 and chapter 7.
20. Ibid., pp. 238–9.

21. For a recent comparison of US and British approaches to casualty aversion, see P. Cornish, 'Myth and Reality: US and UK Approaches to Casualty Aversion and Force Protection', *Defence Studies*, Vol. 3, No. 2, summer 2003.

22. 'Casualties incredibly low, say war experts', *The Times*, 1 April 2003.

23. Macgregor, *Transformation Under Fire*, p. 235. Cordesman, however, suggests that Iraqi casualties could range from 5000 to 20,000: *The Iraq War*, p. 247.

24. Cordesman, *The Iraq War*, p. 254.

25. Ibid., pp. 28–9.

26. See 'Bewilderment and shock at lack of resistance', *Daily Telegraph*, 12 April 2003, reporting on the surprise and anger around the Arab world regarding the lack of resistance by Baghdad.

27. Cordesman, *The Iraq War*, p. 223ff.

28. Dahl, 'Network Centric Warfare, p. 8: 'increased communications capabilities and shared situational awareness will make it possible for senior leaders to direct tactical actions'. For a discussion of the implications of micro-management see P. Cornish, '"Cry, 'Havoc!' and Let Slip the Managers of War": The Strategic, Military and Moral Hazards of Micro-Managed Warfare', NATO/EAPC Research Fellowship Paper, NATO website, October 2002: www.nato.int/acad/fellow99-01/F99-01.htm.

29. See press briefing by Commander Coalition Forces Land Component, Lieutenant General D. McKiernan, 23 April 2003, reported in Cordesman, *The Iraq War*, p. 350.

30. Cordesman, *The Iraq War*, p. 164.

31. C. von Clausewitz, *On War*, ed. and trans. M. Howard and P. Paret, Princeton, Princeton University Press, 1976, p. 605.

32. An excerpt from Stanley Kubrick's film *Full Metal Jacket* has featured in a good deal of discussion of American motives in Iraq: the US Marine colonel explains to the independent-minded private that 'inside every gook [*sic* – referring to Vietnamese people] there's an American trying to get out'.

33. A. Lieven, 'Missionaries and Marines: Bush, Blair and Democratisation', *Open Democracy*, 18 September 2002.

34. For the view of the British Empire as a benign institution, see N. Ferguson, *Empire: How Britain Made the Modern World*, London, Penguin Books, 2003, p. 362. For an assessment of the merits of an American empire see M. Boyle, 'Utopianism and the Bush Foreign Policy', *Cambridge Review of International Affairs*, Vol. 17, No. 1, April 2004.

35. Cordesman, *The Iraq War*, p. 506.

36. Clausewitz, *On War*, p. 87.

37. Ibid., p. 607.

38. For an especially balanced and trenchant assessment of the condition of the US political-military relationship after Iraq, see A.J. Echevarria, *Toward an American Way of War*, US Army War College, Strategic Studies Institute, March 2004.

39. W.S. Churchill, *The World Crisis* (1923), quoted in DG Joint Doctrine and Concepts, *Joint Operations*, UK Joint Warfare Publication 3–00, 30 March 2000, para. 109.

40. R.E. Simpkin, *Race to the Swift*, London, Brassey's, 1988, p. 133, quoted in J.J.A. Wallace, 'Manoeuvre Theory in Operations Other Than War', in B. Holden Reid, ed., *Military Power: Land Warfare in Theory and Practice*, London, Frank Cass, 1997, p. 208.

41. See S.R. Mann, 'Chaos, Criticality and Strategic Thought', in T.C. Gill, ed., *Essays on Strategy IX*, Washington DC, NDU Press, 1993, pp. 33–54.

Index

Compiled by Sue Carlton